FRAMING FEELING
Sentiment and Style in English Prose Fiction
1745-1800

TRISTRAM SHANDY

Plate II.

Published as the Act directs, by Harrison & C.º April 10.ᵗʰ 1781.

FRAMING FEELING
Sentiment and Style in English Prose Fiction
1745-1800

BARBARA M. BENEDICT

AMS Press

New York

Library of Congress Cataloging-in-Publication Data

Benedict, Barbara M.
  Framing feeling: sentiment and style in English prose fiction.
1745-1800/Barbara M. Benedict.
    (AMS studies in the eighteenth century; no. 26)
  Includes bibliographical references (p.) and index.
  ISBN 0-404-63526-1
    1. English fiction—18th century—History and criticism.
2. Sentimentalism in literature. 3. English language — 18th century—Style.
4. Emotions in literature. I. Title. II. Series.
PR858.S45B46 1994
823'.609353—dc20

93-33407
CIP

All AMS books are printed on acid-free paper that meets the guidelines for performance and durability of the Committee on Production Guidelines for Book Longevity of the Council on Library Resources.

AMS Press, Inc.
56 East 13th Street
New York, N.Y. 10003

MANUFACTURED IN THE UNITED STATES OF AMERICA

Farewel great Painter of Mankind
Who reach'd the noble point of Art,
Whose *pictur'd Morals* charm the Mind
And through the Eye correct the Heart.
Epitaph to Hogarth's tomb in Chiswick by David Garrick

TABLE OF CONTENTS

ILLUSTRATIONS

ACKNOWLEDGMENTS

I would like to thank Trinity College and the NEH Travel to Collections Program for grants that allowed me to conduct the research for this book. Part of Chapter 3 has appeared in *Studies in Philology* as "'Dear Madam': Rhetoric, Cultural Politics, and the Female Reader in Sterne's *Tristram Shandy*" (89 [1992]: 485-98); part of Chapter 4 has appeared in *Ariel: A Review of International English Literature* as "The Margins of Sentiment: Nature, Letter, and Law in Frances Brooke's Epistolary Novels" (23 [1992]: 7-25); some of Chapter 6 has appeared in slightly altered form in *ELH* as "Literary Miscellanies: The Cultural Mediation of Fragmented Feeling" (57 [1990]: 407-30); and portions of Chapter 7 and the Conclusion have appeared in *Philological Quarterly* in different forms as "Pictures of Conformity: Sentiment and Structure in Ann Radcliffe's Style" (68 [1989]: 363-77), and "Jane Austen's *Sense and Sensibility*: The Politics of Point of View" (69 [1990]: 453-70). I would like to thank these journals for permission to reprint the material in this book. I would also like to thank Claude J. Rawson for reading the first draft of the manuscript and J. Paul Hunter for early and persistent encouragement and advice. Margaret Anne Doody, John Traugott, and George A. Starr have also generously supported this work in various ways, and Joan Sussler of the Lewis Walpole Library has been of much help. My gratitude also goes to Gabriel Hornstein for his assistance, and to Nancy Sowa and Bob Greene for help in typesetting. My great debt to Mark Miller for his constant help and patience can never be repaid.

INTRODUCTION

Since the eighteenth century, feeling has been at the heart of English prose fiction, from full-length novels to magazine tales. This feeling spans both the emotions of the characters as they waver between internal sentiments and social demands, and the feelings of the audience who reads of their struggles. Despite this central role, however, the sorts of feelings and the ways in which these feelings may be expressed in fiction has always been carefully ordered by literary and cultural conventions. These conventions first take their modern shape in the stories of feeling that flooded the market during the second half of the eighteenth century, the era of sentimental fiction. This book offers an explanation of the stylistic solutions that some of the writers of this period developed in order to satisfy the audience's taste for sentiment while preserving the rules of decorum and restraint revered by their culture. It argues that sentimental literature, in rhetoric and structure, does not simply advocate feeling; it also warns the reader against some kinds of feeling or feelings associated with revolutionary or female culture. Sentimental fiction adheres to a dialectical structure that endorses yet edits the feelings in fiction.

Literary sentimentalism is informed by a loose philosophy of human understanding and social relations that grew from ideas expressed in the early eighteenth century.[1] Drawn from the epistemological theories of John Locke, themselves influenced by the philosophical skepticism of Descartes, and from the moral and aesthetic ideas of Anthony Ashley Cooper, third earl of Shaftesbury, philosophical sentimentalism maintains a belief in the natural sociability of humankind and the importance of impulsive, spontaneous sensibility. In the *Essay Concerning Humane Understanding* (1690), Locke refutes the thesis that human beings are born furnished by God with innate ideas, and argues that all ideas derive from experience achieved through physical sensation and reflection upon that sensation. Locke's epistemology thus defines sensual experience as the very stuff of reality. At the same time, Locke's *Two Treatises on Government* (1690) and particularly his *Reasonableness of Christianity* (1695) defend the "religiosity of the sociable man" while condemning mysticism.[2] Shaftesbury extrapolates from Locke's principles. In the *Inquiry Concerning Virtue, or Merit* (1699), he argues in contravention to Hobbes that human beings instinctively love others as well

as themselves. While reiterating the reasonableness of Christianity, in the
Letter Concerning Enthusiasm (1708) he[1] advocates good-humor, wit, and
ridicule to confute fanaticism. Most influential, his *Characteristicks of Men,
Manners, Opinions, Times* (1711) posits that humans possess an "inborn
conscience" that leads them intuitively to love virtue, detest vice, and feel
altruistic affection for their fellows with whom they are naturally linked
(Todd 25). Moreover, humans reflect on their own actions and discriminate
between good and bad behavior in an exercise of moral judgment that
Shaftesbury correlates with an instinctive aesthetic taste.

Within their discussions of human sociability and individual sensual
apprehension, these early philosophers reveal the contradictions which
structure sentimental stylistics.[3] Both Locke and Shaftesbury couple their
praise of subjectivity and impulse with an emphasis on the role of reflection
and a contempt for enthusiasm. While locating authority within human nature,
Shaftesbury simultaneously relies on common sense--sense shared by
reasonable men--to combat religious extremism. Even while Locke argues
that all people dwell in a common world of material reality in which facts
can be proved through experiment and sensation, his theory also posits a
radical separation between people since each human being experiences
sensation individually and reflects privately. The experience of reality
becomes individual, unique, particular.[4] Shaftesbury attempts to socialize
Locke's definition of experience by endowing humans with altruistic
benevolence, but the strain between these notions of how human beings
experience feeling persists in sentimental fictions.

Shaftesbury's conflation of aesthetic and moral ideas and the definition
of sympathy particularly engaged later eighteenth-century philosophers.
Francis Hutcheson, the Professor of Moral Philosophy at Glasgow, suggested
that natural sympathy restrains human desires in accordance with mankind's
instinctive sense of moral beauty in *An Inquiry into the Original of Our Ideas
of Beauty and Virtue* (1725) and *An Essay on the Nature and Conduct of the
Passions and Affections with Illustrations on the Moral Sense* (1728).[5] His
valorization of benevolence impressed the most influential of these later
philosophers, David Hume, but Hume reintroduced a Hobbesian element of
self-interest into the discourse on sensibility by stressing mankind's
multiplicity of passions, including pride. His *Treatise of Human Nature*
(1740) was widely read when it was simplified and reissued in three volumes,
entitled *An Enquiry Concerning Human Understanding* (1748), *An Enquiry
Concerning the Principles of Morals* (1751), and *A Dissertation on the
Passions* (1757). Hume's work revises Locke's *Essay Concerning Humane
Understanding* by unseating reason in order to grant passions priority in
motivating human beings. Hume also addresses the issue of aesthetic
response. In the essay "Of Tragedy" (1757), he applies his idea of the

complexity of human psychological and emotional responses to art by proposing that audiences experience a combination of pleasure and pain when they watch a tragedy and that these feelings do not contradict, but inform each other.[6] Hume further argues that since we lack sufficient data to prove the existence of the external world or even of ourselves, we rely on the association of ideas, on mental constructions that connect our perceptions, to interpret reality. For Hume, however, human beings also possess natural instincts, notably a tendency to promote the public good and to experience sympathy and benevolence. In *The Theory of Moral Sentiments* (1759), Adam Smith modifies this idea. While arguing that sympathy is the source of all moral feeling, he explains it as the individual's imaginary substitution of himself for the suffering other through spectatorship. By this conscious act of identification, the spectator feels for the sufferer as for himself and thus acts with benevolence, albeit a benevolence balanced by social responsibility; at the same time, just as he sees the sufferer as himself, so the spectator sees himself through the lens of society.[7]

The sentimental fictions of the later eighteenth century reflect not only the central tenets of these philosophers, but also the tensions between their ideas. Although sentimental heroes fashion their own values by means of the individual apprehension endorsed by Locke and Shaftesbury, this individualism is structured and monitored by fictional forms that embody the faculty of reflection and common sense applauded by both philosophers. While idealizing sympathy and benevolence in accordance with the values of Shaftesbury and Hutcheson, sentimental fictions represent the dialectic perceived by Hume between human isolation from the material world and human interdependence. Many sentimental vignettes are designed to elicit from the reader the tangle of aesthetic pleasure and pain moralized by both Hume and Smith. Notably, sentimental literature explores the moral and social consequences of the position of spectatorial sympathy that Smith examined.

Sentimentalism is often called the "cult of feeling." The feelings it cultivates include physical, mental, and emotional sensations. This endorsement of feeling gives unprecedented authority to the individual to determine truth while at the same time threatening the hold of social convention, for society seems to some writers to limit individual apprehension without good cause and to inculcate habits of thought without good effects. Much sentimental writing counters the revolutionary threat to change society that these ideas imply by maintaining that human instincts are morally good, that sympathy demonstrates man's social nature, and hence that emotions exhibit morality. By coopting Shaftesbury's argument that taste--aesthetic discrimination--and virtue are the same, furthermore, sentimental writers allow individuals to experience visual pleasure, indeed to please themselves, as an example of their goodness. Periodicals especially purvey to readers the latest not only in fashionable aesthetics but also in luxurious commodities with the justification that taste manifested by purchasing is a sign of moral distinction. Eighteenth-century sentimentalism not only encourages readers to nurture their feelings, but urges them to cultivate, shape, and train these feelings. Tracing social, moral, and physical experience to sensation, popular sentimentalism reveres benevolence as man's highest moral act, an act of feeling.

Recently, literary sentimentalism has been identified with ideas of social and sexual equality.[8] Pointing to the privileging in sentimental literature of feeling and nature over rationalism and culture, and to Samuel Richardson as the progenitor of sentimental fiction, some feminist literary critics have argued that sentimentalism vaunts female values by locating identity and virtue in responsive delicacy and compassion. Similarly, some literary historians have noted the democratic potential in a sentimental ideal that overturns conventional hierarchy to imply an equality of feeling for all sympathetic souls. Other critics have noted that the popular sentimental themes of familial and domestic harmony define the movement as middle class and therefore congenial to ideals of the progress and refinement of society.[9] Robert Markley, notably, has argued that sentimentalism represents the bourgeois as the heir of the aristocrat by virtue of his naturally paternalistic feelings.[10] In *Sentiment and Sociability: The Language of Feeling in the Eighteenth Century* (Oxford, 1988), John Mullan modifies this view by pointing out the ways in which sentimental novelists "position each private reader as the exceptional connoisseur of commendable sympathies," and establish a privileged discourse of feeling that defines the reader as rare (13). While Mullan illuminates the differences between theoretical sentimentalism and sentimentalism in practice in literature, he confines his analysis to the "languages" of feeling that reflect a philosophical skepticism about sociability. In different ways, these opinions echo the view encapsulated by R. F. Brissenden in his authoritative *Virtue in Distress* (1974). Here, Brissenden identifies the "one basic notion" of sentimentalism as the idea that "the source of all knowledge and all values is the individual human experience"; he thus stamps sentimentalism as radically individualistic.[11] Sentimental literature, however, insistently organizes and channels these individual responses; it controls both skepticism about sociability and individual alienation by adapting sentimental values to conventional rhetorical and structural forms. These discourses and structures signal social feeling and traditional values to the reader despite the portraits of isolated or revolutionary feeling that the characters present.

Although sentimental ideas permeated all literary forms, they grafted peculiarly strongly onto prose fictions and even facilitated the fracturing of generic boundaries by stimulating readers to buy prose miscellanies. Such an effect suggests that prose fiction already possessed features particularly hospitable to sentimentalism and appealed to tastes already established in the novel-reading audience. Until recently, however, critics have polarized the novel and sentimental fiction by modifying rather than challenging Ian Watt's definition of the novel as organized by "formal realism" in language, plot, and character, and ideologically dedicated to the values of individualism and subjectivity. Most recent studies of the readership of novels on the contrary suggest that the prevalence of female and popular audiences, authors, and subjects threatens the hegemony of Watt's definition. Ruth Yeazell, for example, has traced the double discourse on female nature behind the conventional courtship plot of the later English novel to the fictions of the early eighteenth century.[12]

Notably, in *Before Novels: The Cultural Contexts of Eighteenth-Century Fiction* (Norton, 1990), J. Paul Hunter redefines the early novel in a way that clarifies why prose fiction so quickly accommodated sentimental ideas. He observes the novel's inclusion of marvelous, surprising, and inexplicable events, which "test the limits of probability and sometimes the limits of knowledge of natural laws."[13] This characteristic effect of unsettling conventional causality provides an opening for writers wishing to express the radical doubts about the power of human reason and the extent of human perception articulated by Hume. In sentimental fiction, the audience's traditional appetite for startling events is richly fed by the depiction of incidents in a fractured causality that isolates them from a natural sequence and hence imbues them with mystery. Moreover, the sensation of surprise itself is an instinctive reaction, which sentimental theory celebrates. Hunter further points out that the early novel explores taboo arenas of human thought and behavior, specifically sexuality and violence. Since these private, secret, or forbidden areas are precisely where sentimental philosophy locates unspoiled human nature, in sentimental fiction they become the places in which mankind's sentimental impulses are revealed. Sensationalism is easily adapted or softened into sentimentalism, although violence may still be detected in such scenes as the Ghost's vicious pinching of the lapdog at the beginning of Mackenzie's *Man of Feeling*. Sentimental fictions sanction the conventional depiction of such topics by moralizing them as displays of human instinct.

Like early novels, sentimental fictions induce emotional responses in the audience that do not necessarily sustain the umbrella ideology implied by either Lockean epistemology or sentimentalism. Whereas Locke, Shaftesbury, and Hume scorn mysticism, for example, sentimental fictions evoke a form of it by splintered or picaresque plots that invite the reader to marvel rather than to seek an explanation. Several novelists, including Oliver Goldsmith,

Henry Brooke, and Henry Mackenzie, attempt to moralize this sensationalistic feature by Christian innuendo or polemic. Indeed, sentimental fictions always prefer the mystical to the rational. If the early novel "tames violence and sexual aberration within a structure of everyday experience very much as it domesticates the surprising, the unexplained, and the wonderful," sentimental fictions defamiliarize the sensations common to experience to make the quotidian sensational.[14] Early eighteenth-century novels particularly negotiate between the portrayal of lonely, individual consciousness and the depiction of the individual in society. Hunter traces the "novel's addictive engagement with solitariness" to the experience of reading during the early century, which grew increasingly secret because of the cultural disapproval of novels (40-41). For sentimental novelists, this fictional negotiation of individual isolation and social engagement is central, for while sympathy is the moral apex of sentimental philosophy, the sentimental hero or heroine is defined partly by his or her isolation and difference from his or her fellows. Writing in the latter half of the century when the cultural condemnation of novels reached its height, sentimental writers could not remain ignorant of their audience's fear of wild sensationalism. Indeed, it is particularly in reconciling the cultural distrust of sentiment and the audience's desire for it that the stylistic solution of framing adopted by sentimental writers proves so useful. By encasing sentimental perspectives within conventional discourses, sentimental novels placate contemporary moralists and please contemporary readers.[15]

Part of the danger that early novels seemed to contemporary observers to hold lay in their celebration of what later critics have hailed as individualism. Defoe and Richardson present readers with fantasies of the individual personality triumphing morally or economically over conventional values or standards. Robinson Crusoe and Moll Flanders prove delightfully resilient in their unconventional independence; Pamela and Clarissa combat social and parental authority without flinching. Sentimental writers of prose fiction inherit both this emphasis on the power of the individual apart from his or her society and the cultural distrust of such an ideal. By portraying the virtue of the individual as the ability to sympathize with fellow humans, sentimental fictions moralize private experience in an attempt to counter the threat that novelistic individualism offers conventional social relations. At the same time, these fictions define their heroes by their subjective and idiosyncratic responses to various sensations. In sentimental fictions, the social dimension of experience is transferred from the story to the rhetoric in which it is told. Such rhetoric reins the reader back from identifying heedlessly with these apparently rebelliously individualistic heroes.

The emergence of collections of sentimental literature in miscellanies further challenges the notion of the internal coherence of the form of the novel. Despite the critical cliché that novels are "inclusive," little attention has been paid to the way novels provide something for every different taste.

The popularity of sentimental vignettes printed in miscellanies argues that some novel-readers desired particular effects that could be provided by parts of sentimental prose fictions severed from the whole. Possibly, indeed, these sentimental passages better suited readers whose cultural education inclined them toward sympathetic identification than readers whose cultural education inclined them to seek irony. Certainly, separable sections had appeared in Fielding's novels both in such interpolated tales as Wilson's story in *Joseph Andrews* (1742) or the Man of the Hill narrative in *Tom Jones* (1749) and in the narrative passages of stylistic burlesque--themselves a violation of Fielding's asserted theory of probability. This novelistic feature suggests that eighteenth-century novels jumble together different fictional techniques in order to draw myriad readers, letting ideological contradictions fall where they may.

As a hybrid form that includes prose, poetry, and fiction, sentimental miscellanies seem to transgress the generic restriction of this book. In fact, they are at the heart of this book because they exemplify the ambiguities of sentimental literature and demonstrate the link between culture and form. Their recasting of the political, cultural, and sexual innuendos in the literature they reprint, their uncertain literary status, and their reflection of the political realities of the book trade demonstrate the way cultural circumstances, including publishing history, shape sentimental literature and modify the formal categories of literary criticism. Although sentimental vignettes in most prose fictions illustrate an asserted or implied thesis about human nature, they transform into flexible, even unstable, units of meaning in the miscellany. Released from their original context, the sentimental episodes reprinted in miscellanies become raw data, so to speak, malleable to the organizing shape of a new frame. While still pleasing readers by supplying fantasies of individual virtue beaming unnoticed in a cruel world, these episodes can be recontextualized to endorse impulse, to advocate self-discipline, or to illustrate the vice of self-indulgence. The rhetoric they employ does not presuppose or rely on the "form" of the novel itself. Indeed, such vignettes recapitulate the original form of sentimental prose fiction, the periodical episode, which was itself an element in a larger discourse on cultural standards.[16] In popular cultural manifestations, the irony of sentimental fictions becomes absorbed into didacticism. New frames serve the purposes of publishers and public by turning sentimental episodes into pedagogy, and so helping to create a new audience and a new genre. Collected into sentimental miscellanies, these episodes demonstrate that literary and cultural documents released from the author's pen into the cultural whirl of publishers and readers serve a variety of interests, achieve multiple meanings, and change these meanings as the culture of print changes. Miscellanies show the way "high" philosophical or ideological tenets and literary practices fuse with--or are coopted by--traditional culture. While they articulate philosophical tenets in a contemporary idiom, these documents are received by historical readers whose understanding of both the philosophy and the idiom is in flux. Such a reception shapes the meaning of the text itself.

By replacing the formal frame of genre with the material and technical frame of editorial presentation, the literary miscellanies that print excerpted sentimental vignettes challenge and redefine our notion of what genre, in fact, is. Detached from physical form, authorial label, and the narrative of a fiction, sentimental vignettes violate both their ostensible moral message and the implications of the "novel" itself. Their existence suggests that the set of agreements and conventions which we indicate by the term "genre" is highly unstable, largely determined by the conditions of reception rather than by the formal aspects of the works themselves. The ease with which sentimental vignettes drop off, change, or compromise the cautionary frame around sentimental ideology that their novelistic context supplies suggests both the power and the limitations of the device of framing in controlling ideological implication. It is not merely the style of an author which determines the way a text will convey a message, but the context in which that text appears. Once recontextualized in literary miscellanies, sentimental vignettes can change their ideological tendency, their "class" labels, and their audiences. Indeed, these literary miscellanies prove that it is not the formal aspects of literature alone or primarily which determine its ideology; rather, it is the context in which the literary work appears and the way it is presented to the audience. "Genre" thus becomes a label indicating not the formal parameters of a work, but its cultural classification. The sentimental literary miscellanies of the late eighteenth and early nineteenth centuries document the way literary ideas and forms can escape the structures in which they were conceived to permeate literary culture as a whole.

As this is true of the vignettes excerpted from prose fictions, so it is true of entire novels. Both Goldsmith's *Vicar of Wakefield* (1766) and Mackenzie's *Man of Feeling* (1771), for example, confused historical audiences since the specific contemporary discourse both novels used was falling out of fashion or merging with other discourses. Even while acknowledging the unstable irony in the narrative voice, these readers understood the episodes in the fiction as uncritical endorsements of feeling. This historical reception adumbrates the extent to which the device of framing employed by sentimental writers was contrived. In a fashion perhaps not too different from the way Sunday night television frames violent domestic dramas within the moralistic discourse of social improvement, sentimental fictions pander to their readers' fantasies while they claim to instruct them in social morality. Sentimental prose fictions, burgeoning in an era of increased consumption, luxury, and cultural commercialization, try to have it both ways. All the works treated in this book--periodicals, *The Female Spectator, Amelia, The Vicar of Wakefield, The Fool of Quality, Tristram Shandy,* Mackenzie's novels and journalism, sentimental miscellanies, the works of Frances Brooke and of Ann Radcliffe, and Austen's *Sense and Sensibility*--simultaneously sell instinctive feeling and either satirize or moralize it. As miscellanies include literary works from a variety of genres, moreover, so sentimental prose fictions draw their rhetoric from several sources, including periodical journals, sermons, and the novels of the first half of the century. As versions of sentimental miscellanies themselves, Radcliffe's novels even feature poetry as a source of framing rhetoric. This plenitude of fictional languages blurs the generic boundaries of the prose fictions examined in this book.

Literary sentimentalism neutralizes its own philosophical premise of the virtue of individual response through the persistent retention of stylistic and structural conventions that induce and endorse readerly detachment. The sort of feeling that sentimental fiction most seeks to modify is excessive sympathy. Sympathy--identification with another--is dangerous because it violates class divisions and threatens rational self-interest, even individual integrity itself. Moreover, this sympathy is felt for socially or morally marginal characters, those society has rejected, so this kind of sympathy also opposes conventional morality. The notion of "excess," a relative term, also serves as a code for a degree or kind of feeling that injures the self, a kind of feeling that spreads the contagion of the unfortunate other to fresh, healthy hearts. Sympathy and excess are often associated with women in sentimental literature because sympathy is identified in these texts as a form of the social bond that women particularly forge in the domestic arena or exercise in their maternal role; unrestrained by the demands of a public role, such as that available to men, women appear vulnerable to limitless sympathy, which compromises the domestic role itself. Thus, these novels counteract as well as express the new values of a "feminized" culture, a culture endorsing sympathy, sensation, romantic love, instinct, and spontaneity--the behavior of humans unrestricted by education or society. They criticize immersion in feeling by praising the rational and aesthetic pleasures of distance; they tailor sensation by transforming it into a function of spectatorship. Hence, sentimental fiction attempts to refine sentiment to allow spectatorial distance to rationalize instinctive response, to channel the tides of emotion.

The formal conventions and opportunities of genre and irony facilitate this dialectic by providing structures in which to frame feeling. Even a cursory survey of sentimental writing explodes the fiction of "the" sentimental novel.[17] During the second half of the century, sentimental themes and characters in fact weave through a rich variety of prose fictions stiff with their own conventions, including didactic histories, picaresque tales, sensual travelogues, periodical essays and miscellanies, and Gothic mysteries. Many of the fictions written during the second half of the eighteenth century nevertheless share specific thematic concerns about feeling, nature, and society, and express these by a similar formal device--the control of the reader's response to feeling by means of language and structural conventions that conjure a social context and the conventional values of restraint, discrimination, and moral hierarchy. These prose fictions achieve this control most often by the rhetorical organization of the story into episodes severed from the narrative. By using these episodes as examples or illustrations of a philosophy of human nature, these fictions seek to draw the reader back from too fervid an identification with the characters and into a balanced evaluation of their behavior and moral standards. Sentimental vignettes serve as clauses in a periodic sentence arguing the need to reconcile private feeling and public duty by means of refined perception. This technique, however, usually conflicts with the structural conventions of the genre in which the author is working. It is not the specific literary conventions themselves that determine sentimental rhetoric; rather, it is the relationship between these conventions and the sentimental characters that appear framed by them. This dialectic between alienated characters and the socialized language that presents them to the reader constitutes a rhetoric of literary sentimentalism. This rhetoric reveals the contradictory impulses governing the expression of sentiment in didactic prose fiction.

Sentimental fictions, nevertheless, sell feeling. They moralize feeling as both knowledge and virtue, dwelling particularly on love of all kinds--sexual, romantic, familial, fraternal, civic, pious--and reincarnating all sorts of social relations as kinds of love: friendship, patriotism, servitude, and noblesse oblige. Despite this social emphasis, the literature of sensibility presents sensual and moral feelings as private, experienced alone; the physical divisions of the skin enforce the separation of human from human and represent the separation of heart from heart. Even the moment of sexual union that opens *Tristram Shandy* appears simultaneously as a moment of sexual division, as Tristram's mother "interrupts" his father with an irrelevant question.

Sympathy operating through spectatorship, however, is offered to the reader as one way to socialize private feeling. By watching others, one can defeat radical isolation and begin to share their feelings. Sentimental fiction thus corporealizes even ideal love like piety or patriotism, portraying feelings as visible on the body where they can be sympathetically observed. Still, this is a sad sympathy, for the sympathetic spectator knows, as he or she watches, that he or she can only approximate knowledge of the other's feelings. Indeed, the very process by which one vicariously experiences another's feelings reminds one of the distance between one and another. This recognition of distance is also true of reading, for while readers may sympathize with characters, at the very moment of sympathy readers also recognize that they are not the characters for whom they feel. Connection is thus always separation; it is this paradox that makes sentimental heroes melancholy.

Readers, however, can escape much of this feeling. Even while sentimental fictions position their heroes as spectators, they elevate their readers even further above the confusion of sensations by stylistic devices enforcing distance from and control over emotion. This distance is healthy for self and society, for if sympathy counters individual alienation, distance counters sympathetic contagion. While critics like John Mullan and Claudia Johnson have identified the physical "language" of sentimentalism as it appears in the blushes and faints of heroines, they have not examined the rhetoric of sentimental fiction, the language that writers use to present feeling to the reader.[18] By means of this language sentimental fictions attempt ultimately to manipulate the reader's response so that it conforms with conventional social and moral judgments.

This rhetoric includes stylistic features that pull against each other to create a dialectic between formal control and emotional release in the texts of sentimentalism. Notably, sentimental rhetoric employs pictorial language. This device conceals causal connections and moral form while emphasizing the way art shapes or frames impression, drawing the reader away from the dynamic of the plot to spectate the scene instead. Pictorialism has ideological consequences, for it at once externalizes feeling by transforming moral into spectacle and refers to identifiable, familiar images that stimulate traditional responses. Indeed, graphic illustrations of sentimental vignettes themselves come to supplement and to highlight this pictorialism, reinforcing the reader's role as spectator. The emphasis on visual spectacle elevates the value of watching above that of feeling, or redefines feeling as a kind of watching. Likewise, language borrowed from satire, the theater, and sermons serves to evoke a context that modifies the invitation to indulge feeling expressed in the plot. Sentimental rhetoric, by this means, counters the radical privatization of feeling implied in sentimental ideology by describing emotion as spectacle, be this a theatrical, pictorial, or didactic spectacle. Readers are hence directed not just to sympathize, but also to detach themselves from the action and the characters. Similarly, self-conscious structures, such as ironic reportage, pseudo-autobiography, and epistolary exchange, shape stories that reprove the power of feeling as much as--or instead of--recount the feeling itself. Thus, readers are solicited to admire the art that formalizes the feeling. Despite endorsing impulse, sentimental texts rely on stock phrases and images to elicit predictable responses, responses not fresh or spontaneous but conventional. In language, tone, and form, sentimental fictions strain between portraying unselfconscious responses and framing these responses for the reader as moral lessons and aesthetic experiences.

The contradictory impulse to celebrate and to control feeling marks sentimental fiction with formal and tonal fluidity, unevenness, or instability. Men and women of feeling utter broken phrases of sympathetic response, testifying to their sincerity by their inability to articulate emotion in the social coinage of words, yet this drama is explained to the reader through conventional narrative. Such tonal instability is echoed by the narrative techniques of much sentimental literature: interruptions, digressions, and narrative fractures; the tonal combination of pathos and humor; and highly stylized, exclamatory rhetoric.[19] These silences and fragments, however, appear within the conventional narrative frame of the author's chosen genre, a frame often reinforced by narrative irony. Deletions and interruptions, moreover, paradoxically testify to a "whole" story that the distanced reader can perceive, while irony serves to edit sympathy and didacticism so that the reader does not, in fact, feel what the hero is portrayed as feeling.

What is the effect of this stylistic confusion? Certainly, sentimental fiction does celebrate internal experience as the source of knowledge and feeling as the very process of morality. At the same time, the stylistics of sentimentalism persistently shape this celebration of feeling to social ends in a way that undermines the ostensible claims of sentimentalism itself. The conventional language, pictorial diction, tonal instability, structural fragmentation, and multiple narrative voices work to externalize these interior experiences, to deprive them of authority, and to subordinate them within a social frame. Sentimental feeling thus remains firmly a fictional phenomenon, different from, if related to, the experience of the reader. Furthermore, the rhetorical emphasis on spectatorial distance underscores the futility of individual feeling unless it is socialized by being observed, unless, that is, it is useful to or used by others. The reader feels something different from the feeling of the character, usually something better. Hence sentimental stylistics enforce the caution Mackenzie reiterated in his moral essays: sentiment must be restrained, channeled, and employed; it should, indeed, be expressed through society for the public good. The restriction of sentimental expression within the bounds of generic convention represses the sentimental cognizance of the separation between self and other by suggesting that feeling cannot be understood unless it is shared.

This analysis of the stylistics of sentimentalism suggests a politics of sentimental fiction more conservative than might first appear although it would be a pity if recognizing this conservatism entailed ignoring the attention sentimentalism achieved for women in moving domestic and sexual issues to the forefront. At this period, women won a place in the world of letters; their concerns were the concerns of writers, and they were writers themselves, forging a literary culture in opposition to the previous neoclassical literary tradition.[20] As readers, women helped to redefine social values to include domestic relations. Throuĝh literary sentimentalism, women's feelings were figured as a serious subject, one that offered challenges to the social order to reform according to new values. These challenges also drive the formal dialectic in sentimental literature between expression and constraint.[21] Nonetheless, sentimental fiction propagates a role for women that is confining and articulates deep-seated hostility toward the new values women and feminine culture seemed to propound. In her analysis of the novel, Nancy Armstrong argues that the novel legitimizes female desire, an argument sustained but qualified by Felicity Nussbaum. In fact, sentimental fictions often reprove this desire, albeit only after they have represented it. While they also idealize domestic and private life, and laud motherhood and conjugal love, a relatively new phenomenon as Laurence Stone has observed, they do so as a way to cancel the threateningly anarchic possibilities of sentimentalism: the woman's world represents a reconciliation of private feeling and social restraint. Indeed, for sentimental writers, "female values" exemplify the dangers as well as advances of new culture, motivating many authors to use sentimental ideals to advocate female passivity, gratitude, quiescence, and conformity.

Since literary sentimentalism negotiates the relationship between aesthetic convention and sentimental ideology, the issue of taste, of aesthetic preference, is central to sentimental fictions. This issue signals in the eighteenth century the social disruptions of a new system of values, the clash between different classes and sexes.[22] Even at the beginning of the century, Pope had warned that new aesthetic ideas, by changing culture itself and creating new producers of culture, threatened the established social and moral order, a point reiterated in midcentury by Samuel Johnson. By the end of the century, however, sentimentalism was firmly entrenched as popular taste and sold in cheap editions even while it still colored the poetry and prose of "high" culture. Many sentimental writers, preoccupied with taste and its relationship to morality, demonstrate this contemporary confusion of "high" and "low" taste by emphasizing the rarity and emotional cost--or price--of fine feeling. Even while sentiment was seen as universal, it was a mark of naturally high class, as was the aristocratic stance of elite detachment.

This posture of detachment or distance adopted by the ideal reader or spectator in the late eighteenth century has drawn much analysis. John B. Sheriff has fruitfully suggested in *The Good-Natured Man* that, in the writings of the end of the century, such a posture works to naturalize aesthetic attitudes, and thus to revise the old opposition between art and nature as cooperation.[23] This change, nevertheless, involves a redefinition of both terms. Literary sentimentalism accomplishes this redefinition by blurring the old identification of nature with the "lower" classes and presenting a new, aestheticized version of nature as disinterested. As Pierre Bourdieu remarks, "The denial of lower, coarse, vulgar, venal, servile--in a word, natural--enjoyment, which constitutes the sacred sphere of culture, implies an affirmation of the superiority of those who can be satisfied with the sublimated, retired, disinterested, gratuitous, distinguished pleasures."[24] Aestheticized nature, nature redefined as art, imbues the cultivated spectator with natural enjoyment that is yet refined away from nature.[25] By framing the picture of sentiment within the conventions of genre, authors and readers of sentimental fiction demonstrate this refinement.[26]

If detachment guarantees "true" vision, then interest--self-interest, or involvement--blurs the spectatorial eye that can make art of nature. Women, therefore, so runs the discourse, whose sex always "interests" them in fleshly and immediate affairs, have difficulty, as portrayed by sentimental art, in surveying as they should, although they do make a pretty picture. This notion of women as vulnerable to self-interest--the private sphere--is a conventional one in English culture. Derived from antiquity, the idea that women represent immoderation, especially in sexual appetite, reappears in the rhetorical satires of the seventeenth and early eighteenth centuries.[27] In later fiction, women, often involuntarily, tempt the spectator to self-interested feelings that have nothing to do with social good. In Mackenzie's *Man of Feeling*, for example, the hero Harley descends from disinterest into questionable motivations when a destitute prostitute begs him for help. In the late eighteenth century, this link between women and sexual indulgence serves to justify reactionary attacks on the new reading audience, who will learn only promiscuity from books. The literature of sentimentalism must thus separate sexual sensation from benevolence to maintain its ideal of the aesthetic and tasteful control of response.[28] It does so by locating sensation in observation.

This value for distance complicates the conventional ideal of public duty in which each man cares for his fellows as for himself. By the end of the century, in the aftermath of the French Revolution, "sensibility"--the quality of vital responsiveness lauded by sentimentalism--was seen as opposed to the individual's duty to law, and thus to himself and to his fellows. Throughout the history of literary sentimentalism, the laws of fiction, conventions, help to articulate this dialectic between individual impulse and accepted form. One example of this balance is demonstrated by a poetical pamphlet entitled *Sensibility, Provoked by the Rival Pretensions of Pity*, printed in 1819 by the author.[29] In a dense prose preface, the landowning author explains the circumstances behind his prosecution of a peasant for £5 instead of £20 when the peasant, after accidentally killing a pheasant on his land, attempted to take it home to eat. The landowner defends his action as justice mitigated by charity within the limits of the law. The association of law, social superiority, benevolence, and sensibility appears within the first unhappy lines:

I would not enter on my list of friends
(Though grac'd with polish'd manners and fine sense,
Yet wanting sensibility) the man
Who needlessly sets foot upon a worm.

While reiterating the sentimental praise for instinctive behavior over "polish," this verse nonetheless graphically illustrates the social divisions between objects of sentiment and the subject who feels sensibility. Similarly, the reader of sentimental fiction feels rational pity for the sentimental character, a pity that balances the general demands of law or convention with the particulars of circumstance.

In general through the second half of the eighteenth century, sentimental fictions increasingly separate their protagonists from society, feminize them, and portray their unspoken emotions rather than their conversations or confessions. Although sentimental fictions span the last half of the eighteenth century, sentimental vignettes appear as early as the second decade. In the popular periodical *The Spectator* (1711-12, 1714), Addison and Steele lace their cultural criticism with fictional scenes that evoke pity and benevolence from the reader positioned as spectator. While several early periodicals imitated *The Spectator*, *The Female Spectator* (1744-46) by Eliza Haywood (?1693-1756) exemplifies the dialectical strains in sentimental stylistics by encasing sentimental episodes in a moral discourse that opposes experience and spectatorial distance. Although Daniel Defoe (1660-1731) does not use Addison and Steele's technique and Samuel Richardson (1689-1761) uses it only for occasional, dramatic scenes, Henry Fielding (1707-54) structures his novels by means of a detached narrator who quite often describes scenes in sentimental language. His final novel, *Amelia* (1751), dramatizes the conflict between the authority represented by ironic perspective and the authority claimed by sentimental response. While exploring female sensibility, these early fictions retain the frame of a social context that serves as the touchstone of the heroes' values.

In the 1760s, however, sentimental fictions were beginning to recast the relations between the sentimental hero and society, partly by removing their heroes from their homes, from London, or from England. *The Vicar of Wakefield* (1766) by Oliver Goldsmith (?1730-74) and *The Fool of Quality* (1766-70) by Henry Brooke (1703-83) position their male heroes in opposition to society, but both books escape the ideological consequences of this structure by explaining it as a test of the protagonists' worth conducted by a disguised nobleman. This resolution through a form of *deus ex machina* restores, even revives, the social hierarchy, partially in reaction, perhaps, to the threat posed by Sterne's carnivalesque sentimentalism. Laurence Sterne

(1713-68), the least moralistic--if the most critical--of sentimental writers, depicts society as a threat to the sensitive soul in both *The Life and Opinions of Tristram Shandy* (1759-67) and *A Sentimental Journey through France and Italy* (1768). Frances Moore Brooke (1724-89) criticizes social values through female spectators in her periodical *The Old Maid* (1755-56) and her novels *The History of Lady Julia Mandeville* (1763) and *The History of Emily Montague* (1769), which takes place in Canada. Both Sterne and Frances Brooke, partly by contrasting England with other nations in travelogues, nonetheless evoke an idealized society that is the predication for sensibility.

Henry Mackenzie (1745-1831) embodies the contradictory impulses fracturing sentimental prose fiction at the height of the cult of sensibility, the 1770s. His first novel, *The Man of Feeling* (1771), describes the brief career of a sentimental hero through the double frame of two narrators whose spectatorial sympathy complicates the novelistic tone. His periodicals *The Mirror* (1779-80) and *The Lounger* (1785-87) interlard vignettes depicting men and women whose fine feelings have alienated them from society with moral essays on self-discipline. The structural fractures between Mackenzie's moral frame and his sentimental content invited publishers to recycle Mackenzie's stories in different contexts. In the miscellanies of the 1780s and 1790s, vignettes from *The Spectator* and well as *The Mirror* and *The Lounger* appeared reframed by publishers as popular literature.

After the French Revolution, sentimental fictions bury their celebration of individual feeling beneath the rhetoric of enlightened self-discipline. These sentimental protagonists are extraordinary not merely for their capacity to feel, but for their ability to control their feelings. While isolating her heroines from normative society, Ann Radcliffe (1764-1823) relocates normative judgment within their disciplined and educated minds. Both *The Romance of the Forest* (1791) and *The Mysteries of Udolpho* (1794) punish their heroines for their excessive imaginative response and praise them for their rationality. Jane Austen (1775-1817) similarly segregates emotional responsiveness and social responsibility in *Sense and Sensibility* (1811). At the end of the eighteenth century, the sentimental opposition to social values is depicted as a threat to both society and the heroine herself. Nineteenth-century sentimental novelists like Dickens turn this structure to the end of social criticism. Little Nell and Florence Dombey possess an unspoiled sensibility that throws the harshness and hypocrisy of mercenary society into relief, but they are the ones who suffer while the social mechanism grinds heedlessly on.

The poles between which sentimental writers worked can be seen more fully developed in later forms of fiction. Eighteenth-century literary sentimentalism has bred a flock of offspring. Gothic fiction, gloomy father of "slash-and-mash" horror films, and Victorian "sensation" fiction dropping tears on the domestic hearth are two of the most evident. Both simultaneously commemorate and punish feeling as heroic but hazardous. Even these siblings, however, exhibit rival ideas. Borrowing from the rough tales of physical or mental sensation penned by such authors as Smollett and Beckford, Gothic novels revel in anti-social violence, mocking soft feeling and parading perversity in order to rouse the reader to extremes of emotion. On the other hand, much Victorian sentimentality, wallowing in socialized sentiment, depicts the "natural" unity of nature and society in order to prompt the reader's love of virtue; Dickens, for example, banishes perverse characters like Quilp to the moral fringe even while he lambasts society. Different as they are, however, both kinds of later sentimentalism claim to reveal human nature. This heritage raises the questions of what ideas inform the early literature of sentimentalism, and of how these ideas are transformed through the rhetoric of literary texts. How does early sentimental literature in fact view feeling, nature, and society? This book attempts to answer these questions.

Sentimentalism dominated literature throughout the second half of the eighteenth century although sentimental morality precedes 1745 and extends beyond 1800 with its message of self-restraint. Popular sentimental fictions, which often reprinted episodes from sentimental novels or imitations, portray the effects of excess well into the nineteenth century. The "Affecting Histories" published from 1740 to 1850 recount the consequences of "an immoderate attachment to wealth" (1780), of deranged love in "Louisa, the Wandering Maniac" (1804), of extraordinary isolation in the "Duchess in the Dungeon" (1820), and of juvenile delinquency through the tale of Tom Bragwell (1821).[30] Sentimental themes and techniques also appear in eighteenth-century forms other than prose fiction. The shift in contemporary poetry from the rhetorical address of epistle to the reflective mode of the observing poet in, for example, Goldsmith's "Traveller" or "A Prospect on Society" demonstrates this trend toward a belief in the authority of detachment: the poet no longer speaks with an audience, but rather to himself.

In this book, however, I examine widely read fictions from the period in which sentimentalism transformed literature.[31] These fictions range from texts now canonical to novels now scarcely known, all very popular during the eighteenth century and each exhibiting a representative structure of sentimental prose fiction. While these texts are similarly characterized by problematic stylistics that frame feeling as spectacle, they do follow a pattern of change, more of emphasis than of ideas. The earlier fictions evoke an identifiable set of social values to which private feeling should conform; using the moralistic structures of satire and fable, they speak through autobiographical, epistolary, and didactic voices to model the reconciliation of self and society. From the 1770s, however, sentimental fictions become

more pessimistic about the liberating effect of feeling, and structure their
sentiment within detached narratives. In all these texts, however, the
conventions of plot, character, and language that structure genre work to
separate the reader from too unbridled an identification with the sentimental
characters in the story and to criticize excess and feminine feeling.

This book follows a chronological order. By discussing, first, the rhetoric
of Eliza Haywood's *Female Spectator* and, next, of Henry Fielding's *Amelia*,
Chapter 1 identifies some of the ideological and stylistic conflicts and tropes
that mark sentimental rhetoric throughout the century. This chapter explores
the relationship between narrative authority and "female" stories by
identifying the dialectic between reformist and domestic rhetoric, and between
traditional and new ideas, particularly of consumption and display, in
contemporary culture. The following three chapters examine the negotiations
of sentimentalism in the prose fictions of the 1760s, which use intimate
narrative voices both to model and to reprove sentiment. The second chapter
analyses the development of sentimental rhetoric as an open discussion of
aesthetic issues in the works of Oliver Goldsmith and Henry Brooke. Both
these authors, reflecting neoclassical notions of aesthetics and morality, use
moral fable to advocate the control of sentimental excess, vanity, and
consumption. After a chapter discussing Sterne's ironic treatment of
sentiment and perception and his attack on female and contemporary literary
values, Chapter 4 explores the formal consequences of sentimental
spectatorship in Frances Brooke's works, including her periodical and two
epistolary fictions. The fifth chapter explicates the criticism of selfish feeling
and the negotiation between narrative distance and exemplary sentimentalism
in Henry Mackenzie's works. Chapter 6 explores the popularization of
sentimental literature in the context of the literary miscellany by analyzing,
first, the literary contents of three miscellanies and, next, the physical
arrangements and cultural reception of the form. The final chapter examines
the diffusion of spectatorial morality into omniscient narrative in the Gothic
fictions of Ann Radcliffe. The Conclusion uses Austen's *Sense and Sensibility*
(1811) and Richard Payne Knight's optical theory in *An Analytical Inquiry
into the Principles of Taste* (1805) to summarize the attitudes of eighteenth-
century sentimental writers to sentimental spectatorship.

Dialectical conflicts between the apparent ideology and the rhetoric and
structure of sentimentalism constitute the style of sentimental prose fictions.[32]
Literary sentimentalism, like pictorial sentimentalism, shows the audience
how to see so that the audience itself models views and creates aesthetic
effects that interrupt or condition feeling into observation. This style seeks to
counter what was seen as the dangerous commodification of literature and the
rise of chaotic private interpretation by reconciling individual and social
meanings. As this book hopes to show, literary sentimentalism does not free

feeling, but cages it within social limits, advocating moderation and balance over excess, reflection over impulse, and education in Christian and social duty over instinct.[33] Literary sentimentalism frames feeling as the refined response to the spectacle of the individual in society.

CHAPTER 1

Gender and Narrative Authority:
The Female Spectator and *Amelia*

> Life may as properly be called an art as any other;
> and the great incidents in it are no more to be
> considered as mere accidents, than the several
> members of a fine statue, or a noble poem.
>
> Preface to *Amelia*.

The first eighteenth-century fictions of literary sentimentalism were brief vignettes depicting characters expending violent emotions, perceived by the sympathetic but secret, or hidden, observer--the narrator. Common scenes showed lovers, wives, priests, a range of old and young characters exhibiting grief, piety, domestic or filial love, remorse, and gratitude. Such vignettes appeared in a context, periodical journals, that celebrated the power of the observer to shape his experience as art and thus to moralize life. This context included far more than sentimental fiction. As contemporary chronicles of art, literature, and manners, periodicals had already established in the early century the format of providing a dialogue with the silent reader through the voice of the controlling narrator, be this persona a member of a club or the author of letters.[1] Who better to judge manners, culture, and value than a voice that represented a group or club of spectators authorized by their number, by their expertise in literary evaluation, and by the reader's consent? Through such exchanges, periodicals defined fashionable culture as social agreement between refined equals: the persona approved plays and books, described dress and attitudes, popularized new forms of expression, and meditated on social values, all with the implied complicity of the reader. To meet the frequent deadlines and to net a substantial audience, periodicals articulated fairly common ideas that would nonetheless stimulate strong reactions in the reader in a variety of brief forms: letters, narrative visions, poetry, essays, tales, vignettes, parodies, and reveries. Juxtaposed at random with no necessary connection to each other, these forms also prompted various, even conflicting, sympathetic reactions, including especially laughter, reflection, wonder, and tears. The periodical form demands that the reader be able to shift quickly among different reactions as the mode of expression shifts from essay to description, or from hortatory to satirical passages. This context helps to establish literary sentimentalism as a cultural articulation of social cohesion which, by eliciting similar, albeit multiple, personal responses in a medley of private readers, enacts the ideological uniformity of the social body.

Among the favorite topics of the eighteenth-century periodical is social behavior, a topic that pulls together diverse readers and diverse reactions. It is a rich subject for the periodical, a genre predicated on contemporaneity, because manners change with the times and readers therefore require constant updates. To many eighteenth-century observers, manners portrayed the current condition of society. Women's manners, especially, showed social "progress" since women were seen as displaying both wealth and morality on and through their bodies, by their laces, and by their blushes. In *Women and Print Culture*, Kathryn Shevelow has analyzed the way periodicals "construct" femininity by different portrayals of female readers.[2] The very enterprise of this construction, however, is founded on the new set of values and standards embraced by literary sentimentalism. It is the sentimental thesis that response, physical and emotional, reveals morality, that women are peculiarly suited to display that response, and that this display comprises modern manners: the behavior of sensibility. Female manners thus reflect social progress. To observers allied to conventional values, however, sentimental behavior can also be construed as vanity or degeneracy.[3] Thus, while periodical discussions focus on the way female manners pertain to sexual relations, notably prostitution and marriage, they also debate how women should participate in their society, what specific duties or abilities they have to aid the general progress, and whether their sensibility is safe or healthy. This concern about how women should be educated to behave permeates eighteenth-century sentimental fiction.[4]

Eighteenth-century periodicals treat the subject of female behavior with a seriousness that is new. This is not to say that early newspapers had not examined sexual relations. Aaron Hill's *The British Apollo* (1708-11), for example, imitating Dunton's *Athenian Mercury*, represented a scientific "club" of Londoners who promised to answer any questions their female and male audience asked. Many of these letters, invented or modified by the editors themselves to shape as well as reflect popular culture, concern sexual behavior. While most questions involve empirical inquiry--Why are Negroes dark-skinned? How is snow formed?--those that discuss contemporary manners deliberately play for laughs. In number 157, the fifth and final question, bearing no relation to the other inquiries, constitutes the comic complaint of a love-lorn man.[5] The reply, which merits full reproduction here, parodies the exhausted clichés of courtly love.

> Q. *Gentlemen, I have long passionately Lov'd a Lady who for her Excellent Perfections, rather merits Adoration: I have pass'd through all the Probationary Injuuctions* [sic] *requir'd of a Lover, given my self Violent Airs, then Sigh'd, Whin'd, Pip'd under her Window, look'd like an Ass, when* [sic] *slovenly, forgot to blow my Nose and made Verses; nay, I had certainly attempted to kill my self but that I fear'd her Consent to it. Now pray resolve me if this Divine Creature, this illustrious Goddess in regard to all I have suffer'd for her sake, is not obliged in Gratitude, to return Love for Love?*
>
> A. Certainly no--It argues worse than Pagan Stupidity, to expect the Object of our Worship should make Reciprocal Returns, it is sufficient, if she accepts your Off'rings, but Presumption to expect so much as Familiar Conference with a Superior Power: Were she convinced that you was such another Divine Creature, (of which, your going Slovenly and looking like an Ass, gives us little hopes) She might possibly admit of Parley; but even then would not be under the least Obligation of making mutual Returns, for that would encroach on the Freedom of her Choice, and reduce her to a more servile Condition than your own: Therefore if your Goddess be inexorable, the best Advice we can give, is, to comfort your self with *Epicurus*'s Maxim, that your Sufferings cannot be Great and Long: Perhaps She may honour your Ashes with so much Compunction, as to sigh, and say, 'tis Pity--and so call for the Cards.

While deflating artificial manners and words, this reply mocks an issue that sentimental periodicals take seriously: What behavior and language will regulate sexual relations to keep both parties respected and respectful in the new century? The answer provided by sentimental journals is to "naturalize" love, to define love not as a skillful dance organized by stylistic rules, but as a journey of self-discovery. This shift is expressed in form: periodicals increasingly feature what Robert D. Mayo calls "miscellany fiction," short tales that represent "instinctive" feeling in narrative vignettes set in the contemporary world. In this shift from representing love as art to representing love as nature, readers are invited to join the moral circle by experiencing pathos.   The tales themselves, however, characterize women as largely powerless over their sexual behavior; their "instinctive" feelings become both "moral" and dangerous, like nature itself, both disinterested and self-absorbed.

Whereas *The British Apollo* addresses primarily "scientific" issues, many journals specialize in social relations, generally in a progressive or Whiggish spirit, which occasionally leads to practical suggestions at odds with conventional moral discourse. For example, whereas women's vanity might be a moral flaw, it can also be a social virtue by stimulating consumption, as Bernard Mandeville pointed out in "The Grumbling Hive." In accordance with social needs, Sir Richard Steele, in the periodical entitled *The Spinster* (1719-20), urges women to promote Spittlefields's industry by dressing in opulent French fashions made at home. Here, "TISSERANDO DE BROCADE," thanking Steele for his support, prices several luxurious articles of clothing including "A Hat of LEGHORN" for £1 10s, and asks women to spend at least £150 a year on perfume. This connection between economics and fashion, production and consumption, casts women as participants in every level of society. At the same time, women exemplify the commodification of pleasure, which some authors like Goldsmith believed was threatening to replace the sympathetic bond between members of society with the merely expedient bonds of self-interest.

Through their sentimental vignettes, periodicals attempt to reconcile these contradictory or dangerous aspects of modern commercial society by realizing Shaftesbury's formula that taste is virtue. Consumption thus translates as morality. These vignettes sell the latest in aesthetic taste under the guise of moral parable. Within the context of the miscellaneous periodical, these stories are elements in a general discourse on social progress and taste that locates them as stylistic demonstrations of the way to internalize artistic values.

Addison and Steele exemplify this technique in their early periodical *The Tatler* (1709-11). Here, social commentary first becomes identified with elegance of manners and language so that the lines between literary expertise and moral acuity blur. The most influential sentimental periodical, however, is undoubtedly their later *Spectator* (1711-12, 1714). Through a persona acting as the marginalized witness of the follies of people and society, *The Spectator* describes manners, art, social issues and events, and theories of aesthetics and response. These tales of love, death, fear, renunciation, and joy provide models of short, sentimental episodes for such later writers as Frances Brooke and Henry Mackenzie, authors of both periodicals and novels.

In their periodicals, Addison and Steele establish the contextual issues surrounding sentimental fiction--the frame around the feeling--while also defining the characteristics of its rhetoric. Their vignettes illustrate contempo-

rary fashions of art and of response: the way these incidents are described by
the sensitive Spectator demonstrates the way language should express feeling.
Although Mr. Spectator traces the gestures of his distraught characters and
the details of emotion on their faces, he envelopes his stories within the
medium of his own perception, his discourse, his context. This formula
centers on the eye, on the act (informed by art and theater) of spectating, as
the source of interpretation. Like Mr. Spectator, the reader organizes his or
her response by genre scenes, sublime landscapes, and theatrical postures
contextualized in social dialogue. The reader's sense that he or she sees in
company with the authors and with fellow readers frames his or her feeling
within a social context. (See Plate 1.) This context relies on the central
character, the "I" or the eye, which, in turn, establishes the contextual values
of the fiction.

Addison's persona, Mr. Spectator, embodies the ideal perspective
endorsed by sentimental stylistics as well as its contradictions. As we learn
from his introduction of himself to the reader, he is far from theatrical; his
values are not easily seen. Indeed, he defeats superficial judgment, for,
although deemed "sullen" by his peers as a boy, he wins from his schoolmas-
ter the encomium, "*that my Parts were solid and would wear well.*"[6] He holds
his knowledge within himself; he does not spend it in speech or display.
Well-read, curious, and widely traveled, Mr. Spectator is considered "an
unaccountable fellow, that had a great deal of Learning, if I would but show
it." Indeed, so self-possessed is he, we are told, that it is only his friends'
importunities, the social need, that persuades him to converse with the reader.
This self-possession grants him the detachment to see the spectacle of others;
himself content, needing nothing, unattached socially or emotionally,
Mr.Spectator sees clearly. He donates his affection to his friends and his
sympathy to strangers. Containing his own identity, moreover, he can
masquerade as any member of society--politician, merchant, Jew. Mr.
Spectator thus has the power to compare the characters and feelings of
different types of men within and beyond his society. His position, moreover,
almost removes him from the social world: "I live in the World, rather as a
Spectator of Mankind, than as one of the Species" (4). The sentimental
spectator endlessly absorbs experience, accumulates emotion, and educates
himself until his private world mirrors the world around him in diversity and
expanse. Thus, spectatorship--watching, comparing, and so judging--
designates social privilege: the spectator embodies disinterested social values
and judgments.

Addison and Steele's persona represents a fantasy of social control in
which the spectator is everywhere yet eternally private and invisible, learned
yet unprejudiced, detached yet passionate. Such a stance facilitates the
expression of the contradictions in sentimental stylistics. Albeit responding

Plate 1: Frontispiece to *The Spectator* vol. 1 (1711) 1753.
Courtesy of the Watkinson Library, Hartford, Ct.

in private to what he sees and feels, the spectator yet represents the
experience of social alienation paradoxically as a sentimental bond between
the self and the audience. While celebrating the perception of isolated
incidents that allow the spectator to reflect, *The Spectator* links such incidents
by portraying them through the eyes of a single character. This provides a
narrative that emphasizes effect rather than cause, locating morality in
response rather than in responsibility. At the same time, since narrative
normally embodies causality, the spectator's method inevitably connects
events and the moral consequences of them. For eighteenth-century writers,
this causality could indeed best be perceived by someone structurally
detached and disinterested, situated God-like above the action, and so
positioned to see the whole story. Pope, for example, adopts this Olympian
stance in the *Essay on Man* (1733-34) when he explains human dissatisfac-
tion as the failure to see the interdependence of events, which is clear from
the perspective of God. In this sense, narrative represents the language of
law, of social organization, and of order, and, by virtue of his detachment,
Mr. Spectator represents the authoritative narrator. At the same time, Mr.
Spectator and his "club" conjure an ideal society that reflects the individual's
response, and thus broadens the context of the emotional impression.
Sentimental observers cast the impressionistic experience of feeling in a
moral framework. The sentimental structure of periodicals thus forms a
structural dialectic between dynamic narrative and static vignette, between
social cohesion and individual perception, between characters' actions and
spectators' visions, between the reader's engagement and the narrator's
detachment. In the first fully sentimental fictions of the mid-eighteenth
century, this dialectic centers on the topic of sexual love and takes on
gendered implications.

I: *The Female Spectator* and the Moral Gaze

   Among the many journals that imitated *The Spectator*, one of the most
celebrated was *The Female Spectator* (1744-46). Written by the conservative,
popular novelist Eliza Haywood, *The Female Spectator* announces by its title
that it differs from Addison and Steele's journal by virtue of gender. This
difference, however, entails a difference in form.[7] Whereas Mr. Spectator
comments in short essays and tales on many topics and invites the reader to
respond, the Female Spectator, self-consciously addressing only a female
audience, pronounces didactically on the "female" issues of love and
marriage. Rather than a serial publication, which allows quick response to

current events and readers' replies, *The Female Spectator* appears in immutable form, already complete. In place of Addison's praise for feeling, the narrator stresses the morality of restraint and reading through a rhetoric of defense, apology, and warning. Whereas Mr. Spectator exemplifies the right education, the Female Spectator models the wrong one; where Mr. Spectator models the way we should feel, the Female Spectator tells us how not to behave. Rather than being invited to imitate the spectator, Haywood's reader is cautioned to avoid becoming the spectacle.

The Female Spectator appears as twenty-four long essays, each providing an exemplary tale of a faulty woman encased in extensive moral commentary. These commentaries describe the punishment for sentimental indulgence or lack of self-control: shame, ridicule, ostracization, and banishment, all forms of social disgrace. Ironically, the very condition that empowers Mr. Spectator to speak authoritatively on society, his detachment from it, is translated as the cost of female folly: the disempowering or silencing of foolish women. In describing both love and art, the Female Spectator vaunts social over individual values: "I readily agree, that love in itself, when under the direction of reason, harmonizes the soul, and gives it a gentle, generous turn; but I can by no means approve of such definitions of that passion as we find in plays, novels, and romances [in which] the authors seem to lay out all their art in rendering that character most interesting, which most sets at defiance all the obligations, by the strict observance of which, love alone can become a virtue."[8] For Haywood, narrative conveys morality and should enforce self-discipline within a social context. She refigures the responsiveness celebrated by the form of *The Spectator* and by its narrator as moral weakness; correspondingly, it is female error that produces her own narrative. *The Female Spectator* warns women against sensibility, languishing airs, and independent desires typified in "Romances, Novels, and Plays," which show love "impatient of Controul [sic], and trampling over all the Ties of Duty, Friendship, or natural Affection" (1: 10). By opposing "Love" and "natural Affection," Haywood identifies nature with "duty" and society rather than with passion.[9] Throughout the periodical, Haywood indicts female affectation and exhibition as betraying bad taste and inviting social ruin. For her, the woman who stands out is not a spectator but a disgrace.

Haywood emphasizes the function of reading as education and as the exercise of good taste. If writing demonstrates female fault, reading about such faults demonstrates moral and social superiority:

> It is very much, by the choice we make of Subjects for our
> Entertainment, that the refined Taste distinguishes itself from

> the vulgar and more gross: Reading is universally allowed to
> be one of the most improving, as well as agreeable Amuse-
> ments, but then to render it so, one should among the Number
> of Books which are perpetually issuing from the Press,
> endeavour to single out such as promise to be most conducive
> to those Ends. (1: 10)

Haywood thus reiterates the classical formula of instruction and delight in
recommending the use of books like hers for personal improvement. By
watching women and their "Amusements," moreover, the Female Spectator
guards social values. The female audience correspondingly displays its taste
by its literary discrimination; if women read indulgent narratives of female
passion, they pollute or mislead themselves, whereas narratives that cast them
as spectators, not heroines of passion, elevate them socially and morally.

While her periodical provides moral lessons, the Female Spectator
herself does not model correct behavior, although her perspective is laudably
detached. In endorsing the reading of moral narratives yet deploring the
occasions that prompt the writing of them, the Female Spectator puts herself
in a paradoxical position. She exemplifies folly yet she pronounces wisdom;
her morality derives from her immorality. Her defensive language is
symptomatic of the contradictions of her position. She opens: "In order to be
as little deceived as possible, I, for my own part, love to get as well
acquainted as I can with an author, before I run the risk of losing my time
in perusing his work; and as I doubt not but most people are of this way of
thinking, I shall, in imitation of my learned brother of ever precious memory,
give some account of what I am... " (1: 8). While providing a biography of
the periodical's persona is conventional--Frances Brooke and Henry
Mackenzie do the same--Haywood's rationale is uniquely admonitory: she
declares not that her biography will enable the reader to sympathize more
closely with the speaker, but that it will protect the reader as much as
"possible" from deception and waste. She thus adjures her readers not to
identify themselves with the speaker but with other readers.

Her biography underscores this devaluation of the female as writer. In
the process of asserting her narrative authority, the Female Spectator portrays
herself as beyond social concerns, as was her brother, Mr. Spectator. Now
neither beautiful nor young, in the past she has been foolish and shallow: "As
a proof of my sincerity, ... I shall also acknowledge, that I have run through
as many scenes of vanity and folly as the greatest coquet of them all.--Dress,
equipage, and flattery were the idols of my heart.--I should have thought that
day lost, which did not present me with some new opportunity of shewing
[sic] myself" (1: 8). Unlike Mr. Spectator, the Female Spectator had been
dazzled by the superficial values of society: rank, popularity, display.

This experience, however, has contradictory effects. While it prohibits the Female Spectator from serving as a model for the reader, it also hones her perceptions, empowering her to judge society. She explains that, at the risk of her "own interest and reputation," she formed a general if indiscriminate acquaintance which gave her information she lacked, and "also enabled me, when the too great vivacity of my nature became tempered with reflection, to see into the secret springs which gave rise to the actions I had either heard or been witness of;--to judge of the various passions of the human mind, and distinguish those imperceptible dangers by which they become masters of the heart, and attain the dominion over reason" (1: 8). The Female Spectator penetrates the human heart by means of the same talents and experience that she deplores. Albeit urging the morality of reflection, the Female Spectator nevertheless derives her very authority to watch, her spectatorship, from errors that her readers are enjoined to avoid. She speaks from a position of social detachment that is the penalty of bad behavior; both her articulation itself and her position thus demonstrate her moral flaws. The fact of her narrating is itself proof of her "fall," for the only "story" Haywood recognizes for women is the forbidden or reproved story of sexual experience. The alternative "story" has no narrative. In contrast to the Female Spectator, Haywood offers her patroness as an example of flawless behavior. Invoking the social control exercised through the "eyes" of the world, Haywood praises the Duchess of Leeds as an exemplary sight in her dedication: "We beheld with Admiration, how *Reason* outstrip'd *Nature* even in the most minute Circumstances and Actions; but the Crown of all, was the happy Choice of a Partner in that state which is the chief End of our Beings" (1: 4). Even the exemplary Duchess must restrain "nature" by reason, a prefatory philosophy at odds with Addison's sentimental credo. The Duchess, moreover, excels by choosing her husband wisely: her sexual restraint has won her social prominence. She models the ideal reader, the ideal spectacle.

Haywood completes her account of the Female Spectator's authority by endowing her with the voices of other women. Although Addison and Steele give their Spectator a circle of friends, they emphasize the peculiarity of each voice, each type. Haywood, however, stresses the unanimity of the Female Spectator's "Club": Mira, the witty wife; a vivacious widow; and Euphrosine, the accomplished daughter of a wealthy merchant. The Female Spectator assures us that everything she offers to the public has been read and edited by these three whom she urges be "considered only as several members of one Body, of which I am the Mouth" (1: 10-11). Whereas the Spectator embodies cultivated masculine taste by virtue purely of the authority of his voice, the Female Spectator represents female opinion only by delegation.

Haywood's version of Addison and Steele's sentimental *Spectator* sketches the conflicts in sentimental ideology and clarifies the way these conflicts are gendered and identified with certain forms and rhetorical styles. While the Spectator opines, the Female Spectator instructs. The Spectator judges with detachment the picture he sees; the Female Spectator moralizes with urgent purpose the evils she experiences. Mr. Spectator models feeling and judgment; the Female Spectator models self-censorship acquired by error. This dialectic between distance and sympathy, reformism and resignation, characterizes sentimental stylistics. While each spectator possesses the authority to narrate, however, this authority implies an experience that besmirches the virtue of female narrators who win their moral authority at the expense of their social position. Women represented in later sentimental fictions reflect this tension between narrative power or authority and moral power. When they represent virtue or sentiment, they tend not to tell their own tales, but rather to provide spectacles for the reader's and the narrator's contemplation; in later sentimental fictions, even such feminine heroes as Sterne's Toby or Mackenzie's Harley cannot tell their own stories. When women do tell their own tales, however, their reliability is often compromised, for the tales told by women are tales women should not tell, tales of feeling. Women thus serve in fiction more often as sentimental spectacles than as speakers. The powerful voice that frames nature or feeling within art comes from the male spectator. Perhaps the clearest example of this gendered division of ideology and the resulting stylistic medley is the most sentimental of Henry Fielding's fictions, *Amelia*.

II: *Amelia* and Female Influence

Novelistic sentimentalism is most commonly associated with the works not of Fielding but of Samuel Richardson. Richardson's novels assert the importance of personal feeling over social rank, while his epistolary method focuses narrative on the minutiae of experience, defined as impression and emotion, a method used by later sentimental writers like Frances Brooke. It is indeed through Richardson that sentimentalism comes to be identified with the literary expression of feminism. Such critics as Ian Watt, John Richetti, and Margaret Doody have noted that *Clarissa* first establishes the importance of women's internal experience as a subject for moral literature and presents woman as more than her sex.[10] By portraying the process of response as moral, moreover, Richardson popularized the correlations between female internal experience, emotional impressionism, and self-monitored morality.

The wealth of Richardson's endowments to literary sentimentalism, however, have tended to blind critics to those of his rival Henry Fielding. Indeed, critics traditionally have regarded Fielding as antagonistic to sentimentalism, labeling the sentimental themes and tone of his final novel a falling-off from his habitual, stringent irony.[11] As Michael McKeon observes in *The Origins of the English Novel, 1600-1740*, however, "Readers have long recognized that after their initial collision at the beginning of the 1740s, Fielding and Richardson spent the next decade edging closer to each other."[12] He discovers in the works of the two authors a dialectic between "progressive" and traditional ideals exemplified by the heroine Pamela, who both contains and signifies virtue in a fashion similar to Mr. Spectator. Fielding himself plays ambivalently with the sentimental characteristics exemplified by *Pamela*. Although *Shamela* (1740) attacks the form of epistolary sentimentalism for insincerity, Fielding's longer novels flirt with some of Richardson's sentimental ideals. His narrator chronicles the education of nature and the heart through the virtuous characters Fanny, Joseph, and Abraham Adams in *Joseph Andrews* (1742) and through the hero of *Tom Jones* (1749), all of whom respond with instinctive, passionate good-nature. Through his detached narrator, moreover, Fielding articulates the exemplary judgment that is available by means of a distanced perspective similar to that of *The Spectator*; albeit structurally detached from the action, the narrator is yet central to the process of responding to it. The narrator models the right way to see feeling.

Amelia (1751), however, is the novel of Fielding's that most openly asserts sentimental ideals. Its plot, characters, and rhetoric endorse sentimental values. The story traces the life of Captain Booth, a good-hearted free-thinker married to the titular heroine, as he experiences the temptations and corruptions of the city. In the valorization of domestic love, the portrait of ideal womanhood, the exclamations of feeling by the narrator as well as the characters, and the apparent attack upon the corrupt political world, this novel recapitulates many sentimental tropes.[13] At the same time, the structure of the novel opposes its own sentimental ideology. Fielding recounts this story of love and conversion partly through a detached narrator speaking in public, reformist rhetoric, and partly through the unreliable narratives of the characters themselves.[14] While reformism is implied in many sentimental fictions, accusatory rhetoric is a satirical mode. By separating the narrator's perspective from the locus of virtuous feeling, Amelia, Fielding segregates judgment and moral response. He thus dramatizes the oppositions of sentimental ideology and exemplifies the stylistic difficulties of framing feeling.

This perhaps explains why *Amelia* has always been Fielding's least loved novel. Critics complain that the narrator's tone wavers between satire and sentimentality, compromising the reader's sympathy with the hero.[15] Such tonal ambiguity results from the dialectical structure of sentimental rhetoric itself as it solicits both engagement and distance from the reader. As Bertrand H. Bronson notes, in the second half of the century, the ideal of classical detachment and reason did not sink beneath a flood of tears, but, in fact, flourished.[16] Fielding's preference for types over characters rendered from within, his structural reliance on an authoritative narrator, and his references to Virgil's *Aeneid* reflect this neoclassical ideal of art as the portrayal of general nature and of universal standards. While Fielding invites readers to admire Amelia and, if they are female, to emulate her, it is the narrator's Olympian perspective that epitomizes authority. This narrator employs a rhetoric that derives from a tradition opposed to sentimentalism, a neoclassical, oratorical tradition that includes both reformist polemic and what Felicity Nussbaum terms "antifeminist satire."[17] This discourse criticizes women and conventional "female" culture as subversive and destructive: it associates many of the qualities that undermine society--envy, greed, selfishness, materiality--with the hazardous, female side of civilization. Such satire clashes in *Amelia* with Fielding's attempt to celebrate a new kind of femininity seen as private, domestic, and altruistic. In *Amelia*, traditional social values evoked through the narrator's rhetoric qualify the new sentimental ideals expressed in the plot. Through the representation of women in this novel, Fielding voices contemporary anxiety about the influence of new ideals on culture.

Amelia is a novel about women, sex, adultery, and kinds of freedom and limitation. Despite its title, however, it is not really a novel about *a woman*.[18] Rather, Fielding seeks to combine praise for a new feminine ideal with a conventional tale of male inheritance. Indeed, the common complaint about the novel that indicts its structure stems from the divergence between what Aurélien Digeon labels "the center of interest," Amelia, and "the center of action," her husband Captain Booth.[19] This conflict, however, does not so much indicate a failure of control by Fielding as it does express the mixed messages within sentimental discourse itself about the relative values of passion and action, and of women and feminine values. Fielding's difficulties in *Amelia* point out the contradictory demands that a sentimental plot imposes on conventional narrative form.

These contradictions appear nowhere more clearly than in Amelia's role in her own story. The role of Fielding's heroine directly opposes that of Richardson's *Clarissa*. In that novel, the heroine Clarissa occupies center stage; when Amelia embodies female virtue, she remains out of the action, quietly in the house, preparing a private dinner. Richardson's emotional action, the Puritan pattern of self-examination and psychological development, is transformed by Fielding to inaction, stasis, calm. Clarissa refuses to submit to Lovelace; Amelia avoids the rakish Colonel James. Clarissa publicizes herself through her letters; her consciousness comprises the plot. Amelia leaves her self to be narrated by Captain Booth, her husband; his mistakes comprise the plot, as his spiritual rebirth concludes it. Here, it is Booth who recapitulates Clarissa's role, confined, misjudged, and prostituted while he attempts to learn how to discipline himself to live up to his best feelings. Amelia represents the reward of virtue rather than serves as a model of the struggle of consciousness.

John J. Richetti notes Fielding's ambivalence about a method that glorifies a new feminine ideal by stressing his neoclassical techniques: "But even in *Amelia*, Fielding is still committed to traditional generality and concerned to shape his materials towards a controlled and coherent moral purpose. To a large extent, Fielding's moral psychology is interested in the comically predictable aspects of behavior, and his novels tend to exclude the kind of extended portrayal of women which seeks to understand their special mysteries and unique problems."[20] Richetti contrasts this method with Richardson's: "Clarissa is the ultimate woman in eighteenth-century English literature because she seizes the male initiative, transforming her sexual and social degradation into an occasion for her own moral-rhetorical display and replacing the female stereotype with a profoundly independent and transcendent humanity far beyond mere sexual identity" (97). Indeed, *Amelia* does not follow Richardson's lead. Unlike Mrs. Bennet's self-justifying narrative, Amelia's rhetoric is tacit, shown by her reactions not her words. The form and the rhetoric of Fielding's "sentimentalism" tend to recapitulate neoclassical attitudes of satirical disapproval, generality, and idealized distance in opposition to the "sentimentalism" embodied by Richardson. Sentimental fiction, however, borrows from both authors; beneath its attention to the specifics of consciousness lies the neoclassical belief in the universal truth of typical characters, predictable reactions, eternal human nature, and the importance of a departicularizing rhetoric. *Amelia* exemplifies this battle between rhetorical elements in literary sentimentalism through its multiple narrative voices and medley of rhetorical tropes, its critique of unlicensed sentiment, and its paradoxical location of a story of nature in the epitome of culture, London.

The site of this struggle between traditional and sentimental cultural ideals, and the place in which Fielding sets *Amelia*, is the city, the emblem at once of rational idealism and of human corruption. The city is the place of law, of institutions, of restraints; it is also the place of the disciplining of instinct through marriage and "policing," the place that deceives the heart.[21]

In the city, lawyers cheat, squabble, and pander while treacherously fluid, ever-unattainable money dictates power. This is the "realism" of Juvenalian satire in which sexual confusion, social disorder, corruption of nature, and abuse of power coalesce. It is the place where the laws of man overtake the law of nature, characters replace character, and divisively specialized interests war with the general interest.[22] The city thus resonates both in satirical and in sentimental rhetoric.

In *Amelia*, as less extensively in *Tom Jones*, Fielding uses the city as the emblematic location for the conflict between rhetorically gendered systems of value. As a locus particularly hospitable to the rapacious abuses perpetrated by such social institutions as marriage, law, and the army, the city represents the subversion of moral order and "natural" law, undermining economy by display and corrupting even "gentle" men like Colonel Bath into vain puppets. The narrator's rhetoric indicting this urban corruption derives from the rhetoric of moral reformation. Written immediately after Fielding's pamphlet on the "Late Increase of Robbers," *Amelia* suggests that the city requires a reformation of manners that will result from a return to ordered relationships; the restoration of order becomes the restoration of nature. Like Shaftesbury's rhetoric, itself designed to reform society, such language echoes Juvenal's social satire which opposes honesty to public behavior and social values. The classical exhortatory tone is directed toward those who can change society, those whose duty it is to do so: the rulers. There are, however, rulers in the household as well as in the country, as the first chapter establishes. The household, moreover, serves as an allegorical example of the country; this rhetorical analogy asserts the audience's power in the public as in the private realms. In a moral hierarchy echoing the social hierarchy, masculine *virtu* should frame or structure female sensibility, as the head should rule the heart and the public good, guarded by the ruling classes, should rule the city. By modifying the values of sentimentalism that are represented by female power within a structure of paternalistic and conventional public order, Fielding's novel models the discourse of literary sentimentalism itself.

Amelia opens by drawing a significant parallel between the house and society in language that evokes traditional concepts of order. After noting the "Imperfection" of the current constitution despite its creation by "*wise Men*"--a code term throughout later sentimental literature for the decayed establishment--the narrator speaks in the rhetorical tones of the lawyer:

> It will probably be objected, that the small Imperfections which
> I am about to produce, do not lie in the Laws themselves, but
> in the ill Execution of them ... if the same Legislature which
> provides the Laws, doth not provide for the Execution of them,

they act as *Graham* would do, if he should form all the Parts
of a Clock in the most exquisite Manner, yet put them so
together that the Clock could not go. (1: 2, 19) [23]

In this passage, which follows the exordium, Fielding's ironic, distanced, and
controlling narrator proposes an analogy between a faulty watch, a disordered
household, and a corrupt society. All are machines in which the pieces have
been misplaced.

Perhaps, Reader, I have another Illustration, which will set my
intention in still a clearer Light before you. Figure to yourself
then a Family, the Master of which should dispose of the
several oeconomical [sic] Offices in the following Manner: *viz.*
should put his Butler in the Coach-box, his Steward behind his
Coach, his Coachman in the Butlery, and his Footman in the
Stewardship, and in the same ridiculous Manner should
misemploy the Talents of every other Servant; it is easy to see
what a Figure such a Family must make in the World. (19-20)

Through Ciceronian anaphoric analogies, the narrator appeals to the reader
who possesses a timepiece, a household staff, and a classical education: the
gentleman with a regard for order and with the responsibility and means to
create it.[24] The analogy between watch, household, and legal constitution
introduces the issues that dominate this novel: the relationship between
private life and public or state affairs. The passage characterizes this
relationship, moreover, by reducing the great matter of the state to the scale
of household possessions and protocol. Fielding is equating domestic and
political arrangements. Even while implying that the difficulty of ruling the
home reflects the difficulty of ordering society at large, the narrator turns to
"the world" as the ultimate court of judgment: the fear of being "ridiculous,"
or being a public spectacle, should discipline all rulers into sense. The image
of the watch, furthermore, alludes to the neoclassical *typos* of the world as
a time mechanism and of God as watchmaker; here the public-minded private
citizen possesses nearly divine power to regulate life. Private, domestic life
is more than a model of public life; it is part of the public life of the
gentleman.

Fielding's analogy implies that the right hierarchical order will control
both private and public chaos, restoring to their places all of the parts of the
mechanism. People are not cogs and wheels, however, and Fielding knows
that society needs more than a mechanic, even a divine one: it needs feeling
to cement the social bonds. Such feeling, however, like society itself, must

be regulated. This regulation depends on the preservation of established social and sexual roles. Each element must stay in its place to perform its function; each person must maintain his or her established relations in society. In the socially fluid city, however, such stability is threatened as corrupt institutions reflect corrupt manners and values. This corruption elevates weakness and denigrates strength; instead of making private life a model of public order, the city shows public virtues abandoned to private interests. It is when the private becomes public, woman turns man, that all is anarchy.

After his opening analogy, Fielding's narrator supports his theory by describing the felonious cases brought before Justice Thrasher. As his name implies, this judge abuses his role as the dispenser of freedom "within the liberty of Westminster" through prejudice, fear, and cruelty (14). Each case he examines concerns sex or language and reveals the confusion of public and private values. The first comprises a brawl between an underfed Irishman and a stout Englishman; the Irishman's brogue instantly condemns him. While attacking chauvinistic prejudice, Fielding also suggests ironically that a half-starved Irishman who praises England must be abusing the language somehow, for plain common sense and plain talk would surely prove the Irishman wrong. Even patriotic values are awry here. Next, Thrasher condemns as a prostitute a servant running to get a midwife for her mistress. Ironically, she is indeed publicizing sex by exposing domestic affairs on the streets. Thrasher's insincere moralism reverses prurience and domesticity.

The two issues of language and sex coalesce in the next case. A young couple appears before the judge, caught in an act the suddenly decorous narrator "cannot describe." Unable to indict them for lovemaking, Justice Thrasher attempts to imprison the pair for perjury, which Thrasher immediately reinterprets as "rioting." The narrator further glosses the term with a footnote on its legal definition and spelling. Apparently, no legal word exists for "love," but plenty exist for the illegal act. Thus, in this episode, Fielding shows that feeling unlicensed by the state translates as sexual license, transmuted to verbal license, which in court becomes social or political license, and threatens the state order with riot, a carnivalesque reversal of power. The narrator's gloss on "rioting" or "riotting" (with the suggestive innuendo of "rutting") completes the circle, re-establishing the danger as wanton or lascivious sexual behavior. Even while indicting a heartless judicial system, Fielding associates sexual and political behavior. The perverse "professionalization" or specialization of language, the coin of social commerce, facilitates these elisions between social, legal, and sexual categories. A similar play on words occurs later in the novel when Mrs. Atkinson, erstwhile Mrs. Bennet, mispronounces the Greek term for war as "Pollemy," suggesting polygamy, and so blends women's verbal and sexual promiscuity. In Justice Thrasher's court, the woman of the couple, incensed at being named a "whore," excoriates the accusing witness and thus, by her verbal promiscuity, becomes one. Her original šexual liberty breeds verbal and social license; her words label her and stamp her the instigator, as does her sex. In opposition to these liberties and licenses stands the disciplined narrator who "cannot say," nay, "cannot describe" in words the unlicensed sexuality he reports. His verbal withdrawal signals sexual and social management, political control, and the organization of the material and of the reader's imagination by the rules of decorum. He obeys the laws of language, which are the same, it is implied, as those of good taste and of morality. The masculine narrative becomes the regulating moral frame of the fiction.

Fielding underscores the relationship between language and moral authority in the structure of his novel. Unlike his previous novels, *Amelia* contains long narratives told by characters within the story, and uncorrected by the narrator. These narratives work to indict excessive--or excessively justified--feeling. When in prison, Booth, with Fielding's reader, hears Miss Mathews tell her own history. She boasts of an early education that teaches her only contempt for other women and an inappropriate love for her father; using classical and literary allusions, she justifies her morally opprobrious sexual behavior and attempted murder of Colonel James, her lover, by glorifying the depths of her feelings. Her fancy language reveals her pretension and insincerity to the reader, but masks from Booth her vulpine desires and her self-indulgence. Her misuse of classical models signifies the hazards of feminine appropriation of culture; Miss Mathews privatizes the public virtues of epic heroes to make social life a sexual battle.

Booth similarly reveals the distortions of telling one's own tale without spectatorial distance. He recounts wooing and winning Amelia despite her mother's objections. By his own literary allusions and passion, he indicates a humorless sensibility paradoxically blind to its own nature; he lacks the comparative, ironic perspective of the narrator. His account of hiding in a hamper to sneak a view of Amelia, for example, works rhetorically to ridicule his high-flown sentiment while simultaneously stimulating Miss Mathews's passion. These "prison" narratives recount love and sexual desire, legitimizing passions either illegitimate or subversive by their assumption of authority. In a similar fashion, Mrs. Bennet's account of her own history, recounted to Amelia, clouds her moral febrility, weakness, and deceit by its technique of subjective narration. Amelia and the reader must forgive Mrs. Bennet for a moral fall that costs her husband his life because her apologetic rhetoric forms the narrative, the rhetoric of causality which by explaining excuses; yet her dead husband might have a different tale to tell. In all three stories, sentimental experience does not alone guarantee authority, for the perspective of the narrator, which allows a whole view, warns us by contrast of the dangerous titillation of sentimental narratives. Sentimental narrators within this fiction frame feeling to flatter themselves.

Fielding emphasizes the deceptiveness of the authority of subjective narratives by contrasting these tales to that of the narrator, who speaks with the authority of legal language. For example, after listing the victims abused by false justice early in the novel, the narrative proceeds to describe the condemned Captain Booth inside Newgate. Here, a parodic doppelganger of the heroine has been imprisoned: Blear-Eyed Moll. While, as we later learn, Amelia has suffered a crushed nose from a fall from a carriage, Moll has lost hers from syphilis, compounded by a blow in a brawl. Although both are "castrated," these women differ in their public behavior. Despite her grotesque appearance, Moll has been imprisoned for sex "with a very pretty young Fellow" (1: 3, 28). The narrative emphasizes the reversal of sexual power: the "unlovely Creature" has conquered the pretty fellow instead of the fellow's winning a pretty wench as was the case with Amelia. Moll also mirrors Miss Mathews, another kind of actress-whore seducing another "pretty fellow," Booth. Blear-Eyed Moll, with her unapologetic appetites, represents the grotesque inversion of sexual hierarchy implied in Fielding's opening analogy. The narrator calls Moll disgustedly an "actress" who mimics merriment in the face of despair. She serves to indict "public" women: actresses, who had begun to perform professionally on stage only after the Restoration, and women who put on a public posture different from their "private" role. Women in perverted society thus represent doubleness, insincerity, in opposition to the simple and common truth of the *honnête homme* who is the same in public and private.[25] Such activity encapsulates the threat women pose to an ordered, clockwork world: the making of privacy public, and the "immoderate" consumption of pleasures.

The danger Moll represents--of acting, of publicizing--is replicated by the two main female protagonists in the novel, in contrast to the titular heroine. Miss Mathews, who like a Fury or Medea herself is the vessel of savage passions of jealousy and vengeance, blackmails Booth by threatening to reveal their affair. Mrs. Bennet, whose vanity, immoderate passions, and insubordination exemplify the fell consequences of a masculine education, indirectly murders her husband; her licentious behavior leads to his venereal infection and the consequent hysterical violence that kills him. This story reverses typical roles as the innocent man dies from the promiscuity of the woman. Mrs. Bennet also masquerades as Amelia to earn her second husband a promotion. Both she and Miss Mathews, moreover, tell their own tales with a hyperbolic, self-serving language that contrasts with the public rhetoric of the narrator. The third protagonist, Amelia herself, pretends ignorance of Booth's affair throughout the novel and consents to Mrs. Bennet's masquerading as herself although she feels that even attending a masquerade would compromise her own virtue. While complying in morally ambiguous behavior, however, Amelia remains silent. She is a trope in the narrator's discourse, not a rival storyteller herself--a sentimental example not a sentimental narrator.

The three marriages in the novel also reflect this female threat, as all are corrupted by "unnatural appetites" and the perversion of appearances or public laws. The pimping Trents, who seduce and extort lustful men, have turned the institution of marriage into a license for prostitution and vice. The frigid and ambitious Jameses, who lust only after the unattainable, have hollowed it into an empty word, designating no bond. The destitute Booths have a disordered household: the woman not the man heads it. Consequently, it is vulnerable to internal and external attacks from lust and vice. The pairing and mirroring of marriages and women in the novel sketches a structure that continually reinforces the possibility that a loose domestic union will create unhappiness and corrupt public values and behavior.

It is women, moreover, who model the central thematic flaw in the novel: the trust in appearances. Throughout *Amelia*, Fielding's narrator condemns women for vanity, deception, and pretension, all vices that conventional satire attacks and that value appearances over truth. Mrs. James conceals her frigidity in fine clothes; Mrs. Ellison conceals her immorality in kindly rhetoric. Dr. Harrison, with narrative authority, teases even Amelia for personal vanity, and Amelia demonstrates her superiority to all her sex by not denying it. Miss Mathews betrays her vain desire to dominate through her jealousy of Amelia and abuse of Colonel James who "loves," or rather lusts after, her. Mrs. Bennet exemplifies vanity in her pride of her learning, the implied root of her inability to enjoy domestic harmony. Aping men, she violates the subordinate role that would ensure harmonious relations. Women's vanity, pride in their appearance or achievements, and thus ambition lie at the heart of the sexual reversal of corrupt London. Fielding implies that, by applauding women as "the" public, by encouraging their consumption of luxuries--including literature and dress--, and by publicizing and rewarding their values, society inverts virtue; vanity and display replace modesty and containment, and the virtue of feelings is squandered. The publicizing of women, moreover, reverses the hierarchy of man and wife on which depends the social and political order.

As a model of the city, Newgate contains characters representing other city vices. With Booth, the narrator and reader see an inverted world that mirrors Defoe's gutter Newgate in *Moll Flanders* and Hogarth's scenes of Bedlam, of riotous elections, and of disordered households. Miserable souls here gambol in fevered delight like fettered puppets or demons in hell. We see vignettes of despair, madness, lunatic arrogance, and sexual perversion.

While Fielding's palpable details and allegorical resonances, such as Moll's blear-eye, evoke Bunyan's Vanity Fair, the narrator's moralizing structure envelops the chaos he depicts within a rigid moral panoply. This panoply condemns sentimental license. After observing Blear-Eyed Moll, the narrator describes Robinson, the free-thinking gambler. Like his namesake Robinson Crusoe, this Robinson reveals mutable moral principles reflected in free speech; he discourses on fatalistic necessity while he robs Booth who is pontificating on the passions and, in one speech, makes the opinions of others, the bubble reputation, metonymic with himself, a possession. Like Richardson's Pamela, Robinson becomes his own signifier and contains his own property. He is the disenfranchised male within the city, alienated from public service or duty. In later literary sentimentalism, this containment of sentiment as property within the self is often associated with the man exiled from the city, the man of feeling whose lack of public role indicates a feminization of social standards. Fielding foreshadows this shift through Atkinson, "the man of feeling" in the novel, as Simon Varey observes: "innately good-natured, benevolent, naturally modest, and bashful enough to be socially awkward, like Joseph Andrews."[26] So too is Sterne's Uncle Toby and Mackenzie's Harley. Fielding, however, criticizes unlicensed sentiment even in such virtuous characters. Booth's own sexual and fraternal feelings create evil when they are undisciplined and uninformed. Atkinson himself stimulates in Amelia feelings that threaten her marriage and would disturb Booth were he to know them. This is the price of sentimental license, but this threat is controlled by the bond of marriage and the narrator's frame; we know it through the narrator, not through the action. By making sentiment a possession rather than a narrative principle, Fielding models the way in which many texts control the "license" of sentiment.

Fielding continues to describe vignettes or episodes that carry emblematic as well as socially specific meanings. Like the fragmented structure of later sentimental fiction, this series of portraits omits a linking narrative, serving rather to elaborate examples of the moral point stated by the narrator at the novel's opening. The next example of disorder is a man whose imprisonment has induced his pregnant wife to hurl herself from a window. This incident reveals the state injuring private life. Then a pretty young girl opens her mouth and spews forth verbal filth; Fielding's characteristic example of deceptive appearances again joins sexual and verbal license. After this, we meet a Guardsman who has unjustly imprisoned his young daughter-in-law for threatening his life. This incident doubly inverts social hierarchy: in the nightmarish world of the city, the daughter seems to threaten the father, who ought to represent the powerful state, so that both sexual and generational hierarchies are reversed, and the nation abuses its power by using public systems to avenge private grievances. This pattern of feminized and so endangered inheritance reappears in Mrs. Bennet's history. She usurps her father's place by assuming a learned wisdom and condemning his imprudent marriage. Furthermore, she recounts that the young woman who controlled Mr. Bennet's fortune kept it, an incident that once more demonstrates the inversion of social relations. Even the inheritance laws so stringently arranged to keep wealth in male hands can be abused once women are given power. Mrs. Bennet's tale again demonstrates the inversion of social relations as women dictate inheritance and reinterpret the "will" of their fathers.

Newgate thus symbolizes perverse society, the epitome of the female place, the city itself in *Amelia*. It is "Moll's place," confining and corrupt, the source of values that oppose those embodied in *Tom Jones* by Allworthy in the free, wind-scoured countryside. In Newgate, Blear-Eyed Moll and her companions "discipline" a man imprisoned for "unmanlike practices." Sex or pleasure becomes punishment; women punish men for behaving like women, and thus women usurp male privilege, reverse sexual valuation, and invert sexual hierarchy. Here, women have the money and the power, exemplified by Miss Mathews; men serve their desires. In prison, carnival and charivari rule: prisoners roar for the spectacle of a beating, usurping the place of state discipline, subverting society's categories, and turning punishment into pleasure. In doing so, they coopt the stance of privilege and transform themselves from victims into spectators.

While the novel reproves the feminization of values through the plot, through the themes of fatalism, sentiment, license, and deception, and through narrative control, it is the motif of the "box" that encapsulates the double power of women. This image suggests confinement and secrecy, the values associated with corruption and female power, as well as sentiment. The enclosed, box-like world of London has reappeared in small several times.[27] Compelled to secrecy by Mrs. Harris, Amelia's tyrannical mother, Booth enters Amelia's house boxed in a wine-hamper, only to be ejected without seeing his love. With high pathos, Booth relates this comic vignette in Newgate to a Miss Mathews quivering with some form of "sympathy". Not only does the tale illustrate the indignity of secrecy, even in matters of sentiment, but it also symbolically prefigures Booth's confinement by Miss Mathews, herself an example of the fate that might have befallen Amelia had she succumbed to Booth before marriage. These examples suggest a symbolic connection between the box and sexual imprisonment.

The box, however, also represents and contains property. Clarissa plays grimly on this old joke when discussing her casket in Richardson's novel-- possibly the pun to which Fielding is alluding--and Congreve's *Way of the World* (1700) is also hinged on boxed property. The use of a box to represent fetishized sentiments in *Amelia* coalesces with the literary image of the box as the object of self-revealing choice: the fairy-tale boxes of gold, silver, and iron from which Portia's suitors must choose in *The Merchant of Venice*. As Shakespeare demonstrates, however, the box deceives by appearances: what lies within is what is valuable. Booth's cherished iron snuffbox, signifying his sexual chastity and sentimental purity, is stolen upon his arrival at Newgate and empty when he recovers it; so too will his virtue be stolen and emptied. Sterne's Parson Yorick will later protect his chastity with the horn snuffbox given to him by the Monk in *A Sentimental Journey*, and Pope offers another parodic reading of released sexuality when Sir Plume opens his snuffbox in *The Rape of the Lock* (1714). Amelia's precious "casket," given to Booth to preserve him when he rides to war, represents a similar kind of property. This casket contains medicines and a lock of Amelia's hair, mementos of health, protection, and love; symbolically, it contains Booth's fortune, or rather Amelia's fortune to which Booth will become heir. In the casket also lies a portrait of Amelia encased in a frame of gold set with diamonds, which the lovelorn Atkinson steals. The loss, return, pawning, and recognition by Robinson of this portrait results in the recovery of Amelia's fortune, the restoration of the Booths' place in the country, and Booth's inheritance of Amelia's dowry. This casket encloses an ideal, Amelia's love, just as the valuable frame around Amelia's portrait encases an invaluable ideal, Amelia herself. Fielding's legalistic precision, however, reworks this romantic trope. As Simon Varey notes, the final question of inheritance rests on the laws defining property; it is the *box* in which the legal documents testifying to Amelia's inheritance lie that constitutes the property, not the documents themselves. Like the authoritative narrative itself, the frame or box defines the value of the thing inside it and at the same time contradicts or negates that value.

In *Amelia*, Booth must choose between sentiment and strength, between feminized urban education and the classical education in *civitas*, emotional restraint, and duty, represented by Dr. Harrison--between kinds of boxes. Mrs. Atkinson, known as Mrs. Bennet, most clearly embodies the cultural dilemma Fielding addresses and the choice Booth faces in a world of changing values. She stands morally between the two women and between Amelia and Booth as a mean and an obstruction; she is educated both as a male like Miss Mathews and Booth in the classical languages, and as a sentimental female like Amelia through suffering, disaster, and self-confession. She tells her own story. In fact, she retells it, unintentionally and often, through her vanity of learning. As a modern woman, she serves to expose another central theme and context for *Amelia* and for sentimental discourse: the context of the debate on women's education. This context explains the ambivalent attitude to progress of sentimental texts, including *Amelia*.

From 1760 to 1820, "courtesy books on women" surged and with them printed opinions on what and how women should learn, which cut across social lines.[28] Long before then, however, the debate on women's education and especially on whether they should learn the classics had stimulated such arguments as Bathsua Makin's *Essay to Revive the Antient Education of Gentlewomen* (1673). This treatise advocates Latin as the language of power for women. Fielding deplored such an idea, partly because learning might cause contention within the household by replacing sexual hierarchy with competition, as he argues in *Amelia*, and partly because a little learning is a dangerous thing. But he also opposed female education because he feared that too great a love of the learning of men might lead to too great a love for their bodies: humanism might be taken literally. The ideal of *virtu*, moreover, achieved through classical reading, entails potency, privilege, membership in a restricted class, strength, tradition, the protection of the past, and the mergence of public and private responsibilities; it is social power. While Fielding resists conferring such privilege on women, he also defends the ideal of this education, and deplores the alternative education in empty manners--appearances--offered through current literature on women.

This strained relationship between the classical education, which produces the civic man, and the education of the city appears in an interchange between Booth and an "unlearn'd" author. They are discussing Cato, the exemplar of civic and domestic duty and Booth quotes, "*Urbi Pater est, Urbique Maritus*," which he translates as "Cato is ... Father and Husband to the City of Rome" (8: 5, 327). The author instantly reiterates admiringly, "Not only the father of his country, but the husband too," and they proceed to wrangle on the exact relationship between Cato and his country. Booth glosses the quotation to mean that Cato "became a Father and a Husband, for the Sake only of the City"; in other words, he shaped his private life to conform to public values. The author, however, repeats "*Urbis Pater est ... Urbis Maritus*," annihilating motivation but admiring a private relation made public (328). Metaphorical and literal meaning become confused; the relationship between the public and private duty blurs. Booth supplies the interpretation that unifies public and private experience, but in the very language of privilege, of public identity: Latin. The author mouths a cliché that figures the city as a child and wife, a woman. This concept reveals his confused notion of hierarchy.

Fielding reiterates this tension between sentimental and traditional values in his rhetorical climax toward the end of the novel. Instead of himself wanting to break out of his box, prison, Booth sees the world attempting to break into his house, the seat of value. When Booth is about to listen to the contrite Robinson, the narrator records: "[Robinson] was just entering upon his Story, when a Noise was heard below, which might be almost compared to what hath been heard in *Holland*, when the Dykes have given Way, and the Ocean in an Inundation breaks in upon the Land. It seemed indeed as if the whole World was bursting into the House at once" (12: 7, 522). Dr. Harrison rushes to tell Booth the good news, that his fortune is recovered, all now openly known, all restored. Booth, possessed of wealth and status, becomes public. Indeed, his private world becomes *the* world. The world, the water, at this moment rushes up rather than gravitating down. This climactic moment when the world rushes in where even Dr. Harrison earlier feared to tread is apocalyptic, sexual, and carnivalesque. Fielding here follows the Aristotelian notion of sudden contrasts, popularized six years after *Amelia* in Burke's treatise on the sublime, by juxtaposing the isolated and trembling, guilty Robinson with the enthusiastic turmoil of the world. This rhetorical technique, of course, reappears throughout sentimental literature, but it is important to note here that it is the narrator, reader, and Booth--with his "firmness of mind"--who observe this contrast, not the fearful and fainting Robinson or the delicate Amelia. We are placed in the locus of value, and we watch the spectacle of guilt facing innocence from privileged moral distance.

Once Booth recovers Amelia's inheritance, he assumes his proper role as leader, and order is restored to his household. By becoming Mrs. Harris's son, he becomes the friend of Dr. Harrison who replaces Amelia as his moral guide. Far from exhibiting the female vices of display and extravagance, as he did in buying a carriage in his first essay at country living and thus offending his neighbors by his pretentiousness, he now apportions information and money to Amelia; nonetheless he delays telling her of their changed fortunes and thus establishes authority over the fortune. This shift in Amelia's role appears through the difference in the narrator's rhetorical descriptions of her. When Booth confesses his adultery to her and Amelia shows him Miss Mathews's scurrilous letter telling of the affair, which Amelia had concealed, the narrator remarks, "Amelia never shin'd forth to Booth in so amiable and great a light; nor did his own unworthiness ever appear to him so mean and contemptible, as at this instant" (508). This is the language of contrast, of extremes, a language marking the later development of "antifeminist satire" by setting up a polarity between the degenerate Miss Mathews or the guilty Booth and the angelic Amelia.[29] The end of the book, however, revises the beginning, restores Booth's authority, and demonstrates an ordered society and household. A benevolent judge entertains the Booths at home since their private affairs now conform to public rules. After Booth has accepted his fortune, the narrative shifts from Booth's perspective to an authoritative, masculine narrative that bonds reader, hero, and narrator in one point of view. From this perspective, Amelia is reborn as a bride and described as

restored to physical perfection, or virginity, a condition promising moderation, "neatness," and control, an example of all that opposes modern vice:

> Amelia was then in a clean white gown, which she had that
> day redeemed, and was indeed dressed all over with great
> neatness and exactness; with the glow therefore which arose in
> her features from finding her husband released from his
> captivity, she made so charming a figure, that she attracted the
> eyes of the magistrate and of his wife, and they both agreed
> when they were alone, that they had never seen so charming
> a creature; nay Booth himself afterwards told her that he scarce
> ever remembered her to look so extremely beautiful as she did
> that evening. (536)

Magistrate and wife, Booth and reader, are joined in the purified admiration
of Amelia dressed in redemption. This is the aesthetic and moral perception
of beauty, not the divisive look of lust that throughout the novel has turned
Amelia's charms into destructive forces; it is the disinterested sentimental
spectator's gaze. Indeed, the repetition of "charming" indicates this sexually
neutralized description, for the narrator only uses "beautiful" to describe the
legitimized sexual admiration of her husband. Amelia's "charm" even stimulates the Justice to the liberality applauded by sentimental theory. The Justice
reverts to his right role of acting justly when Booth reverts to his role of
leader and man.

Fielding dramatizes his criticism of feminine values by his structure. He
includes morally ambiguous, autobiographical tales narrated by women--Miss
Mathews and Mrs. Bennet--within a narrative apparently conducted by a
narrator representing moral certainty; this structure opposes two narrative
voices and thus questions the moral authority of the least comprehensive one,
the female narrative.[30] Fielding also uses the rhetorical technique of
describing multiple, non-narrative vignettes as proofs of an implied argument
and examples intended to stimulate the reader's emotional response. Like the
sentimental texts that follow it, *Amelia* reflects hostility toward new values
intimately associated with women even as it panders to the female audience.
Through images of the evil city and of sentiment as a possession, as well as
through the themes of female education and social reform, it attacks
consumption and display, disrupted hierarchies, the self-serving confusion of
public and private, and unlicensed sentiment.

As Nancy Armstrong has recently observed, the genre of the novel
suggested the "rise of female authority" as literary attention shifted from the
male world of political authority to the female world of emotional authority.[31]

Although Fielding's final novel predates this "rise," it anticipates contemporary skepticism about the morality of this 'authority. It thus introduces some of the issues and images which vibrate in the dialectical structure of sentimental rhetoric. Through the voice of an authoritative narrator representing social values and through the causal conventions of plot, *Amelia* reasserts the values of self-restraint, hierarchy, discrete social and sexual roles, and ironic control even over the celebration of sentimental experience within the domestic world of the city. The themes of confinement, education, deception, acting, license, and language express the conflict between public duty and modern corruption. The confessional passages of female characters are framed by the spectatorial and authoritative gaze of the keeper of secrets, the public moralist, the narrator, for in this novel, the ironic narrator does not disclose his secrets but asserts his right to keep them.[32] Prototypical in assigning evil to an environment run by money and in focusing on a sexual fall, *Amelia* initiates the rhetorical device of signifying an implied morality by means of the aesthetic perspective of violent contrasts that characterizes literary sentimentalism. Significantly, however, Fielding's narrator in this novel must battle female narrators to win the reader's trust; their ambiguous narratives compromise the authority even of his narrative. Like Haywood's *Female Spectator*, Fielding's *Amelia* separates social authority from female narrative; the private story of women's experience becomes a topic in a tale of self-control, and sentimental narrative is told from a masculine perspective. Both works warn women against indulging their feelings and laud the power of spectatorial distance.

CHAPTER 2

Fools of Feeling:
The Vicar of Wakefield and *The Fool of Quality*

> The whole conversation ran upon high life
> and high lived company, with pictures,
> taste, Shakespear, and the musical glasses ....
> *Vicar of Wakefield*

The formal problems faced by Samuel Richardson and Henry Fielding led the next generation of sentimental authors to try a different form for reconciling static vignette and moral plot: the didactic fable. Both Oliver Goldsmith and Henry Brooke present prose parables advocating Christian humility with deliberate simplicity, but both are forced to resort to rather confusing explanations of the details of their involved plots to resolve their stories. Through a plot structure that chronicles the trials and final reward of faulty but virtuous men in autobiographical or didactic narrative, these authors finesse the moral complications of their form.[1] While these plots support a progressive ideology that locates virtue in experience, passages of satirical virtuosity hint at a less hopeful, darker, and more ironic vision; stylistically worked spectacles, supplied for the reader's sublime contemplation, of folly, deceit, grief, gratitude, and love show the characters facing betrayal both from the world and from their own natures. Neoclassical values battle with sentimental techniques. These novels show pictures of eternal human experience encased within an ostensibly particularizing plot.

This dialectic between a causal plot and a rhetoric that resists causality invigorates images and themes familiar from periodical fiction and recaptured in Fielding's *Amelia*. In Goldsmith's and Brooke's sentimental fables, the city again appears, not as a triumphant site of human progress, but as the scene of fashionable pretence and deception in which society loses the struggle between civic virtue and selfish appetite. Here, human nature, coded by gender, displays its constitutional weakness and vanity. The Christian virtues of gentleness, obedience, modesty, chastity,, and honesty mark only extraordinary men in extraordinary circumstances: those "men of feeling" who are banished from social intercourse, whether by internal or external compulsion. Neither of these novels, moreover, depicts conversation in the manner of earlier eighteenth-century writing, as either the display of sociability or the social exchange of values. Rather, Goldsmith derides it as vainglorious deceit--boasting or lying--while Brooke coopts it as pure pedagogy, the vehicle by which to indoctrinate the young. Such distrust of verbal communication to facilitate mutuality undermines the authority of the narrator's explanation. Still, it is essential to remember that both writers address an audience familiar with the conventions of periodical discourse; like periodicals, their fictions participate in an ongoing debate about taste and virtue. The question both authors address does not ask merely how to reform manners, but how art should achieve this by shaping feeling.

This question took its shape through discussions at "The Literary Club" -- or just "The Club" -- dominated by Samuel Johnson. Including such disparate aesthetic practitioners and theorists as Sir Joshua Reynolds, Edmund Burke, and Oliver Goldsmith, the "Club" supplied a moral rationale for literary sentimentalism that accorded to art the power to organize the reactions of an increasingly anonymous audience. Reynolds reiterated the necessity of self-discipline to produce good history paintings; Johnson both modelled and advocated through his periodical essays the ability of sensitive critics to monitor their own actions and reactions. In his influential *Philosophical Enquiry into the Origin of Our Ideas of the Sublime and Beautiful* (1757), Burke argued that aesthetic principles induce profound, even philosophical, realizations.[2] By emphasizing the moral effect of the experience of an artwork on individual feeling and on public behavior, this rationale married social relations with personal experience and elevated art to a moral guide. By interweaving aesthetic, philosophical, and literary categories, moreover, the "Club" constructed a model of the right way of experiencing art: aesthetic spectatorship.

While the "Club" raised sentimentalism into high art, however, the rationale its members supplied and much of their work paradoxically suppress the ideological implications of sentimentalism itself. Despite valorizing individual response, for example, the "Club" maintained that all readers experience the same sensation, which conveys the same moral meaning. This universal response confirms the authority of a central body of moral concepts, derived from previous literature; in so doing, it may endorse the individual experience of reading, but it also limits response to conventional moral categories and reiterates the notion of a universal human nature. This limitation also appears in the repetition throughout sentimental literature of specific tropes and familiar images to prompt predictable reactions. Moreover, by figuring experience and emotion as phenomena not only to be felt by the reader or viewer, but also to be "read" for their significance through their signs on the character in literature or art, these sentimental authors mystify individual reality.[3] Their sanctioned method of "reading" reality, even if celebrated as "instinctive," must be learned through the observance of art. In depicting common human feelings as heroic, these sentimental novels, like genre paintings, emphasize the contrast between the unselfconscious characters and the sensitive reader or viewer; this reader, by virtue of a broader perspective that imposes epic significance on domestic details, demonstrates elite moral taste. Thus, in literary practice, "common" feelings are heroicized as uncommon. Finally, by locating the route to moral comprehension as a distanced aesthetic perception that allows rarefied imaginative sympathy, literary sentimentalists establish distance as the prerequisite to moral feeling and a comparative process akin to formal analysis as the technique to structure response. It is the reader of feeling recognizing juxtapositions and contrasts who interprets the pathos of a scene; this reader must have leisure enough to stand and watch and remain disinterested enough to see the scene as a whole.[4]

Despite this similar ideology, the fictions of Goldsmith and Henry Brooke employ different rhetoric. Oliver Goldsmith's *Vicar of Wakefield* (1766) has puzzled critics for over two centuries by its blend of irony and sentiment. Still, it has found its way, if only by honorable mention, into the canon of eighteenth-century literature. Although increasingly attracting critical attention, Henry Brooke's *The Fool of Quality*, first published in the same year, has not.[5] Whereas Goldsmith exemplifies the ambivalence of literary sentimentalists toward a philosophy that praises instinct and common experience, Henry Brooke uses sentimentalism to promote a social education in Christian morality, adopting a didactic tone that alienated several readers. Both authors, nevertheless, demonstrate the nostalgia for a vanished past of ideal relations, which Rousseau articulated and which R. F. Brissenden identifies as the mark of sentimentalism. Both also express this ideal in the form of a fable that endorses the role of informed judgment and educated perception in balancing instinctive response. Through spectatorial narratives presenting sentimental pictures to disinterested readers, both fictions counteract sympathy with aesthetic evaluation: they frame feeling as a conversation on the standards of taste.

I. *The Vicar of Wakefield* and the Talk of the Town

Goldsmith's prose fable contains several of the most typical characters, scenes, and themes of sentimental fiction, the tropes of the following forty years. These include a young woman caught "in the struggle between prudence and passion," who consents to a clandestine marriage, and, deserted, turns wild-eyed and repentant[6]; a disguised high-born Man of Feeling whose benevolence is screened by misanthropy and a love of children and child's games; a sequence of sudden misfortunes and tragedies stripping the kindly speaker of family, fortune, home, and freedom; and a narrative language blending appeals to Christian compassion with simplicity, humor, and domestic affection. Set in country scenes of rural modesty, Goldsmith's fable seems to celebrate sentiment.

Goldsmith, however, compromises all these thematic clichés by depicting them through a rhetoric informed by satire. Domestic fidelity appears as constant, if amicable, wrangling between the weak husband and the crude wife; village relations become merely rivalry for money, display, and social power; female susceptibility results not from good instincts but from bad education; even the clerical speaker, Dr. Primrose, displays a vanity and self-ignorance like that of Fielding's Parson Adams, within a rather less forgiving narrative structure, since he tells his own tale and hence remains uncorrected and unredeemed by any detached narrator.[7] The countryside itself transforms into a social scene, not a romantic retreat shielded from the vices of human nature. This rhetoric undercuts or interrupts the episodic structure of the sentimental vignettes by evoking a Fieldingesque, reformist narrative. It does not, however, work solely to ridicule the sentimental ideal, as Robert H. Hopkins has argued; rather, it frames sentimental values within a familiar set of references that contextualize sentiment within society.[8] Since it allows a myriad of readers to enjoy the story while also attacking the vices of luxury, this flexible rhetoric serves a practical purpose.

These conflicts perhaps contributed to the difficulty Goldsmith's original audiences had in understanding his novel. Although the book grew extremely popular after 1779, thirteen years after its publication, scanty reprinting and mixed reviews mark the puzzlement of early readers. Contemporary critics condemned Goldsmith for lack of originality.[9] Modern audiences, on the other hand, object to the contradictory messages in the book, mainly debating whether or not Primrose is ridiculed or Goldsmith confused.[10] These different criticisms may express similar responses in their rejection of Goldsmith's method and may result largely from two causes. First, the dialectic of sentimental rhetoric itself compromises both sentimental and reformist ideals by endorsing conservative cultural values.[11] Indeed, sentimental heroes are usually ridiculed to some degree because sentimental writers portray in them conflicting values. Similarly, since sentimental authors negotiate opposed cultural ideals within sentimental works, they may appear, if not confused, at least inconsistent. Although contemporary audiences, perhaps less insistent on formal purity in prose fiction than modern ones, did not object to Goldsmith's structure, they share with modern readers the perception that Goldsmith was adapting familiar tropes to a rhetorically uneven text. His ambiguous attitude toward sentimental ideals, moreover, is borrowed as much as his tropes are from previous sentimental fiction. The second reason for this reception may lie in Goldsmith's use of the character types, language, and tone of periodicals within a narrative structure that resists periodical topicality. Goldsmith reproduces this journalistic style openly in the conversation between the player and the parson who debate public culture, a passage similar to the set pieces in *Joseph Andrews* (260-64), and in the discussion of town topics when we meet "the philanthropic bookseller in St. Paul's church-yard," whom readers would recognize as John Newbery (91). Such exclusive references were a typical device of periodical fiction, titillating the reader with in-group gossip. *The Vicar of Wakefield* combines this journalistic discourse with the language of artistic comparison. In this rhetorical formula, sentimentalism merges with the discourse on taste, and thus the praise of responsiveness juxtaposes the praise of discrimination.

As a hack journalist, Goldsmith had considerable experience at wooing a faceless audience through conventional forms. His Chinese Letters from *The Citizen of the World* demonstrate his mastery both of the familiar letter and of topics of current interest on the model, again, of *The Spectator*.[12] His poetry also expresses an idealistic sentimentalism: "The Traveller: or A Prospect of Society" (1764) and "The Deserted Village" (1770), through the voice of a speaker authorized by detachment, mourn the desolation of the countryside and of old England as new mercantile values encroach.[13] His plays are clearly sentimental: *She Stoops to Conquer* (1773), for example, combines comedy with an emphasis on expression, emotion, and delicacy. In his novel as in his poetry, he exhibits the nostalgia for a unified culture, which Richard Sennet notes is itself a characteristic of sentimental discourse.[14] Yet, Goldsmith like Johnson himself continually denigrated long fiction for its emphasis on the love theme, its distortions of reality, and its idealization of human happiness.[15] As conventional criticisms, these charges articulate not only Goldsmith's literary philosophy but also the conservative, stoical aspects of literary sentimentalism itself.[16] His own novel is motivated as much by the desire to reform the genre as to imitate it, as much by the ambition to reform the taste for sentimental fiction as to feed it.

The Vicar of Wakefield addresses the issue of taste directly, linking it with the social theme of conversation.[17] 'In both, the ideal is to preserve decorum, maintain generic distinctions, and balance individual with social perceptions. Goldsmith also seeks this ideal balance in the tone and form of his novel: as Robert H. Hopkins has shown, he freshens his feeling with irony, a tonal medley that dilutes sentiment. Similarly, Goldsmith structures his evocative scenes within a narrative frame that enforces a moral lesson. For example, he combines lessons on taste and behavior through the comic "fable" of Lady Blarney and Miss Carolina Wilelmina Amelia Skeggs, the whores dressed as ladies. This masquerade, in itself a convention contrasting city and country manners, is plotted as true literally, not merely metaphorically, in order to contrast false values with the true taste of the sentimental autobiographer, Dr. Primrose.

Like most men of feeling, Primrose does not perceive the masquerade; dazzled by fashion himself, he is fooled by simple appearances. Nevertheless, he does recognize bad taste. He condemns the expression, "by the *living jingo*, she was all of a muck of sweat" as "very coarse."[18] Recording bemusedly these women's "reserved" conversation ("blarney"), in which "they would talk of nothing but high life, and high lived company; with other fashionable topics, such as pictures, taste, Shakespear, and the musical glasses," Primrose notes that they frown at Burchell's bluntly sexual "conversation"; as a *naif*, he exposes their hypocrisy (46-47). Their false modesty, or counterfeit gentility, reveals their false values in both the costumes they wear and the costume of their thoughts, their words. Dr. Primrose discovers in their swearing, or verbal abuse, "the surest symptom" of their fashionableness, adding that their "finery ... threw a veil over any grossness in their conversation" (46-47). He also remarks in the voice of the hack writer of a periodical: "But as every reader, however beggarly himself, is fond of high-lived dialogues, with anecdotes of Lords, Ladies, and Knights of the Garter, I must beg leave to give him the concluding part of the present conversation" (54-55). Such a remark satirizes, as Goldsmith does in his criticism, the taste for female fiction--romance--and for gossip, the fevered ambitious dreams of imaginary high culture.

It is left to the high-born sentimentalist, Sir William Thornhill, himself disguised as blunt Burchell, to identify the true nature of the whores' discourse. Throughout their talk, Burchell intersperses "*Fudge!*," reproduced in parentheses in the text; his antisocial language is fit reply to theirs. By using social intercourse to advance their own interests, the whores masquerade as much in their language as in their dress. They cannot distinguish high life from high living, high culture from popular entertainment, "reserve" from the manners of a Mrs. Slipslop. At the end of the conversation, Miss Skeggs compliments her companion on her "own things in the Lady's Magazine," initiating the offer to take Primrose's daughters to town as "companions" or fellow whores (56). Women's writing, the decay óf manners, and masquerade coalesce as features of the city which confuse culture with prostitution; they oppose values of the patriarchal and paternal countryside, upheld by the exemplar of true values, the traditional country gentleman. Since Goldsmith himself contributed to the *Lady's Magazine* in 1760 and 1761 and served as its editor under the pseudonym of the Honourable Mrs. Caroline Stanhope, he may be teasing the reader with an in-joke, which also points up the masquerade of the entire, pseudo-autobiographical narrative mode.[19]

Since these whores both are and are not "fine ladies," they both symbolize the corruption of false city values--pretentiousness, luxury, the disease of faddism--and parody them. They link the social abuses of the "upper" classes with the moral degeneracy of those lower down. While the journalistic discourse on the decay of manners serves here to distinguish the uncorrupted taste of the sentimentalist from the false values of the city, however, it does not define "true" taste or social conversation. The simple taste of the naive, moreover, is not incorruptible. The fell contagion of these women breeds middle-class ambition; their influence, manifested as taste, immediately conquers "temperance, simplicity, and contentment," presented here as issues as much of class as of taste. Primrose's family fills its windows with "washes for the neck and face," coopting the boundary between a domestic arena, their home, and public space (49). Again, "the whole conversation ran upon high life and high lived company, with pictures, taste, Shakespear, and the musical glasses" (49). This rhythmic incantation of the subjects of tasteful discourse echoes the mystified nature of this conversation; words become trophies, not means for the exchange of ideas. The family, moreover, violates its social position by mimicking "fashionable ladies." They exemplify the bad taste characteristic in periodical literature of the socially ambitious merchant--without even the money to pay for such display.

This attack on the social and moral hazards of bad taste extends to literature. Like Goldsmith's periodical *The Bee* (1759), *The Vicar of Wakefield* includes a variety of literary genres, including ballads, stories, revised Biblical parables, and historical tales. These genres fall into gendered categories reflecting the varied audience of literary culture; while some readers like Mrs. Primrose are entertained by country songs, and formal renditions of the superstitious dreams and habits associated with women, others may prefer the more classical discourse on central issues of taste that appears in male conversation (50). Burchell and Primrose discuss together and separately such topics as ancient and modern education, standards of taste, and kinds of fiction and literature, subjects as far from Lady Blarney's tales in "The Lady's Magazine" as possible in form and content. Goldsmith nevertheless advocates the reform of literary taste to include popular genres, valued for their "simplicity" and clarity. As a model of the rational conversation on taste, Burchell likes "old ballads" (30), and appreciates even flawed greatness in poetry and painting (75); to educate his reader, Goldsmith also includes in his text the long ballad of recovered love and disguise unveiled, "Edwin and Angelina" (39-44).[20] This expansion of the borders of literary merit allows more cultural variety to be encompassed within the moral theory of sentimentalism. If such variety legitimizes the literary experiences of a wider audience, however, it also narrows the range of response by redefining such genres as literary expressions rather than imitations of life. Whereas the "popular" audience, like Mrs. Primrose, listens naively entranced by the fiction, the educated sentimentalist from a distance admires the formal qualities of the expression of experience. Such literature must be either authentic, written naively, or composed with refined sophistication to be acceptable. Lady Blarney's attempts to cater to modern taste are, by implication, sloppy fakery.

This contrast between pretentious, female culture and "honest" values, between self-aggrandizement and social balance, is reiterated through the trope of painting. Burchell articulates the neoclassical ideal reiterated throughout sentimental literature when he cites Horace's analogy comparing poetry with painting. In rude contrast to this stands Primrose's tasteless family portrait, the result of the competition between Primrose's family and Farmer Flamborough's: "one large historical family piece" that is cheap, "genteel," and fashionable, "for all families of taste were now drawn in the same manner" (78-79). The portrait Primrose commissions and purchases is, of course, appalling in all ways.[21] Too large to fit on the walls, glaringly colored to gratify Mrs. Primrose, it portrays a masquerade: Primrose's wife as a richly jewelled Venus, with her two youngest children as Cupids, while Primrose as a stately clergyman offers her his books on monogamy. Added to the confusion of historical and mythological genres is the ironic contradiction between Primrose's learning and his taste; both artificial, neither truly represents his character. Instead of displaying a universal moral, this portrait flaunts individual vanity and competitiveness as the Primroses ape aristocratic tradition. In contrast with this morally meaningless elaboration of images--a picture without a narrative--Primrose hangs a framed epitaph to his wife over the chimneypiece, "where it answered several very useful purposes" by reminding the couple of duty, fidelity, and mortality (13). While ironically framing Dr. Primrose's own vanity in urging monogamy after death, this narrative without a picture vies with the grandiose mythological painting in representing distorted taste. It exemplifies the moralism in much popular culture and stimulates Mrs. Primrose's "passion for fame." Goldsmith implies that an alternative to both meaningless allusion and blunt didacticism is needed.

In *The Vicar of Wakefield*, women often represent and encourage the perversion of values. Deborah Primrose stands at the center of the portrait: it is her ambition that created it. Her Biblical name adumbrating ironically her failure of Christian companionship, Deborah models the socially ambitious, vulgar wife whose taste refuses refinement. Discussing dinners instead of ideas, she speaks in a language close to slang, rocks with laughter at her own coarse, country humor, yet obsequiously flatters misperceived images of high culture: the rakish Squire Thornhill, degenerate nephew of Sir William, and the two whores dressed as ladies. Dazzled by ornament and blind to the honest worth of Sir William Thornhill, Burchell, she exemplifies the traditional, or reactionary, discourse on upstart middle-class taste, worshiping mutable fashion over fundamental forms.

At the same time, Goldsmith was aware that women comprised the vital, new audience for sentimental literature. Periodical literature, including his own, flattered women as the heroines of fine feeling and models of sympathy, and in his novel Goldsmith repeats this double discourse concerning women and their "modern" education. In *The Vicar of Wakefield*, even while women define the audience and initiate the discussion of aesthetics that punctuates the tale, the opening sentence satirically indicts their importance: "I was ever of opinion, that the honest man who married and brought up a large family, did more service than he who continued single, and only talked of population" (9). Beneath this praise of domesticity as the remedy for the social problems worrying contemporary society lies a patent joke: the "honest" husband "does more service"--has more sex--than the libertine bachelor who talks a good game but probably sees little action. At the same time, the power inversion implied by the man "servicing" the woman indicts modern social relations in which women, or female culture, dominate men.

Goldsmith's tone vacillates between traditional bawdy satire and the new gentility of sentimentalism. The prurient joke is continued as Primrose reveals that sexual desire, screened as social duty, motivated him to marry quickly, and to marry a durable woman who would encase him well. It is a joke at Primrose's expense, however; like Abraham Adams, he does not know his own feelings and hides natural impulse behind social theory.

> From this motive, I had scarce taken orders a year before I began to think seriously of matrimony, and chose my wife as she did her wedding gown, not for a fine glossy surface, but such qualities as would wear well. To do her justice, she was a good-natured notable woman; and as for breeding, there were few country ladies who could shew [sic] more. She could read any English book without much spelling, but for pickling,

> preserving, and cooking, none could excel her. She prided
> herself also upon being an excellent contriver in house-keep-
> ing; tho' I could never find that we grew richer with all her
> contrivances. (9)

Deborah appears as "the notable woman," the boastful but disastrous kitchen
economist, itself a common character type illustrating the corruption of
practical education.[22] A version of the comic, domineering stereotype, who
breeds even without "breeding," this eighteenth-century caricature possesses
a specific social dimension that associates the female sex with materialism.[23]
This notable woman fails to refine or to improve either her "taste" or her
patterns of consumption; her double failure of taste and value suggests that
good taste means good value and thus makes both moral and economic sense.
Thus, while women's "modern" education exemplifies the decay of values,
an "improved" education in good taste is necessary for social survival.

   The Vicar of Wakefield includes conventional remarks and jokes about
female education in order to dramatize contemporary debates on the question.
Olivia, the strikingly beautiful eldest daughter, is so named, instead of
"Grissel," because Primrose's wife Deborah "had been reading romances"
while pregnant. This false education reappears in Olivia's fate: she falls for
promises, agrees to a secret ceremony, and suffers desertion, following the
pattern of a romantic heroine who mistakenly trusts the power of love over
social values. Olivia, moreover, reads *Robinson Crusoe* and *Tom Jones*, as
well as Defoe's *Religious Courtship* (on the necessity of marrying religious
spouses); from this reading, she assumes the right and power of controversy,
and from the novels she learns to indulge her romantic passion, and to trust
that love conquers all (37). Although Primrose indulges this education,
Goldsmith implies a more complex view. Even while his schematic story
parodies contemporary fears that women learn subversive lessons from
modern reading, it also justifies these fears. He shows that reading induces
self-indulgence and grants women the power to argue and dispute; it
encourages them to subvert authority and decorum and to become whores, as
Olivia might easily have done had she not been saved by the self-interest of
a villainous witness. Olivia's education exemplifies the false values of
sentimental romance where imaginative involvement overwhelms judicious
distance and idealism replaces sense.

   The conflict between romantic and "sensible" values results, in
Goldsmith's text, from the difference between sexual and disinterested
perception and from the difference between male and female perception.
After puzzling over his perceptive daughter Sophia's preference for the
apparently destitute Burchell, Primrose remarks in the objective voice of a
chronicler, "The two sexes seem placed as spies upon each other, and are

furnished with different abilities, adapted for mutual inspection" (45). The scientific language of observation here privileges a perception beyond that weighted with sexual interest: as the sexes watch each other, the sexless and disinterested speaker observes their behavior, which implies that women, defined by their sex and thus incapable of disinterested perception, cannot serve as arbiters of taste. Sophia may see with her heart, and such a perception may indeed be sound, but she cannot judge beyond the questions of sex. Such general or social judgment belongs to the educated spectator. Primrose demonstrates both disinterested and sexually implicated vision when he stands "a calm spectator of the flames" of his house, but "could not continue a silent spectator of [his wife's] distress," and hence scolds her (126-27). Disinterest can, however, entail moral misjudgment. He attempts to amuse his daughter with the tale of the calm disinterested stance of a condemned soldier as he approaches death, but such artificial accounts of neoclassical stoicism only sadden her further. The final scene in prison, in which the wretched revel in glee, further exemplifies false feeling, as it does in *Amelia*; their disinterest is uninterest, resulting from despair, not philosophical perspective. These false forms of detachment highlight the delicacy of a true, sympathetic taste that sees sentiment within a social and moral frame. Women may see too much with their sex, but men may see too little with theirs.

Goldsmith's central device to dramatize aesthetic perspectives and issues of taste is his speaker, the naive, chatty, confessional Dr. Primrose. Despite his coherence as a character, this speaker sometimes exhibits and sometimes employs irony and humor, depending upon the function he serves in the narrative. As a character, Dr. Primrose, like such periodical characters as Sir Roger de Coverley or Mr. Homespun, models fashionable flaws and voices risible notions for the educated reader's pleasure. As a narrator, he describes social follies with wit and taste.[24] The fact that he vacillates between these two roles, sometimes even combining them, might confuse the reader--and seems to have done so--but it is not uncharacteristic of the mixed mode of long sentimental works or of eighteenth-century prose fiction.

Primrose most often plays an exemplary observer when he describes scenes or people. Explaining the poor but happy friends gathered around his table, he says that "this remark will hold good thro' life, that the poorer the guest, the better pleased he ever is with being treated: and as some men gaze with admiration at the colours of a tulip, or the wing of a butterfly, so I was by nature an admirer of happy human faces" (10). While this deliberate conflation of social duty, moral action, and aesthetic pleasure defines Dr. Primrose as a benevolent spectator, a sentimental hero, the analogy reiterates a neoclassical formula that associates society and nature. Deducing a general maxim from experience on human nature in balanced phrasing, Primrose

underscores the vanity not only of the rich, but even of the poor who cherish
the delusion that they are "being treated'" as a favor. His language models
distanced perspective. At the same time, Primrose exposes his own weakness,
the delusion of detachment. As Hopkins observes, this passage also reveals
the parson's vanity as he plays "great man" to beggars.[25]

Primrose, moreover, draws an analogy between the observation of the
surface spectacles of nature, the delusive play of colors, and his own pleasure
at observing the surfaces, the faces, of pleased objects of his benevolence.
Such discourse is typical of sentimental literature and demonstrates the
ambivalence in sentimental rhetoric toward valuing appearances. Even while
documenting the power of reflective benevolence as the beggar's face reflects
the benefactor's virtue, this trope repeats the warning that surfaces, faces, and
masks deceive. Primrose's image also recasts the issue of benevolence, the
cardinal virtue of sentimentalism, as one of aesthetic debate.[26] While his taste
runs to variegated and bright colors, a preference for contrast that echoes
Burke's theory of the sublime, he articulates the sentimentalist's faith in
appearance, the reduction of motive and character to flat type.

> Mere outside is so very trifling a circumstance with me, that
> I should scarce have remembered to mention it, had it not been
> a general topic of conversation in the country. Olivia, now
> about eighteen, had that luxuriancy of beauty with which
> painters generally draw Hebe ... Sophia's features were not so
> striking at first; but often did more certain execution; for they
> were soft, modest, and alluring. ... The temper of a woman is
> generally formed from the turn of her features ... Olivia wished
> for many lovers, Sophia to secure one. Olivia was often
> affected from too great a desire to please. Sophia even represt
> [sic] excellence from her fears to offend.... But these qualities
> were never carried to excess in either, and I have often seen
> them exchange characters for a whole day together. A suit of
> mourning has transformed my coquet into a prude, and a new
> set of ribbands has given her younger sister more than usual
> vivacity.... (11-12)

Despite Primrose's asseverations to the contrary, this "portrait" specifically
correlates character with appearance, reading fiction as art. "Mere outside"
is an essential clue. In this description, moreover, Primrose's aesthetic
perspective on his daughters Hebe and Sentiment defines their "tempers" and
changes when their costumes change; these women mirror artistic stereotypes
and become literally objects of spectatorship. They do not masquerade when
they change costumes, for no "inside" exists to oppose the "outside." This
perspective establishes the "family likeness," which Dr. Primrose defines as

"one character, that of being all equally generous, credulous, simple, and inoffensive" despite describing his daughters by'their looks and his sons by their education (12). Regardless of Dr. Primrose's own vanity and blindness to the dangers of his children's "miscellaneous education," the principle by which he deduces general character from aesthetic observation is not challenged. Dr. Primrose, like the persona of a periodical, models the privileged distance that sees these fictional appearances as shortcuts to character and foreshadowings of plot.

Goldsmith provides another model of the impressionable surface in Burchell. As Primrose demonstrates the aesthetic response to surface, Burchell, the "Man of Feeling," demonstrates the physical response in terms the physician Smollett would use to describe Matthew Bramble in *Humphry Clinker* (1771). He describes his state as physical hypersensitivity: "Physicians tell us of a disorder in which the whole body is so exquisitely sensible, that the slightest touch gives pain: what some have thus suffered in their persons, this gentleman felt in his mind. The slightest distress, whether real or fictitious, touched him to the quick, and his soul laboured under a sickly sensibility of the miseries of others" (21). Burchell also criticizes his own selfish motives which blended with his "sickly sensibility" and led him to abuse his fortune and talents. In Burchell and Primrose, undisciplined sensibility thus endangers self and society by veiling vanity with high ideals. Our detached narrator Primrose "love[s], laughe[s] at, and pitie[s]" Burchell (10). As an example of benevolence inducing benevolence, Burchell is still somewhat impotent and comic. By ignoring hierarchies of value and response, sensibility thus signals emotional disorder and waste--false aesthetics and false economy--even as, by being the characteristic of the highborn, it points to moral elitism. Burchell represents the fine values of an age of personal responsiveness. Goldsmith shows us that this age has passed.

The Vicar of Wakefield merges discourses from periodical literature on class or social status, sentimental excess, female or modern education, taste and social duty. Like Addison, Goldsmith vaunts the spectatorial stance that allows the correct, because detached, judgment of life, but warns against the moral pitfalls of this stance including an excessive regard for appearances. Inset pieces such as the fable of the venerable, silver-locked elder who turns out to be a con man (67), and rhetorical flights such as the jargon on liberty (95) and the arguments on taste and on the power of "contrast" (38-39) counteract any reader's impulsive response by eliciting his or her power to discriminate between surface and substance. Goldsmith thus pulls the reader back from unselfconscious sympathy with the narrator. *The Vicar of Wakefield* employs sentimental tropes to do something different from evoking the reader's feelings. Just as Primrose himself structures his sentiment within a fable and edits feeling with irony, so Goldsmith presents contemporary

issues of aesthetics, culture, and social values and relations as topics within
a moral narrative. Even while soliciting' a sentimental reaction, the novel
includes the pragmatic advocacy of rational economy, of a balance between
individual and social expression and interest, and of the preservation of
decorum in aesthetics,   social intercourse and emotional response. The
sentimental tale is framed by a conversation on art and morality.

II. *The Fool of Quality* and Didactic Dialogue

Friend of Swift, correspondent of Pope, and author of pedagogical
fables, satirical and neoclassical drama, moral verse, and political pamphlets,
Henry Brooke was famous in his own time for his religio-scientific poem
"Universal Beauty." He is now rather remembered as a "sentimental"
novelist.[27] Yet his five-volume novel *The Fool of Quality; or, the History of
Henry Earl of Moreland* (1766-70) is less an articulation of sentimental
ideology than a pedagogical treatise on Rousseauistic education and on
Christianity. Because of its conservative message and form, it shows clearly
the way sentimental structures and rhetoric can support traditional values. By
means of chatty exchanges between Author and Friend, or reader, Brooke
moralizes the sentimental episodes in his novel. While celebrating sentiment
as virtue, the novel justifies artistic and social patronage, hierarchical, even
feudal, social relations, lower-class passivity, and upper-class charity; it
further demonstrates that nature in the high-born--endowed already with
innate courtesy, patriotism, and leadership--will result in Christian and social
excellence. Despite his theoretical republicanism, Brooke imagines glory in
traditional terms as monarchical, hierarchical, and religious. The book indeed
defines good feeling as feeling fitting the social order, for Brooke sentimentalizes his reformatory rhetoric to make satire work to advocate social
sympathy. Designed to educate children and self-consciously pedagogical,
The Fool of Quality exemplifies the tendency of sentimental literature to
control, rather than to release, response.[28] Brooke's form, a fable that
illustrates lessons by fictional episodes, elicits feeling to persuade the reader
to moral self-discipline.

The Fool of Quality resembles Goldsmith's fiction in its debt to the
conversational topics and tone of the periodicals. Within the episodic account
of Harry's education, we encounter the open discussion of matters of current
debate, including literary theory; character types like Sir Christopher Cloudy,
Sir Standish Stately, fat Lady Childish, and Squire Sulky; and witty rhetoric

by the narrator, as in, "These were the principle characters. The rest could not be said to have any character at all" (1: i, 45). Characters themselves also discuss philosophical or physiological ways to read experience, debating, for example, if blushing shows guilt or virtue, shame or modesty (2: 101-102); and if physiognomy reveals or conceals man's nature (2: 110-32; illustrated in 4: 33). Sentimental ideas appear as didactic statements, or "sentiments": "Benevolence produces and constitutes the heaven or beatitude of God himself," Brooke's sentimental mouthpiece Clinton asserts (3: 242), and "The language of love is understood by all creatures" (1: 2, 52). Such pronouncements evoke periodical treatments of similar issues.

Brooke's "Author" discusses not only morality, but also method with "Friend," the reader. This discourse on literary procedure leavens the religious polemic with an appeal to taste and universal aesthetic values. As the first chapter ends, Friend interrupts with a question on the plot, to which the Author replies, "wait and see," further asserting that the characters have the right to preserve their secrets until they wish to disclose them (1: 50-51). This pretense of the characters' actuality is, of course, a conventional game with the reader. Similarly, at the end of the second chapter recounting the rejection by our hero Harry of the luxurious toys given to him by his father, the Earl of Moreland, "Friend" debates with the Author on the wisdom and the probability of Harry's behavior (1: 67-70). This device allows Brooke to defend not merely his ethical notions, but also his fictional plan. Significantly enough, they are seen as separate, although certainly related; the virtue of Rousseau's educational method does not automatically assure the "probability" of literary method. We are deliberately pulled from the fiction to attend to the art and the moral.

Brooke includes philosophical dissertations in his dialogue with the reader. These passages underscore the author's control over the meanings in the fiction. The debate following Chapter 3 covers matter and spirit, superstition and Cartesian reason, providing a philosophical key to the fable of Harry's encounter with a pretended ghost (1: 81-89). Author and Friend also discuss the definition of a hero, vaunting a "builder" like Lycurgus, Peter the Great, or even Kate, Peter's washerwoman, who "humanized the man that humanized the nation" (1: 151). When Author admits that his greatest hero was "a madman" and his greatest "lawgiver" was "a fool"--Cervantes' idealistic hero Don Quixote and his earthy companion "Sancho Pansa"--Friend claims that Author exhibits both qualities, madness and folly. Adopting the satiric convention of praise-by-blame to justify the simple fable he tells and to indict critics who condemn it, Brooke thus relies on conventional irony and literary allusions to structure the morality of his fable and to organize his sentimental rhetoric (1: 152).

Fictional examples also illustrate Brooke's sentimental principles of aesthetics as well as morality. After Author and Friend defend "irregularity" as both natural and spirited in opposition to mechanical rule (a formula proposed by Pope in *Essay on Criticism*), Brooke recounts the "History of a Man of Letters." A typical inset tale, reprinted separately through the end of the century, as was "David Doubtful," the "History" describes the corruptions of a city education on the unfortunate Clement, titular "Man of Letters": hack authorship, debt, false friendship, and the rape by the degenerate Lord Stivers of his virtuous wife Arabella, who subsequently stabs her rapist, is imprisoned for the crime, and only escapes poverty and hanging with Harry's help.[29] In most of its details and themes, this tale mimics Fielding's *Amelia*: the dangerous masquerade, the lord's betrayal of his social position in abusing the innocent middle-class couple, misunderstandings between Clement and his father, salvation through love. However, it also includes melodramatic incidents such as the starving and desperate Clement's attempt at robbery (repeated by Mackenzie in *Man of the World*), and the supernatural, supervisory figure who warns the desperate hero not to sin again. Framed by the Author-Friend dialogues on method, this tale serves as a self-declared allegory illustrating man's progress through the world and the eternal possibility of grace, rather than merely a kind of "biography," which Brooke scorns in his preface. Self-conscious "literariness" frames the sentimental story.[30]

Brooke uses his self-conscious method to flatter his female audience, conjured as tolerant of didactic and exemplary literature. They, presumably, favor the conflation of literary probability and sentimental philosophy in the prefatory dialogue of volume 2, in which Clement's story continues. Here, Friend objects to unnatural characters, especially Arabella: "such an exaltation of female character is of evil influence among the sex...their vanity will be inflated, and they will rise, on the stilts of Arabella, to a presumptuous level with their natural lords and masters" (2: 83). Leaving this inflammatory rhetoric unreproved, Author instead defends the low station of his Christian hero, and defines woman as the "civilizor, governor, polisher, and companion" of man, not merely his cook, bedmate, and children's nurse (2: 83). Brooke thus redefines "natural" sexual relations by elevating women to mothers, while comparing them to Christ in their humility. As always, a fable follows to illustrate this apparently bold iteration of female independence and equality. This fable illustrates that woman is not only stronger than wine, but even more powerful than a King at persuading men. The illustration makes, in fact, a rather different point from the Author's sentimental declaration. Rather than demonstrating women's independence, it lauds women's role of exercising power through men and of asserting their physical and political dominance only through domestic love. While Brooke's message remains sentimental, however, his tone wavers between the pedagogical and the ironic; by continually reminding the reader of the politics of literary method and of literary production, Brooke compromises his own assertions of the value of simplicity and unselfconscious impulse. Women, specifically, represent both the consuming audience demanding flattery, and the center of sentimental value, never demanding but always giving love.

Juliet Grenville: or, the History of the Human Heart, Brooke's three-volume epistolary novel published in 1774, also portrays women ambiguously as Brooke interlards his sentimental rhetoric with misogynistic humor.[31] Despite the novel's worship of love, Brooke uses the sophisticated Countess of Cranford to utter witticisms designed to appeal to a literate audience, replaying the Augustan attitudes of his *Fables for the Female Sex*: "Women...are in the nature of towns. To speak in the general, they neither have forces within, nor fences without. But, happily, on the other hand, they have little worth attempting. Yet they pride themselves in having escaped pillage, and ascribe it to their being guarded against surprise" (1: 3). Through an analogy associating women with urban or mercantile culture, Brooke satirizes women for vanity and self-consciousness, which is the traditional jibe of neoclassical literature.[32] Brooke also attacks women's influence on culture, particularly the political and moral tendency of novels written about women. Juliet Grenville, the titular heroine of this novel, reads Richardson's *Pamela; or, Virtue Rewarded* (1740), and, after conceding Richardson some artistic power, condemns his sexual explicitness and his morality, concluding with a satirical jab at Richardson's admiration for wealth and social power (3: 92). Condemning Richardson for pandering to the public appetite for sensationalism and materialism in place of adjuring readers to spirituality, Brooke defines sentimental literature not by its endorsement of sexual or female themes, but as moral education intended especially for women and children whose emotions most need guidance. He thus differentiates, sometimes deliberately, sometimes not, between the literary culture suited to his female audience and the literature his own sex reads. This difference dictates plot and method: Brooke acknowledges that literary method sculpts sentimental simplicity to portray the way women and children should feel. Probability thus becomes a matter both of philosophy and of method.

Issues of literary decorum and social decorum merge when Author and Friend discuss the definition of a "gentleman." They establish six principles: charity; delicacy to women; yielding to others; concern for others as for oneself; honor; not envying superiors (2: 195-205). These cardinal virtues emphasize social responsibility and stability, urging complacency, not the independent ambition of a Pamela Andrews. As a Christian moralist, Brooke locates sentimental virtue in obedience to religious injunctions; sentimental behavior can be learned by imitating the manners of the elite. Author remarks: "As Aristotle and the Critics derived their rules, for epic poetry and the sublime, from a poem which Homer had written long before the rules were formed, or laws established for the purpose: Thus, from the demeanor and innate principles of particular Gentlemen, art has borrowed and instituted the many modes of behaviour, which the world has adopted under the title of good-manners" (2: 197). Echoing the preface to Fielding's *Amelia*, Brooke argues that sentimental behavior is analogous to art, and mimics aristocratic virtues; good manners become goodness and social leaders become moral models. Codified instinct constitutes sentimental behavior. History, the past, and example, rather than mechanical rules, determine virtue; yet, even while like most sentimentalists Brooke rejects "system" or law (as his daughter observes in the Preface of his *Poetical Works*), he appeals to a universal human nature deeper than law but equally rigid. This faith in a fundamentally stable nature, coupled with the rejection of "artificial" rules, resembles the artistic method that Pope constructs in his *Essay on Criticism*. Moreover, Brooke celebrates imitation, not only in art, but also in response. Indeed, Harry's father, modeling sentimental reading, prods the reader to imitate his sentiments when he caps Clement's tale by saying, "Your story...has been generally conversant in middle, or low life; and I observed that there is scarce a circumstance in it, which might not have happened to anybody, on any day of the year. And yet, in the whole, I find a chain of more surprizing and affecting events, than I have ever met with in history, or even in romance" (1: 92). In this stilted praise of universality within uniqueness, Brooke attempts to reconcile the neoclassical value of generality with the sentimental narrative of particularity, the true with the new. He argues that the virtue of art is that it structures history to accord with, and to respond to, eternal principles of morality.

The Fool of Quality blends this discourse on literary theory with lessons advocating social and classical virtues. These lessons reinforce Brooke's conservative message while revealing his ambivalence toward his audience and toward the politics of fiction. A lengthy account of the little Harry's education by a benevolent uncle in disguise, Harry Clinton, the novel advocates physical activity, friendship, rationality, observation, and morality, especially in volume 4 where our intellectual necessity for doubting is explained (4: 82). Long passages on politics, religion, history, and social order intersperse accounts of Harry's fights with his little friends, defense of his weaker brother, and compassion for beggars or unfortunates. We are informed that we have a right to property, but a duty to society, which "succors and strengthens" man (4: 96, 82). Brooke manifests the conflict in sentimental rhetoric between triumphant individualism and social duty in his "Dedication." By mimicking the conversational tone of Pope's Horatian imitations and the theatrical prologues of Restoration comedy, this dedication defines Author as the beleaguered, lone voice of social justice and integrity; at the same time, Brooke mocks his own idiosyncrasy and undercuts the validity of any lone voice. Addressed "To the Right Respectable my antient and well-beloved Patron the PUBLIC," the dedication opens with the question in quotation marks, "Why don't you dedicate to Mr. Pit?"[33] To this interlocutor, the voice of reader and public, Brooke's "Author" replies, "Because, Sir, I would rather set forth my own talents than the virtues and praises of the best man upon earth. I love to say things that no-one else ever thought of, extraordinary, quite out of the common way. I scorn to echo the voice of every fellow that goes the road. Whether the vessel of the commonwealth shall sink or swim; what is it to me? I am but a passenger" (1: iii). By declaring that love of fame and of singularity motivates his dedication, the speaker satirizes the fashion for originality as social dereliction. In another example of mock modesty, the Author adjures the public to dedicate "lasting monuments" to Pitt, "the patron of my patron," rather than desire the dedication of a mere novel. Then, the dedication proper begins. Brooke has identified himself with the individual reader, the "passenger," yet also against this reader as an "extraordinary" voice.

This dedication establishes openly the moral and political motivation of the novel, identifying the credentials of the author. Developing the theme of social relations as systems of patronage, the author commences his dedication to the public in mock humility. Imitating Sterne's elusively ironic voice, he isolates the "race of readers" from the complicitous "Dedicator" and "Dedicatee," who manipulate language and literary convention for personal gain. Brooke associates the literary hack who pens dedications with a tradesman, elaborating the analogy between clothing and language as signs of opulent and decadent culture: "The trades also, incumbent upon [dedicators], are manifold, such as of painting, patching, and plastering; of embroidery, shaping, and shaving; and of tyring, trimming, and tayloring; in order to smooth and garnish the man, "whom it delighteth them to honour," and to furnish him with a full suit of praises" (1: iv-vi). Such satire indicts the reciprocal self-interest and hypocrisy of corrupt social relations and the politics of culture. As his novel shows, however, it is not patronage to which Brooke objects, but praise wasted on vain upstarts, proud of being "respectable" rather than virtuous. His novel brims with examples of the social necessity of moral patronage to improve the behavior of the poor and undereducated and of financial patronage to improve their living conditions. At the end of the novel, for example, Harry symbolizes the true "Gentleman" in becoming the peoples' leader. Now Earl of Moreland, husband and adoptive father, he exemplifies physical, social, and moral leadership: "Slow as Lord Moreland moved the multitude strove to retard him, by throwing themselves in his way, that they might satiate their eyes with fulness of beauty. Bended knees and lifted hands, prayers, blessings, and exclamations were heard, and seen on all sides; and all the way as they went, thousands upon tens of thousands, shouted forth the hymenial [sic] of the celestial pair" (5: 299-300).

Harry becomes Christ on earth: "Harry walked between the ranks, his heart exulting in the sense of it's [sic] own divine humanity" (5: 297).

As author, Brooke requires a different kind of sentimental virtue to justify his role as narrator: the virtue of opposing, rather than of reforming, society. To establish this, he declares himself as socially inept as, for example, Goldsmith's Burchell: "There is, also, a kind of delicacy requisite in tickling the ribs of vanity. I am at best but a downright sort of a fellow; and should I, awkwardly presume to dash your merits, full, into the chops of your modesty, I might deserve but ill at the hands of your Respectableness" (1: vi). As an *honnête homme* like Pope and Horace, the author refutes effeminate "delicacy" for coarse truth. In warning us that this story will feel more like a blow in the face than a tickle of the ribs, he echoes the traditional warning of the satirist: this moral fable is no sentimental flattery. Later, he characterizes himself as simple and honest rather than mercenary and cunning, confessing he hopes for remuneration from the Public for his advice, since he is an "ass at this business of getting money," as a "cunning" fortune-teller had predicted when he was a boy. Brooke thus opposes public values with truth in the tradition of Juvenalian satire; his instincts and values define him as the last honest man in a corrupt world.

Brooke's sentimental values extend to broader issues than the endorsement of domestic love or the education of the reader in literary values. The faults he condemns include luxury, familial neglect, irreligion, and frivolous modern indulgence. These beggar the state and the soul, replacing English glory with the soft seductions of European fashion. In recounting Public's rejection of lessons in "moderation, content, self-denial" which even lead him to sell his mother (1: ix-x), Brooke voices a nostalgia for a glorious, "Spartan" past; now, however, Public, decked in foreign finery--"your linen of the Netherlands, your point of Spain, your ruffles of Dresden, with a full suit in the cut of France, and trimmed like that of the three brothers in a Tale of a Tub"--fritters away his time watching Italian puppet shows, gaming, and cockfighting on Sundays, unlike "the days of queen Bess" (1: x-xii). Acknowledging that other countries, as other times, also suffer from this "distemper" of "the sensuality of the Body, and the Corruption of the Mind," Brooke proposes as "medicine" the "Temperance and Patriotism of the primitive Romans" (1: xxi, xxii). Brooke sentimentalizes his neoclassical ethic, however, by arguing that patriotism, the strength and glory of the Romans, formed "an invisible chord which ran from man to man, and united all as one in the Love of Country" (1: xxii). In Brooke's rhetoric, sympathy confutes self-interest, replacing the discourse of profit with the praise of public service.

This service includes improving the public's taste, for literary values are seen to reflect social values. Readers should eschew, along with such literary low-life as the "strumpet Biography," the urban, professional, materialistic culture of degenerate display, competition, and legality (1: xxvii). Brooke indicts the conflation of commercial literature and public morality in a fashion that echoes the moral oppositions of *Jonathan Wild* (1743), Fielding's ironic biography of the "heroic" coward and "public" figure of a notorious thief. Defining "fool" as either one man, or the world, and "Wisdom" as worldly ambition, cunning, and greed, Brooke sets individual virtue, "Folly," in opposition to contemporary culture:

> It is the Tarantula that spins a web, whereby innocence is entangled. It is a politician who opens a gulph for the swallowing up of the people. It is a lawyer who digs a grave for the burial of equity. It is the science of Hocus Pocus, that bids happiness come and pass, by the virtue of cups and balls. It is a syllabub of fasting-spittle for the fattening of the Virtuosi. It is a robe with a pompous train. A wig spread to the rump. A beard lengthened to the girdle. It is a ditch of puddle, with a hoary mantle, that will not be moved to merriment by any wind that blows. It is an ass in a sumpter-cloth. An owl, solemnly perched, amidst solemn ruins, on a solemn night.
> Descend to me, sweet Folly! (1: xxxvi)

Brooke's style here embodies this message, as he replaces didactic prose with exclamatory rhetoric. Whereas Wisdom, or worldly interest, walks in the trappings of power and age, Folly, implied to be the goddess of simplicity, appears in his subsequent prayer as "ever joyous, ever young" (1: xxxvii). This conventional figuration of "new" Christianity opposed to the decadent old world defends sentimental nostalgia. Heaping images borrowed from propaganda and contemporary art of political and cultural degeneracy upon one another--the spider, the charlatan, the pudgy degenerate Virtuosi, the old men who rule culture, all playing with the toys of power--Brooke uses an impressionistic, fragmented rhetoric that reduces culture to static emblems. While leavening his lesson with a stylistic spectacle, this rhetoric advertises the liberation of feeling from convention; its fragments articulate impression and annihilate connection. Here, in contrast to the highly causal structure of his novel, Brooke marries his message to a sentimental method.

Henry Brooke recasts the tonal medley and the themes of periodical literature to advocate the reform of culture. Indicting modern selfish commercialism, he blends a conservative praise of simplicity with the admiration of "instinctive" manners. His mixture of religious allusion, neoclassical values, and Rousseauistic moralism defines one of the main strands in sentimental rhetoric: the criticism of culture corrupted as a consequence of the indulgence of the wrong values. He also interlards his vignettes with rhetorical flourishes and religious polemic to evoke the network of social concerns implied by sentimental ideology: literary values, public behavior, social relations, and the role of nature. His fictional structure urges readers to learn social responsibility by disciplining feeling and observing the consequences of social actions. This sentimental novel, in style and subject, endorses social hierarchy--albeit one based on merit--, and Christian humility. Only the satirical author retains the right to stand alone in his judgment.

   The Vicar of Wakefield and *The Fool of Quality* indict the desire for luxury, ambition, and display as symptoms of diseased will. This disease not only corrupts individual behavior, but it also perverts literary and artistic values. Both authors suggest that the conventions of art provide models for structuring feeling that will confute sentimental indulgence and provide an escape from the vanity and blindness of selfish individualism. It is only through the self-knowledge achieved by aesthetic refinement and a detached, inclusive perspective, often signaled by irony, that feeling can be translated into social virtue. It is, moreover, by recognizing the conventional rules that structure sentimental portraits that spectators can identify the universal in the particular and make morality out of emotion. This ironic perspective is modeled by the narrators, not by the fictional exemplars. Since, however, these narrators also act as exemplars in the fiction by virtue of their autobio-graphical and didactic voices, they occasionally exhibit the flaws they condemn, notably, self-deception. Thus, the structure of these fables compromises the sentimental simplicity both narrators assume. The center of sentimental perception is seen to lie in the consciousness of the art maker, not in the virtuous behavior of the characters he shows the reader. It is these cautious observers, these sophisticated spectators, who become the heroes of sentimental fiction, and these spectators can include the reader who creates his or her own moral sensibility by framing sentimental feeling within a social context to "make the happiness he does not find," as Samuel Johnson would have it. Both *The Vicar of Wakefield* and *The Fool of Quality* advocate the channeling of feeling to conventionally moral ends that identify individual virtue with social benefit, but both show that this channeling requires distance and relies on art for success. It is the narrator who truly turns experience into art, simplicity into sentiment. Reconciling virtue and feeling, he is the spectator who escapes feeling like a fool.

CHAPTER 3

The Sensitive Reader:
The Life and Opinions of Tristram Shandy
and *A Sentimental Journey Through France and Italy*

> Nature is shy, and hates to act before spectators.
> *A Sentimental Journey*

The "confessional" voices of sentimental pseudo-autobiographies, like Goldsmith's *Vicar of Wakefield*, dramatize the processes of feeling in the language of social intimacy. This blend of public and private rhetoric is useful for conveying sentimental ideology because it portrays the way the conscious mind of the writer makes sense of experience and feelings; thus, it can model both the sensitive apprehension of reality and the sensible adaptation of that apprehension to social rules. This dialectical tension between sensation and control, between sympathy and irony, characterizes the style of no writer more powerfully than Laurence Sterne. His sentimental fictions explore the oppositions between the modern world and the ideal of sympathetic unity, using sexual divisiveness to represent the decay of culture.

Sterne is typically considered the foremost sentimental novelist. Both *The Life and Opinions of Tristram Shandy* (1759-67) and *A Sentimental Journey Through France and Italy* (1768) exploit the themes of compassion and benevolence, sensation and impression, that characterize sentimental philosophy. Both also balance on the delicate line between parody and pathos.[1] Ostensibly, rules are mocked and feelings celebrated, as they are in Henry Brooke's *Fool of Quality*, and later by Rousseau and Goethe.[2] In *Tristram Shandy*, the "modest," sympathetic Toby exemplifies sentimental delicacy, although it is Walter Shandy who stands as the "man of sentiment" or of "opinion" in the book, and the narrator Tristram, like Goldsmith's and Brooke's narrators, who blends confession with rhetorical virtuosity. Sterne's later novel, *A Sentimental Journey*, explores sentiment in the travelogue, recasting tourism as Yorick's experience of sensation not scenery. Nevertheless, even while Sterne lauds sympathetic connection, his novels describe alienation in a world where divided interests divide affection itself, a world producing not pity but prurience. Sterne's fractured form, ambiguous tone, and empty antitheses establish a sentimental rhetoric that condemns the very sensuality that organizes his stories. His style sabotages his structure and thus articulates the contemporary conflict between the patriarchal tradition of neoclassical order and the current chaos of a feminized literary culture.[3]

Defining Sterne's sentimentalism as Humean sympathy, John Traugott explains the "philosophical" basis of *Tristram Shandy*:

> As we perceive actions in others similar to our own, we form an idea of the emotions of others, and the idea is transformed into an impression, and becomes through association with ourselves a real passion of our own. But still the emotion or passion is not directed toward ourselves, but rather, we feel for and with the object of our intuition. For Hume man is always a social being, neither egoistic nor selfless but always in some sympathetic relation (in normal behavior) ... This philosophical sentimentalism is the real sentimentalism of *Tristram Shandy*; it is the real order of *Tristram Shandy*.[4]

While such sympathy may represent Sterne's ideal, his book is peopled with characters who demonstrate the limits of reason and language, preferring gesture and tacit sympathetic identification to explanation, even falling into the solipsism and relativism Hume warned against.[5] His rhetoric, moreover, condemns extremes of feeling or behavior that betray an inadequate marriage of selfish and social interests: solipsism on the one hand, and prostitution on the other. Sterne's rhetorical strategies are myriad. John Traugott has explained his philosophical rhetoric, and Richard Lanham has noted his traditional oratory, while John M. Stedmond has explored Sterne's formal innovations by exposing his debt to the classical models of the satirist, the clown, and the *rhetor*.[6] Developing this connection between Sterne's form and his rhetoric, John Mullan points out Sterne's ambiguous address to the publisher and the critics, his exhortations both for and against patronage, and his flattery of the "private reader" that establishes a privileged relationship between text and interpreter.[7] While Mullan explains this privilege as that of the "true feeler" against "the herd," and cites a number of Sterne's "distancing" techniques, he portrays Sterne's audience as a unified whole (158). In fact, Sterne establishes several exclusionary rhetorical strategies that define different readers against each other. These classify readers according to gender, class, and education; in so doing, they revive quarrels between neoclassical and "modern" aesthetic, social, and cultural values.

The most notable theme and rhetorical strand in *Tristram Shandy* is sex. Some of the time, Sterne uses sex as an analogical symbol for communication or sensation; some critics have labeled it the weapon in a rhetorical attack on false communication, figured as logic.[8] At other times, however, it symbolizes the reverse: lack of communication, the absence of sympathy.[9] Women often represent the insistent, consuming, demanding audience--the Widow Wadman to Tristram's literary Toby, the aggressive reader who interferes with the private communication between civilized men mated as fellow souls. In noting Sterne's persistent tonal ambiguity, critics have tended to ignore sex as the attribute of women, real women readers as well as literary stereotypes. Sterne's view of sex, however, provides the key to unlocking his attitude toward "the female sex," both as readers and as literary tropes; sex, moreover, represents not merely his relationship to women, but also the relationship of author to audience, for "dear Madam," the quintessentially intrusive reader, is the repeated butt of Tristram's rhetorical jokes. By the middle of the century, women constituted an audience and a topic for literature as John J. Richetti explains.[10] As female readers comprised part of the audience, the "female" value for the "particularized facts of social experience" was valorized in modern literature (68). Such an aesthetic preference rubs against neoclassical tenets promoted in the schools and universities men attended, which endorsed universal or general portraits. Henry Brooke, softening Sterne's formula, yokes these conflicting literary values in *Fool of Quality*, partly by didactic theorizing. In Sterne's sentimentalism, however, this conflict becomes a sharp battle between kinds of culture and between values, both gendered by the rhetoric of the novel. Sex thus dramatizes several vital themes that interweave sentimental discourse: the relationship between public and private, between author and audience, between observation and consumption, and between aesthetics and pragmatics.

In *Tristram Shandy*, women and sex serve as rhetorical opponents to the values men of feeling hold dear, whether those values seem applauded or mocked. This is comically exemplified by the relationship between Walter, called "the man of sentiment" several times in the book, and Mrs. Shandy. At the insistence of Toby, that other sentimental man, Walter insists on a clause in his marriage contract that limits Mrs. Shandy's "right" to lay in at London: if she should ask to be taken to London on a false call, she forfeits her right to give birth there. The assumptions beneath this clause--that women's bodies constitute their laws and hold their "rights", that women use their bodies and child-bearing mysteries to win "unfair play," as Toby calls it, that they love the city, and will deceive honest affection to gallivant there--are the assumptions of the Augustan moral-rhetorical tradition Richetti notes (1: xv, 35).

Sterne, of course, mocks these assumptions as he attacks modern abuses of nature and learning, particularly through Walter. Walter's obsessive resentment of Mrs. Shandy's maternal "authority" exposes the nature of his hobbyhorse, as the quarrel about generation exemplifies the futile division between artificial antitheses--man and woman, art or law and nature (2: vviii, 114-15; 4: xii, 227; 4: xxix, 262). In his advice to Toby "upon the nature of women, and of love-making," Walter urges concealment, deception, and artificial seriousness to promote yet control lust (8: xxxiv, 476-78). Walter incorrectly assumes Mrs. Shandy's lust as she peers through the keyhole when in fact she seems frigid; it is his own prurient spectatorship that he reveals. She advocates "love" and children when he contrarily condemns sex (4: xxxix, 379; 8: xxxiii, 474). Unlike the system-mad Walter, she "truest of all the *Poco-curante*'s of her sex!" cares not how something is done as long as it is done (6: xx, 355). The very persistence throughout the novel of the problem of penetrating Mrs. Shandy's body with mechanical instruments to extract Tristram highlights the contrast between false science and female nature. Mrs. Shandy's nature shows up Walter's denatured "method".

Nevertheless, Sterne plays rhetorically with antitheses that are revealed to be as delusive and unsatisfying as all formal structures. The replication of the flaws of father and of mother in Tristram do not make him the unquestioned "authority"; his double-talk points to a further, if slippery, authority in the language itself, for Sterne hints that the author's authority may not be the last word. The false "authority" that Walter models, however, directly opposes female "authority." While establishing this opposition between the corruptions of male learning and female nature, Sterne reinforces the distinction between male sentiment and female pragmatism, between the delicacy and difficulty of male feelings, and the bovine simplicity of natural women. Mrs. Shandy's pragmatism, torpidity, coldness, and conventionality are not virtues; she is not a heroine because Walter is a fool. Similarly, Walter's meanness, revealed in his "grave" expression upon hearing of Toby's intention to leave a pension to Trim, does not justify female avarice (4: iv, 221). We learn that Tristram's great-grandmother wins a handsome jointure from her husband because of his "little or no nose," and Walter has had to pay her £300 a year for twelve years after his father's death (3: xxxiii, 174-75). Even while Sterne satirizes both male impotence and Walter himself for resenting this expenditure, he also revives the traditional association between women's sexual and commercial appetites, between a man's "paying" a woman physically and financially. The literary stereotypes of women, sex, and sexual relations serve to highlight the unique characters of the Shandy men. The center of interest is not, in fact, female nature but male nature, not the woman's body but the man's mind, as conveyed in print.

The most typical sentimental example of the rhetorical function of type-cast--or typed--women to tease out sentiment is "poor Maria," who reappears in *A Sentimental Journey* and throughout sentimental fiction until Jane Austen cures her as Marianne Dashwood in *Sense and Sensibility*. Driven mad by frustration after her marriage bans were forbidden, she has become "The love and pity of all the villages around," and the cause of "the full force of an honest heart-ache" in Tristram as he eludes death on the Continent (9: xxiv, 522-23). As Michel Foucault has noted in *Madness and Civilization*, this type populates eighteenth-century literature, representing uncontrolled sensibility, imagination run free, and alienation from the immediate (219-20). In sentimental literature, the mad wandering girl also serves as an emblem of purified nature, sexuality that has regressed to childhood and thrown off civilized arts. She confirms reader and writer within safely civilized bounds; by pitying her and by recognizing her emblematic qualities, we establish an artful frame around nature and the implied criticism of society the mad girl suggests. Indeed, in *Tristram Shandy*, Maria's story is actually what Mullan calls "parenthesized" by appearing in a separated text, "The Invocation," addressed to Cervantic humor.[11] Tristram, moreover, further emblematizes Maria by labeling her "Misery," whose "venerable presence" reproves his Rabelaisian wit and assures his pure motives to the "candid reader" (9: xxiv, 523). While the "poor hapless damsel" dwells alone in her isolated world of music and madness, Tristram and the reader return to the world of writing, of words, of civilized laughter and the "Gentle Spirit of sweetest humour" (521). She serves as a rhetorical opportunity to reassert the values of the male literary tradition, which include an emblematic and generalized understanding of nature and of learned wit.

An equally powerful female type stands in opposition to poor Maria: the Widow Wadman. Whereas Maria's madness stems from eternal virginity, the Widow's keen sanity results from her sexual experience and knowledge. Her "worldliness" appears in her reluctance to admit her love of Toby, whereas Toby exhibits his virtue by openly declaring his love (8: xxvii, 468). If Maria is alienated from immediate, physical reality, the Widow is only too well aware of it when she asks Toby where he got his wound and blushingly protests when he promises her that she will put her hand upon the place. As opposite extremes prominent in sentimental literature, these two types frame Mrs. Shandy, yet "my mother" remains a cipher, even a hole or a blank like the Widow's portrait, who serves merely to draw out the characters of the Shandy men. Her rhetorical style and function is mere reflection: just as she agrees automatically with whatever Walter asserts, so Sterne uses her as a mirror to portray Walter's irritable self-absorption. As throughout sentimental literature, women serve in *Tristram Shandy* to expose the workings of sentiment in men.

As rhetorical opponents, of course, women can also work to satirize falsely rigid or inhuman abuses of learning. They are features in sentimental discourse who change function with the intentions of the speaker--but their role as the tabula rasa of male meanings and their place as the nexus of satirical innuendos persists throughout that discourse. Women and sex traditionally represent the threat to conventional and established structures of authority and standards of taste. Their taste--their "peeping" and their perception--threaten literature, social relations, conventional hierarchies, wit, indeed whatever needs defending at the moment. Like Widow Wadman, they are carnal or trivial when true value lies in the intellectual; like Mrs. Shandy, they are distracted when the moment calls for physical response. Traugott says, "The core of Sterne's sentimentalism lies in his insistence that by certain public signs--conduct, reaction, and attitude--we can come to understand individuality. Far from any romantic notion of the private personality, this conception is rooted in Aristotle's *Rhetoric* and the whole classical tradition of predictable human behavior" (75). Women, however, in Sterne's rhetoric represent the insistently private, personal, concealed, original. Since it is the perception of these public "signs" that ensures communication, the way one sees, as well as what one sees, becomes a central issue in the battle on taste. Sterne sexualizes the opposition between idealized, innocent vision and practical perception. When one sees the text as a "pure" reader, one should see Tristram's signs, not the omitted or hidden, which Madam always seeks--although Sterne slyly suggests that real readers always snoop. Through the theme of perception and by contrasting different aesthetic values, Sterne creates a rhetorical opposition between sentimental and feminine interpretations of value.

Sterne's women incarnate the principle of contrast. They represent the carnivalesque opposite of true values, even to the extent of satirizing the weakness of these "true" values in the "real" world. They embody disorder if order is the order of the day; they are self-absorbed when a benevolent wide view is needed.[12] If Mackenzie endows his "hero" Harley with risibly female weaknesses to attack degenerate social standards, Sterne borrows, albeit ambiguously, a neoclassical antithesis to attack modern corruption in the form of female culture. Critics have noted Sterne's Augustan touches, especially attacks on the abuses of learning, or false wit.[13] These abuses in Sterne's day included false taste in reading, or reading for bad reasons or in the wrong way, as Richard Payne Knight deplores in his *Inquiry into the Principles of Taste* (1805).[14] It is not merely the dog-star-mad authors who batter at the door with their vulgar literature as in Pope's *Epistle to Dr. Arbuthnot*, but the audience ruling the market who now corrupts taste. Sterne uses sexual opposition to represent this fervid yet futile opposition between the producers and the consumers of literary culture who are, in fact, mutually dependent.

The form of *Tristram Shandy* itself embodies this opposition. The confessional format evokes the authenticity and intimacy of autobiography, already established as the genre of individual expression and associated strongly with tales of adventure, experience, or education. When Tristram invokes "ye POWERS" who "preside over this vast empire of biographical freebooters," he mocks the mysterious order of self-revelation that is, in fact, disorder (3: xxiii, 164). Indeed, Tristram in mock-horror avoids turning his "book apocryphal" into "a profess'd ROMANCE"--a female genre--by violating the probability of time (2: viii, 84). Sterne of course outdoes Richardson, writing to the second where *Pamela* contents itself with the minute; as other critics have noted, identity, let alone individuality, is reduced to absurdity by Tristram's attempts to find the beginning of life. At the same time, Sterne lambasts the morality-mongering and Scriblerian generic distinctions of current literature.

By coalescing a parody of women's literature with an attack on the abuses of learning, Sterne condemns feminized literary culture, not least because it usurps authority from male culture, as Nancy Armstrong observes.[15] At the same time, in the fashion characteristic of the dialectic of sentimental stylistics, Sterne attacks masculine rigidity, resistance to female culture, and impotence through both Tristram and Walter, who can father successfully neither the son, Tristram, nor the book, *Tristapaedia*. Tristram has his own problems with literary culture. For example, he confesses his intention to flatter any kind of reader early in the book in a passage that contrasts with his parody of sycophantic criticism in "The Author's Preface" (3: xx, 153-54):

> I know there are readers in the world, as well as many other
> good people in it, who are no readers at all,--who find
> themselves ill at ease, unless they are let into the whole secret
> from first to last, of every thing which concerns you.
>   It is in pure compliance with this humour of theirs, and from
> a backwardness in my nature to disappoint any one soul living,
> that I have been so very particular already. As my life and
> opinions are likely to make some noise in the world, and...will
> take in all ranks, professions, and denominations of men
> whatever,--be no less read than the *Pilgrim's Progress*
> itself--and, in the end, prove the very thing which *Montaigne*
> dreaded his essays should turn out, that is, a book for a
> parlour-window;--I find it necessary to consult every one a
> little in his turn. (1: iv, 7-8)

While parodying the pretentiousness, unctuous flattery, and soulless commercialism of contemporary literature, this passage also lambasts the taste such literature feeds: the appetite for exhaustive, "secret," and private information and the use of literature for quick morality and status. When Tristram longs to write a "chapter upon sleep," but despairs because it is an exhausted topic, preferring "buttonholes," Sterne satirizes the fashion for novelty over significance (4: xv, 230-232). Tristram boasts that his novel is full of mysteries, both "progressive and digressive" at the same time, and possesses a hidden structure that his wondering reader can only imagine (1: xxii, 57, xxv, 63). This pride in novelty and disorder insinuates plaints against modern, immoral literature. It also, however, portrays the disorganization of a sentimental world, a world structured by response instead of by rule. Tristram remarks that he will add a map to his twentieth volume "not to swell the work,--I detest the thought of such a thing," but to explain passages susceptible to "private interpretations, or dark or doubtful meaning" (1: xiii, 31). His own Scriblerus, Tristram also mocks the way in which self-important and money-grubbing authors exploit ignorant readers in a literary climate which celebrates length and particularity while selling universal morality. Tristram serves simultaneously to mock and to indulge anxiety about the effects of sentimental ideology of literary culture.

The parody of genre operates to parody the specific form in which women's tales achieved respectability: the novel of individual experience, which accords ultimate authority to the subject and so flatters readers who, like Arabella in Charlotte Lennox's *Female Quixote* (1752), identify with the fictional hero.[16] *Tristram Shandy* is both a triumph and a failure as such a novel because it relies utterly on an individual authority that it constantly undermines. Tristram addresses "Sir," a "perfect stranger," as "my dear friend and companion" when he allows Tristram to tell his story his own way and pities his "fool's cap" and his tarrying (1: vi, 10). Flattery of the author produces flattery of the reader. Similarly, modern literary culture vaunts individual values. Tristram's sycophantic dedication to "my Lord" satirizes the commercialization of literature and the degradation of "public duty" to private pleasure--a joke reinforced by Toby's assertion that Walter performs sex "out of principle," not pleasure (1: viii, 13-14; 2: xiii, 93). Narratives of individual experience are shown to please the self rather than serve society, and while Sterne criticizes this, he also begs the question of whether any literature ever did, or could do, otherwise. While she becomes the source of bawdiness in contrast with the learned or sympathetic "Sir," Madam signals false rhetoric, thus linking sex and a certain kind of literary language as reciprocally false methods of communication, both represented by female narratives. It is "Sir" to whom Tristram appeals, using a generalized rhetoric, in excusing Toby's submission to Widow Wadman--"So Sweet!--so exquisite" in "Nature"--but this aesthetic appeal contrasts both with female sexuality and with women's pretense that sincerity appears transparently in self-assertions (6: xxxviii, 378). Neoclassical male literary culture uses a rhetoric and structure opposed to the novels of female individuality.

The attack on women's taste, standards, demands, and incursion on male literary culture is launched primarily through the "conversations" with "Madam," the female reader. These "conversations" constitute rhetorical attacks on the female reader for sexual preoccupation--itself an ironic example of the subjective being objectified through oratory. In her first appearance, Madam is inquiring into Walter Shandy's sex life, asking why he could not have conceived Tristram earlier than the fatefully interrupted night that starts the novel (1:, iv, 9). The traits this question exposes-- prurience, calculation, a gross concern with quantity and with sexual satisfaction--are conjured by Tristram in all Madam's queries. In discussing Yorick's horse (or hobbyhorse), Tristram declares, "And let me tell you, Madam, there is a great deal of very good chastity in the world, in behalf of which you could not say more for your life" (1: x, 16). It is Madam whom Tristram addresses when defending Toby's "modesty in the truest sense" against the charge of verbal hypocrisy (1: xxi, 54; 6: xxix, 365-66). He assures Madam that "We can conceal nothing ... worth shewing" under "our" short coats and trunk-hose, or under our rhetoric, implying his value for public over hidden or private values (3: xiv, 147). After describing shredded breeches, he requests Madam to govern her fancy (9: ii, 488). Although he declares obstinately to Madam "'That both man and woman bear pain or sorrow (and, for aught I know, pleasure too) best in a horizontal position','" Walter's walk in reaction to the news of Bobby's death disproves this and his assertion (3: xxix, 171). By Madam's leave, Tristram relates Slawkenbergius's tale in which a "nose" becomes a word and a thing, anything but a nose (3: xlii, 193). After asking Madam to clarify Slawkenbergius's description of "the lambent pupilability" of whispering, he tells her that only "the sentimental part" of a conference has value; the rest is not "worth stooping for" (4: i, 218-19). "Sentimental" is here defined as public, while Madam stoops for the private(s). Madam questions the "strange tale" of the Abbess of Andouillets and Margarita, who swear by syllables in order to move their mules and save their virginity, only belatedly observing that Tristram is wearing his fool's cap (7: xxvi, 410). Throughout, Madam notes the verbal promiscuity and sexual innuendo but misses the rhetorical tone.

Madam is also, like "my mother," curious. This curiosity is the sign of Madam's lineage from Eve, her upstart impulse to inquire into the forbidden. This cultural ambition corrupts public values, even while it could also be said to create culture. Slawkenbergius blames "CURIOSITY" for opening the city's gates, as Pandora opened her box, and curious women begin the tale

by wondering at the size of his nose (4: j, 217). Identifying "curiosity" as
"the weak part of the whole sex," Tristram links "my mother" with Madam
and with every "lady" (5: xii, 295). Entering a long "caveat in the breast of
my fair reader," Tristram defends himself from the charge of being "a
married man," as the moral judge Madam opines, merely because he has
referred to his "dear, dear Jenny":

> All I plead for, in this case, Madam, is strict justice, and that
> you do so much of it, to me as well as to yourself,-- as not to
> prejudge or receive such an impression of me, till you have
> better evidence...--Not that I can be so vain or unreasonable,
> Madam, as to desire you should therefore think, that my dear,
> dear *Jenny* is my kept mistress;--no,--that would be flattering
> my character in the other extream [sic]...All I contend for, is
> the utter impossibility for some volumes, that you, or the most
> penetrating spirit upon earth, should know how this matter
> really stands.--It is not impossible, but that my dear, dear
> *Jenny*! tender   as   the   appellation   is,   may   be   my
> child.--Consider,--I was born in the year eighteen.--Nor is there
> anything unnatural or extravagant in the supposition, that my
> dear *Jenny* may be my friend.--Friend!--My friend.--Surely,
> Madam, a friendship between the two sexes may subsist and
> be supported without -- Fy! Mr.*Shandy*: -- Without any thing,
> madam, but that tender and delicious sentiment, which ever
> mixes in friendship, where there is a difference of sex. Let me
> intreat you to study the pure and sentimental parts of the best
> *French* Romances;--it will really, Madam, astonish you to see
> with   what   vivacity   of   chaste   expression   this   delicious
> sentiment, which I have the honour to speak of, is dress'd out
>   (1: xviii, 42).

In language shifting from the legal to the aesthetic, Tristram attacks not
merely the sexual hypocrisy of the reader, but female readers and female
literary culture, exemplified by Continental "Romances" and expressed
through the unstable term "sentimental". This female literary culture appears
preoccupied with prurient sex masked as morality or sentimentalism; it allows
the reader to envision only wife or mistress, not friend or child, despite
pretensions to sentimental friendships and familial values. Tristram
underscores the double standards beneath Madam's sexual values by refusing
to call "Jenny" his "kept mistress" out of declared modesty: this is a dig at
the licentious sensationalism of romantic fiction.

Sterne also sexualizes and opposes ways of reading. In another famous passage, Tristram scolds Madam for "inattentive" reading when she fails to gather from an obscure hint *"That my mother was not a papist"* (1: xx, 47). While the penitent Madam re-reads the previous chapter, Tristram converses with the other reader, who must be "Sir," on the

> vicious taste which has crept into thousands besides herself,--of reading straight forwards, more in quest of the adventures, than of the deep erudition and knowledge which a book of this cast, if read over as it should be, would infallibly impart with them.---The mind should be accustomed to make wise reflections, and draw curious conclusions as it goes along; the habitude of which made *Pliny* the younger affirm, "That he never read a book so bad, but he drew some profit from it".
>
> (1: xx, 48)

Again, Sterne uses Tristram's joke to mock both hypocritical readers and the platitudes of a current moralism that separates virtue from entertainment. At the same time, his rhetorical strategy does separate the female readers who doggedly follow his instructions from the male readers who sit back awaiting their return and moralizing on modern degeneracy and the excellence of classical culture. The two aspects of reading remain rhetorically segregated. Tristram further adds, "I wish the male-reader has not pass'd by many a one [subtle hint], as quaint and curious as this one, in which the female-reader has been detected. I wish it may have its effects;--and that all good people, both male and female, from her example, may be taught to think as well as read" (49). Although this mock-pious wish seems to equate male and female readers, Sterne has, in fact, reinforced the distinction between impression-hungry female readers and their kinds of books and the witty literature of male culture. Reading for pleasure, like reading for sex, becomes characteristic of modern female literary culture, even if reading for any other reason, or "out of principle," as Walter has sex, is an absurd extreme. Once again, the antithesis of male and female readers collapses into an implied third term: a balance of pleasure and principle that constitutes neoclassical doctrine.

Sterne teaches his audience how to read. Both in his digressions and in his rhetorical ploys, Tristram establishes a "conversational" style. The rhetorical aspects of this style have been noted, even its association with gossip as typically female discourse.[17] The relationship that the author establishes with the audience is, however, primarily authoritarian, indeed schoolmasterly, as J. Paul Hunter has observed.[18] The text resists allowing readers to determine the moral value of the recounted experience for themselves since Tristram scolds, cajoles, and dictates to the reader many if not all of the possible meanings of his book, and so reiterates a classical, albeit precarious, control over his rhetoric.[19] When these techniques fail, Tristram tries another kind of authority: he beseeches the "gentle" reader for sympathy and tolerance in his literary endeavor (4: xxii, 239). While mimicking the pleas of literary hacks, Sterne rhetorically associates pity with cultural privilege: it is the "gentle" who have the room for tolerance; it is those who can judge who can forgive. "Sir" condemns the bookbinder for omitting chapter twenty-four of the fourth volume (251), but the "gentle Critick" (not the "hypercritick") patiently awaits explanation. It is to "good folks" that he promises the juicy tale of Jenny, if "your worships and reverences are not offended" (4: xxxxii, 269-70). Tristram further distinguishes between "the Christian reader" and "Sir," who by contrast stands, not as irreligious, but as impartial or classical (6: xxxiii, 370). All these rhetorical distinctions enforce a way of reading--expansive, leisured, broad-minded--associated with the literary values of a nonprofessional culture in contrast to the literalistic and pragmatic readers of the current market.

This way of reading requires a guide. Sterne underlines the importance of relying on a central authorial voice to control interpretation. In adjuring "my unlearned reader" to "Read, read, read, read," and thus "read" the marbled page, Sterne emphasizes the laxity of a contemporary literary culture that demands little learning from its members (3: xxxvi, 180-82). At the same time, this command underscores the pointlessness of learning and reasserts Tristram's authority since no reader, whatever his learning, can "read" the unwritten. We must have signs. Sterne thus casts the reader into the role of the ignorant Madam; such a role does not excuse his or her ignorance, but rather legitimizes Tristram's authority. Tristram reassures the "gentle reader" that he will use him kindly now that he holds him in the power of his pen (7: vi, 390).

Tristram Shandy revels in the rhetorical technique of addressing the reader and thus prompting his or her reactions. These reactions, however, paradoxically dramatize the separation of the reader from the fiction, the characters, and even the narrator. Whereas Fielding characterizes his reader as an honest companion, innocently naive at worst, Sterne shifts his rhetorical addresses to suit his subject. When unsexualized, the reader is flattered, often ironically, for precisely the same qualities as Sterne reveals are moving his characters at that moment. He has "a thorough knowledge of human nature" which tells him that Yorick must have been dunned by creditors (1: xii, 24). He has justly "observed ... my father's great good sense," yet he condemns, according to his humor--whether "cholerick," "mercurial," or "saturnine"-- Walter's belief in the importance of names (1: xix, 43). He is "learned" when Tristram warns him against fixed ideas,   but "gentle" when he understands Walter's disasters (1: xix, 45, 47). He is "penetrating" when he suspects a hidden cause for Toby's abrupt shift from uncomplaining passivity to peremptoriness with his surgeon (2: iv, 75). Thus the reader reflects Tristram's own descriptive analyses: pragmatic and cunning in worldly affairs, idiosyncratic and hasty in personal, passionate matters, wise on learned issues, pitying the pitiable, visionary when the hidden comes to light. The reader, in short, is rhetorically compelled to experience the feelings of the characters themselves through sympathetic identification, yet the self-consciousness of Sterne's rhetoric perpetually pulls the reader back from this identification.[20] The rhetorical frame of Tristram's "conversation" with the reader distances this reader from the characters, segregating observation and witty allusion from sympathy and identification.

> Writing, when properly managed, (as you may be sure I think
> mine is) is but a different name for conversation: As no one,
> who knows what he is about in good company, would venture
> to talk all;--so no author, who understands the just boundaries
> of decorum and good breeding, would presume to think all:
> The truest respect which you can pay to the reader's
> understanding, is to halve this matter amicably, and leave him
> something to imagine, in his turn, as well as yourself.
>
> (2: xi, 87)

Both the stylistic similarities to Fielding and the analogy with   "good breeding" stamp this "conversation" as a privileged discourse between equals within "just boundaries of decorum." As Sterne's method demonstrates, however, conversation or communication paradoxically marks alienation, and Tristram continually attempts to coopt all the imaginative possibilities in the text. Decorum perpetually fractures. Writing is as much a sign of the separation of author and audience as it is of their communication.

Sterne's novel exemplifies several other rhetorical techniques that articulate the tension between alienation and sympathy, fragmentation and connection, that characterizes literary sentimentalism. One typical device is pictorial description, which personifies impressions or feelings and slides into panegyric. Tristram begins one chapter, for example, by objectifying mood or atmosphere as mythic action: "STILLNESS, with SILENCE at her back, entered the solitary parlour, and drew their gauzy mantle over my uncle *Toby*'s head;---and LISTLESSNESS, with her lax fibre and undirected eye, sat quietly down beside him in his arm chair" (6: xxxv, 373). The elegiac description allegorizes a domestic portrait so that this moment of intimate observation becomes public. After recounting Toby's loss of his hobbyhorse, Tristram shifts to lyricism:

> ---Softer visions,--gentler vibrations stole sweetly in upon his slumbers;--the trumpet of war fell out of his hands,--he took up the lute, sweet instrument! of all others the most delicate! the most difficult!--how wilt thou touch it, my dear uncle *Toby*? (6: xxxv, 373)

This scene evokes classical literary oratory, the language of public imagery; these formalizing conventions counter the intimacy of the speaker's address to "my dear uncle." In a similar style, Tristram describes Heaven's tolerance for uncle Toby's sentimental pity. When he has sworn an oath to help Le Fever, "--The ACCUSING SPIRIT which flew up to heaven's chancery with the oath, blush'd as he gave it in;--and the RECORDING ANGEL as he wrote it down, dropp'd a tear upon the word, and blotted it out for ever" (6: viii, 341). A version of a seventeenth-century allegory contrasting human justice with divine mercy, this picture supplies a conventional and public context within which the detail of Toby's oath appears. By allusion, this rhetoric generalizes the meaning of the incident and places Toby's idiosyncratic sentiment within a humanistic tradition of values.

This interfusion of emblematic or public meanings with private descriptions saturates Sterne's prose, as classical references animate the inanimate. A form of personification, this rhetorical technique usually endows domestic objects with emotions rather than confers the power to act on grand natural phenomena, as classical personification does. Whereas winds howl or skies rage in Homer and Virgil, in literary sentimentalism small, purchasable commodities--books, mementos, poems, portraits--serve as receptacles of feeling. In Goethe's *Sorrows of Young Werther* (1774), Werther receives Lotte's pink ribbon as a birthday gift, and Yorick in *A Sentimental Journey* uses the Monk's gift of a horn snuffbox as a moral emblem ensuring humility, while St. Aubert weeps over his sister's miniature in Radcliffe's *Mysteries of Udolpho* (1794). Victorian fiction also exploits the sentimental significance of objects to attack or, sometimes, to advertise the relationship between feeling and commercialism, but in Sterne's novels this technique marks the fusion of older, allegorical ways of expressing meaning with the new objectification of psychological significance derived from empiricism. It works in eighteenth-century novels to express the uneasy bridging of public and individual meanings that forms one of the preoccupations of sentimental fiction.

The confusion of words and things throughout *Tristram Shandy*, however, allows Sterne to challenge both public and private meanings.

Commenting on the blank page he has supplied for the reader's portrait of Widow Wadman, for example, Tristram exclaims, "Thrice happy book! thou wilt have one page, at least, within thy covers, which MALICE will not blacken, and which IGNORANCE cannot misrepresent" (6: xxxviii, 378). The formal exclamation and address "thou" belong to conventional rhetoric, while the neoclassical personification of the evil forces of the social world echoes the plaints of Pope and Horace. At the same time, Tristram's exclamation interprets the blank page as innocence, a tabula rasa that the reader's prurient portrait will stain. Tristram thus characterizes both words and fancies as simultaneously physical and potential. "Happiness," moreover, is attributed to the "book" and encompasses both objective and subjective meanings. While the book is "happy" in the classical sense of fortunate, it is also imagined to experience the sensation of happiness that Tristram envies. This rhetorical ambiguity signals an increasingly ambiguous reciprocity between actor, emotion, and object, between the feeling person, what he or she feels, and the thing that represents what he or she feels.

Such linguistic instability dramatizes the conflict between educated and naive perception that comprises one of the battles between traditional and new literary culture. How to read entails the question of how one should see. The visual tricks in the novel play with the relationship between the physical and the metaphorical. Asterisks, pointing printer's hands, blank, black, and marbled pages, dashes, squiggles, and scrawls all draw the reader's attention to the surface of the work, as many critics have noted.[21] This technique reinforces the thematic attention to painterly perspectives, and, indeed, to aesthetics. After asking the reader, "Sir," to peruse Hogarth's treatise on beauty, for example, Tristram asks, "Pray, Sir, let me interest you a moment in this description" (2: ix, 84-85) and proceeds to "paint" Obadiah in detail. The description of "my father" prostrate on his bed in sorrow at Tristram's misfortunes carefully highlights significant, even emblematic details--his hand, his right leg, the chamber pot's handle are all composed to illustrate his "attitude" (3: xxix, 171). In the chapter headed "*De gustibus non est disputandum*," Tristram declares himself "both fiddler and painter," but not a "wise" man; quoting a classical dictum on the idiosyncracy of taste, Tristram vaunts his love of the sound and sight of things--of beauty--above the tangled arguments of philosophers (1: viii, 12-13). Aesthetic sensitivity becomes a philosophy itself, urging tolerance over argument. Later, however, Tristram compares "Writers of my stamp" with "painters": "Where an exact copying makes our pictures less striking, we choose the less evil; deeming it even more pardonable to trespass against truth, than beauty.--This is to be understood *cum grano salis*; but be it as it will,--the parallel is made more for the sake of letting the apostrophe cool, than any thing else,--'tis not very material whether upon any other score the reader approves of it or not" (2:

iv, 74). Tristram here suggests that an aesthetic preference for beauty reflects the author's pride, as biographers or autobiographers prefer their own beauty to truth. This apparently sentimental preference for effect is undermined by the cold-water advice "*cum grano salis*," and by the underscored emptiness of the words, written to fill the unattractive space. "The reader" is solicited to take the statement only in the present context and expected to distrust this ostensibly simple formula. The writer, moreover, who notes his own deviations from "truth," invites the reader to question all his "truths." Once again, Sterne's self-consciousness sabotages the illusion of his fiction and parodies the insincerities of contemporary novels. The wise reader will never forget the difference between the book--beauty--and life.

The rhetorical associations coloring the aesthetic values in *Tristram Shandy* extend even to the question of how to see not merely art, but also life itself. By dividing approved from disapproved aesthetic attitudes, Sterne establishes a distinction between approved and disapproved perception, a distinction that again works to exclude certain readers and to flatter others. This rhetoric of distinction and exclusion reflects again the strains in contemporary literary culture, including rivalry between scientific and humanistic empiricism, sometimes gendered as male inquiry and female nature. In chapter 2 of the first volume, Tristram ironically distinguishes between the views of "the eye of folly or prejudice," which laughs at the homunculi, and "the eye of reason in scientifick research" which respects it (1: ii, 7). Part of the joke lies in the subject; the story of Tristram's interrupted conception and the consequent scattering of the "animal spirits" in mid coitus by Mrs. Shandy's thoughtless question. Toby tells Tristram this story, having heard it from Walter, and Tristram addresses it to "dear Sir"; Mrs. Shandy knows nothing of it. Thus, confined entirely to secret male conversation, the story develops a male topic of a male act from a male perspective, seriously regarded by men: the scientific "eye of reason" then contrasts with the moral "eye of folly and prejudice." The main joke lies in the realization that "reason" here appears merely another form of "folly and prejudice," peeping indecently into the internal workings of creation. Scientific perception is another kind of superstition.

More often, however, *Tristram Shandy* opposes the narrow view attributed to women and women readers with the general, laughing, philosophical view of men and male readers. Tristram himself explains, "This is the true reason, that my dear *Jenny* and I, as well as all the world besides us, have such eternal squabbles about nothing.--She looks at her outside,--I, at her in--.How is it possible we should agree about her value?" (5: xxiv, 306). Female perspective here is characterized as being preoccupied with appearances, the forms of things, while the lover sees eternal nature, as much a prurient as a philosophical view. She sees herself; he sees her, the other.

This opposition associates materialism with women and spiritualism with men in accordance with neoclassical rhetorical tradition. Tristram sees "in," however, only when looking at the fundamental and spiritual essence of things; his penetration is part of his inclusive vision. This resembles the thoughtful "observations" of Yorick in contrast with the narrow, gynecological view with which the novel opens--the perverse vision of the doctors (1: x, 17). At the beginning of volume six, Tristram and "my dear Sir" "look back upon the country we have pass'd through," the story so far, and marvel at its absurdities from a distance (6: i, 329). Tristram also conducts "Sir" on a "tour" through the world in order to determine how people fare in different countries, saying, "if you hold your hand over your eyes, and look very attentively, you may perceive some small glimmerings (as it were) of wit, with a comfortable provision of good plain *household judgment* ..." (3: xx, 156). Both incidents use the language of cultural tourism to describe metaphorically the proper view of human nature and past experience. This "wide, equal survey," however, relies on the perception of contrast and on an internal stock of learning, for "*your curious observers are seldom worth a groat,*" Tristram claims, since they perceive according to their idiosyncracies and vanities without a philosophical frame (5: vi, 288). The right view here looks out, not in.

The curious perspective represents the wrong way to look--the perspective of feminized or degraded culture. In contrast to the wide view of nature traditionally claimed as the neoclassical perspective, it is figured as "peeping." Paul-Gabriel Boucé has noted the myth persistent in the eighteenth-century that women who caught a glimpse of a man's sexual organs were tormented by lust, an idea reiterated by John Marten in *Gonosologium Novum* (London, 1709); this idea runs through Sterne's association between women's peeping and their self-interested prurience.[22] When the Widow Wadman determines to enchant Toby, she insists that he look into her eye, into the depths of her pupil--the bottomless hole. Tristram deplores this perspective; he exclaims, "Honest soul! thou didst look into it with as much innocency of heart, as ever child look'd into a raree-shew-box; and 'twere as much a sin to have hurt thee.--If a man will be peeping of his own accord into things of that nature--I've nothing to say to it---" (8: xxiv, 465). "Raree-shew-box[es]" provide the illusion of distance. So, indeed, Widow Wadman's eye deludes Toby into believing she has great "humanity" and disinterest. (See Plate 2). In fact he sees only his own reflection, and like most sentimental physiognomists, falls in love with the sight of himself in the other. Tristram describes Widow Wadman's eye as eloquent, varied, a "cannon," in a long mock panegyric that effectively strips it of any quality but literary conventionality (8: xxv, 466). He addresses this panegyric, moreover, to Madam, who is eyeing his text, as he does his defense of his

Plate 2: WIDOW WADMAN'S Plan of Attack on UNCLE TOBY, 1785.
Courtesy of the Lewis Walpole Library, Farmington, Ct.

mother as she peeps through the keyhole with her "thin, blue, chill, pellucid chrystal" (9: i, 485). The female reader is looking into her own "eye."[23] Tristram, moreover, declares to Madam that "we live amongst riddles and mysteries" that even the "quickest sight cannot penetrate into" (4: xvii, 233). Even while indulging and ironically applauding this appetite, Sterne associates the desire of the eye with vanity, illicit inquiry, and women's sexual hunger.

Peeping, or a perverted perspective, is also associated with abuses of learning, and hence not only with curiosity, but also with blindness. Walter shares this flaw. Indecently curious, he wears spectacles (5: xxvii, 307): his perspective is myopic, for as Tristram remarks, he could not have understood his brother even "Had my uncle *Toby*'s head been a *Savoyard*'s box [a hurdy-gurdy], and my father peeping in all the time at one end of it" (3: xxvi, 170). Walter sees his stature in relation to sex or to women, for he remarks that all the household women grow "an inch taller" when one of them is pregnant; Toby, humble where Walter is proud, sees men sinking an inch (4: xii, 227).[24] While "my mother" wishes to look through the key-hole at Toby and the Widow "out of *curiosity*," "my father" wants to peep from prurience (8: xxxv, 479). Both Shandys, like their son, seek secret sights.

Doctors, also, like to peer into the innards of things. Mocking scientific causality, Tristram tells us that when his brain is dissected, "you will perceive, without spectacles" the "large uneven thread" that his father left in his brain (6: xxxiii, 371). Sterne further attacks the idea of empirical peeping into human nature through his ironic allusion to Momus glass and the dioptrical bee hive; as Momus was expelled from heaven for his criticism, so those who scrutinize human nature should at least be taxed for peering into the heart. Human curiosity produces neither knowledge nor tolerance, but merely more criticisms. Tristram avoids this method and the other methods of mad Academics who, like Swift's in Book 3 of *Gulliver's Travels*, attempt to know human nature by "extractions" or by mechanical replication through "Pentagraphs." Instead, he "draws" Toby's character (1: xxii, 57-58). This contrasts the "natural" or humanistic method of Tristram's "pencil" with inhuman, modern corruptions and opposes aesthetic perspective to the hungry peeping of the curious.

It is the marginalized, those who cannot legitimately look, who peep. These include women, hypocrites like Madam the reader and, occasionally, Walter, and the uneducated classes characterized as children, unable to understand or act upon what they see. Their view is countered by the aesthetic view of the detached narrator. Whereas Corporal Trim, for example, caters to Toby by "prying and peeping continually into his Master's plans," for which he has no license but love (2: v, 77), from Tristram's perspective, he strikes a "painterly" attitude, becoming, like women, the subject of art (2:

xvii, 96-97). Indeed, Tristram even uses Trim as the rhetorical occasion to attack the grandiose absurdities of politics (and Humean causality) when he declares that "the preservation of our constitution in church and state,--and possibly the preservation of the whole world--or what is the same thing, the distribution and balance of its property and power, may in time to come depend greatly upon the right understanding of this stroke of the corporal's eloquence..." (5: vii, 289). By pointing to the corporal as the voice of politics, Tristram links his childlike ignorance with fate and the fall of kingdoms; children and servants rhetorically expose the futility and chaos of organized society. The narrator uses the private life of the sentimental character to illustrate his general philosophy. It is Trim who sketches the line of liberty as an unregularized flourish, specifically not "trim": it is nature without art and hence quite meaningless except insofar as it denies meaning (9: iv, 490). Even his "real" name--James Butler--reasserts his function as a servant and his substitution for the wife Toby contemplates, although this "reality" is, of course, fiction. Through this character, Sterne endorses the paternalism of sentimental ideology while his emblematic rhetorical method emphasizes marginal status of the sentimental character-as-object. At the same time, Sterne undercuts the reformist rhetoric of sentimental literature by highlighting its artificiality.

Tristram Shandy establishes rhetorical methods that will characterize sentimental literature until the end of the century. The techniques of exclusionary allusions, false antitheses, literary stereotyping, metaphorical emblematization, didacticism, and shifts in perspective counteract the sentimental appeal to the reader to identify with the characters by supplying a frame within which to position or "see" these characters. Tristram also discusses his own procedures in framing feeling through language, articulating the dilemma of sentimental fiction that rejects yet relies on words for communication. Beneath the illusion of intimacy lies the firm frame of public perspectives and privileged humor which ensures that reader and author stay in their place, looking at the characters.

A Sentimental Journey (1768) contains many of the themes of literary sentimentalism within a structure that criticizes sentimental indulgence. As Arthur Hill Cash suggests, it is not a burlesque of sentimental fiction, but an example of it, applauding natural benevolence, noting natural selfishness, and reproving Yorick's self-indulgence, for "Sterne thinks reason ought to *sanction* every moral decision."[25] Nostalgia for nobility appears in the tale of the Marquis who redeemed his fortune through commerce and returned an old man to claim his sword and service for the king. The praise of passive resignation supports the tale of the destitute Chevalier de Croix whose modest humility finally won him a pension from the king. The English starling in his French cage who chirps "I can't get out" parrots the words of Liberty.[26] The "woman's weakness" and powerlessness of Yorick, the speaker, seem to praise feeling over action; similarly, Maria, lost for love, demonstrates that we can do nothing except sympathize with the afflicted, thus reiterating the passivity of conservative sentimentalism at odds with Henry Brooke's ethic.

Stylistically, the book also employs a range of sentimental techniques. Rhetorical addresses to poor Maria and to "dear Sensibility" cast sentimental impressions within allegorical language, and blend praise of feeling with praise of nature. The fragmented narrative emphasizes static vignette and reduces causality to a minute scale of impressionistic reflection and refraction. The aesthetic values of sentimentalism appear in Yorick's praise of variety and diversity and in his attraction to faces that reveal a sublime contrast between happiness and present degradation (42, 114). The frame of the travelogue form, the fragments of La Fleur and the Notary, and the confessional and conversational sections all vaunt impressionism, the internal stock of a sentient being, while the initial discussion of the function of traveling and the final panegyric on the "great Sensorium" structure these impressions by public rhetoric within a cultural context. Ironic jokes, literary puns and allusions, constant class distinctions, and especially the hidden attacks on sex, money, and current literary culture indicate the rhetorical assumptions of Sterne's literary sentimentalism.

As the epigraph of this chapter demonstrates, *A Sentimental Journey* vaunts the privacy of sentiment. While women often supply the occasions for sentimental thrills, they stand on the margin between the public and private realms by virtue of their simultaneously public and private identity as "women." The sentimental occasion they provide is thus rhetorically opposed to the feeling itself. The same is true of all experience. Love letters, for example, are opposed to real feeling--and hence to the writing of the *Journey*--because, like the French themselves, according to Yorick, they lack nuances, relying on a conventional relationship between author and audience, woman and man. The form letter supplied by La Fleur to satisfy the importunities of Madame de Rambouliet satirically undercuts the pretense that every relationship, or "Friendship," is unique. Similarly, at the opening of the book, Yorick, sitting alone in his *Disobligeant*, categorizes travelers in a parodically mechanical, comprehensive list: "Idle Travellers," "Inquisitive Travellers," proud, vain, "splenetick," etc. (34-35). Like other parodic references to travelogues, this catalogue satirizes not merely such writers as Smollett, but also modern writing modes themselves. The occasion for sentiment tends to blunt that sentiment because it is so common.

The tensions of this paradox in *A Sentimental Journey* work to conflate languages of sentiment and of interest or money. These two forms of exchange, emotional and mercenary, continually overlap, confusing the question of charity and benevolence, indicating the mixed motives behind gestures of kindliness, and resurrecting the buried satire behind Sterne's sentiment. The initial incident of the Monk, for example, explores the themes of benevolence, public duty, and sex. Despite feeling generous when warmed by wine, albeit merely two-livre a bottle, Yorick freezes at the thought of charity to the Monk. The ironic contrast serves to satirize Yorick's self-approval, but also to introduce the overlap of money and feeling. It is when the ill-tempered Yorick, who has refused charity to the Monk, sees the Monk conversing with a woman that he determines to alter his behavior and act charitably--in order to preserve himself from the lady's scorn, since she, he repeats, is clearly one of "a better order of beings" (40), and hence he feels "benevolence toward her" (41). She represents public opinion, but also offers him private interest since he is imaginatively attracted to her. Sterne here dramatizes the contradictions between social and selfish motivations that sentimental philosophy attempts to reconcile. Within the ironic joke at Yorick's self-interest lies another rhetorical figuration: the woman represents the interference of the outside world, listening to secrets (as the Monk talks privately to her) and judging Yorick. Like feeling, money connects us to the world yet we fear to lose its protection.

Yorick further claims that "When a man is discontented with himself ... it puts him into an excellent frame of mind for making a bargain" (32). While this creed reiterates the sentimental ethic that we feel about others as about ourselves, so that self-love induces love of others and self-hate malice to the world, it also mocks the facility of Yorick's earlier claim that, feeling good himself, he could not then be mean to any man. The structural irony deliberately undercuts simple sentimentalism by reminding us of the need for self-discipline. This irony recurs when Yorick gives his last sou in delight at the flattery of being named "*my Lord Anglois*," and thus neglects worthy and necessitous people (60). However, it also underscores the relationship between commerce and feeling; money becomes a social text of benevolence, the coin of feeling, but it also becomes the condition or circumstance in which benevolence or sensibility flourish. Keeping it is sensible, albeit giving it away shows sensibility.

Yorick himself introduces the language of trade as ironic metaphor for feeling:

> It will always follow ... that the balance of sentimental commerce is always against the expatriated adventurer: he must buy what he has little occasion for at their own price--his conversation will seldom be taken in exchange for theirs without a large discount--and this, by the by, eternally driving him into the hands of more equitable brokers for such

conversation as he can find, it requires no   great spirit of
divination to guess at his party--. (33)

This partly satirizes travelers who too closely count the cost of their travels
and therefore lose the value of them by spending their time with their own
countrymen. It also mocks the pretence that sentimental conversation pleases
all equally; like other forms of exchange, it contains a scale of values that
each conversationalist recognizes. Tongue in cheek, Yorick compares
traveling for the sake of "saving money" (34) with traveling to gain
"knowledge and improvements" (36). Although both motives are
self-interested and expressed in mercenary terms, the one vaunts keeping, the
other expending. Such cautious valuations modify Sterne's apparent
recommendation to indulge feeling.

Money is the form of "sentimental commerce" plied to the lower-class
women Yorick meets as a "sentimental" substitute for sex. Indeed, Yorick
gives money instead of sex, but Sterne does not applaud this: he laughs at
Yorick's transferred sexuality with innuendo throughout--the same kind of sly
joking as appears in a literary context against "Smelfungus" or "Mundungus".
The incident with Grisset, the shopkeeper who sells Yorick gloves too large
for him and only overcharges him by a livre for her wares, exemplifies a
sexual joke translated into sentimental language. After feeling her pulse,
Yorick buys her gloves; this sexual exchange precedes a financial one, in
which the language shifts from conventional praise--"a beautiful creature"--to
battle: "I found I lost considerably in every attack--she had a quick black eye
and shot through two such long and silken eye-lashes with...penetration" (77).
Like the Widow Wadman, Grisset wants something very material for her
satisfaction: here, however, it is money, not sex. Moreover, this married
woman's overstretched glove and her husband's complaisance touch the story
with social and sexual satire. Yorick is taken in by his own susceptibility.
Similarly, the innocent *fille de chambre* who sews a special pocket that just
fits his crown, and returns to sew his sock in the blushing room provides
Sterne with the chance to blend sexual, commercial, and political metaphor.
Such "innocent" figures contrast with Janatone, the landlord's daughter, who
receives an "ecu" from an English Lord for unspecified services (53). Sterne
underscores the prurient innuendo by showing the landlord himself reproving
Yorick for "entertaining" a young woman in his room in the evening, selling
"lace and silk stockings and ruffles" (121)--all the trifles Yorick buys from
his "innocent" women. Yorick's protest that he did not "look into" his
visitor's "bandbox" cements the implication. The innuendo also appears
when Yorick converses with Eugenius on the occupation of "*taking a
woman's pulse*," which suggests that one could do "worse," presumably, by
"taking" her "purse" instead (75). Only poor Maria is beyond sexual

knowledge, and hence charity: she is beyond exchange, dwelling on the border of sanity. Needing nothing, she exists for Yorick in the dependent, unsexualized role of daughter.

If servants and lower-class women want money, upper-class women, having it, want flattery. Indeed, the French *politesse* becomes merely the language of the exchange: sex is bought with soft words rather than hard cash. The Marquesina who continually makes room for Yorick as he moves aside for her exemplifies ludicrous *politesse* and perverted flattery; the beggar who wins twelve sous apiece from rich women by flattering them exemplifies the underside of benevolence. We pay for our pleasures, Sterne implies, and women, even while stimulating sentiment, also exemplify the selfishness of those pleasures and the crudeness of their calculation and cost. In *A Sentimental Journey*, Sterne modifies his celebration of delicate sensation by casting it in language that emphasizes its materiality. Albeit sensitive, Yorick is also a fool who gives away too much and gets in return too little.

Sterne blends satire against literary consumerism, sex, and social mores into the very language of sentimentalism. In *Tristram Shandy*, he satirizes a female audience that contributes to the degeneration of values; in *A Sentimental Journey*, he satirizes a culture in which sentiment is merely another commodity. Throughout both books, he preserves a slippery flexibility and multiplicity of rhetorical attitudes that attempt simultaneously to applaud and to attack the new influences on literary culture and the traditional values opposing them. His types, his rhetoric, and his strategies of description and innuendo establish a conspiracy between author and implied audience that conjures an illusion of communication (or exchange) undermined by the elusive language and ambiguous tone. He shows that sensation may remain private, but satire is public; through this satire, he cautions the sensitive reader against delusive modern values. These techniques construct a stylistics of sentimentalism that undermines its own liberal claims for instinct and sociability by exclusionary and fragmented rhetoric. Sterne's sensual stories chronicle the chaos of sense when language used self-indulgently makes feeling into spectacle. It is the task of the reader to reconstruct from Sterne's satire the public context that rationalizes feeling into true exchange.

CHAPTER 4

The Margins of Sentiment:
The History of Lady Julia Mandeville
and *The History of Emily Montague*

> The great science of life is, to keep in constant
> employment that restless active principle within
> us, which, if not directed right, will be eternally
> drawing us from real to imaginary happiness.
> Ed Rivers, *The History of Emily Montague*

In the eighteenth century, the most popular form of literary sentimentalism written by women, and so part of the literary culture that Sterne satirized,
was the epistolary novel. Unlike the novels of Goldsmith, Henry Brooke, or
even Sterne, epistolary novels usually do not describe experience through the
voice of an ironic narrator; rather, they use the epistolary form to present
sentiment even as it is being experienced and thus to stir the reader's
response.[1] This technique centralizes the responsive internal consciousness of
the sentimental spectator so that characters marginalized by sex, status,
circumstance, or culture can nonetheless serve as touchstones of morality.
Like Samuel Richardson's *Pamela* and *Clarissa*, epistolary novels also
portray the process by which the sensitive writer translates desire into
narrative and disciplines this desire by moral rules. This process shows the
reader how to confine nature by the strictures of society, art, and morality,
by the letter and by the law. Thus, these novels do not simply present
sentiment; they present sentiment structured by morality and disciplined by
experience.

Two of the most popular such novels, *The History of Lady Julia*
Mandeville (1763) and *The History of Emily Montague* (1769), by Frances
Brooke, exemplify epistolary sentimentalism. Through letters that explain the
characters' feelings in a language directed at a distant correspondent, Frances
Brooke organizes response into moral perception. All experience is framed

by the margins of the letter and the artistic power of the narrator. Both *The History of Lady Julia Mandeville* and *The History of Emily Montague* juxtapose descriptions of nature, art, and sentiment that illustrate the function of rules and conventions to structure response, a function simultaneously liberating and confining. Whereas *Julia Mandeville* glosses literary texts to enforce a sentimental ideology advocating the disciplined expression of the wild desires of the human heart, *Emily Montague* uses travel narrative to show sentiment controlling the wilds of physical nature. At the same time, this control violates or muffles certain kinds of imaginative experience at which Brooke hints in the tragic emotions of her characters and their experiences of a nature--their own and physical nature--which overleaps the bounds of art. Nonetheless, Brooke shows that art must and should shape nature as the letter shapes communication and that both comprise civilization itself, the rational control of feeling.[2]

Daughter of a Lincolnshire curate, and wife of another curate, Frances Brooke, *née* Moore, was a recognized, if herself marginal, figure on the literary scene, known both to Samuel Johnson and to David Garrick.[3] She wrote heroic tragedy, started a periodical journal, translated French works, composed poetry, and finished three, possibly four, novels of her own, including the first Canadian novel.[4] It is her periodical that first explores the liberties and restrictions that social isolation provide. Published weekly from late 1755 until July 1756, this periodical, *The Old Maid*, appeared under the pseudonym Mary Singleton and sketches sensibility and taste through both vignette and moral commentary by a persona who addresses a friendly audience.[5] Its thirty-seven issues comment on the social world, politics, theater, and current events. Like Haywood's *Female Spectator*, they also discuss the "female" questions of love and marriage, and like Addison and Steele's *Spectator*, they trace the tales of a medley of character types from the comic stage. These include the central commentator, the apologetic, kindly Old Maid, her niece Julia, infatuated with the impoverished but well-born officer Belville, Julia's country friend Rosara, Belville's uncle Dr. Hartingley, and his student and friend, Sir Harry Hyacinth. Like the exemplary, if not necessarily heroic, characters in her novels, these good-natured and sensitive types express themselves through conversation or writing rather than by action. They are defined by their relationships to each other rather than by social position, yet it is their social position that provides the tension in the various plots by obstructing marriage and advancement. This sentimental opposition between character or desire and social convention similarly informs Brooke's novels; there, as here, she recommends compromise and caution rather than rebellion.

Brooke's "Old Maid" Mary Singleton attends and records these stories. In her first number, like her "brother" Mr. Spectator, she explains her qualifications: it is her very distance from the bustle of politics and love that licenses her to comment disinterestedly on society, for she avers that as a spinster she is otherwise useless to society. While implying that literary "productions" parallel biological ones, this claim also emphasizes Mary Singleton's unique privileges. If she is sexually unengaged, she is also politically pure; marginalized by her sexual irrelevance, she also stands clear of confusing emotion and special interests to judge society according to its own ideal values. Like Mr. Spectator, her sentiments--in theory, at least-- represent in the internal space of her consciousness the sentiments of society. She remains untainted by the bribes of social power.

It is the role of disinterested supporter of the arts that Frances Brooke advocates for women in *The Old Maid*. Suggesting that antiquated virgins should busy themselves by submitting papers to her periodical instead of passing strictures on giddy girls, Mary Singleton suggests that social action should constitute literary endeavor, not defensive reproach. She thus maintains that the frustrations of being marginalized can be shaped produc- tively. By arguing that traditionally women have encouraged artistic merit, pointing to the great poetry that flourished under the reigns of such queens as Elizabeth and Anne, she transforms art into a demonstration of female power, albeit a vicarious one. Brooke adds that such a role of artistic judge is fashionable: "A French woman of distinction would be more ashamed of wanting a taste for the Belles Lettres, than of being ill dressed; and it is owing to the neglect of adorning their minds, that our travelling English ladies are at Paris the objects of unspeakable contempt, and are honored with the appellation of handsome savages" (*The Old Maid*, no. 3, 29 Nov. 1755). Again, when a reader signing himself "Spectator" complains to Brooke that a lady's laughing in the audience disconcerted an actress at the theater, Brooke apologizes for her sex and bids them guard their public behavior more closely (*The Old Maid*, no. 15, 21 Feb. 1756). Women's mental improvement should improve their public behavior since it is internal morality that, in the sentimental ethic, conditions culture. It can also influence others. Brooke suggests that women applaud artists with real merit instead of the flighty singers with temper-tantrums who attract men's applause. Brooke moralizes women's role as spectacles into the role of guardian of culture.

It is, moreover, not only what the Old Maid says but also the way she says it that qualifies her as social critic. Her brevity, decorous diction, choice of topics, and disinterested tone proclaim her ability to organize social experience into moral commentary. The frontispiece of Brooke's periodical illustrates the power and precariousness of her position: a Roman matron sits at a writing table, with the city's turrets looming in the background, listening to a warrior and a bard recite their tales. This picture reproduces one of the common illustrations of travelogues in which the Muse transcribes tales of adventure; the writer translates culture, as well as records others' heroic deeds.[6] (See Plate 3). In this case, by portraying the audience's own culture as remote, the periodical centralizes the marginality of its "author," the Old Maid: a Roman--i.e. selfless patriot--she locates value in hearing about, rather than in experiencing, sensation. Like the reader, she understands experience by means of its communication through language and thus in terms not so much of its own significance as of its significance to society. While depicting the reader, like the author, as detached, distanced, and literally "outside" the action, this image of the Old Maid simultaneously counteracts the individual-istic and isolated experience of sentiment by presenting it through epistolary communications or social encounters. Paradoxically, it is by their marginality that the Old Maid, and the reader, serve as centers of social value.

   The Old Maid correspondingly advocates the social role of feeling and of rational, female independence.[7] Mary Singleton embraces feminist issues: she defends the rights of daughters, praises literary women, supports equality in marriage, and reproves social attitudes that denigrate spinsters.[8] While Belville discusses the "masculine" topics of politics and war, the Old Maid defends the civilizing influence of women on bellicose culture. This theme reappears in Brooke's novel *Emily Montague* where women or feminized men soften the rude processes of colonization by moralizing them into advances of civilization. In both of these texts, Brooke uses the epistle to supply a language that mediates between the two sides of nature: love and war. Both kinds of physicality--violence and sexuality--are channeled into sentimental discourse. The independence of unattached women also earns mixed treatment from Brooke. She mocks the fear, entertained by Goldsmith among others, that if women enjoy too great an independence, they might thin society by failing to keep up the birth rate and pollute the ideal of social service with the corrupt values of self-interest. Many issues bear epigraphs ironically apologizing for the deficiencies of a virgin or spinster. The Old Maid repeats confessional attacks on old women as, "except an old batchelor, the most useless and insignificant of all God's creatures" who must "service" the "public" to compensate for their selfishness (no. 1, 2-3). In fact, Mr. Town welcomed this self-abnegatory language by launching a prurient attack against the first issues of *The Old Maid* in *The Connoisseur*. He missed the point. By identifying writing and childbearing, Brooke playfully overturns the tired metaphor to endorse women's writing and social, rather than sexual, service; this strengthens her commitment to the association of art with (female) nature against the destructiveness of masculine passions. Both art and sex become public acts binding women and society, feeling and function.

   Brooke reiterates this point by comic hyperbole. In the first number, the Old Maid declares that she will write because "every body knows an English woman has a natural right to expose herself as much as she pleases; a right

Plate 3: Frontispiece to the *London Magazine*, 1760.
Courtesy of the Lewis Walpole Library, Farmington, Ct.

some of us seem lately to have made a pretty sufficient use of; and since I feel a violent inclination to show my prodigious wisdom to my contemporaries, I should think it giving up the privileges of the sex to desist from my purpose" (*The Old Maid*, no. 1, 2-3). Rhetorically conflating sex, liberty, and writing, this passage mocks discourse attacking female authorship as prurient exposure and rebellious, even violent, indulgence. While the extravagant language of this teetotaling, good-humored old lady mocks contemporary fears of female expression, the argument confirms that women act in the service of society, defending the English right of free expression. Brooke suggests that it is, in fact, the artful control of her "natural right" of feeling that qualifies the Old Maid to speak to society.

Brooke honed her sentimental style in her translations of Madame Ricconi's epistolary fictions. In 1760, she translated the epistolary novel of sensibility written the previous year, *Letters of Juliet Catesby, To Her Friend Lady Henrietta Campley.*[9] Here, Brooke describes the heroine looking out at a garden or estate and transcribing her reactions through the self-regulating process of a letter. These letters at once formalize the heroine's reactions, and frame them in social language.

> I write to you, from the most agreeable Place, perhaps, in Nature: From my Window I have a View of Woods, Waters, Meadows, the most beautiful Landscape imaginable: Every thing expresses Calmness and Tranquillity: This smiling Abode is an Image of the soft Peace, which reigns in the Soul of the Sage who inhabits it. This amiable Dwelling carries one insensibly to reflect; to retire into one's self; but one cannot at all Times relish this Kind of Retreat; one may find in the Recesses of the Heart, more importunate Pursuers than those from whom Solitude delivers us. (10)

Written from the country estate of a benevolent patriarch whose wisdom the ordered landscape reflects, this letter records Juliet's desire to make her inside mirror the outside, to reconcile human and physical nature within artful borders. While the beauty of her surroundings penetrates her and "carries" her "to reflect," her heart also contains a society of "Pursuers." These "Pursuers" are those desires that have not been tailored to fit social forms, renegade flutterings of individual need resistant to the penetration of the ordered world before her. The story of her heroism is the story of subduing these desires. These epistolary heroines thus chronicle and illustrate the correspondence between surveying placid scenes of artfully ordered nature and experiencing internal calm, an ideal that appears both in Brooke's journal and her novels.[10]

In her first novel, *The History of Lady Julia Mandeville*, Brooke rewrites *Romeo and Juliet* in a fashion that permits her to indict not familial pride, but the flaw of undisciplined passion. (See Plate 4.) Unlike Shakespeare's tragedy, the book contains no objective rationale for the tragedy: instead, misunderstanding and panic drive the hero to unnecessarily desperate measures that lead to the deaths of the young people. Thus, it is not social relations but internal economy that fails the hero. Nevertheless, within the story of the tragedy lies the lurking possibility that social forms--be they epistolary, legal, or behavioral--cannot encompass or express the passions of the young heart.

Both in form and plot, this novel advocates self-discipline. By turning the play into a novel and substituting letters for actions, Brooke emphasizes the importance of contemplative, self-disciplined thought; moreover, she chooses a marginalized spectator to model clear perception and balanced evaluation, Lady Ann Wilmot. In contrast to Lady Ann's wit and detachment, the hero, Harry Mandeville, fails to confine his spontaneous effusions within the borders of his father's will, or within the margins of the letter; he thus fails to express or explain himself to those he loves or as to the reader. Fearing that he is too poor to win Julia's father's consent to his marriage, he conceals his love and embarks on a military career whose meaningless procedures frustrate him. Just as he is unable to discipline his actions to the rules of the army, so he violates the rules both of society and of morality by forcing an unjust duel in which he is slain. We learn tragically that both his father and Julia's father wished him to marry her, had he but trusted them.

The novel opens with a letter from Harry Mandeville, the generous, noble hero, which introduces the tensions between practical and idealistic values characteristic of sentimental fictions. After enjoying a Rousseauistic education in art, culture, and love, Harry writes to a friend expressing thanks to his father for beggaring himself in order to "stor[e] my mind with generous sentiments and useful knowledge, to which his [father's] unbounded goodness added every outward accomplishment that could give grace to virtue, and set her charms in the fairest light." [11] While this education prompts his love for the perfect Julia, however, it does not teach Harry the social skills of negotiation, self-control, or patience. It may be that his father gave too much for this result and loves his son not wisely but too well. Harry, moreover, is writing to the wrong audience: to his friend, not his father. Throughout the novel, he fails to communicate with those on whom his fate and fortune rest, and this failure leads to his death.

Harry's uncle, Lord Belmont, seems to contribute to the disaster by preserving aristocratic prejudices about the importance of birth. While praising Belmont's virtues, Harry remarks, "If there is a shade in this picture, it is a prejudice, perhaps rather too strong, in favour of birth, and a slowness

Plate 4: Frontispiece to *The History of Lady Julia Mandeville* vol. 1, 1764.
Courtesy of the Watkinson Library, Hartford, Ct.

to expect very exalted virtues in any man who cannot trace his ancestors as far back, at least, as the conquest" (1: 8). Harry's irony rebounds on himself, however, for it is Lord Belmont's very indifference to money and respect for birth that induce him to find Harry the ideal match for his own daughter. At the end of the novel, Belmont writes, "Humbled in the dust, I confess the hand of Heaven: the pride of birth, the grandeur of my house, had too great a share in my resolves!" (2: 200). This self-knowledge promotes the social responsibility that Belmont already possesses, and leads him to combine individual and social interests so that all society becomes Belmont's family. In reflecting on the sadness of his wife and niece at Julia's death, he remarks, "There is one pleasure to which they can never be insensible, the pleasure of relieving the miseries of others: to divert their attention from the sad objects which now engross them, we must find out the retreats of wretchedness; we must point out distress which it is in their power to alleviate" (2: 203). The novel concludes with his pious resignation to God's will. Brooke thus recommends the discipline of selfish ambition by social duty and by identification with a broader social scene.

Despite his final punishment for this weakness--he loses his heir--Brooke legitimizes Belmont's prejudice by endowing aristocrats with sentiment. Praising Lord Belmont for benevolence and the "hospitality of our antient English nobility," Harry describes an ideal aristocrat: "tall, well made, graceful; his air commanding, and full of dignity; he has strong sense, with a competent share of learning, and a just and delicate taste for the fine arts; especially musick, which he studied in Italy.... His politeness is equally the result of a natural desire of obliging, and an early and extensive acquaintance with the great world" (1: 7-8). His liberality, European ease, paternal care, patriotic zeal, loyalty, and polite and tender husbandly attention combine with "the noblest spirit of independence": he is a Briton on the old model, but, like Horace and Burlington, he also "knows how to live." (1: 34) This ideal type exemplifies disciplined feeling.[12]

Brooke enforces her moral lesson through her aesthetic form. She preserves the pleasure of drama, that very pleasure that Hume identifies as a combination of sympathy and distance in his essay "On Tragedy" (1757). As Hume specifies, Brooke provides the spectacle of strong emotions, but she controls the reader's imaginative sympathy with these feelings by describing them through the perspective of a spectating character, Lady Ann Wilmot. In witty and subtle letters to her fiancé Bellville, Lady Ann blends empathy with irony, analyzing the heroes' love-agonies from a self-consciously aesthetic perspective. Lady Ann thus exemplifies the control of strong emotion by artful organization: she models the way to derive aesthetic pleasure from experience.

Throughout the novel, aesthetic and moral judgments coalesce. It is Julia's father, the benevolent Lord Belmont, who represents the transformation of life into art, of chaos into order, of an unjust society into an Eden. As both Harry and Lady Ann somewhat tediously repeat, Lord Belmont has created a Utopia in which social relations are perfectly regulated in a perfectly designed environment. He balances in a pattern of ordered irregularity--a paradox itself encapsulating Brooke's ideal fusion of sentiment and restraint--public conversation and private contemplation, the art of music and the grottos of cultivated nature, regular schedules and delightful surprises. His guiding principle is "variety" of amusements: his guests read, walk, ride, converse, play, dance, sing, join the company, or "indulge in pensive solitude and meditation, just as fancy leads; liberty, restrained alone by virtue and politeness, is the law, and inclination the sovereign guide, at this mansion of true hospitality" (1: 11). Lord Belmont, however, provides the varied structure of amusements: his plan keeps their "liberty" lawful, their "inclination" and taste "polite." The aesthetic of balance and control structures the picturesque variety.

Lord Belmont directly represents a monarchical ideal, in which power is vested in established hierarchy. Both Eden and England, his estate provides a political and moral lesson. In one of many such passages, Harry remarks that

> His estate conveys the strongest idea of the patriarchal government; he seems a beneficent father, surrounded by his children, over whom reverence, gratitude, and love, give him an absolute authority, which he never exerts but for their good; every eye shines with transport at his sight; parents point him out to their children; the first accents of prattling infancy are taught to lisp his honoured name; and age, supported by his bounteous hand, pours out the fervent prayer to heaven for its benefactor. (1: 13)

Harry pictures Christian ideals: in a perfect state, "absolute authority" is a gift instinctively awarded to natural goodness. Described as a genre scene, this benevolence affords a pleasure as much aesthetic as moral--indeed moral because aesthetic. Harry admires Lord Belmont's virtues through sympathetic observation:

> The surprize, the gaiety of the scene, the flow of general joy, the sight of so many happy people, the countenances of the enraptured parents, who seemed to live over again the sprightly season of youth in their children, with the benevolent pleasure in the looks of the noble bestowers of the feast, filled my eyes with tears, and my swelling heart with a sensation of

pure yet lively transport, to which the joys of courtly balls are
mean. (1: 13-14)

While Harry learns by empathy, Lady Ann characteristically edits Harry's
enthusiasm. For example, she laments of Belmont's estate, "Really, this place
would be charming if it was a little more replete with human beings; but to
me the finest landscape is a dreary wild unless adorned by a few groupes
[sic] of figures" (1: 46). With flippant understatement mocking the substitution of aesthetic for social ideals, Lady Ann articulates the moral ideal of the
book: the socialization of sentiment by irony, of sympathy by distance, of
solitude by society.

Although this balance between individual expression and self-discipline
represents the ideal of the novel, the rhetoric of aesthetic judgment and of
sentimental feeling often contrasts with the conceptual language both Lady
Ann and Harry use to discuss ideas of society, education, and marriage. Such
contrasts create a tension in Brooke's sentimental rhetoric between the
ostensible model of virtue, represented by the flawless heroes, and the way
to appreciate this virtue, represented by the detached spectator. The issue of
marriage is a good example of this conflict between reformist and aesthetic
expressions. Like Richardson, Brooke includes extensive discussions of
marriage in her novel, echoing the themes of her periodical. Lady Ann's own
history condemns marriage for money since her boorish husband, an old
country gentleman, abused her to such a degree that she now shrinks from
marrying even the admirable Bellville (1: 10-11). Criticizing parental
interference and social convention, she carefully defines a good marriage and
argues against bad ones in a passage echoing Congreve's ideal of equality
and mutual respect in *The Way of the World* (1700), an ideal exemplified by
the Belmonts' marriage. These passages defend marriage for love, using
example to support precept.

This rational discourse, however, juxtaposes descriptive passages that
resurrect conventional and static ideals of love. Harry writes,

> Lady Julia then, who wants only three months of nineteen, is
> exactly what a *poet* or *painter* would wish to *copy*, who
> intended to *personify the idea* of female softness; her whole
> *form* is delicate and feminine to the utmost *degree*: her
> complexion is fair, enlivened by the bloom of youth, and often
> *diversified* by blushes more beautiful than those of the morn-
> ing: her features are *regular*, her mouth and teeth particularly
> lovely; her hair light brown; her eyes blue, full of softness, and
> strongly *expressive* of the exquisite sensibility of her soul. Her
> countenance, *the beauteous abode of the loves and the smiles*,

has a *mixture* of sweetness and spirit which gives *life and
expression* to her charms. (1: 15; my italics)

Harry describes Julia as the painting of an idea, even bedecked with the
fashionable baroque conceit of "loves."[13]   Harry again shows his artistic
perception by describing Lady Julia as typical of high art: he writes to
Mordaunt, "-- paint to yourself the exquisite proportion, the playful air and
easy movement of a Venus, with the vivid bloom of an Hebe. -- However
high you raise your ideas, they will fall infinitely short of the divine original"
(1: 15). While rehearsing the conventional pictorial metaphor of admiration,
this language effectually erases rational negotiation, the contract between
lovers that Lady Ann asks of her fiancé Bellville; instead, it presents love as
courtly convention.

This convention provides a traditional context for sentimental expression, and thus forestalls readerly reproach. For example, when Harry deduces
Julia's character from her appearance, he interpolates moral qualities that
legitimize aesthetic or sexual attraction.[14] "As her mind has been adorned, not
warped, by education, it is just what her appearance promises; artless, gentle,
timid, soft, sincere, compassionate; awake to all the finer impressions of
tenderness, and melting with pity for every human woe" (1: 6). Harry detects
these social virtues, this ideal female complacency, through the physical
evidence of Julia's loveliness; his sentimental rhetoric identifies appearance
and behavior. Such rhetoric prohibits irony or social consciousness, both of
which result from the disparity between appearance and behavior, to proffer
as ideal an absolute unity between experience and appearance. Julia is
transparent; she is what see looks to be, and this is the condition for heroism.

Nevertheless, such transparency is not the condition for sentimental
experience. It dangerously misrepresents the complexity of female response
in a world ruled by men; moreover, true perspective, the perspective that
moralizes experience, derives from distance and the power of contrast. Lady
Ann models the way to learn from experience. After Julia's death, she
recounts to Bellville,

> I am now convinced Emily Howard deserves that preference
> Lady Julia gave her over me in her heart, of which I once so
> unjustly complained; I lament, I regret, but am enough my self
> to reason, to reflect; Emily Howard can only weep.
>   Far from being consoled for the loss of her lovely friends,
> by the prospect of inheriting Lord Belmont's fortune, to which
> after Colonel Mandeville she is intitled [sic], she seems
> incapable of tasting any good in life without her. Every idea of

> happiness her gentle mind could form included Lady Julia's
> friendship ... without her she finds the world a desart [sic].
>
> (2: 176-77)

Lady Ann finds happiness, or at least contentment, within her "self" through
reason and reflection; the alternative, immersion in feeling and dependance
on others, leads to misery. Sentimental friendship thus entails the loss of the
self in a fashion as dangerous to society as to the individual.

Brooke reiterates this warning against immersion in feeling by a method
later employed by Radcliffe: the emblematic episode.[15] After describing
Emily's beautiful grief, an ideal portrait which the reader likewise admires,
Lady Ann recounts her own deviance from reason into delusive fear beyond
the bounds of the civilized estate: "Pleased with the tender sorrow which
possessed all my soul, I determined to indulge it to the utmost; and, revolving
in my imagination the happy hours of chearful friendship to which that
smiling scene had been witness, prolonged my walk till evening had, almost
unperceived, spread its gloomy horrors round; till the varied tints of the
flowers were lost in the deepening shades of night" (2: 179-80). Her
imagination possessed by indulgent feeling, Lady Ann transgresses the
boundaries of day, of cultivated nature and of reason:

> Awaking at once from the reveries in which I had plunged, I
> found myself at a distance from the house, just entering the
> little wood loved by my charming friend; the every moment
> encreasing [sic] darkness gave an awful gloom to the trees; I
> stopped, I looked round, not a human form was in sight; I
> listened and heard not a sound but the trembling of some
> poplars in the wood; I called, but the echo of my own voice
> was the only answer I received; a dread silence reigned around
> me, a terror I never felt before seized me, my heart panted
> with timid apprehension; I breathed short, I started at every
> leaf ... my limbs were covered with a cold dew; I fancied I
> saw a thousand airy forms flit around me, I seemed to hear the
> shrieks of the dead and dying; there is no describing my
> horrors. (2: 180-81)

By abandoning control of her fancy, Lady Ann becomes as vulnerable as a
sentimental heroine, isolated and frightening herself with her own voice.[16]
This is an example of the wrong way to "feel," yet it is also an evocative
passage of stylistic virtuosity that challenges the hold of "reason" on the
imagination.

Lady Ann, however, soon recovers from this temporary indulgence in order to model for the reader the right way to feel: by evoking contrast and deriving a moral from detached comparisons: "Bellville, you are coming to Belmont, once the smiling paradise of friendship. Alas! how changed from that once happy abode! Where are those blameless pleasures, that convivial joy, those sweet follies, which once gave such charms to this place? For ever gone, for ever changed to a gloomy sadness, for ever buried with Lady Julia" (2: 121). In this elegy, fear filtered by detachment becomes melancholy, itself testament to the simultaneous perception of what was and what is. This is the way to aestheticize feeling. Indeed, Ann herself comments on the aesthetic pleasures of tragedy:

> Whether it be that the mind abhors nothing like a state of inaction, or from whatever cause I know not, but grief itself is more agreable [sic] to us than indifference; nay, if not too exquisite, is in the highest degree delightful; of which the pleasure we take in tragedy, or in talking of our dead friends, is a striking proof; we wish not to be cured of what we feel on these occasions; the tears we shed are charming, we even indulge in them; Belville [sic], does not the very word *indulge* shew [sic] the sensation to be pleasurable? (2: 121)

Directly addressing her lover, Lady Ann moralizes the effects of the aesthetic or literary representation of sorrow; she indeed comments with the theoretical apparatus of Addison and Hume on the reader's own experience of the very novel in which she appears. Representing herself as a spectator of experience, like the reader, Lady Ann thus cautions against indulgence even in the pleasures of fiction.

Brooke's second novel, *The History of Emily Montague* (1769) focuses the question of how to shape feeling by instructing women on how to choose a husband wisely. By juxtaposing letters from characters with different perspectives, Brooke creates a dialogue debating the nature of sexual relations, marriage, and liberty. Two central correspondences contrast cynical and sentimental discourse in a parallel pattern. The titular heroine Emily writes only once she is in love, only of her love, and almost only to one correspondent, her friend Arabella. In contrast, Arabella describes physical and social scenes to many correspondents in Canada and London with a witty and allusive style that fences feeling with irony and distance. Colonel Ed Rivers moralizes colonization and love to his crony John Temple in London, who replies with polite sophistication. Brooke thus endows the female spectator with a general and socialized perspective while the male hero articulates sentiment.

She structures this debate by means of a comic plot that banishes the central characters to the "wild," Canada, where, shedding their social defenses, they recognize their true natures and pair off before returning to cultivate their gardens in England. While Emily must face social disapproval for breaking her engagement with the wealthy, handsome but insensitive Sir George Clayton, she is rewarded for her fidelity to her feelings by marriage to the laudable Colonel Ed Rivers and by a rich inheritance from a newly discovered father. Most of the drama and suspense, however, arises from the fears and misunderstandings caused by love, not the prejudices of society: the action is internal. Inset sentimental vignettes dilute this sentimental plot by depicting the hazards of excessive feeling. In Canada, a hermit forever distraught from the loss of his love demonstrates that feeling can make the world a wilderness, while in England, the virtuous Fanny, poor foster-mother to the love-child of her sentimental friend, recounts the fatal costs of loving not wisely but too well.

The most cogent critique of both sentimentalism and society, however, comes from the persistent comparison between the native Canadian Indians, the Canadian French, and the newly arrived English colonials. Generally, the English balance raw nature represented by the Indians and corruption represented by the French, opposite extremes linked by their use of marriage as a political rather than a sentimental contract. One of the central points of comparison is sexual relations, which Brooke stresses by constrasting the perceptions of a female and a male observer. Whereas Arabella admires Huron women's freedom to wander without the permission of their husbands, Ed condemns their manners, vowing to Temple, "You are right, Jack, as to the savages; the only way to civilize them is to *feminize* their women; but the task is rather difficult; at present their manners differ in nothing from those of the men; they even add to the ferocity of the latter" (118-19).[17] By teaching women to love their children, Ed hopes to civilize them. Ed illustrates that sentiment is a civilized luxury when he applauds Huron purity of morals and manners before their "conversion" by the Jesuits "except in what regarded the intercourse of the sexes: the young women before marriage were indulged in great libertinism, hid however under the most reserved and decent exterior" (34). Still, "liberal to profusion of their charms before marriage, [Indian ladies] are chastity itself after" (11), perhaps because, as Ed records, the Hurons dissolve their marriages upon mutual agreement. In a parallel fashion, as Ed notes, French women, chaste before marriage, wed for convenience and play the libertine afterward: "Marriages in France being made by the parents, and therefore generally without inclination on either side, gallantry seems to be a tacit condition, though not absolutely expressed in the contract" (84). On the contrary, Arabella criticizes the "peasants" of Montreal as "ignorant," lazy, dirty, and stupid beyond all belief; but hospitable, courteous, civil," especially insofar as they "leave their wives and daughters to do the honors of the house," for "all the little knowledge of Canada" is confined to women (18). In both the Huron and the French Canadian social systems, marriage separates husband and wife instead of unifying them.[18]

These alternatives suggest that the "English liberty" of a woman's right to marry whom she pleases is not merely a sentimental, but also a sensible principle to preserve social morality. When she learns of their system of marriage, Arabella recants her praise of Huron freedom:

> I declare off at once; I will not be a squaw; I admire their talking of the liberty of savages; in the most essential point, they are slaves: the mother marry their children without ever consulting their inclinations, and they are obliged to submit to this foolish tyranny. Dear England! where liberty appears, not as here among these odious savages, wild and ferocious like themselves, but lovely, smiling, led by the hand of the Graces. There is no true freedom anywhere else. They may talk of the privilege of chusing [sic] a chief; but what is that to the dear English privilege of chusing a husband? (56)

By mingling the jargon of marital engagement--"declare off"--with that of politics--"tyranny," "true freedom"--Arabella demonstrates the overlap between politics, manifested by law, and domestic relations or sentiment. Her literary reference to the Graces further suggests that sentiment, "English liberty," and civilized refinement are interconnected. Sentiment is not the product of such sublime nature as the Huron display; nourished by female instinct, it is the fruit of culture.

Brooke further explores the limitations both of nature and of civilization by comparing Indian and English politics. The Huron political system represents a version of Rousseauistic natural law with "no positive laws"--no written statutes. As one Indian avers, "'we are subjects to no prince; a savage is free all over the world.'" Ed confirms that

> they are not only free as a people, but every individual is perfectly so. Lord of himself, at once subject and master, a savage knows no superior, a circumstance which has a striking effect on his behavior; unawed by rank or riches, distinctions unknown amongst his own nation, he would enter as unconcerned, would possess all his powers as freely in the palace of an oriental monarch, as in the cottage of the meanest peasant: 'tis the species, 'tis man, 'tis his equal he respects.... (33)

Living in the state of nature, adhering to epic virtues of hospitality and courtesy, as well as warlike ferocity, the Hurons escape European hierarchies of class and gender. Ed notes that the chief's power is limited and reasonable since it is always obeyed, while "The sex we have so unjustly excluded from power in Europe have a great share in the Huron government" since women choose both the chief and his council of assistants, for "women are, beyond all doubt, the best judges of the merit of men" (34). Just as he persistently praises sexual equality in marriage, Ed condemns English politics as uncivilized tyranny: "in the true sense of the word, *we* are the savages, who so impolitely deprive you of the common rights of citizenship, and leave you no power but that of which we cannot deprive you, the resistless power of your charms" (34-35).

Brooke illustrates the contrast between Canadian nature and European politics through the letters of Arabella's father, Captain William Fermor. In describing the political and cultural conditions of Canada to the Earl of--, William Fermor contextualizes the lovers' sentimental accounts of Indian freedom and personal relationships within the parameters of conventional social values. After Fermor records that, since they always long to return home, the English will not settle well, Emily and Rivers discuss whether they can afford to leave the "exile" of Canada (224). Implicitly blaming the "Romish" religion, Fermor condemns the reveling, "Sloth and superstition" of Canadians (208-9), advocating universal religion and rational labor in place of the religious pluralism and native freedom his daughter admires. While deploring the softness of the English who cannot "bear the hardship" of settlement, he recommends winning the Canadians "by the gentle arts of persuasion, and the gradual progress of knowledge, to adopt so much of our manners as tends to make them happier in themselves, and more useful members of the society to which they belong" (220-21), a perspective that highlights the romantic indulgence of the lovers' praise of Canadian liberty. He also attributes the "striking resemblance between the manners of the Canadians and the savages" in their indolence in peace and "ferocity in war" to infection of the French by "savage" "manners," whereas Ed admires the independence of the Indians in resisting European influence, even while he also condemns their indolence. In condemning Indian drunkenness, Fermor protests that "It is unjust to say that we [Europeans] corrupted them" since "both French and English are in general sober" (272), an argument that rationalizes Arabella's tale of taking wine to Indian women and watching them get drunk while she asked them questions. Indeed, Fermor's perspective resembles his daughter's in its faith in cultivation: "From all that I have observed, and heard of these people, it appears to me an undoubted fact, that the most civilized Indian nations are the most virtuous; a fact which makes directly against Rousseau's ideal system" (272). At the same time, Brooke demonstrates that the conventional perspective Fermor adopts, with its firm definition of "virtue," does not penetrate nature. When he describes scenery, he uses technical rather than picturesque language, finally admitting, "I am afraid I have conveyed a very inadequate idea of the scene ... it however struck me so strongly, that it was impossible for me not to attempt it" (236). An enlightened father, he advocates conversation between the sexes to educate women to be "the most pleasing companions," and recommends moralists "expand, not ... contract, the heart," yet he claims possession over Arabella's affections: "Notwithstanding all my daughter says in gaiety of heart, she would sooner even relinquish the man she loves, than offend a father in whom she has always found the tenderest and most faithful of friends" (244-45). Fermor reiterates the conventional tenet that, although English women may refuse their parents' choice of husband, they may not marry where they will, yet Arabella's letters, "all she says," suggest that she embraces complete freedom of choice in marriage. Brooke emphasizes this contrast by juxtaposing Arabella's teasingly hyperbolic declaration of passion and secret marriage to Fitzgerald with Fermor's account of Fitzgerald's birth and fortune, the very standards of value all other characters, including Arabella, condemn as English corruption.

If Fermor, albeit enlightened, exemplifies the patriarchal values opposed to sentimentalism, Ed also reveals the effects of "male" education. Despite his sympathy for their "natural law," Ed does not reflect Indian morality. To women, he attempts to act with an internal delicacy that the stoic Indians do not share, yet his function in Canada is colonization. He opens the novel by declaring himself ruler of the wilderness: "My subjects indeed at present will be only bears and elks, but in time I hope to see the *human face divine* multiplying around me; and, in thus cultivating what is in the rudest state of nature, I shall taste one of the greatest of all pleasures, that of creation, and see order and beauty gradually rise from chaos" (3-4). Although Brooke repeatedly identifies his behavior with "female" softness--"You ... really have something of the sensibility and generosity of women," declares Arabella (347); "my heart has all the sensibility of woman," confesses Ed (133)--she also points out the link between his attitude toward sexual opportunity and his exploitation of land.[19] Ed judges women as a sentimental connoisseur, as Arabella describes scenery:

> I hate a woman of whom every man coldly says, *she is handsome*; I adore beauty, but it is not meer features or complexion to which I give that name; 'tis life, 'tis spirit, 'tis imagination, 'tis--in one word, 'tis Emily Montague--without being regularly beautiful, she charms every sensible heart; all other women, however lovely, appear marble statues near her:

fair, pale (a paleness which gives the idea of delicacy, without destroying that of health) with dark hair and eyes, the latter large and languishing, she seems made to feel to a trembling excess the passion she cannot fail of inspiring: her elegant form has an air of softness and languor, which seizes the whole soul in a moment: her eyes, the most intelligent I ever saw, hold you enchain'd by their bewitching sensibility.

(1: 20-21)

Ed proves his picture of her indeed describes her nature by remarking her "attentive politeness" in conversation and her "desire of pleasing." His cultural power of observation, moreover, makes him a "philosopher" not merely of physical scenery, but of human scenery too: "As I am a philosopher in these matters, and have made the heart my study, I want extremely to see her with her lover, and to observe the general increase of her charms in his presence; love, which embellishes the most unmeaning countenance, must give to her's [sic] a fire irresistible: what eyes! when animated by tenderness!" (21).

Brooke punishes Ed for believing he can observe beauty unmoved by making him fall in love with Emily, but his detachment also hurts another sentimental character, Madame des Roches. Madame des Roches enters the story when she asks Ed for legal help in adjudicating a property claim, a request Ed passes on to his rakish London crony, the lawyer John Temple. This first encounter outlines the nature of their relationship: he is master of the rules that define territory, be this wild land or natural feeling.[20] In a letter to Temple which light-heartedly acknowledges the loss of his old flirt Lady H--, Ed adopts the jargon of connoisseurship to describe sexual relations in society:

Widows were, I thought, fair prey, as being sufficiently experienced to take care of themselves.... A woman in the first bloom of youth resembles a tree in blossom; when mature, in fruit; but a woman who retains the charms of her person till her understanding is in its full perfection, is like those trees in happier climes, which produce blossoms and fruit together. You will scarce believe, Jack, that I have lived a week *tête à tête*, in the midst of a wood, with just the woman I have been describing: a widow extremely [sic] my taste, *mature*, five or six years more so than you say I require, lively, sensible, handsome, without saying one civil thing to her ....(84-5)

Although Ed contrasts this cultivated appreciation of women as products of
nature to his feelings for Emily, he fails to recognize that his behavior affects
Madame des Roches: believing he loves her, she loves him. When he learns
of her love, however, his response employs the language of imperialism: "I
was at first extremely embarrassed: but when I had reflected a moment, I
considered that the ladies, though another may be the object, always regard
with a kind of complacency a man who loves, as one who acknowledges the
power of the sex, whereas an indifferent is a kind of rebel to their empire"
(158). His sexual language mirrors his political behavior. Brooke again
reminds the reader that men confuse sex and power when Ed's friend
Temple, now married to Ed's sister Lucy, after praising his wife in a
rapturous letter, hastily concludes, "Lucy is here. Adieu! I must not let her
know her power" (373). This echoes Ed's own misogynistic clichés: when he
begins to love Emily, he calls her a "little tyrant" who wishes to add him "to
the list of her slaves" (24).

Brooke reinforces this disturbing criticism of colonial attitudes by
silencing Madame des Roches. Like the Indians, she possesses no first name,
exhibits sublime nature in her obdurate passion, and speaks only through
translation in the letters of the English. Only Arabella, as a disinterested
spectator, passes on her words when Madame des Roches congratulates
Emily and vows eternal fidelity to Rivers, and even Arabella paraphrases
them: "I thought of sending her letter to [Emily and Ed], but there is a certain
fire in her style, mixed with tenderness ... which would have given them both
regret, by making them see the excess of her affection for him; her
expressions are much stronger than those in which I have given you the sense
of them" (282). When a jealous Emily has behaved rudely both to Ed and to
Madame des Roches, Arabella undercuts Emily's complacent self-criticism
with the addition of a parenthetical comment that adumbrates the implicit
"colonization" of Ed: "I have been with [Emily] again ... she ... was peevish
with me, angry with herself ... said ... that *her* Rivers (and why not Madame
des Roches's Rivers?) was incapable of acting otherwise than as became the
best and most tender of mankind" (163-64). Arabella questions Emily's
possessiveness, which, like colonial ambition, desires to dominate nature. In
contrast, Madame des Roches, the embodiment of wild nature, is banished to
a solitary life in Canada, and even to madness (283).

Brooke stresses her point that sentiment, like Burke's "beautiful," relies
on art as well as nature by linking it with law, language, and literature. The
Indians have no "positive laws" because they "have no idea of letters, no
alphabet, nor is their language reducible to rules: 'tis by painting they
preserve ... memory" (85-86).[21] Ed notes that they sing only on the subjects
of war and male friendship, except for a single, "short and simple, tho'
perhaps not inexpressive" lyric, which he quotes:

"I love you
I love you dearly,
I love you all day long." (11)

This emotional efficiency contrasts with both the ritualized language of
complimentary courtship borrowed from the French, which Temple and
occasionally Ed himself use, and with the stylized literature of sentiment
quoted and imitated by Arabella in her literary letters. Indeed, Indian
illiteracy demonstrates the degree to which sentiment, women's "power,"
relies on language, especially epistolary language, for just as Indian women
lack sentimental language--itself a commodity of modern literary culture--,
so they lack sentiment. So, too, do those men who lack sensibility. "Adieu!
I never write long letters in London," asserts Jack Temple as he plays the
roué at London assemblies (83). William Fermor apologizes for discussing
his personal matters to his correspondent, the Earl of--, by blaming the nature
of letters: "Your good-natured philosophy will tell you, much fewer people
talk or write to amuse or inform their friends, than to give way to the
feelings of their own hearts" (162). Similarly, after a long description of the
Huron, Ed entrusts communication to women with a characteristically
professional metaphor: "What a letter have I written! I shall quit my post of
historian to your friend Miss Fermor; the ladies love writing much better than
we do; and I should perhaps be only just, if I said they write better" (39). By
chronicling the progress of love and self-realization through letters by women
or feminine men, Brooke suggests that women regulate their reality,
sensibility, through letters as men regulate theirs, property, through law.
Epistolary language connects experience and reflection, and thus constructs
the very morality the Indians lack: private memory and public history.

It is Arabella Fermor who exemplifies epistolary power. She articulates
the balance between French artifice and Indian instinct, between masculine
judgment and feminine sympathy, between literary and spontaneous language.
While Brooke names "Rivers" and Madame "des Roches" after nature, the
ideals of the beautiful and of the sublime respectively, Arabella is named
after Pope's model for Belinda in *The Rape of the Lock*. Like her namesake,
Arabella loves cards, masquerades, and coquetry; almost like Pope, she
"wrote pastorals at seven years old" (387). She is thus both her own artist
and artwork; her creation is herself where Ed aims to create a kingdom
(80).[22] Arabella blends wit with her sentiment, reflection and observation with
her flirtation. As she herself observes, "[Emily] loves like a foolish woman,
I like a sensible man" (198). While she comes to acknowledge Emily's love
for Rivers, she warns her not to "fall into the common error of sensible and
delicate minds, that of refining away your happiness" (45). She acknowledges
"a certain excess of romance ... in my temper," and, in the midst of a letter

on the rival claims of physical and moral beauty, quotes Montesquieu and teases herself for vanity (280).[23]

A kind-hearted spectator who deliberately disengages herself from excessive sentiment, Arabella is the only character to describe the physical nature of Canada; moreover, she does so in picturesque language that contrasts the wild sublime and the pleasingly beautiful: "There are two very noble falls of water near Quebec, la Chaudiere and Montmorenci: the former is a prodigious sheet of water, rushing over the wildest rocks, and forming a scene grotesque, irregular, astonishing: the latter, less wild, less irregular, but more pleasing and more majestic" (29). Albeit temporarily "Montmorenci-mad," Arabella, like Rivers, ultimately values English beauty, "the lovely, the smiling" (151), over "the savage luxuriance of America" (300). Like her favorite Horace and like Ed, she "cultivates her own garden" (132; 408).

Arabella's admirable perspective on nature and art is preserved by her style, which, brimming with literary allusions and philosophical argument, permits her to retain her "independence" of judgment. This style contrasts with Emily's descriptions of emotional vacillation. In one letter enclosing a missive from Emily confessing dislike of her fiancé, Arabella concludes not only that Emily should be released, but also that "long engagements ... [are] extremely unfavorable to happiness" and that she will not consent to one (131). Her ability to "read" others' feelings allows her to decide her own course; she judges from observation and education, not just sentiment. She also extrapolates both from her own feeling and from literary authority to determine the nature of social concepts, including the delicate issue of religion. Quoting a passage from Nicholas Rowe's *Tamerlane* arguing that all people worship the same God despite their differences, Arabella paradoxically raises a distinction of gender:

> I should doubt the sex of an unbeliever in petticoats. Women are religious as they are virtuous, less from principles founded on reasoning and argument, than from elegance of mind, delicacy of moral taste, and a certain quick perception of the beautiful and becoming in every thing.
>   This instinct, however, for such it is, is worth all the tedious reasonings of men. (107)

In correlating the "natural taste" for virtue and religion with gender, Arabella articulates a tenet of literary sentimentalism; at the same time, her argument that women act from instinct cultivated by good breeding locates religion in civilized sensibility rather than in wild nature. Her own reflections thus modify the literary authority she cites. Indeed, throughout the novel, Arabella's disinterested observations on nature and culture, punctuated with general reflections, exemplify Locke's ideal of judgment as the result of reflection on the data of empirical observation and of sensation.

European women like Arabella, Emily, and Madame des Roches, are "softened" not only by nature, but also by education into dependence on the sensibility and courtesy of men. The ubiquitous comparison between English and Indian women underscores Brooke's point that female softness is the luxury of a "civilized" society and therefore should also be its responsibility. Brooke thus demonstrates that sentiment is neither a natural nor an entirely good quality, for, although it supplies an internal moral system more reliable than the regulations of society, it weakens women in a world ruled by the laws of men.

Brooke's final novel, *The Excursion* (1777), satirizes sensibility and points to the way that sentimental prose fictions will transform into bildungsroman, foreshadowing Jane Austen's *Northanger Abbey* and *Sense and Sensibility*. Written in the voice of an authoritative, ironic narrator, the story opposes twins, the mild, blue-eyed sentimental heroine Louisa and her "wild" sister Maria Villiers, who travels to London and reforms her romantic expectations. When Maria asks her father, Mr. Dormer--allusive of Chester-field, whose *Advice to His Son* typifies worldly education--for permission to go, the narrator remarks: "He cautioned her, not against the giants of modern novels, who carry off young ladies by force in post-chaises and six with the blinds up, and confine free-born English women in their country houses, under the guardianship of monsters in the shape of fat housekeepers, from which durance they are happily released by the compassion of Robert the butler; but against worthless acquaintance, unmerited calumny, and ruinous expense" (1: 34).[24] Mocking Richardson's *Pamela* as Austen mocks Radcliffe's *The Mysteries of Udolpho* in *Northanger Abbey*, Frances Brooke reasserts the dangers of the social, tangible world in a fashion foreshadowing Frances Burney's *Evelina*. Romantic adventures teach nothing, she implies; moral literature warns of the world, as *Tom Jones* did. Once again, rationality must restrain fancy.

Indeed, Brooke's narrative voice mingles ironic spectatorship with morality in Fielding's style: "A Thousand moralists and philosophers have declaimed on the joys of solitude, on the advantages of silent contemplation. May I be allowed to suspect them of affectation, if not of falsehood? For my own part, I had rather be a beggar happy in the converse of my fellow beggars, than a princess condemned to solitary greatness. My heroine, for which I love her, thought, or rather felt, in the same manner" (1: 34). As Austen bares the fictionality of her heroine--"my Fanny"--in *Mansfield Park*, and as Fielding links his fiction with the current debates on man's nature, so Frances Brooke here models the way to read her own novel: with ironic detachment. By referring to a fable, moreover, the narrator asserts her identity with the ordinary reader; at the same time, she stands above her foolish heroine. Brooke plays, in addition, on the overlap between "thinking" and "feeling" for young heroines who express themselves in ignorant hyperbole. She thus adopts the perspective of amused detachment in order to narrate--interpret--the story. In this novel, Frances Brooke abandons epistolary models for an objective narrative voice that curtails sentimental expression.

Influenced by the sentimental fictions of Madame Riccoboni, Brooke locates her sentimental ideal in Utopian, pastoral estates where nature and art inform each other in rational balance. Beyond the borders of these estates, her youthful and romantic heroes and heroines undergo confusion and fear as their feelings lead them to misinterpretation. In Brooke's tragic novel *Julia Mandeville*, these excursions prove fatal to the hero even as his monomaniacal letters transgress the rules of communication; it is left to the detached spectator versed in literary and social art to interpret the tragedy for the reader through her letters. In *Emily Montague*, the hero disciplines his sensibility in the wilds of Canada by adhering to political, moral, and religious laws, echoed by his moralistic narratives to his London crony. As Ed says, "The great science of life is, to keep in constant employment that restless active principle within us, which, if not directed right, will be eternally drawing us from real to imaginary happiness" (407).

Frances Brooke uses aesthetic theory and description, literary allusion, and pictorialism to advocate the control of feeling into charitable, socially useful forms. While her heroines model sensibility, her voices of authority urge ironic distance. Brooke demonstrates that both civilization and right sentiment ultimately rely on the power to judge with a detached perspective, the power to write the scene as art. These epistolary novels are the artistic expression of socialized feeling, of individual perception and emotion translated into social communication. Through aesthetic description, emotion becomes spectacle; through epistolary intercourse, private experience becomes communicable. The figures who exercise social or internal command--the patriarchs and the marginalized commentators--exemplify Brooke's morality. At the same time, Brooke's didactic style occasionally conflicts with her implied ideological endorsement of feeling. She sometimes stifles the vivid transcription of moral process so that her novels structure sentiment into sententiousness; alternatively, the wild feeling that inspires her romantic figures sometimes escapes being moralized neatly into a lesson on self-control. Style thus dramatizes the strain between the sentimental value for feeling and for restraint.

CHAPTER 5

The Fictions of Sentiment:
The Man of Feeling and
Mackenzie's Periodicals

> But hence, to some parts of an audience, the
> danger of a drama such as this [Schiller's *The
> Robbers*]. It covers the natural deformity of
> criminal actions with the veil of high sentiment
> and virtuous feeling, and thus separates (if I may
> be pardoned the expression) the *moral sense* from
> that morality which it ought to produce.
>
> "Account of the German Theater"

Henry Mackenzie is best known today as the author of the notoriously
sentimental *Man of Feeling* (1771). He was also, however, a shrewd lawyer,
a member of the inner circle of the Edinburgh elite, and the "Scottish
Addison," the editor and major writer for two popular periodicals, *The Mirror*
(1779-80) and *The Lounger* (1785-87). Concerned both professionally and
personally about social morality, Mackenzie even recommended censorship
of the very kind of sentimental literature with which critics have associated
his novel. Mackenzie, successor to Goldsmith and Boswell, advocates a
reform of manners that yet reinscribes the necessity of social control.[1] In the
epigraph above, as in *The Man of Feeling* (1771), Mackenzie divides "some
part of the audience" from others, and private feeling from public action.[2]
This division worried him, however, for he wanted the two to reinforce each
other. In both his novels and his periodicals, therefore, he hedges private
sentiment with irony and encases it within a structural frame that limits, even
undermines, its authority. For Mackenzie, sentiment may demonstrate refined
sensibility, but it can also erode civic virtue.

Despite his popularity in his own day and on his own Scottish ground, most modern scholars of the eighteenth century have ranked Mackenzie as an imitative, third-rate novelist whose works repay only an historical or philosophical interest in the theory of sentimentalism.[3] Brian Vickers exemplifies this view. Tracing Mackenzie's characters and scenes to the stock types and situations mastered in Goldsmith's *Vicar of Wakefield* and his narrative method to Sterne's chef d'oeuvre *Tristram Shandy*, Vickers denies that Mackenzie presents "a divided or ironic response at any point--it is tears, tears all the way.... *The Man of Feeling*," Vickers shrugs, "has little absolute literary value, yet if we use it mainly to gauge 'the tune of the time' we must grant that Mackenzie caught it with some sensitivity."[4] "A divided or ironic response," however, indeed sounds a strain in "the tune of the time"; such a response is entailed by the ambiguities of narrative method and of language within sentimental discourse itself. Mackenzie's very talent for garnering sentimental clichés--what Vickers and others indict as his lack of orig-inality--ensures the repetition within his work of the contradictions within sentimental literature between reverence for feeling and distrust of it. Although this novel uses irony rather than didacticism, like his other works it is consistently informed by his desire for a stable social order and his distrust of sentimental literary values, especially the formula that feeling guarantees virtue. Through sentimental novels and periodical vignettes that expose the way vanity and selfishness masquerade as benevolence and morality in the fashion for feeling, Mackenzie criticizes the fictions of sentiment for ignoring the discipline of virtue.

The Man of Feeling exemplifies the ambiguities of sentimental irony. Through fragmentary chapters pinned together by an "editor" from a "discovered" manuscript, the book recounts the adventures of Harley, a sensitive, bashful youth who travels to London in an attempt to gain his inheritance. Between meeting social types, including a beggar, a cardsharper, a misanthropist, and a "benevolist," he restores a starving prostitute to her distraught father and views the traditional roster of mad types in Bedlam, each displaying a form of imaginative excess. Disappointed in his political and financial hopes by the corruptions of the city, he returns to the country, and on the way encounters Edwards, an old servant whom disasters have stripped of his home and family. In pity, Harley assists him by tilling his land until, debilitated by nameless causes which seem to include physical exhaustion, moral disgust, fever, and frustrated love, he dies.

Through structural irony, puns, and parody, *The Man of Feeling* condemns the literary refinement of feeling that replaces judgment with a self-regarding emotion wrongly portrayed as sympathy. Mackenzie presents the tale through the double frame of two narrators, each of whom represents an ironic variation on the theme of the title. This device allows the author to parody sentimental conventions. The first narrator, the Editor, exemplifies the self-conscious, literary taste for "private" feeling, although his role is confined to an "Introduction" and a few editorial notes. The second, "The Ghost," who tells Harley's tale, resembles the "man without a skin" of Smollett or Goldsmith's Burchell; his sentiment is the sensation of outraged morality. Harley, morbidly sensitive yet filled with romantic respect for feeling, blends faults from both narrators. Mackenzie supplies no model of balanced feeling; rather, he condemns several literary types of sentiment for sifting feeling out of social reality.

Mackenzie opens the novel by mocking through puns the sentimental enthusiasm for idiosyncratic meanings. In his "Introduction" recounting his discovery of the manuscript, the Editor conflates spiritual and material terms. We learn that the Editor has gone hunting with his friend, a portly curate; the language warns us that this hunting is not only physical but metaphysical, a hunt for "birds" and for meanings that is not going well.

> It was a false point, and our labour was in vain.... There is no state where one is apter to pause and look round one than after such a disappointment. It is even so in life. When we have been hurrying on, impelled by some warm wish or other, looking neither to the right nor to the left--we find of a sudden that all our gay hopes are flown; and the only slender consolation that some friend can give us, is to point where they were once to be found. And lo! if we are not of that combustible race, who will rather beat their heads in spite, than wipe their brows with the curate, we look round and say, with the nauseated listlesness [sic] of the King of Israel, "All is vanity and vexation of spirit."[5]

This extrapolation from daily experience to grand philosophy parodies the literary language and method of sentimental literature, especially Henry Brooke's evangelism in *The Fool of Quality*, a text Mackenzie read and ridiculed before he wrote his own novel.[6] In this passage, Mackenzie also highlights the sentimental emphasis on individual response rather than on social circumstance; the Editor contrasts two ways to "feel" in response to loss, but offers no program to forestall loss. "Combustible" people, like the "Ghost," spite themselves physically in order to match their mental pain; sentimental or spiritual readers, like the Editor or the audience, find sermons in stones or stories. Both responses address individual suffering but ignore social context.

By his self-conscious clichés, dense puns, and typical scenes, however, Mackenzie demonstrates that such private responses themselves adhere to general standards, the agreements or "conventions" of literary sentimentalism. The trouble for Mackenzie is that these conventions valorize unique feelings or meanings at the expense of social values. This passage sets up the Editor as the model of the sentimental reader, whom Mackenzie mocks for being conditioned to respond according to rules yet deluded into thinking none exist. The Editor tells us that, as he paused in the "hunt," he stood upon a "stone" to observe Harley's sweetheart, Miss Walton; on learning that the curate has Harley's "history," he exchanges for it his own text, a copy of "the German Illustrissimi." The manuscript is marred by holes where the curate tore it to plug his barrel when using it as gun wadding, just as the Editor used his German treatise (5). This detail creates a comic analogy between the physical and the spiritual treatment of texts, parodying the literary convention of authenticity that presents manuscripts as physical objects beaten by time.

The analogy also parodies the thesis of sentimental reading that presents private feeling as faith, if not, indeed, as truth. The curate, the public man of faith, loads his "gun" or argument by shredding the manuscript on feeling, which he himself terms a "sermon," yet he values the German logical treatise "for the curate was a strenuous logician" (5). This anticlerical allegory rehearses one of the central tenets of philosophical and literary sentimentalism, repeated by Rousseau, Henry Brooke, and Sterne: that conventions, "rules," and logic abuse the human spirit. Like the Editor, the contemporary reader learns from exemplary fiction, read privately, not from rational proofs: faith, the Holy Ghost or Ghost's holey script--or spirituality, lies not in the mechanical services that the fat curate performs, but in the narrative the reader is offered. Mackenzie suggests that this process flatters rather than informs the reader.

Before presenting the Ghost's script, Mackenzie slips in a final criticism of sentimental readers and authors for confusing self-regard with the regard for and of nature. Mackenzie almost steps out of his fiction when his Editor ends by admiring this

> bundle of little episodes, put together without art, and of no importance on the whole, with something of nature, and little else in them. I was a good deal affected with some very trifling passage in it; and had the name of a Marmontel, or a Richardson, been on the title-page--'tis odds that I shoud [sic] have wept; But
> One is ashamed to be pleased with the works of one knows not whom. (5)

In praising the text for affecting him, the Editor unwittingly reveals that the "affected" reader of sentimental literature admires his own feelings, himself, when he admires sentimental art. Mackenzie thus ironically suggests that sentimental texts artfully dramatize to the reader his or her own morality. Since Mackenzie published the book anonymously, this advertisement also challenges the audience to trust their private literary judgment without the sanction of the literary establishment. By citing Marmontel and Richardson, Mackenzie further teases his timid audience, for both writers idealize independent judgment, yet the audience who demands to know the author's name before praising a text signally fails this ideal. Richardson also appended letters praising *Pamela* to his text, a self-congratulatory practice Mackenzie imitates here. Thus, in the Editor's "Introduction," Mackenzie mocks the hypocrisy of the sentimental reader who pretends that art is nature and self-interest disinterest.

Throughout the text, the Ghost at once criticizes Harley's over-refinement and deplores the abuses Harley himself detects. This dialogic dynamic entangles any overt assertion of value in the web of irony.[7] The Ghost begins by comparing Harley's manner with both modern and past ideals of civilized behavior, explaining that Harley's debility results from British isolation. Whereas other "nations" rub off the "rust" of social awkwardness, "in Britain, it often goes with a man to his grave; nay, he dares not even pen a *hic jacet* to speak out for him after his death" (7). Contrasting social "polish" to British bashfulness, the Ghost defines Harley's sentimental manner as the cost of an undeveloped or fragmented society. When the Ghost's friend Silton distinguishes two kinds of "bashfulness," one resulting from insensitivity and the other from over-sensitivity, Mackenzie reinforces his satire; both kinds of manner fail to express individual feeling in social form; the two extremes meet.

As a member of the "combustible race," the Ghost eulogizes a social type opposed to Harley: Silton, the baronet of Silton Hall, who represents the ideal of an earlier, uncorrupted England.

> He is now forgotten and gone! The last time I was at Silton hall, I saw his chair stand in its corner by the fireside; there was an additional cushion on it, and it was occupied by my young lady's favorite lap-dog. I drew near unperceived, and pinched its ear in the bitterness of my soul; the creature howled, and ran to its mistress. She did not suspect the author of its misfortune, but she bewailed it in the most pathetic terms; and kissing its lips, laid it gently on her lap, and covered it with a cambric handkerchief. I sat in my old

> friend's seat; I heard the roar of mirth and gaiety around me;
> poor Ben Silton! I gave thee a tear then: accept of one cordial
> drop that falls to thy memory now. (8)

Deploring that the representative of hearty, harmonious England, the "silt" of the earth and good old dog, should be replaced by a lady's lapdog, the Ghost mourns the contrast between the past "roar of mirth" and the effeminized present in which a woman rules with the accoutrements of refinement--cambric handkerchiefs and toothless dogs.[8] To emphasize the analogy, Mackenzie's Ghost narrator even calls Harley a "bashful animal" (9).

At the conclusion of the novel, Mackenzie again attacks sentimental reading, but this time through the Ghost who "reads" his own story as we return to the scene of the Editor's introduction: the graveyard. Sitting in the "hollow of the tree," an experience "worth a thousand homilies," and feeling a "virtue" in "every beat of my heart," the Ghost pities "the men" of the world, yet he warns the reader that Harley's death "will make you hate the world" (132-33). By juxtaposing the Ghost's private "virtue" with the reader's social "hate," Mackenzie emphasizes the irrelevance of sentimental virtue to the social world and the severance of response and responsibility in literary sentimentalism.

The most important criticism of sentiment in the novel is, of course, through Harley. Contemporary book illustrations portray Harley as a languid, sighing youth whose aristocratic gestures stamp him as too refined for success in the bourgeois world of competition and corruption. Using the trope of physiognomy, Mackenzie himself portrays Harley's sentimental "performance" as self-regard. Harley is shown to be perpetually the fool of one flaw: he sees the world as himself and loves it accordingly. In the chapter entitled "His skill in physiognomy," Harley spies "a fresh-looking elderly gentleman" looking "piteously" on a beggar and lamenting that he cannot help him. The narrative continues,

> there was something in his physiognomy which caught
> Harley's notice: indeed physiognomy was one of Harley's
> foibles, for which he had been often rebuked by his aunt in the
> country; who used to tell him, that when he was come to her
> years and experience, he would know that all's not gold that
> glisters: and it must be owned, that his aunt was a very
> sensible, harsh-looking maiden-lady of threescore and upwards
> (43-44).

While rewarding the beggar, Harley admires the stranger's benevolence. Showing his vanity by seeking to display his own perspicacity in rewarding merit, he even comments that "charity to our common beggars is often misplaced; there are objects less obtrusive, whose title is a better one" (44). When the stranger agrees that many "of the worthless" may be merely unfortunate, Harley "blesse[s] himself for his skill in physiognomy" (44) and accompanies the stranger to an inn where the stranger fleeces him at cards. It seems that his "harsh-looking" aunt is right: good looks do not reveal good thoughts. As an acquaintance scoffs, "as for faces--you may look into them to know, whether a man's nose be a long to a short one" (44), a sentiment shared by Henry Fielding's innkeeper in *Joseph Andrews* as he laughs at Parson Adams.

Harley's "foible" is one that deludes many a sentimental hero: the belief that he can read a person's character in his face and that this character is benevolent.[9] In his superficial reading of social surfaces, Harley exemplifies the naiveté and solipsism of sentimentalism, which mistakes self-regard for sympathy. What he in fact sees in the face of the "other" is himself, his own benevolent impulses reflected. Mackenzie illustrates this by the comic disjunctions in Harley's conversation with the cardsharper; Harley contradicts his own actions by reproving "common" "charity" while giving alms to an "obtrusive" beggar, and the sharper reverses Harley's words by suggesting not that there are hidden objects of charity, but that "obtrusive" or "worthless" beggars may be merely unfortunate. This is not a dialogue; it is a counter-point of sentimental clichés that reveals Harley's self-absorption. The face and words of the cardsharper reflect back to Harley his own dreams.

Such a pleasing reflection flatters the "man of feeling." The Ghost emphasizes this by comparing Harley's perspective with that of the archetype of vanity, a woman gazing in a mirror:

> Though I am not of the opinion with some wise men, that the existence of objects depends on idea; yet I am convinced that their appearance is not a little influenced by it. The optics of some minds are in so unlucky a perspective, as to throw a certain shade on every picture that is presented to them; while those of others (of which number was Harley) like the mirrors of the ladies, have a wonderful effect in bettering their complexions. (25)

The Ghost suggests that in reading the face of a trickster as benevolent, Harley unwittingly reads himself: self-tricked by the false picture of benevolence. In contrast to Harley's self-flattery, Mackenzie provides a portrait of true benevolence in the story: the incident of Mountford who enters the prison of a poor family he had assisted "with a look in which was

pictured the benign assurance of a superior being" (121). This is a true
portrait of benevolence because it reflects good deeds, not merely good
feelings; moreover, the tale is narrated by a friend who was moved to virtue
by the incident. In implying that the benevolent face reflects divinity,
Mackenzie also anticipates the popular physiognomist Johann Caspar Lavater
in hinting that the original benevolent face is the face of Christ.[10] Mackenzie
hints here, as elsewhere, that humanity needs the discipline of Christianity as
well as the sacrifice of Christ; sentiment alone will not save society or the
soul.

A few pages before he meets the cardsharper, Harley meets another
character who reflects back to him his self-regard. On his journey to the city,
he encounters a begging fortune-teller who roams the "open" countryside in
bare feet with a faithful, albeit stolen, dog. Trusting "the plump appearance
of good humour" in the man's face, Harley invites him to tell his tale: a
barefaced account of duplicity in which the fortune-teller learns the habit of
"idleness" after losing work when he was "seized with a jail-fever ... for I
was always curious to get acquainted with the felons, because they are
commonly fellows of much mirth and little thought, qualities I had ever an
esteem for" (21). Apparently imitating this model, the fortune-teller explains
that when he "told his misfortunes truly," they were "seldom believed," so he
"changed his plan, and, instead of telling my own misfortunes, began to
prophesy happiness to others. This I found by much the better way: folks will
always listen when the tale is their own; and of many who say they do not
believe in fortune-telling, I have known few on whom it did not have a very
sensible effect...every one is anxious to hear what they wish to believe" (21-
22). Even Harley hesitates to reward so manifest a parasite, yet "Harley had
drawn a shilling from his pocket, but virtue bade him consider on whom he
was going to bestow it.--Virtue held back his arm:--but a milder from a
younger sister of virtue's, not so severe as virtue, nor so serious as pity,
smiled upon him: His fingers lost their compression" (22). Harley's
benevolent sensibility overcomes a "virtue" concerned for society and
outstrips even "pity" as Harley pays for his pleasure in a Sternean gesture
described as physical weakness. Flattered by the beggar's assumption of
"honest" roguery, Harley is deaf to the truth the fortune-teller tells: "every
one is anxious to hear what they wish to believe" (21).

Mackenzie also attacks the self-regard in sentimentalism by parodying
sentimental attitudes toward love. The Ghost describes Miss Walton, the pale,
elegant vessel of sentiment and the picture of maternal care, as earning
Harley's chivalric love not for her "mild" beauty and "good-humour," but for
her mind:

> Her beneficence was unbounded; indeed the natural tenderness
> of her heart might have been argued, by the frigidity of a
> casuist, as detracting from her virtue in this respect, for her
> humanity was a feeling, not a principle: but minds like
> Harley's are not very apt to make this distinction, and general-
> ly give our virtue credit for all that benevolence which is
> instinctive in nature. (16)

Opposing "feeling" to "principle," the Ghost reiterates Shaftesbury's tenet that
true goodness is instinctive, yet Mackenzie's technique of praise-by-blame
uneasily complicates this sentimental truism by suggesting the reverse: that
virtuous principles should shape "natural tenderness" and that Harley would
do well to learn this. Ironically, Miss Walton models this formula.[11] Noting
his shyness, she pays particular attention to him: "it was a mode of politeness
she had studied, to bring to the line of that equality, which is ever necessary
for the ease of our guests, those whose sensibility had placed them below it"
(16-17). Miss Walton's manners socialize the feelings of benevolence. At the
novel's conclusion, Harley does act benevolently by helping Edwards, but his
lack of self-knowledge--knowledge of his own limitations and abilities--leads
him to his death. He fails to exercise either social or self-restraint.

In contrast to Miss Walton's ideal instinct tempered by politeness,
Mackenzie shows the social and moral consequences of unprincipled
sentiment in the tale of the prostitute Emily Atkins. Emily's instinct has been
misled by a faulty education in freethinking and sentimental literature. Before
learning this, however, we perceive her as an urban temptation when she
solicits Harley outside a brothel, and he accompanies her inside. Her pale
face showing beneath her "artless" "paint," however, wins Harley from his
"bad motives" of lust to the chivalry of benevolence, and he makes an
appointment with her, not to buy her services but to hear her story (49).
However, Mackenzie counterpoints the sentimental lesson with structural
irony. Before keeping his appointment, Harley learns from acquaintances that
he has been fooled by the physiognomy of the cardsharper in the chapter
entitled "His skill in physiognomy is doubted." Mackenzie reminds us that
faces and feelings fool Harley.

Emily's tale undermines the authority of Harley's sentimental ethic.
Despite the "colder homilies of prudence" that counsel caution, Harley keeps
his appointment with Emily, declaring that "to calculate the chances of
deception is too tedious a business for the life of man!" (53). This maxim is
proven doubly wrong. Not only has Harley just lost his money because he
failed to calculate the deception of the cardsharper, but Emily's story proves
the tragic consequences of heedless trust. She traces her fall to her fashionable education. Taught by her father to ridicule religion, she reads "plays,

novels, and those poetical descriptions of the beauty of virtue and honour, which the circulating libraries easily afforded," and becomes a model of social politeness (55). (See Plate 5, which, drawn after the French Revolution, portrays *The Man of Feeling* as an invitation to debauchery.) Still ignorant of both the world and her own susceptibility to flattery, she falls for a heartless roué, crediting "to his sensibility that silence which was the effect of art and design" (58). Her metropolitan education leads her to ruin. Believing her lover's asseverations that "genuine love should scorn to be confined," she becomes his mistress and then his deserted whore. Her unlicensed ideas lead to unlicensed behavior; mental induces physical prostitution. Her freethinking father has taught her ideal, rather than concrete, values, severing principle from feeling and feeling from social convention.

In his other novels and his periodicals, Mackenzie urges the point that sentiment needs structure, albeit without the dialogic irony of his first work. The sequel to *The Man of Feeling*, *The Man of the World* (1773), dramatizes the hazards of undisciplined feeling in an elaboration of the Emily Atkins plot. Here, the dissipated Sindall destroys the Annesly family and almost debauches his own daughter through uncontrolled lust; significantly, their ignorance of the world and their own human weakness also contribute to the Anneslys' disaster. Whereas *The Man of Feeling* addresses an audience of sentimental readers, *The Man of the World* criticizes the gentry and nobility for a moral irresponsibility that leads to social decay. In both novels, however, Mackenzie uses the technique of interpolated narratives to illustrate alternative ways to express feeling. In *The Man of Feeling*, Sedley's story of Mountford's benevolence contrasts with Harley's ineffective feelings, and in *The Man of the World*, the rustic Jack Ryland offers stylistic alternatives to refined sentiment. In *The Man of the World*, Mackenzie contrasts the self-indulgence of both the villainous Sindall and the virtuous Anneslys with "The Stranger's Story," the tale of Richard Annesly's son's capture by the noble savages of America, in which their fantastically harsh treatment teaches him stoicism and earns him respect. Like *Emily Montague*, true sentiment is disciplined on the margins of civilization where social values are less mediated by false language. These inset incidents were sold in reprinted collections as exemplary fictions of moral virtue.[12]

In his last novel, Mackenzie represents the tragedy of excessive feeling. *Julia de Roubigné* (1777) imitates Richardson's novels in plot and method. An epistolary account of the love of two men for a woman, resulting in murder and suicide, the novel is presented by an "editor" who asserts that, having assumed the responsibility of publishing these letters, he must also take responsibility for their moral tendency. Specifically, the heroine's sit-

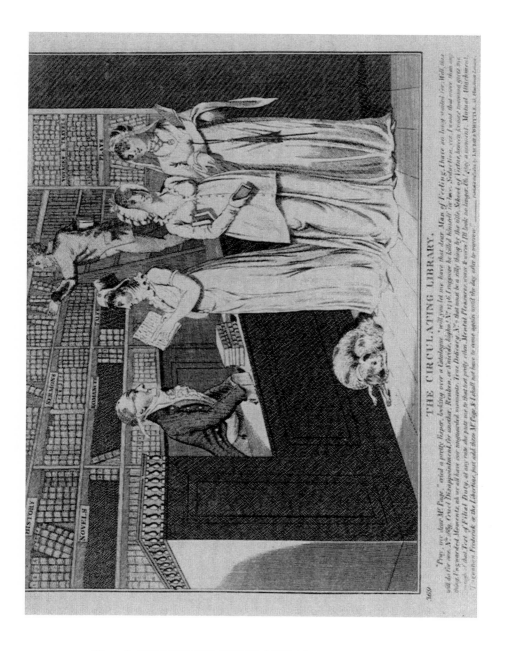

Plate 5: THE CIRCULATING LIBRARY, 1804.
Courtesy of the Lewis Walpole Library, Farmington, Ct.

uation and character mimic Clarissa's: gentle, reverent, passionate, but earnest, she suffers from the theft of her letters, which we peruse as spies on the original thieving spy. Julia's final scene imitates Clarissa's: sitting at her piano and listening to the angels above, she hears heavenly music and she sees visions of her ancestors beckoning. Mackenzie tries to control the morality of the fatalistic and sensational plot, however, by interlarding letters that reiterate conventional views, most notably on the duties of women.[13] Such moral messages ground the heady image of the sentimental heroine in domestic reality. At the same time, Mackenzie knew that his structure adulterated the effect of his tale. In his introduction, Mackenzie directly addresses the problem of finding a moral form for fashionable sentiment: "I found it a difficult task to reduce [these memoirs] into narrative, because they are made up of sentiment, which narrative would destroy."[14] By suggesting that narrative--causal prose--vitiates "sentiment," Mackenzie opposes feeling and understanding. This method and message anticipate the final form for his sentimental fictions: the periodical.

In *The Mirror* and *The Lounger*, Mackenzie uses sentimental fictions and the fictions of sentiment to punctuate his discussions of feeling, moral education, and social behavior. These periodicals grew so popular that they were reprinted in collections almost immediately and sold into the nineteenth century. *The Beauties of Mackenzie* (1813), for example, vended sentimental vignettes from Mackenzie's works to youthful readers. Nevertheless, even "Father Nicholas," his version of Addison's "Theodosius and Constantia," shows Mackenzie's concern that sentiment be framed by sense. Although Mackenzie presents this story to prove that example rather than precept persuades readers to virtue, he nevertheless doubts the permanence of sentimental impression on ill-educated minds: "Natural disposition or acquired habits regulate the tenor of our lives; and neither the sermon that persuades, nor the relation that moves, has any permanent effect on the actions of him who listens or who weeps."[15] He supplies the story of Father Nicholas for, "I never felt so strongly the evils of dissipation, nor ever was so ashamed of the shame of being virtuous" (58). This sentimental assertion appears only after the power of habit and the importance of "gracious" language have been announced: Mackenzie thus emphasizes the roles of art and education, not merely feeling, in molding behavior.

These periodicals address a female audience who wishes to improve their social behavior by an education in manners and morality. Many of the letters these readers sent to Mackenzie pun on the concept of a "mirror," distinguishing vanity from moral self-regard. "Sophia Sensibilis," for example, reproaches Mackenzie for discussing "ancient poets" who treat nature rather than society, and asks that Mackenzie's "Mirror" reflect "myself, represented as I am, in my truest Colours & most exact attitudes, that if anything is wrong I may attempt an *Amendment*."[16] Another recounts her family's discussion of Mackenzie's purpose. After the youngest child exclaims, "O dear mama, I fancy the gentleman who writes this paper intends it only for us ladies, for you know we laugh at the men who consult their mirror," the wise mother rejoins,

> a gentleman who spends the morning in the operations of the toilet, and is so fond of his mirror as to carry it in his pocket, for the important purposes of adjusting a disheveled lock ... is justly an object of laughter .... But a looking glass ... which shows the beauties and deformities of the mind as well as the body may be consulted with equal benefit by both sexes.(1-2)[17]

She concludes by begging Mackenzie to print some "wholesome strictures" on the current female abuse of wit. Other letters praise Mackenzie's moral conversation or ask him to discuss education and behavior. These letters show that readers understood that Mackenzie's *Mirror* not only supplied sentimental stories, but also reflected faulty feeling and behavior.

In his periodicals, Mackenzie consistently advocates an education in religion, wise reading, and reflection, deploring "too refined an education" for a woman's social expectations and warning women that "reading [novels] and refinement, far from enabling the female mind to grapple with its situation, have rather a tendency to soften and enfeeble it."[18] He illustrates this message perhaps most powerfully in the epistolary story of Sophia M--, subtitled in later editions, "A wife seduced by her husband" (*Lounger*, no. 75). Banished to Avignon, Sophia asserts that she will write her tale with impersonal distance as if she wrote of a third person. This technique resembles that of both Eliza Haywood's *Female Spectator* and Frances Brooke's epistolary novels. By portraying a woman moralizing her own life, Mackenzie urges his readers to control their sentiment with understanding and education and to resist the fiction that unrestrained feeling produces unlimited pleasure or virtue. Like Emily Atkins in *The Man of Feeling*, Sophia employs a biographical chronology that implies causality. The child of a gentleman, she was educated by her high-born, extravagant, and undisciplined mother, who sells her in marriage to the worldly, sharp Mr. M--. He speaks to her "in commonplace language" of his love, and to her mother "in the language of the world" of her dowry (298). After bearing him a son, Sophia falls in love with him, but they move to the city where he ignores, betrays, and abuses her; she becomes "part of his establishment" like a servant. Neglected, accompanied only by women, the vain companions of the evil city, she finally commits adultery (as her husband has done long since) and is instantly discovered and banished. Declaring that she now "cultivates her mind" and praises Providence with humble resignation, she nevertheless ends her letter in a style reminiscent of Richardson's spirited Pamela with a reminder of the sexual injustice of her husband and of society: "But it would be more dignified in him, as well as more just, were he to forget, rather than reproach, the woman whose person he bought, whose affections he despised, whose innocence he corrupted, whose ruin he has caused!" (300).

This story exposes several of the fictions of sentimental literature. By portraying Sophia wounded by virtuous feelings and betraying when betrayed, Mackenzie contradicts the sentimental notion that love equals virtue. By stressing the social inequality of the sexes, he also warns women that they cannot afford the luxury of failing to "calculate deception," as Harley does. Both the parental and the conjugal guidance Sophia receives corrupt her by failing to supply principles to control feeling; like Julia de Roubigné, Sophia finds that her feelings hurt, not help, her.

In another popular story from *The Mirror* (nos. 108-109), "Louisa Venoni," Mackenzie uses sentimental convention to eulogize moral education. The titular heroine, low-born but the model of filial and domestic fidelity, succumbs to the blandishments of the high-born Sir Edward. As her conscience attacks her, she begins to fade, but she never abates her careful, good-humored conversation and comfort to her lover. Finally, Sir Edward realizes her value and promises to marry her, declaring, "forgive me, my *Louisa*, for rating your excellence at a price so mean. I have seen those high-born females to which my rank might have allied me.... Profligate in their hearts, and, amidst affected purity, they are slaves to pleasure without the sincerity of passion; and, with the name of honour, are insensible to the feelings of virtue" (3: 310-11). Here, Mackenzie uses the sentimental fiction that virtue will be its own reward in order to advocate domestic values and good manners: the real "accomplishments" of society should reinforce the achievements of the heart--the love of virtue. It is the education in morality, sincerity, pleasing others, and serious thought that he seeks and advertises in his periodical fictions.

The social context of sentimental literature persistently concerned Mackenzie. A year before the French Revolution, indeed, he criticized sentimental literature both for its social effects and for its cultural causes when he identified the "danger" of Schiller's play *The Robbers* as the severance of feeling from social action. A drama like *The Robbers*, Mackenzie argued, "covers the natural deformity of criminal actions with the veil of high sentiment and virtuous feeling, and thus separates ... *the moral sense* from that morality which it ought to produce" ("Account of the German

Theater" 192). Mackenzie traces this immoral message to an immoral method: "in the metaphysical refinements of sentiment ... the feelings are created, not the characters; and we have no leading radical idea to which we can refer them, to which we can discover that intimate relation, which it is the great excellence of the poet to preserve, and the great pleasure of the reader or the spectator to trace" (164). Mackenzie argues that by severing the description of a feeling from a radical context for it, sentimental literature severs effect from cause.

This "metaphysical refinement" violates "nature," but it also reflects social fragmentation, for Mackenzie attributes the fashion for literary sentiment to social disengagement: "This prevalence of highly refined sentiment [in Germany and mid-eighteenth-century England] seems commonly the attendant of newly-introduced literature, when letters are the property of a few secluded men, and have not allied themselves to the employments or the feelings of society" (192). For Mackenzie, the social dislocation which sentimental fictions reveal mirrors the separation of feeling and understanding that literary sentimentalism promotes. Mackenzie blames the literary elite who claim that feeling alone constitutes morality for eroding rational values: "an audience may admire what it does not perfectly understand, if a few sentimentalists of high name do but shew [sic] it what it ought to admire. In sentiment, as in religion, enthusiasm is easily communicated. High refinements which go far beyond real life, catch with a rapidity of infection. They are the creed of a sect, which is always propagated with more ardour and bigotry than the rational belief of a community" (192). Here, as elsewhere, Mackenzie condemns sentimental literature for ignoring social reality and misrepresenting religious feeling.

Mackenzie was not alone in fearing that the fashion for sentiment would corrupt social values, nor was he unusual in using irony to criticize the very sentiment his works evoked. Both Sterne and Goldsmith also laughed at their own tears. Mackenzie, however, exemplifies the use of the literary taste for sentimental vignette to warn his readers against injudicious feeling, confronting the danger that sentiment would coopt religious feeling. *The Man of Feeling* uses linguistic and structural irony to point out the difference between good feelings and good deeds. This irony addresses an audience familiar with fashionable sentimental fictions and their stylistic signatures of successive narrative frames, fragmentation of the story and the manuscript, and the trope of physiognomy. In his later works, Mackenzie manipulates the conventional vignettes of sentimental fiction in order to advocate moral education and to condemn unlicensed or uncontrolled feeling. Both *The Mirror* and *The Lounger* warn the female audience that the current rage for fine feeling can lead to unhappiness, immorality, and social chaos. For

Mackenzie, sentimental fictions brim with fictional sentiments that sell the readers a false faith in feeling and recommend an ideal refinement dangerous to the moral fiber of real society.

CHAPTER 6

Selling Sentiment:
Pictures of Feeling
in Sentimental Miscellanies

> A lasting wreath of various hue,
> Deck'd with each fragrant flow'r.
> Epigraph, *Literary Miscellanies*

Literary sentimentalism in the eighteenth century not only permeated virtually every conventional genre, but it also helped to transform the popular genre of the literary miscellany. Since the Restoration, ephemeral collections of brief literary works had sold the latest in literary fashion to wealthy, middling, and relatively poor audiences. These miscellanies were usually short, cheap, topical pamphlets that skimmed the "best" from fashionable literature and presented it in a quickly digestible form. With the popularity of novels, these pamphlets shifted from printing poetry to printing prose vignettes, thus attracting an even wider audience. In fact, this genre appealed to the very readers Mackenzie thought should not "consume" sentiment: women, merchants, tradespeople, and even servants. The tremendous popularity of sentimental novels and of new periodicals, coupled with rising literacy, moved publishers to provide this "consumable" form of literature in several varieties--series, serials, long and short volumes--all requiring constant renewal and revision, and stimulating--in theory--constant profit. The selections reprinted in this new genre tended to be the self-contained, vivid vignettes from longer fiction that exhibited extremes of feeling, although many publishers balanced such scenes with stories of social virtue. Because these episodes were published out of context, however, the moral frame of the surrounding story was lost. Scenes that originally criticized the corruptions of feeling that sentimentalism derides--display, indiscriminate consumption, excess--might now appear to celebrate both fashion and feeling. In order that sentiment not be severed from sense, or not be perceived as inviting behavioral license, however, and in order that parents might buy these books for their children, publishers often reproduced a context that, like the original, kept the dangers of sentiment within moral and social bounds. This context repressed the individualistic ideology of sentiment in favor of emphasizing its function as moral training.

While varying in format to appeal to specific audiences, these miscellanies all aim at the vast, fluid middle class attempting to ape the classes above them by consuming the right kind of literature.[1] Some, like *Elegant Tales, Histories, and Epistles of a Moral Tendency* (London, 1791) call to socially ambitious, middle-class women with examples of genteel reading. Several, like R. Whitworth's *Polite Miscellany* (Manchester, 1764), Thomas Davies's *Miscellaneous and Fugitive Pieces* (London, 1774), and William Creech's *Edinburgh Fugitive Pieces* (Edinburgh, 1791), offer history and manners, leavened with anecdote and epistle, cheaply to the middle-class consumer. Others such as James Mitchell's *Sentimental Tales, &c.* (Newcastle, 1801) seem designed for the lower end of the social scale, featuring marvelous folk narratives, balladic poetry, and historical snippets that advocate social conformity and political quietism. Many address the newly profitable market in children's literature with a coy eye to the ambitious parent. In this category fall such books as *The Moral Miscellany* (London, 1758), the ubiquitous *Moral and Improving Tales*, reprinted throughout the last thirty years of the century, and the ambitious twenty-volume *Literary Miscellany* of George Nicholson (Stourport, 1812). Whatever the specifically intended audience, however, all reflect the ways in which sentimental literature echoed social and political conservatism in the last half of the eighteenth century.

Sentimental miscellanies mingle characteristics from "high" poetic compendia, popular collections of wit, and inexpensive collections of prose. In presentation, illustration, and contents, they offer morality and manners à la mode, the classics au courant, the lasting and the latest. For the final one-third of the eighteenth century, and into the nineteenth, this fashionable taste was feeling. Probably bought by the very audiences that fifty years earlier had read chapbooks, religious tracts, or periodicals, but who now aimed to learn gentility and rise in society, these literary potpourris mediate current culture by means of the reassuring and familiar signals of popular literature. They package sentimental literature as high--yet conventional--culture.

During the first half of the century, prose miscellanies comprise sheafs of political tracts, essays on parliamentary debates, taxes or religious issues, or practical georgics on such country topics as husbandry. Subsequently, however, the "miscellany" came to connote variety and brevity: a selection of short, light pieces, often humorous or satirical, into which the educated reader could dip at convenient moments for a literary lift.[2] The popular

miscellaneous collections of poetry promoting Dryden and Pope, produced by
Jacob Tonson from 1684 to 1709 and by Bernard Lintot from 1712 well into
the eighteenth century, had already established that the miscellany could
become a vehicle for literary verse, but it remained a vehicle of uncertain
status. In his *Dictionary*, Samuel Johnson derives "miscellany" from the Latin
for "a dish of mixed grain," a derivation similar to "*satura*" for "satire,"
defining it as "A mass formed out of various kinds," which he illustrates with
the following examples:

> I acquit myself of the presumption of having lent my name to recom-
> mend *miscellanies* of works of other men.
>
> > Pope.

> When they have join'd their pericranies,
> Out skips a book of *miscellanies*.
>
> > Swift.

These examples suggest that the word designates not merely a new literary
endeavor, but also a dubious one, at least one scorned by the literati of the
first half of the century.

A typical example published in London in 1744, *The Modern Miscellany*,
explains this reputation. As its title indicates, this miscellany is designed to
appeal to current tastes. Blotted and splotched, printed on rough ragpaper for
the "Will o' Wisp at the Sign of the *Man* in the *Moon*, in the *Ecliptick*," it
provides three literary pieces for one shilling and sixpence, bound:

> I. The Genuine Life and Confession of *Richard Walton*, a *reputed*
> Conjuror, who was fourteen Years confined to his BED, notwithstanding
> which, he was drawn out thence by a Rope and hanged for *Horse-stea-
> ling*, at Warwick. *Wrote by himself*. II. The *Blind-Man's* Meditations
> and Diversions, consisting of Poems on various Occasions; with Poetical
> Paraphrases on several parts of the *Holy Scriptures* and other *Divine
> Subjects, Composed* and *Dictated by him since he lost his Sight*. III. A
> *Scripture Catechism*, being a Compendium of the Principles of the
> Christian Religion. (Title)

By combining a rogue's biography, a blind--i.e. unread--man's thoughts on
religion, and a catechism, the publisher offers the reader the literary forms
most popular with the under-educated both of the city and of the countryside.[3] Like a chapbook, this miscellany both purveys the prestige of literature,
and advertises religion as entertainment with the epigraph: "Who'ere Variety

approves? / We hope will here find what he Loves." Richard Walton's
confession, a plain account of venality interspersed with repentant prayers,
is followed furthermore by "A Poem on the DEATH of Richard Walton,"
which echoes the ambivalence of the popular audience toward rogues who
cheat the system:[4]

> Death is the common Lot impos'd on all,
> The Brave and Virtuous with the vulgar fall ...
> The Vulgar die in Beds: to the[e] 'twas given,
> To swing in open Air the nearest Heaven.

The self-advertisement, cheap price, combination of sensationalistic and
conventional content, and shoddy presentation of *The Modern Miscellany*
indicate the low cultural status of the form during the first half of the
century. Miscellanies seem designed for an audience who are lured by the
marvelous, the new, and the usefully religious.

This audience quickly came to want literary excellence, or at least
prestige, as well as moralism. Miscellanies comprising collections of pieces
written by a single, renowned author were thus also popular, although early
in the century these tended to preserve formally the anonymity of the author.[5]
Hence, Swift's miscellanies appear only under the publisher's name, while
later in the century, miscellanies of Fielding and Johnson appear under their
own names. These miscellanies include the author's light, short, or occasional
pieces. Toward the end of the century, such miscellanies of a single author's
works tended to become representative collections: the "beauties" of
Mackenzie or Sterne, for example, collections advertised for their sentimental
value.[6] These miscellanies, the first to print extracts from longer works on
principle, supply the buyer with a convenient crib of vignettes and "sentiments" from novels, letters, poetry, and essays, indiscriminately jumbled
together under alphabetical categories. Such collections may imply the moral
frame of the author's opus, but they do not reproduce it.

Most literary miscellanies of the end of the century, indeed, include
excerpts or extracts, not merely short pieces. Publishers reprinted periodical
essays and character sketches, especially from Addison and Steele's
Spectator, and vignettes from full-length novels, imitating and plagiarizing
apparently without much effort at concealment.[7] Extracts from works by
Johnson, Goldsmith, Henry Brooke, Collins, Mackenzie, Langhorne, Pope,
and Parnell abound in the high-brow miscellanies; anonymous tales and
poetry dominate the more popular ones. These texts were collected by the
publisher, not the author, and prefaced with tendentious flattery of the reader

veiled as moral purpose. By announcing that he has designed this collection of "beauties" for the reader's appreciation, the publisher recontextualizes the literature for the reader and presents it as constructed by responsive reading rather than by authorial control. The observation of these "beauties" initiates the reader into sentimental virtue. These volumes, moreover, preserved the promise of the earlier miscellanies of providing easy fare, but they no longer offered mere entertainment, nor deliberately appealed to the limited audience who would catch a political or social reference. These miscellanies solicited various, newly literate readers whose knowledge was far less determinate. In addition, this audience wanted moral miscellanies that would retain their value beyond the amusement of the current scandal. These were not for amusement--or at least not solely for amusement--but for instruction. Publishers thus created a rhetoric that advertised permanence while selling novelty and implied a morality of self-discipline while offering examples of excessive feeling.

I. Canonizing and Popularizing Sentimental Literature

One miscellany that caters to the socially ambitious middle and lower middle classes who wished to consume rather than to collect literature is the series *The Literary Miscellany: or, Elegant Selections of the Most Admired Fugitive Pieces and Extracts from Works of the Greatest Merit: with Originals: in Prose and Verse*, published by George Nicholson in Manchester and sold in London at least from 1793 through 1802. Nicholson, as his remarks in this and later editions reveal, was a modern thinker and business-man. Apparently producing one slim edition about every month, at least for the first year, this series includes selections from both renowned poets of the previous fifty years and recently famous sentimentalists. Indeed, Nicholson's popular series, reprinted in bound volumes in 1812 and 1825, underscores the similarities between them, and presents all the literature he provides as the moral advocacy of moderation and good manners.

Nicholson's selections display the conservative and minatory nature of many literary miscellanies, for only works that reiterate and urge convention-al messages belong here. Indeed, although he includes works by authors themselves of dubious sanity or morality, cautious biographical sketches clarify both the limits of the editor's faith in such men and the principles of selection for the *Literary Miscellany*. After describing the demise of William Collins (1721-59) in a lunatic asylum with only the English Testament as his

companion, for example, Nicholson remarks, "Dr. Johnson has spoken of the
productions of Collins in severe and injurious terms. A very different opinion
of their excellencies, is, however, maintained by critics of unquestionable
reputation."[8] This self-advertisement from 1796 is reinforced by the
description of Collins's piety and misfortune so that the story of the author
joins with the productions of his pen in illustrating sentimental pathos, and
the reader joins with the editor in understanding and appreciating this pathos,
in feeling like a person of taste. Somewhat disconcertingly, however, the
editor adds on the overleaf of the title page, as a final gloss on Collins's
biography that conforms to Johnson's judgment, "The pieces omitted in this
selection are such as abound with too much obscurity and absurd traditions."
This hardheaded editorial policy reiterates the sentiments expressed on the
title leaf by the following excerpt from "Visions of Fancy" by Dr. Langhorne
(1735-79), himself a very popular poet at the time, contributor to this series,
and the editor of the first collected edition of Collins's works:

> Sweet Bard! belov'd by every Muse in vain,
> With powers whose fineness wrought their own decay:
> Ah! wherefore, thoughtless, didst thou yield the rein
> To Fancy's will, and chase her meteor ray:
> Ah! why forget thy own Hyblaean strain!
> "Peace rules the breast, where reason rules the day."

In Langhorne's classical imagery of the "day," or chariot-driven sun of
reason, Collins himself here is made to reproach his own "excesses" and join
with the editor and the readers in praising moderation, self-control, reason.
Collins is thus framed, or reintroduced to the reader, by a more moderate
poet; he is presented in a rationalized and familiarized context. This process
is analogous to the way the wealthy collectors of eighteenth-century art
repositioned this art within their estates to make it their own.[9] Such a
domestication of Collins's dangerous muse permits the reader to relish
guiltlessly his selected works, which accord with the bias of this series
toward short, correct lyrics on fashionable themes: the "Oriental Eclogues,"
"Odes" to Pity, to Fear, to Simplicity, to Peace, On the Passions for Music,
On the Death of Mr. Thomson, the "Dirge to Cymbeline," and a "'Song': the
sentiments borrowed from Shakespeare."

In a similar fashion, Nicholson glosses the unsuitable aspects of another
poet condemned by Johnson on moral grounds, Soame Jenyns, the Augustan
roué. Early in the biographical sketch on the overleaf of the title page, he
writes, "The poems not inserted in this selection consist of a translation of
Browne de animi Immortalitate [sic], a mysterious and controverted subject;

pieces adapted to particular times and occasions, which have become nearly uninteresting by the lapse and change of times; and of rapturous descriptions of the charms of earthly goddesses, and of the sighs and dying pains of love." Thus eschewing topics too esoteric, topical--or "fugitive"--, or graphic, Nicholson avoids religion, politics, and sex, a sound policy in polite conversation. Faced, however, with the necessity of explaining Jenyns's life, he implies that Jenyns' first, mercenary marriage induced further laxity in matters religious and social, despite his laudable liberal politics. Nicholson hastens on to the happy ending with a description of Jenyns's perfectly Christian death and summarizes the lesson thus: "Gradually losing ground in faith, he wandered into obscure paths and became a professed deist. He, however, returned to the comforts of rational Christianity. He shrunk not from death as an evil or a punishment, but met it with decent firmness; as the kind release from what was worse, the kinder summons to all that is better" (overleaf). Through short sentences and conventional imagery, Nicholson interprets Jenyns's life for the reader as a moral tale, even a sermon.

The selection comprises five poems of Augustan flavor. The "Art of Dancing," a long, sprightly social satire dedicated to Lady Fanny Fielding, evokes Gay's *Trivia* in its domestic details and comic characterizations. The inclusion of this poem reflects the preoccupation with the etiquette of the gentry typical of the socially ambitious middle classes. At this period, indeed, manuals on manners, especially on dancing, abound, and even William Creech includes some epistles from a dancing master in his miscellany. Like the ubiquitous "Chesterfield's *Advice to His Son*," which reappears in literary, moral, and pedagogical miscellanies, Jenyns's poem merges high literary culture with pragmatic middle-class advice.[10] Because he concentrated so much on the advertised and literal subject of the poem, and presumably expected his audience to do likewise, Nicholson overlooked the figurative implications of its language, for such passages as the following remain unedited:

> Nor need I, sure, bid prudent youths beware,
> Lest with erected tongues their buckles stare,
> The pointed steel shall oft their stockings rend,
> And oft th'approaching petticoat offend. (11.47-50)

The prurient innuendo, merging the schoolboy rudeness of a stuck-out tongue with mature male rudeness, finds more euphemistic expression in Jenyns's verses "Written in Mr. Locke's Essay on Human Understanding," also included. These verses describe woman in the form of Eve, after naming the animals and mastering nature with her knowledge, staring into a pool with

Locke's assistance and catching sight of her own reflected eyes; we learn that her ill-gotten sexual knowledge pales before this deeper knowledge of herself provided by the philosophic man, John Locke. It is interesting that Nicholson considered neither the "Art of Dancing" nor this verse vignette irrelevant to his modern audience, despite their specific reference to issues and manners prevalent fifty years earlier. Rather, the topics of social conduct and female education dominate, reflected in selections that emphasize the fame of the authors.[11]

The selection of Jenyns's work also includes the poetic "Epistle to Lord Lovelace," whom an editorial footnote elaborately identifies as Soame Jenyns's lifelong friend, on the testimony of private letters now in possession of the relative of his Lordship's sister, Lady Harry Beauclerc. Both the ostentatious reference to nobility and the redemption of Jenyns's character further indicate the readers of this work. They are not people informed by knowledge of the literary climate of the previous hundred years; rather, they are those who have picked up the common fashion for sentiment and heard the famous names of some dead poets but understand them in the context of the current climate. This "Epistle" recalls the Golden Age of honest man and manners in the fashion of Swift, with humorous, informal portraits of modern corruption. It is followed by "Virtue," a Popean effort on the folly of fear, and the selection concludes with Jenyns's famous Epitaph on Dr. Samuel Johnson, labelling him "Christian, and a Scholar--but a Brute." This Epitaph articulates a somewhat outdated concern for conduct over content, social over moral behavior, but it is framed by Nicholson's moral biography. These verses exemplify the flowers for the "lasting wreath" of sentiments, impressions, and maxims that *The Literary Miscellany* promises to provide its audience.

From its initial number, *The Literary Miscellany* also contains works by poets revered through the eighteenth century and anthologized ever since. In 1793, Nicholson printed Gay's *The Shepherd's Week* (1714), and Goldsmith's "The Traveller; or, a Prospect of Society" (1764), and "The Deserted Village"(1770). In addition, John Lord Lyttelton's "Monody on the Death of His Lady" appears, an unexceptionably neoclassical and mournful panegyric of conjugal love, as does Matthew Prior's "Henry and Emma," a bombastic dialogue of humility and love with a happy ending, which was frequently engraved. Nicholson printed Pope's *Pastorals* and *Eloisa to Abelard* in 1794; in 1795 we find selections from Thomas Gray's poetry, and in 1797 Robert Blair's "The Grave."

Nicholson also publishes verses which cross the boundaries of age and class, like Dr. Thomas Parnell's poetic fable "The Hermit," printed in 1794.

Reminiscent of chapbook tales of disguised kings, and representative of the fad for "picturesque" hermits, this poem resonates with allusions.[12] It relates the story of a hermit who doubts the ascendancy of virtue in the world and sets forth on a journey of discovery "To find if books or swains report it right" (1.22). The situation recalls classical myths and medieval romances when a fair-faced youth joins him and abuses the hospitality of the three houses in which the pair take refuge: the youth robs a generous wealthy man of a golden cup, which he gives to a miser; and he then murders the only son of a man whose mansion,

> neither poorly low nor idly great;
> It seem'd to speak its master's turn of mind,
> Content, and not for praise but virtue kind. (11.131-34)

This portrait of "The Uses of Wealth," so similar to Pope's poem yet cast in a narrative, then exploits its classical origin: the youth turns into an angel, while "Surprise in secret chains [the hermit's] words suspends" (1.183). The theme of hospitality merges with the portrait of disguised Zeus and Hermes traveling to try the temper of the countrymen, a popular chapbook episode; the classical notion of "secret" as unseen (evocative of Milton) rather than illegitimate surfaces in the language. The poem ends with a definite moral-- "God's will be done,"--a specifically Christian notion, of course, but also one that requires no immediate, indeed no future, action at all. Interestingly enough, however, we learn that "books" rightly report men's behavior, not the "authentic" tales of men themselves; the poem thus promotes the moral and pragmatic virtues of this miscellany and of literate culture itself. Like the rest of the selections, this poem is accessible to a popular and unlearned audience, advocates political and religious quietism, and employs literary qualities popularized by sentimentalism in its simple, rustic tale of rural innocence and the mysteries of faith.

The Literary Miscellany also features prose works that socialize and moralize feeling. In 1793, Hugh Blair's sermon "On the Duties of the Young" urges "moderation, vigilance, and self-government" as "duties incumbent on all" (2). In contrast, he observes, the young, "Impelled by desire, forward they rush with inconsiderable ardour: Prompt to decide, and to chuse [sic]: averse to hesitate, or to inquire; credulous, because untaught by experience; rash, because unacquainted with danger" (2). This describes Mackenzie's *Man of Feeling*. Indeed, Mackenzie shares much with Blair; both were Scottish, Edinburgh-educated Moderates, albeit Mackenzie of a younger generation, and both are included in this series. Blair makes clear, however, that this sentimental character, however noble its impulses, must be changed by time, for he announces; "Whatever be your rank, Providence will not, for your sake, reverse its established order" (4). This absolute assertion of conservative politics appears in the same context as Mackenzie's excerpted "Story of La Roche" and "Story of Old Edwards" (1793 and 1795, respectively). Indeed, the underlying political attitude is the same. The admirable impulses of noble and generous nature must be pruned, honed, and refined through education, self-discipline, and experience--although that experience may, as these books demonstrate, occur through the sympathetic identification of the audience with an oral narrative or of the reader with a written one. Framed by this moral and pedagogical context, sentimental impulse becomes a characteristic of foolish youth.

The Literary Miscellany also published in 1794 George Horne's "A Picture of the Female Character, as it ought to appear when formed." Horne, Bishop of Norwich, uses as his text Proverbs 31: 10: "who can find a Virtuous woman? For her price is far above rubies." Summoning the authority of "antiquity," he cites the benefits of a "properly formed woman." First, the preservation of the husband's possessions, which will free him to work and prevent him from robbing or plundering others, including other nations. The logic of necessity here obscures the possibility that man's nature is destructive; it is not that man wishes to rape and plunder, but rather, we see, that the spendthriftiness of an ill-formed wife drives him to it. Following this, Horne cites the advantages a proper wife will bring: she will keep her husband in a good mood, be industrious, and promote her husband politically. The virtuous female character "thinks before she speaks": "To express the whole in a few words, she says nothing that is foolish, and nothing that is illnatured" (6).[13] Finally, she displays charity rather than the vanity, folly, and extravagance typical of her sex. This subordination of the woman to a housekeeper on the basis of antiquity accords with the tendency of the other selections and does not violate the sentimental spirit of this turn-of-the-century series. On the contrary, the image of domestic control implies the possibility of adolescent excess in the sentimental husband--although even this possibility is carefully delimited by political quietude and social flattery.

This sermon articulates yet another important, hidden opposition within the sentimental format exemplified by Nicholson's entire series: the conflict between "poets" with their libertine views and "wise men" with their sober counsels of control. Although the former seem to express sentimental attitudes, in fact the latter represent sound truth in most literary miscellanies. Poetry is appreciated as a diversion from the solemn stuff of life, a decoration, an entertainment, an ornament of culture very far from the expression of a way to live. Moreover, truth must be revealed by a vetted

authority rather than merely perceived by just anyone. Mackenzie demonstrates this conservative strain in sentimentalism. In *The Man of Feeling*, the
narrator opposes the views of "wise men" to the views he seems to advocate
and to his sentimental applause for bursts of emotions and demonstrations of
feeling. Yet Mackenzie's plot shows that the "wise men" who counsel
restraint and experience end up saying truly: Harley dies from lack of self-
control and of the knowledge of the world that alone permits rational life. In
"The Story of La Roche," the philosopher's wisdom opposes the minister's
enthusiastic sentiment. Here, Mackenzie specifically associates philosophy
with unfeelingness, or stoic resignation, yet the story ends with a compromise, both praising the philosopher for feeling and praising the sentimentalist
for self-restraint in the face of his beloved daughter's death. Sentimental
literature thus implies a respect for social conduct and authority at variance
with its ostensible tenets.

In this sermon, Dr. Horne associates poetry with beauty, sex, and worldly
affairs: "But let beauty have it's [sic] due praise, and suppose what you will
of it--suppose all that the poets say of it be true: still the wise man tells you,
it is *vain*, it is in it's nature transient, fleeting, perishing... The grave is
already opening for the most elegant person that moves, and the worms are
in waiting to feed on the fairest face that is beholden" (7). Implied in this
ghoulish description is the deceit of appearances, manifested in *The Man of
Feeling* by Harley's foolish belief in "physiognomy." Just as Harley must
learn by being cheated and mocked that he cannot tell truth from pretty
vision, so here the divine tells us that the beauty of poetry, of women, is
delusive. Horne's language evokes Locke's distrust of flowery metaphor, the
seductive power of poetic diction; like elegance, it veils the truth. Note also
that he employs the logic of hypothetical argument--like Marvell for a rather
different purpose in "To His Coy Mistress"--to confute the charms of sensual
impression. This is not the technique of sentimentalism, but it is the
traditional rhetoric of the fathers of religion. Horne concludes by echoing
Locke in the language of the liberals: "Such is the female character, and such
the importance of forming it by education. Without education, it cannot be
formed; for we are all born equally ignorant, and are what we are by
instruction" (8). Women, like children, need their impulses formed for their
duties; men, however, need their sympathies expanded by impressions. Again,
women and literary culture are joined and associated with transient, deceptive
pleasures. Both must be shaped by men and by traditional values, just as the
true man of taste must be a gentleman.

The fictional prose in the series is equally moralistically conjured. Unlike
the poets, no author of this sentimental prose is named (Mackenzie deliberately preserved his anonymity as the author of *The Man of Feeling* until the

end of the 1790s). Nor is any distinction made between entire essays drawn from periodical journals and excerpts from sentimental novels. This lack of differentiation reflects the persistent denigration of fiction dating from the sneers against novels at the beginning of the eighteenth century and continuing into the nineteenth.[14] These prose works represent current, fashionable taste, provide easy reading, and offer moral applause to the under-educated; while supplying samples of current literary chic, they do not provide direct access to high culture, as the Augustan poets do. Mackenzie's stories of La Roche, the enthusiastically pious minister who befriends the philosopher, and of Father Nicholas, the erring monk, both appeared originally in periodicals: *The Mirror* and *The Lounger*, respectively. "Father Nicholas" specifically evokes Fielding's interpolated tales in *Joseph Andrews* and *Amelia*--the heroine's name is even Emilia. Both tales draw tears for past injuries, although the story of La Roche reproaches the arbitrary fate of God and that of Father Nicholas reproaches the erring ways of a man who ruined his happy life through succumbing to the evil city and heartless companions. The "Story of Old Edwards" from *The Man of Feeling* includes no particular introduction. While the audience might have known the novel, or at least have heard enough about it to know that this was an extract, the episode functions as a complete sentimental tale ending with the moral of the interdependence of duty and happiness (a laudatory rather than a minatory sentiment). "Father Nicholas" also ends with the moral "Be virtuous and be happy." The story of La Roche is less moralistic, but its "moral"--God's will be done--equally generally applicable.

Extracts from Addison's and Steele's periodicals also work to moralize the tone of the miscellany. "The Story of Theodosius and Constantia," attributed to *The Spectator*, describes the pious remorse of the daughter of a nouveau-riche miser for seeming to waver in her troth to the son of her father's aristocratic rival. Beneath the romantic veneer, this story reiterates the maxim that seeming to sin is tantamount to sinning itself: Caesar's wife must be above reproach. Such a moral well accords with the concern for manners and appearances of the readers of *The Literary Miscellany*. Addison's tale of the deaths of the faithful pair--the disappointed suitor as a fervent religious father, the repentant maiden as a nun consoled by the purely religious comforts of her former lover, now a friend--confirms the superiority of friendship to love and revises Pope's passionate "*Eloisa to Abelard.*"[15] The story also reiterates class and sexual hierarchies while seeming to proclaim a merchant equal to an aristocrat. By blaming the tragedy on the daughter's inadequate resolution and her father's upstart pretensions, since his character is ruined by success, the tale indicts middle-class ambitions.

Recontextualized vignettes also echo contemporary literary fashion. The Catholic trappings, religious theme, and romantic language of "Theodosius and Constantia," for example, resemble the features of newly fashionable Gothic fiction. The stylistic similarities with Radcliffe, Beckford, or Walpole are particularly apparent. For example, the juxtaposition of narrative with sentimental conventions in the following passage awkwardly marries impersonal language with highly emotional content. After receiving Theodosius' hasty farewell letter written on very little evidence of infidelity but much lack of communication, the narrator remarks: "This letter was conveyed to Constantia that very evening, who fainted at the reading of it" and continues breezily "and the next morning" (4). Here, the sentimental tendency to describe exaggerated passion conflicts with the narrative conventions of rapid action. In a later passage, the descriptions of the tearful confession of Constantia to her hidden ex-lover display sentimental pictorialism and excessive emotion:

> She here paused, and lifted up her eyes that streamed with
> tears towards the father; who was so moved with the sense of
> her sorrows, that he could only command his voice, which was
> broke with sighs and sobbings, so far as to bid her proceed.
> She followed his direction, and in a flood of tears poured
> out her heart before him. The father could not forbear
> weeping aloud, insomuch that in the agonies of his grief
> the seat shook under him. (6-7)

Despite the lachrymosity of this episode, the father-lover "commands" and points the "direction," his grief so strong it actually shakes his chair. Such characterizations, language, and physical detail evoke pictorial scenes of Catholic passion, especially in Radcliffe's novels, which similarly strain between impersonal narration and sentimental detail. The tale ends with this comically polite epigram, italicized: "*They were lovely in their lives, and in their deaths they were not divided.*" The pretense of authenticity here follows that of the early novel; this is a true tale for the education of the young. Here, sentiment rules sex, friendship ousts love, and obedience replaces self-expression, as the tale is told from the perspective of a repentant Constantia, albeit in the third person. It is with the heroine that the audience is expected to identify, and from her remorse to learn to moderate passion. This tale, with its romantic utopian setting and customs, its sentimental descriptions, its evocation of current literary fashion, and its conservative ideology, fairly represents the tendency in the fiction of this series.

Finally, the romantic tale of "The Story of Abbas" by Dr. Langhorne, also published in 1793, demonstrates the pedagogical strain in sentimental miscellanies. This excerpted prose vignette describes the encounter of a Muslim and an English merchant with a hermit, who efficiently combines several of the stereotypical figures of the time by also being a misanthrope. The extract opens abruptly in the middle of the story, as the merchant remarks after the Muslim has finished his morning devotions: "The God of nature seems to have given us these sympathetic feelings, to link our affections in the great chain of society: hence, social virtue is not left to depend solely on the moral will, but is founded on the principles of our nature" (4). The proclamation of the philosophic basis of the tale is instantly tested by the companions'--and the reader's--sympathetic response to the hermit's tale of being wronged by law, society, and friends. "'The narratives of age,' replied the hermit, 'are seldom agreeable to youth; but as instruction can be gained only from experience, you will do wisely to learn it from the misfortunes of Abbas.'" The reader is thus also instructed to learn through the "experience" of sympathetic identification with the narrator, in other words, through the education of the story. Books replace experience, as they did in Parnell's "The Hermit." The reader, however, is also expected to learn not to rely on this means of education, that men are not always sympathetically linked or generous in their sentiments and nature. Sentimentalism here is ringed with caution. The extract ends with Solyman, the Muslim, rashly excoriating all mankind while the English merchant urges caution in his opinions. In valorizing the English merchant, in recommending the wisdom of age to impatient youths, and in arguing for the educational efficiency of narrative over experience, this tale melds the chauvinistic and class biases of chapbooks with conservative ideology within the frame of fashionable orientalism. Further, by appearing in the context of *The Literary Miscellany*, the fable merges several audiences: youth, the merchant middle class, and new consumers of literary culture. The story recapitulates the themes characteristic of the series and of sentimentalism as a whole of experience, education, and the cautious formation of judgment through rationally controlled sympathy. Nicholson's *Literary Miscellany* reframes sentimental literature as neoclassical literary culture.

In contrast to Nicholson's late eighteenth- and early nineteenth-century literary miscellany, which was beginning to replace its signals of popular culture with the discourse of enlightened liberalism, James Mitchell published a collection in 1801 that emphasizes political and social resignation, entitled *"Sentimental tales &c.*, viz. Harley's Visit to Bedlam. The Military Medicant [sic]. Montford; or, The Generous Man. Poetry, The Orphan Boy's Tale.

Faithful Negro. Etc. Etc."[16] Extremely poorly printed, on thin paper in faint ink, full of typographical, spelling, and printing errors, this collection clearly aims at a poorer audience whose access to politics comes through publicized topical or sensational issues. Despite the sloppy production, Mitchell's miscellany includes a frontispiece by Thomas Bewick depicting Harley, Mackenzie's Man of Feeling, drooping between two supporters within the crest of two Roman arches, with the sunlight streaming on his head from the barred windows, and the poor mad girl kneeling at his feet, holding up her hands imploringly. Inscribed beneath is her speech "Do you weep again?" The picture imitates a *pietà*, with Harley as Christ within the domains of madness, the prison of worldly pain. Opposite, an unframed engraving of a bush with a hat and a gloved hand resting on it--an image of "natural" manners--recalls the engraving of Chesterfield's "Advice" in *The Literary Miscellany*. Variations of such illustrations continue well into the nineteenth century. (See Plate 6.) While announcing the theme of the series, this wood engraving suggests that the emblems of formal dress and high class have been laid aside as the aristocratic speaker ventures into nature--human nature symbolized by physical nature. The suggestion is that nature strips people of their false distinctions of dress; the reader of this collection stands equal to the writer in sentimental literature. Nowhere in this text is Mackenzie's name mentioned; the engraving replaces any authorial attribution with an emblem indicating the kind of literature this is. Although Mitchell does name the other authors, whose pieces embrace a wide variety of "sentiments" and forms, he intends to sell not only culture, but also sensation. While this cheap collection aims at a popular audience, it reflects the definition and importance of sentimentalism at the turn of the century--especially, since it was published at Newcastle-on-Tyne, to a local readership including the Scots who had native authors to revere. This miscellany shows that sentimentalism may proclaim class equality, but the authoritative narrative voice, the class-specific pictorial language and decoration, the persistent theme of the importance of charity and benevolence to those racially, nationally, or socially disadvantaged, and the conservative structure blending nostalgia and paternalism all remind readers of their class status. In a sense, this literature is presented as charity to be read as alms: it educates the less literate by the generosity of the well-educated.

The collection comprises fables, rewritten parables, or poetry with overtly moral--even political--intent. Following "Harley's Visit to Bedlam," the first and most prominently advertised piece, "The Military Me[n]dicant; or Benevolence Repaid," by Mr. C. I. Pitt, relates a fable of the rewards of

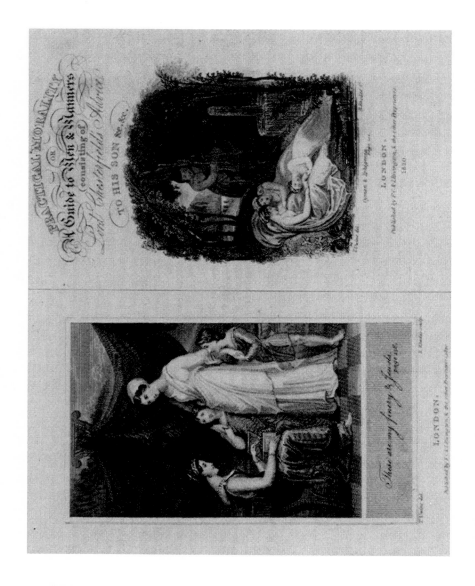

Plate 6: Frontispiece and title page to Lord Chesterfield's *Practical Morality; Or, a Guide to Men and Manners.*
Courtesy of the Lewis Walpole Library, Farmington, Ct.

generosity. Beginning *in medias res* of a journey, the story traces the life of hardship and sacrifice endured by a pious, brave, inadequately rewarded soldier, whom misfortune in farming and the ingratitude of his country have beggared. Through a complicated and hurried set of explanations at the denouement, he inherits an estate and rewards the poor curate, who generously gave him a guinea, with the living he desires. This plot, however, which imitates, if it does not plagiarize, Fielding's *Amelia* and Mackenzie's "Story of Old Edwards," is not the main interest of the tale. Rather, the chatty disquisitions of the Fieldingesque narrator who vacillates between coy worldliness and sentimental exclamations give the story meaning by framing the narrative within a specific moral context. The ostensible meritocratic tendency of the plot is sabotaged by the coincidence that enables the soldier to meet the selfless executor of his brother's estate and by the prevalence of benevolence in the characters of the story. It is also undermined by the narrator's own tone and attitude, which rather observes the rarity of benevolence and the duplicity of appearances than sentimentally expects goodness. For example, he pulls back the veil of narrative to analyze the motives of the landlord who lies about his own military experiences. After informing us in a scandalized aside that he was in fact "*drummed* out," the narrator continues in Sternean rhetoric flavored by Fielding's moralism, "'For what?' asketh thou. Peace, untoward spirit of Curiosity! seek not to bring to light the misdeeds of thy brother, which time has kindly left in oblivion:-- Alas! I am guiltier than thyself. I set thee an example. How frail is man! how vain his reasoning!" So excessive a sentimental moralizing over so trivial an incident might be read as satire, but in this piece it functions rather to exemplify the self-examination requisite of the religious and moral man of feeling. The audience never learns the answer to the question of the landlord's past; such inquiries, the attempt to perceive the underlying truth, are best left to those with the right, talent, or obligation to order society's morals. The external picture, as it were, is sufficient to convey the moral to the ordinary audience even if a more subtle picture might be available to the experienced reader.

The narrator first appears after the opening remark, "I wish thee success," uttered by the benevolent curate Dr. Kind to the old soldier Roach. He launches into an almost mock-heroic description of the soldier's "greasy vellum pocket-book," which, "unlike modern friends," keeps the secrets of the soldier's life (11). The narrator explains, "Over these faithful memorials he frequently shed a tear, which sweetened the hour of distress, and bestowed a consolation only to be imbibed by minds attuned to the delicate harmony of Sensibility, at the refined touch of Virtue" (11). The present object and Roach's absent arm both serve as reminders of the past and as testimonials

to suffering, and therefore to morality. They also replace action with
introspection or reading, the arm with the armchair. Such a valorization of
education over military strength replaces the ancient justification for the
aristocracy on military grounds--so disastrously and publicly disproved by the
Civil War and the growth of mercenary soldiers--with educational ones:
moral leadership rather than military. At the same time, this endorsement of
internal satisfaction lards political quietism with prestige. The narrator
resumes, "Grant, Almighty Disposer of events! that *my* heart may ever be
awake to the still voice of honour; that the season of calamity may not be
rendered more irksome by the inquietude of conscience" (11). The narrator,
moreover, adjures the reader to a secular goodness blending piety and elitism.
'Virtue' is personified and the audience defined as honorable, refined, and
sensitive. At the conclusion, the narrator shifts to a personal prayer as a
demonstration of the moral application of the tale; he models the way to learn
from experience and to read the sermons in sentimental objects like the
vellum pocketbook. This narrator consistently interjects comparisons between
the simple goodness of his heroic characters and the invidious hypocrisy of
the world.

Further moralistic clichés marking the narrative style are sprinkled
throughout the tale. These enforce the political and social advocacy of
humility, resignation, and private charity as the means of reward. As usual
in sentimental rhetoric, such sentiments as "Success is not always the reward
of industry" contradict the apparent moral of the tale, for whereas the story
suggests that financial reward follows worldly generosity, the narrator reveres
the insubstantial pleasures of feeling, be this the generosity of a benevolent
gentleman or the resignation to God of a poor servant, soldier, or reader.
"The hand of Providence seemed against them; but the ways of heaven are
inscrutable!" runs another moralism recommending passivity on religious
grounds (10). The tale ends with a passage that employs the language of
sentiment for religious and social instruction: "in presenting the rectory to the
benevolent doctor, [Roach] experienced the sublimest gratification of a noble
heart, from the consciousness of having, by promoting the independence of
virtue, discharged the obligations of Gratitude" (20). The words "sublime,"
"noble heart," and "discharged the obligations of Gratitude" elicit the
sentimental creed of the virtue of pleasure and the pleasures of virtue and
duty. In this way, the plot, language, and narrative structure of this tale
reflect the interlacing of sentimental and traditional interpretations of morality
and education. The entire discourse--plot, language, rhetorical stance of the
narrator, and frame of religious moralism--indicates that this is a narrative
translation of a sermon, designed to teach the audience to revere generosity

and practice mercy and humility. It is included as a sentimental tale because it calls upon the audience's love of virtue and dwells on the vignettes in the tale, rather than on the course of the plot. The formal rhetoric blends religious and sentimental discourse.

As in Nicholson's *Literary Miscellany*, fashionable genres associated with anti-rational impulse appear in this miscellany. For example, the anonymous "The Hermitage; or, An Account of an Interesting Occurrence in the Rhoetian Alps; with a general Character of the Tyrolese," clearly excerpted from a long, and even duller, travelogue, describes an innocent Roman Catholic girl placing a wreath on the head of a statue of St. Mary in a small church in the Alps while thunder rocks the skies and lightning illuminates her; she does this in the belief that this repeated action for three years will cure her accident-crippled miner father. This vignette prompts the narrator to moralize on the simple purity of these mountain folk, whose superstitious religion is as yet uncorrupted by politics or rationalism, and finally to observe that the Alps make a nice holiday spot.

Many selections testify to the popularity of certain attitudes associated with charity. "The Military Me[n]dicant" precedes "Dr. Johnson's Famous Letter to Lord Chesterfield, on Declining his Offer of Patronage" (7 Feb. 1755). This uncivil epistle is neatly finished by an illustration of a cherub holding a wreath to full up the page; nothing beyond Boswell's explanation of the circumstances of the letter further frames it. Why is this "sentimental"? It is sentimental partly because it displays strong emotion and class independence, partly because it snubs a middle-class nose at the nobs and proves success outside the patronage system--the triumph of true values. Indeed, in Johnson's characterization, the profligate Earl almost begs the poor but moral writer for the prestige of his name. At the same time, the literary and cultural renown of Dr. Johnson half a century later may further contribute to the editor's reasons for including it, particularly since the Scottish Boswell introduces the letter. Primarily, however, it is included because it was written by Johnson, the exemplar of private charity.

Most of the rest of the contents similarly praise traditional class hierarchy by means of sentimental conventions that again emphasize charity. The periodical excerpt "Montford; or, the Generous Man" comes next: a tale of a wealthy, benevolent philanthropist who aids a beggared young lover who has fallen for the daughter of an employer while teaching her French. This tale fleshes out the sketch of Mountford in Mackenzie's *Man of Feeling*. The son of a businessman with pretensions, Wilson (the youth) earns and loses a fortune in diamonds working as a secretary to a man in the East Indies; Montford relieves his wants; they meet his old, faithful love Clara by chance in Hyde Park, and all is well, since Montford decides to disinherit his relatives for this youth. Despite its praise of the merchant hero, the lovers rely on patrician wealth, not middle-class pretensions, to survive. Furthermore, the narrator nostalgically regrets the desolation of Hyde Park, where "our forefathers were wont to exhibit their equipages and gallantry" (38). The printer completes the unfinished page with an engraving of an eagle eating a snake on a rock, a conventional emblem not merely of natural appetite but of natural control. Like the high-flying eagle, the Generous Man devours the evil and clears the path for the worthy.

The final prose selection, a "Petition of The Wife of an Hindoo Prince, said to have been presented to the famous Warren Hastings, late Governer [sic] General of Bengal," similarly endorses conservative values. In its epistolary immediacy, a generic feature hospitable to sentimentalism, it resembles Dr. Johnson's letter. Written in neoclassical language that attempts to recall the primitive simplicity of a noble non-Christian race, the letter pleads with the brutal Governor to spare the innocent life of a Hindu Prince and be content with all his lands and goods as gifts instead of prizes won by violence. The angelic wife asks only to labor as a common servant on the lands she once ruled. Hastings's case translates here into a political attack on unlimited and exploitative power, the power of business administered without restraints. It is the old, aristocratic order that is disrupted by the new economic forces; sentiment allies with inherited rights and domestic love against bureaucracy.

This piece introduces the poetry, which similarly addresses charity to alien, alienated, or underprivileged recipients. "The Orphan Boy's Tale," a song describing a father's death under Nelson in the Nile, ends with the orphan ecstatic at the listening lady's gift of "cloathing, food, employ" (1.38). This is a celebration of private charity for public service that only implies reproach to the government for neglect or bloodthirstiness. The next poem, "The Faithful Negro" by Charlotte Beverly, recapitulates in heroic verse this political philosophy, seen before in the "Indian Petition." The poem describes the suicide of a distraught slave when his cruel second master sells the wife whom his kind first master allowed the slave to marry. The final selections are Burns's "John Anderson, My Joe; or Domestic Happiness Exhibited," a panegyric on the happiness of the loyal poor, and "Lines" by Collins, which recounts wandering in a ruined grove, finding a lone rose, emblem of his desolate heart, and losing bliss but retaining "Patience." All the selections (except for Johnson's epistle) repeat the political message of private charity, resignation, domestic peace, and trust in the benevolence of the aristocracy.

If Nicholson's miscellany seeks to lift sentimental literature into the canon, and Mitchell's *Sentimental tales, &c.* seeks to politicize sentimental resignation, both nonetheless appeal to a popular audience. A similar miscellany exemplifies the overlap of popular and sentimental culture. In 1806 in Newcastle-upon-Tyne, James Mitchell prints another slim collection entitled *The Interesting Story of Louisa Venoni. By Mackenzie*. It includes not only "Louisa Venoni" and "The History of Sophia M--" by Mackenzie, but also "A Signal Instance of English Fortitude," "Anecdote of Sir Matthew Hale, Lord Chief Justice of the King's Bench in the Reign of Charles II," and "Anecdote of Professor Junker, of the University of Halle," comprising in all only thirty-six pages. The frontispiece depicts a seated maiden beneath a gnarled oak overlooking a river, her hand to her mouth, her elbow resting on a stump; in the background, lurking behind the brush, is the curly beaver hat and watching face of Sir Edward, spying on the innocent and natural Louisa. Inscribed beneath the engraving runs a quote from the text, cited as page 10: "Louisa sat down on a withered stump ... and burst into tears." The contents, however, transgress this stereotypically sentimental trope; attracting both female and male readers, they blend the marvelous, the moral, and the nationalistic as they confirm the power of social authorities to define the identity of individuals.

Here, historical anecdote and fiction are equated as narratives of extra-ordinary feeling. Mitchell reproduces and attributes Mackenzie's stories accurately, even quoting Shentstone's "Ah Vices" epigraph to "Louisa Venoni" and allowing Mackenzie almost half of the space in the volume. The other pieces, however, remain anonymous and thus are understood to be true. The five-page "Signal Instance of English Fortitude" describes the resistance of the English to the French and Spanish siege of Alicante in the 1709 war from the perspective of an unnamed ally of the English whose ship bearing relief comes too late. The account concludes its detailed history with this nationalistic salute: "The Spanish and French historians speak of this action with all imaginable regard to the gallant defense made by the besieged.... The Spaniards magnified their [English] heroic conduct, and called the ruined castle the monument of English courage" (28-29). Eulogizing heroic surrender and recording enemies praising each other in the manner of the ancient Greeks, this anecdote proclaims the ethic of death before dishonor.

The five-page "Anecdote of Sir Matthew Hale" celebrates justice and uses the traditional trope of disguise to restore right within a legalistic idiom. Indeed, the legalistic terms in the tale overwhelm its Biblical allusions to Cain and Abel and the Prodigal Son, redefining identity as a legal construct, as in the story of Martin Guerre. Efficiently told in a journalistic style, the anecdote describes the judge's assumption of the disguise of an "honest" miller to expose the corruption of a bribed judge and jury, in order to restore a disenfranchised elder son to his rightful estate, of which his younger brother had attempted to defraud him. The question of motive, which would dominate a narrative modeled on Fielding's method, is never addressed; as in chapbook literature, the motive is assumed and the marvelous strategies and trickery of confounding it are examined.

In the tale, the elder son had gone wandering on the seas, away so long no one knew him; he is therefore himself disguised. The judge consents to participate in the affair doubly disguised: as a miller and as a juror. The lawyer prosecuting the case for the elder brother consents to assume it with the risk that, if he loses, he gains no money but only the opprobrium of the town, whereas if he wins he collects one thousand pounds from his grateful client. The story of the brothers' struggle now becomes the story of the Justice's triumph, as the lawyer's actions and the abuses of bribery at the court take over the narrative, including details of the amount of bribe money (10 carolines for each juror except the miller, who receives only 5, thus emphasizing the further injustice of class prejudice within the outrage of legal abuse). The miserable plaintiff, the disadvantaged elder brother, is told by Judge Hale to exercise "the right and privilege" of "every Englishman" to object to one juror without giving cause; this allows the court to decide on the substitution of an "honest man," who is the miller (disguised judge), chosen apparently by virtue of his old country trade. The judge trying the case apparently has the power to refuse the plaintiff his legal right if he feels like it; thus, it is his own arrogance that fells him. The suspense ends abruptly when the outraged King's Bench Judge Hale steps out of his miller's costume, and "unravelled all the sophistry to the very bottom, and gained a complete victory in favor of Truth and Justice" (33). This plot preserves the status quo by testifying to the right of the higher judge to judge the lesser, and of the elder brother to inherit over the younger son; it also establishes a bond between the courts of power and the "little man," the honest miller, as against the mercenary and corruptible middle classes and upstarts. As is often the case in sentimental fiction, the plot actually violates its ostensible moral: Judge Hale wins the case through the exercise of his superior authority and power, not through logical argument. The legal system, in fact, breaks down, and arbitrary (or, rather, well-chosen) authority saves justice. This is as conservative a message in the legal arena as the "Signal Instance of English Fortitude" is in the military one.

The final anecdote also depicts right feeling triumphing over misused authority. In this story, the somewhat absentminded anatomy professor Junker, working late one night, is startled by noises issuing from his sitting room where he has stashed the corpses of two criminals while he writes up some notes late into the night. Entering the sitting room, he perceives one of the bodies sitting in a chair, following him with its eyes. Terrified, Junker drops his candle, and in the darkness rushes out of the room, pursued by the corpse. When it has cornered Junker in the bedroom, the corpse falls to its knees, and, begging like a sentimentalized Frankenstein's monster, beseeches the executioner to spare him. To this point, the unacknowledged narrator has told the story with a light-hearted ghoulishness that as much pokes fun at the professor as it does arouse the fears of its audience. Now, however, the brief tale assumes the tone of a moral fable. Moved by compassion for the escaped criminal, a deserter who inexplicably escaped execution (probably through fainting with fear) and who now pleads for help, Junker dresses him as himself and contrives his escape, while the deserter thanks him in the language of sentimental excess. Years later, on a visit to Amsterdam, Professor Junker is hosted by a rich, married, and sober merchant who reveals himself finally as the rescued deserter and proclaims: "Henceforth, look upon my house, my fortune, and myself, as at your disposal" (36). The story ends with the following sentimental tag, probably written by Mitchell himself: "Those who possess the smallest portion of sensibility, can easily represent to themselves the feelings of Junker" (36). This final line framing the marvelous tale as sentimental flatters the audience for being familiar with the wordless language of sentiment, and the feelings of gratitude and benevolence that characterize the elite. By illustrating that benevolence literally reforms or revives the cowardly, criminal, or unfortunate, this anecdote advertises the social benefits of sentiment.

In this miscellany, traditional narrative themes and forms are adapted to include sentimental ideas in order to attract a wide readership. The collection itself does not aim solely at female readers, despite the frontispiece and title, since only Mackenzie's pieces address domestic or sexual topics, and even "Sophia M--" emphasizes the penalties (an adulterous wife) incurred by philistine and inconsiderate men who do not treat their wives as they ought. The other pieces address the several realms in which men encounter authority in society: in traveling, in the military, in the courts, in academia, and in private petitions for benevolence. These tales warn readers of the hazards of these realms of society. By using the form of the marvelous tale, these stories entertain and instruct young, new, and poor readers in the sentimental ethos.

II. Presenting and Representing Sentimental Miscellanies

The popularity of these literary and moral miscellanies results partly from their packaging. Booksellers and publishers were skillful in targeting the

new audiences to which these books are addressed. Richard D. Altick
remarks that

> cheap illustrated editions of the works of standard authors, old
> as well as recent, began to multiply in the wake of a court
> decision in 1774 that, by abandoning the concept of perpetual
> copyright, threw into the public domain a large body of
> literature that certain publishers had hitherto claimed as their
> exclusive property. In addition to separate editions of single
> works and collections of individual authors, publishers brought
> out long series of pocket-sized volumes with the same con-
> tents. Their low prices, convenient formats, and illustrations
> recommended them to many middle-class readers whom the
> generally high prices of books had barred from participating
> in the steady expansion of the reading public.[17]

The forms in which this newly accessible literature appeared are also vital to
its appeal. By including many short pieces, miscellanies can be read by those
whose attention span is limited, for some reason: servants, children, the
partially educated or semi-literate.[18] Those printed in small sizes, moreover,
and reasonably priced could be carried with the reader. Size and price
contributed to the privacy of their consumption; these were pleasures to be
digested alone, in contrast to the rowdy and public amusements of Vauxhall
or the public masquerades noted in Fielding's *Amelia* or Fanny Burney's
Evelina. At the same time, they represent a means of ascending the social
ladder by supplying cribs of fashionable culture. These miscellanies testified
to the reader's morality, Puritan predilection for self-improvement, and social
gentility without demanding too much time or concentration. They provided
material proof of the reader's moral virtue beyond the pages of the books
themselves.

These miscellanies equate culture, sentiment, and class. Indeed, sentiment
serves to replace education and qualify the reader as a consumer of elite
culture. Thus, they include "high" literature in a form that evokes "penny-his-
tories" by its visual elements, editing, and introductions.[19] Woodcut
illustrations, varied typescripts, footnotes, and prefaces that contextualize the
contents as accessible, universal morality counteract the formality of the
literature itself. These miscellanies, as we have seen, also mirror the
topicality of much Augustan literature by including "fugitive" pieces, informal
or specific essays, letters, and poems, which both reflect the fashion for folk
or native literature and provide a local reference for a politically conscious

audience. Such pieces frequently echo the riddles, jokes, and jests of chapbooks. *The Merry Miscellany: or, Humourous Companion* (London, 1805), for example, proffers "Smart Repartees, Excellent Humbuggs, Pleasant Stories, Comical Quibbles" and many other short jesting genres "Collected from ... the last and present Age." Examples of such wit appear in literary and moral miscellanies from the 1750s to the end of the century. This combination of the generally true and the politically or socially specific prevails markedly in the miscellanies of Scotland where chauvinistic cultural nostalgia, a determination to mimic the French Enlightenment, a flourishing chapbook industry, and comparatively slow growth in literacy combine to provide publishers with a rich crossover audience. Literary miscellanies reprint not only poems by the Augustan and fashionable poets, but also popular or folk forms of moral maxim, verse, and fable.

While many poetic miscellanies, like Nicholson's series, include well-known pieces from the "Graveyard Poets" or from Pope, Jenyns, and Phillips, miscellanies of specifically sentimental literature do not aim at improving the literary judgment of their audience. Rather, they present fragments of feeling, small vignettes that should stimulate the reader to virtue by softening the heart with stories of heroism and pathos. Of course, the renown of their selections suggests an overlap between moral and literary merit parallel to that in poetic compendia, but readers of sentimental collections are not taught to recognize aesthetic features. Instead, they are advised to note the behavior and emotions of the characters in order to emulate virtue. Similarly, careful selections from French or German authors--particularly Voltaire and Marmontel--present vignettes of selfless civic heroism, bowdlerizing the atheistical or revolutionary hints in the plot and language into the familiar form of an heroic fable glossed with the rhetoric of rationalism. These Continental selections intended primarily for children blend neoclassical ideals with the conservative tendency in sentimentalism--its nostalgic praise of the feudal past, its privatization of action, its emphasis on individual feeling.[20] By directing the reader to ignore the style in favor of the story, these miscellanies replicate the moral procedure familiar to readers of folk and popular literature, which offers tales as exemplary rather than as stylistic spectacles. Nothing threatens convention-al morality except the privilege accorded to individual buyers to exercise it by reading.

This is not to deny, however, that "modernity," as J. H. Plumb defines it, did not also contribute to the popularity of sentimental miscellanies. Indeed, the packaging and presentation of sentimental literature in these miscellanies exemplify the way conservative messages about sexual behavior, class, social order, and conformity fuse with liberal discourse praising social mobility, current literature, and the benefits of change. "Enlightened" discourse on freedom from past errors, rationality over superstition, and new education permeates the upscale literary miscellanies. Miscellanies, moreover, exploit fashion by appealing to the eye. The popularity of this genre coincides with the invention of the jigsaw puzzle in the 1760s, an activity which requires visual skills to replicate the pattern of the external world from a pile of fragmented pictorial details rather like the patchwork fields newly created by enclosure. The child playing with a puzzle thus reorders the external world according to his recollection or point of view. The tremendous psychological and epistemological implications of this game, which is very hospitable to sentimental narrative perspective and fragmentation, reverberate in the new children's literature and the burgeoning world of visual spectacles and exhibitions designed for children, who were leading their parents in understanding new ways of looking at the outside.[21] "Raree" shows, exhibitions in which the audience peered through a peephole with background lighting to increase the effect of "realistic" perspective, grew as a popular street entertainment during the last quarter of the eighteenth century. Magic lanterns, zogroscopes, all forms of projected optical effects appeared. In the second half of the eighteenth century, moreover, the servant and middle classes not only attended popular entertainments, but also displayed their status by buying "inessential" status objects, including portraits and engravings that might well mimic the commissioned paintings for which the wealthy middle classes conceived a passion.[22] In addition, with the development of the "engraved woodcut" by Thomas Bewick, illustrations of great delicacy and detail could embellish even inexpensive texts.

These developments led to new attention to visual stimulation in the miscellanies. Partly, the illustrations and engravings reproduce the traditional emblematic woodcuts that decorate chapbooks and provide interpretative and generic clues for the barely literate. Partly, these visual details mirror the consumer desire for decoration as a symbol of class; in owning a book with engravings or elaborate woodcuts, the consumer also owns paintings. Indeed, in the late seventeenth century, in a parallel fashion, the chapbook audience would tear the illustrations from their bindings, and pin them up on the walls. The visual variety of these miscellanies is a response to new fashions and an appeal to a wide and varied audience. Most significantly for the history of sentimental literature, however, this visual detail could adumbrate the pictorialism of sentimental stylistics. Readers who possessed illustrated texts became spectators of sentiment; the presentational form of the story itself, evolved from market demands and fashion, shaped the way the story was read. Sentiment became spectacle.

The actual composition of these pictures in the miscellanies of the end of the century clearly demonstrates their social and moral function. Two essential iconographic types of picture dominate, both sentimental: the pastoral scene in which one or two figures appear in the lap of untrimmed nature; and the internal domestic scene in which a group, generally of three, appears floodlighted in the foreground and gesticulating to indicate pain, surprise or violent grief. The pastoral scenes invariably lack a frame; the engraving retreats into outlined sketches and trailing shapes disappearing into the blank page. (See Plate 7). It is the figures in conversation, or a single figure communing with grief, that attracts the eye, firmly centering meaning on human exchange within nature. The internal scenes, on the other hand, are encased in a square frame which is replicated within the pictures themselves by the borders of the room, and frequently by other frames such as those of the pictures on the walls, or of the furniture. (See Plate 6 and Frontispiece). This iconographical design mirrors the visual intertextuality of Hogarth and later of the Royal Academy. These engravings, however, lack the irony of sophisticated artistry, instead representing paintings as signs of domestic success--comfort and ownership--not as debris from the past or examples of the misguided values of conventional representation.[23] Indeed, the emblematic function of these pictures within pictures peaks in Nicholson's elaborately illustrated *Literary Miscellany* of 1812. Here, both portraits and generic illustrations of sentimental incidents within the text appear framed by an oval space, itself encased within a thick hexagonal medallion frame. By supplying both picture and frame, these illustrations, if not intended to be torn from their texts, faithfully reproduce the fashionable servant and lower middle-class forms of fine art of the turn of the century.[24] Both types contextualize sentimentalism within a cultural frame.

The engravings themselves also indicate the conservative nature of the audience and presentation. Altick notes that paintings with literary subjects came into vogue in the 1770s and 1780s, but within books themselves were quickly dominated by the abstract and idealized style from the Continent.[25] The inexpressive uniformity of these book illustrations proved very useful for the publishers of literary miscellanies. Their neoclassically rounded figures both evoke the high art of the previous fifty years and also generalize and impersonalize the characters so that the illustrations themselves signal a particular kind of literature--simple, exemplary sentimentalism. For publishers, this meant that the same basic figures or scenes could illustrate a number of sentimental tales. Nicholson, indeed, boasts of the uniqueness of his miscellany by announcing that he has commissioned specific engravings for it; in fact, these actually merely imitate the commoner ones. For the audience, it meant that the tale could appeal to children, with the unsexualized figures

Plate 7: Title page to Sterne's *Sentimental Journey Through France and Italy*, 1798. Courtesy of the Lewis Walpole Library, Farmington, Ct.

representing prototypical youth, as well as to those ambitious to mimic the good taste of the gentility. Furthermore, such generic illustrations warned the reader of the nature of the literary material and prodded his or her response. The similarity of the illustrations advertised the predictability of the contents: in method and moral, these tales replicated all the others identically illustrated.

These illustrations do express the central values of sentimental literature. They not only replicate the classic postures of, for example, the *pieta*, but they also indicate emotion by gesture rather than by expression. This, of course, was typical of theatrical acting at the time; moreover, book illustrations themselves began as illustrations and advertisements for plays.[26] This technique, however, strongly characterizes sentimental literature, in which the body expresses the "language" of emotion and thus makes visible to the spectator the concealed processes of feeling. The figures in these illustrations of sentimental scenes, furthermore, do not indicate by their particular dress or postures any specific incident, nor any delicate or unusual emotion; they serve rather to counteract the particularity of the text with general representations of the emotion or situation. Like pictorial rhetoric, they identify the specific incident with a universal trope. When pictorial details do occur, they generally record the surroundings, especially household interiors, faithfully replicating the possessions of the distraught characters. As the figures' stylized gestures evoke the visual displays in the theater or paintings with which the audience might be familiar, so the detailed background represents the audience's immediate surroundings, the urban home for in-servants or middle classes. Once again, the familiar context is emphasized.

Full-length pictures are not the only form of pictorial illustration: woodcut emblems also clue the reader visually to the nature of the literary material. Celtic lyres indicate lyric poetry, so common an emblem that when George Nicholson commissioned a new emblem, his engraver W. Craik virtually replicated the standard design, with a few more wafting ribbons and leaves. A funerary urn indicates a sentimental tale in prose in almost all miscellanies; it is particularly interesting as a symbol of perhaps moribund, classical culture, associated with "classic"--even "classy"--texts. Other emblems indicate very loosely the nature of the literary piece they accompany: a young boy's head suggests a moral lesson, a drooping daisy implies a love story, a flowery garland indicates a marriage, or a happy ending. These emblems appear generally to fill up the empty space at the end of a page, and they are not always correctly correlated with the story; in the more elaborate miscellanies, they head the print. The simplicity and uniformity of these emblems, and the laxity with which they are applied, again mirror the practices of chapbook printers who would fill up a page by stamping on it standard cows or dogs. They provide a context and a clue to the interpretation of the story for the reader.

In addition to illustrations, these miscellanies excite the eye of their audiences with the available variety of typescripts. These also advertise the nature of their literary contents. Elaborately cursive titles, for example, mimic ladies' delicate handwriting and reflect Henry Mackenzie's observation that women had to write in "a sort of long-shaped, hair-stroke hand; it was deemed masculine to write any other."[27] By representing an informal penstroke, the publishers of these miscellanies evoke the familiar, authentic, and interior world of female epistolary novels. So many of these novels are concerned with etiquette and the manners and morals suitable for one rising in society that the script with its connotations becomes virtually synonymous with moral literature on conduct. Thus, the feminine script would attract a socially ambitious audience, as well as a female one, although only Fanny Burney's *Cecilia* appears excerpted with any regularity from the panoply of female novels from the 1770s to the turn of the century.

Other scripts counterbalance the female one, including block capitals shaded into three dimensions to suggest classic permanence. Leigh Hunt's *Classic Tales* (1806) emphasizes its title still further by adding pillars and pediment to the title page. These multifarious scripts represent visually the multifarious contents of the miscellany and balance the formality of "classics" with the informality and privacy of women's tales. Most importantly, they help to condition readers to expect nothing new or unconventional from their books.

Just as the iconographic engravings evoke familiar religious and moralistic symbols and scenes, so the size of the miscellany signals its intention. These miscellanies do vary in size. Those designed for men of the upper end of the social spectrum appear in the more expensive quarto, large octavo, or folio size. Most literary miscellanies, however, come out in small octavo or duodecimo, suitable for a pocket or reticule. This small size reflects both the political tendency of the sentimental tales within and the ideology of the audience beyond. These are collections designed to educate the social response of the reader, yet to be consumed in private. Unlike the splashy and expensively bound volumes on the library shelves of the gentry, these miscellanies could provide individual and private instruction wheresoever the owner was compelled to go, even if she had no club in which to read. This size also achieves three connected and significant effects: it emphasizes the private, almost secret, way in which these stories should be read, and it defines the scope and nature of their didactic message, and it serves to train readers rapidly and privately in social response. The size consequently blunts any public or advertised class association; and it imitates "little books for little people"--the elf-sized books for children, which are still produced today. In *Small Books and Pleasant Histories*, Margaret Spufford observes that seventeenth-century schoolboys, hungry for chivalric tales and laden with pocket-money sufficient to buy the tuppenny histories, mediate between high and popular culture as their books provide a basic literary background for both audiences. The market was especially large for "Tales," whose morality was claimed as a sop to convention.[28] This is also true for the literary miscellanies of the eighteenth century.

This association between children's literature and sentimental vignettes becomes more and more important in controlling and trivializing the political and social threats of sentimental literature. As the inheritors of modernity, children could lead their ambitious parents up the social ladder through their literature. Many of these miscellanies thus blend signals aimed at children with those attractive to the parents who bought their books.[29] The chapbook size equates children, women, and the under-educated classes, all of whom, sentimental philosophy claims, react with spontaneous sympathy yet lack the worldly wisdom for self-guidance.[30] The resemblance to chapbooks also underscores, or advertises, the morality of sentimentalism; these miscellanies replace older forms of didactic literature to control and educate the audience. Spufford notes the wide appeal of the chapbooks of the seventeenth century, which included audiences "from merchants down to apprentices in towns, from yeomen to in-servants in the countryside."[31] Similarly, the miscellanies of the eighteenth century include topics, forms, and illustrations that borrow from chapbook, folk, and "high" cultural traditions to broaden their appeal and to translate the material of high culture into fare for less well-educated audiences.

Number 60 of the weekly periodical *The Lounger*, published on Saturday, 25 March 1786, provides a suggestive definition of these miscellanies, their audience, and their status in the literary world. Appearing at a time in Scotland when the growth of literacy and of the printing industry seemed to threaten the patronage of the arts and the stability of class divisions, *The Lounger*, as the organ for that select group of Edinburgh lawyers to which Mackenzie belonged, voiced the aesthetic, social, and literary preferences of Edinburgh's in-group as the high era of sentimentalism began to draw to a close.[32] Despite its polyglot intentions, the periodical focuses on the topic of sensibility; it sandwiches Addisonian character sketches and sentimental tales between essays warning women of the dangers of sentiment and adjuring them to correct their tempers, habits, reading, and education. It is in this context that Number 60 appears.

Although we cannot know certainly, it seems very possible that the author of Number 60 was the Scottish publisher and printer William Creech, contributor to both *The Lounger* and *The Mirror*, friend of the Edinburgh Moderates, author of a sociological analysis on Edinburgh, and publisher of his own miscellany, *Edinburgh Fugitive Pieces*.[33] It would take someone who knew both the taste of the town in sentimental literature and the prejudices of the literati to compose so sophisticated and topical a satire on miscellanies; Creech's own miscellany, furthermore, includes numerous satires on women and modern culture. By speaking as an old-fashioned literary opportunist who has caught the wave of sentimentalism, Creech here voices the fashionable sneer against "wise men," the cold-blooded rationalists of the previous generation, while simultaneously condemning those who exploit sentimentalism for cheap ends. In the tradition of Enlightenment moderation, his ironic persona thus serves to mock both extremes: the old fogies and the new jackals.

Entitled "Scheme of a literary projector for a new sort of periodical publication," this essay comprises a brief satire imitating Swift's "Modest Proposal." The literary projector's proposed publication turns out to be a "Miscellany" with the apparently unique feature of catering exclusively to women: female subscribers, contributors, and topics only would be permitted. We learn that the monomaniacal speaker is qualified for his task from his previous accomplishments in politics, criticism, and "treatises":

> Another performance of mine is an Essay deducing the degeneracy of present manners from electricity and the feudal system. The one I consider as the first or primary, the other as the promoting and assisting cause. From the latter proceeds the subordination of ranks, and from the former that inundation of feeling which was formerly confined to children, and fine ladies like children, but has now deluged the army, the navy, ministers of state, shoe-blacks, and footmen. (235)

Like Scriblerus, the speaker is expert in science, history, and social observation. Like Swift's Modest Proposer, he offers mechanical solutions to modern problems: taxes that benefit the state but burden the people; a formula to remedy the superiority of the ancients, with their three epics, over the moderns, with none; and here an impersonal, inorganic, and absolute cause for behavior that blames the influence of the corrupt past.[34] While his language echoes the pretentious objectivity of natural philosophers, he also conflates two clichés: condemnation of the decay of modern manners and condemnation of "that inundation of feeling" that indicates childlike or uncorrupted sensibility. By a reference to Swift, we readers are warned that this unreliable speaker caricatures disapproved, modern attitudes of mechanical, antihumanistic calculation through the device of ironic reversal; therefore, if he condemns modern manners, we approve them, and if he scorns feeling, we indulge it. This seems simply another way of selling sentimentalism.

Like Swift's irony, however--indeed, like all irony--the reversal is not without ambiguity. The scorn for women and the association between the degeneracy of modern manners and the prominence of female values leaps from the text when this clownish speaker announces his aim to begin a miscellany designed for women. He defends his design by explaining what model he means to follow: "My hopes of success are founded on the wonderful avidity with which mankind receive weekly and monthly Miscellanies. These are generally good things, translated from the French, copied out of old authors, or altogether new and original, the production of modern writers" (235-36). This is, perhaps, the best short description we have of the nature of the collections, or miscellanies, so popular in the last decades of the eighteenth century. Like periodicals, they appear regularly, feature borrowed or stolen pieces, as well as new ones, and appeal to an audience who has not read the original "old" or French authors. "Good things" comprise short works of literary talent, moral merit, or both.

This ambiguity between aesthetic and ethical standards reflects the confusion of the audience emulating sophisticated discourse. Obviously, this audience hungers for works that smack of high-class sophistication, be this classical, Continental, or fashionable. What matters is not the worth of content but the prestige of the source. When this speaker remarks the "wonderful avidity" with which the audience gobbles up these collections, he implies that their greed for sensation, like a sweet tooth, spoils their appetite for substantial literature and ruins their taste. As a pimp of literary prostitution, the speaker advertises the merits of his project. The sustained innuendo identifying editorship with seduction establishes the central theme and trope of the essay: publishing women's writing is prostituting them. He writes,

> My plan is entirely new. I wish to be director in a work of this kind [a miscellany], more adapted than any thing that has yet been published, for the improvement of the *fair sex*. On no account will I admit any but female subscribers; and, excepting in some of the departments wherein I must toil myself, I will admit of none but female writers: For I incline

> to have this work altogether perfect, classical, and feminine. I
> consider this as the winding up of a long life; and I shall
> certainly lie down in my grave in more peace, reflecting that
> I have added to the republic of letters one half of the human
> species, whom our foolish prejudices have hitherto in a great
> measure excluded. (236)

Like Swift's speaker, our literary projector stands to gain something from
his idea, despite his asseverations to the contrary: following the fashionable
trend, he will make money by catering to women, or even through women.
He feeds their desires, becoming effeminized, as the literary culture that
panders to female will is effeminized.[35]

To subvert the speaker's degeneracy, the author, Creech, conveys irony
through the classical rhetorical devices of zeugma, allusion, and pun. Such
techniques, of course, rely on the sophisticated literary education of an
audience unlikely to buy such miscellanies in place of organs such as *The
Lounger*, an audience allied to classical values. This same audience, however,
was reading in the periodicals that women should be "classically" educated
rather than trained in fashionable talents that fostered displays of singing,
needlework, and so on. In projecting a work "altogether perfect, classical, and
feminine," the speaker thus teases his audience by yoking categories that are,
if not mutually contradictory, at least conventionally opposed; in this context
particularly, where women, denied their place in the "republic of letters,"
finally may publish modern works, "feminine" and "classical" stand in direct
conflict. Uncertainties of class identity are translated into sexual jokes.

The moral claims of sentimental miscellanies are also mocked. The
phrase "the improvement of the *fair sex*" (his italics) conceals both a prurient
and a political *double-entendre* since the term "improvement" at this period
signalled the ambitions of the nouveau riche to beautify and modernize the
estates they have purchased from the old gentry by replanting, relandscaping,
rebuilding, and redecorating. It is a code word for commercial aesthetics.
"Improvement," however, is also associated with revolutionary politics,
Jacobin hopes for reforms in education and society.[36] This innuendo on class
echoes the innuendo on sex: women who have been "improved" have been
educated by morally lax, modern standards; if "improved" by the speaker,
then "educated" sexually by him. The speaker's indiscriminate publication of
women's works, furthermore, parallels his indiscriminate enjoyment of their
sexual charms. He will "wind up a long life" by "lying down." This link
between education and sex resurfaces obsessively in the periodical essays of
the 1780s, and hence appears in the literary miscellanies of the period.[37]

When this speaker marries his "project" with the moral intention of redressing sexual inequality and restoring "one half of the human species, whom our foolish prejudices have hitherto ... excluded" to "the republic of letters," he anticipates the very words of Mary Wollstonecraft's *Vindication of the Rights of Woman* (1792) with the political echo of her *Vindication of the Rights of Man* (1790). The speaker here adopts the language of late eighteenth-century radical feminism, reviled by the conservative literati of Scotland. Creech, the author, ridicules such language by juxtaposing it with the language of sexual innuendo, publicized in the sentimental works of Laurence Sterne; the phrase "some departments wherein I must toil myself" particularly echoes Sterne's sermon the day after his wedding, a gloss on the verse from St. John.[38] Thus, the stylistic conventions of both classical and sentimental literature, apparent to an audience educated in neoclassical poetry and modern fiction, oppose the language and values of revolutionary theory. This miscellany for women epitomizes the subversive ideas of women's education and publication, of political republicanism, and of commercial art.

The interplay between sex and writing resurfaces in the final passage of the satire. The speaker explains that the last, "largest and most useful," segment in his miscellany will present "Freethinking," a religion he advocates for women and that, from the middle of the century, had been virtually synonymous with "free sex."[39] He concludes with a promise to include in each edition an engraving of a woman who has distinguished herself by behavior or writing. Not only does such a "free gift" satirize the literary miscellanies that advertise their engravings rather than their literary judgment as inducements to the purchaser, but it also slurs the motivation for women's writing. Under the aegis of the "sisterhood of the arts," these promised engravings emphasize the vanity of women writers and the self-display of writing. The reader of this periodical essay might well remember Lely's "Court Beauties" series and the tradition of painting women whose behavior with famous men had led to such "distinction." In this case, moreover, it is not the literary subject but the literary author who would be depicted: not the story but the writer. This projector's objectification of the female author echoes his earlier assurances that "similar assistance will be given to the artists of the female figure, and the inventors of female decoration" (239). Women authors thus become art objects, themselves the subjects of art instead of the creators of it. This is the same theme variously treated by Eliza Haywood and Frances Brooke. With a pun derived directly from Sterne, the speaker finally signs himself "Projector Literarius," in case we have neglected to "project" the meaning of the text, or to identify his literary projection. This satire suggests not only that the publication, the making public, of women's sensibility equals their prostitution, but also that the process by which their sensibility is published is itself prostitution.

In advocating this literary project, our unreliable speaker has exposed the danger of leaving literature in the hands of the uneducated projectors. This view implicitly reiterates the complaint of Pope, Swift, and the Scriblerus Club and the worries of Goldsmith, Henry Brooke, and Sterne: that literature, as a moral commentary on society, should be practiced only by the moral few--by "men of taste." Tasteless men, like our speaker, or women might turn sensibility into sex, inner feeling into feeling others. Especially since both publishers and women are mediators of culture, producing imitations and counterfeits, they symbolize the loss of the "genuine" in an age of replications.[40] The "degeneracy of modern manners" represented by the degenerate Projector also results here from the flattery of women, which stimulates the Projector's entire project. Flattery of women accords with freethinking, he insinuates, and helps to castrate culture.

The apparent corruption of taste exemplified by the literary miscellanies that Creech attacks becomes still clearer as the projector outlines his six sections of contents. First, the projector includes "Foreign Intelligence," that is scandal, interspersed with travelogues describing exotic marriage ceremonies. This ridicules "female politics," the power mongering of women obsessed with sex and marriage, which in this corruptly feminized culture replace the "true" politics of the man's world, as the battles and negotiations of Belinda's cardtable parody those of the court in Pope's *Rape of the Lock*-- a very popular text in the miscellanies of the early century. Secondly, he proposes a section on "Sketches and Interesting Anecdotes of private characters, with the Tea-table conversations, and the Fashions of the principle towns in Great Britain," including a "Dictionary" of French phrases and recent cant, and plates like those in architectural manuals, displaying "Fronts," "Backfronts," "Arches and Abutments," "designs for Frizes, Stucco-Cornices, and Pilasters" (237-38). While mocking the claim of indiscriminate miscellanies that gossip and fashion constitute "literature," this passage also condemns the substitution of "private" revelations for public information. Intimate, personal, and specific "Anecdotes of private characters" here replace the impersonal, scientific sketches of foreign countries, customs, and coastlines so popular at the end of the century. This glorification of "feminine" knowledge is conveyed through concrete metaphor by the puns on the female body, a body that mirrors--or rather supplants--both the civilized structures of men, and the accounts of external, physical nature.

The third section offers the efforts of "Female Essayists": "little affecting histories, to animate the female world to virtuous and worthy deeds" (239).

These, like those already published, he adds, would include both the bad and the good consequences of action since only by witnessing both can a woman decide how to act (239). By reiterating sentimental jargon with its emphasis on fictional example over stern precept, Creech indicts both the banality and the insincerity of the moral pretensions of female literature. His spurious explanation highlights what was considered the moral ambiguity of such tales, indeed of sentimental literature itself, by hinting that they arouse feeling by exploitative scenes of sexual ruin and deceit; this innuendo echoes the familiar outcry against novels for "inflaming" the rebellious passions of young women. It is for this reason, the projector implies, that sentimentalism appeals to women and that he is promoting it. The projector underscores his commitment to the feminine side of culture by explaining that his fourth section, "Critical Review of Books," would not evaluate philosophy, belles-lettres, or history, since he dares not encroach on this "male property" (239). Presumably, such topics disregard sex, seen here as the defining feature of female reality. While men "own" history, philosophy, and fine writing, women's "property" is "Novels, Plays, and Soft Poetry," which he would tacitly critique by means of extracts, rather than commentary, while devoting his fifth section perforce "to the Female Muse" of poetry as required by the form of the miscellany (239). Women, one can infer, do not evaluate, but instead experience literature.

By encapsulating in the literary miscellany the infamous triad of the feminine, the sentimental, and the modern, Creech implies that the very form of the miscellany reflects the sins of decadent culture. The ability of the publishers to extract representative pieces demonstrates that the literary works are neither written nor read as sustained, whole, and organic forms the way Swift, for example, as a humanist would have preferred. It is the middlemen, furthermore, who determine the form of this literature, rather than the artists, so that production--or reproduction--edges out creation. By tossing together "fugitive" pieces, essays from the periodical journals, sections of novels, and patches of verse, miscellanies violate literary decorum and the hierarchy of literary merit so bitterly defended by Pope. In fact, Creech's satire on literary miscellanies recapitulates the old battleground of the ancients versus the moderns: those whose works represent and improve the whole person, as opposed to those that cut and hack and address little bits of the person with little bits of fragmented knowledge. Further satire of the quality of the poetry included in these miscellanies grows into indictment of the quality of all its literature and spills over into derision of the literary taste of women as a whole, the literary taste for women, in fact the literary taste promoted by female writing. Finally, the disorder or lack of hierarchy of the miscellany evokes the leveling tendency of republican politics, actually articulated in several prefaces. Thus, modern taste, feminine values, and the

political implications of sentimentalism coalesce in the form of the literary
miscellany.

Creech's parody sketches not only the form and contents of the literary
miscellanies of the time, but also the political, social, and sexual composition
of their audience, and their status in the world of letters. These miscellanies
offer the ambitious middle classes, women, and those not educated in the
classics the chance to catch up: they are the *Reader's Digest* of the 1780s.
As the parody further demonstrates, women, the middle classes, and
freethinking merchants roused the hostility of the more traditionally educated
classes by usurping with their modern standards the old province of the
gentry. A vital and ubiquitous element in these miscellanies is sentimental
literature. This literature, juxtaposed with "the classics," advertised as
"classic" itself, and popularized in these collections, both flattered the
"uncultured" and satisfied their appetite for culture. Their audience was the
social upstart.

Creech thus exposes the contradictions faced by these well-born, male
sentimentalists in the two related areas of morality and audience. On the one
hand, these men advocate an instinctive, universal, and natural virtue
exemplified by private, untutored female sensibility; on the other hand, they
desire to protect and preserve their province of high art, written by and for
men of taste. They fear that female sensibility made public and flattered by
their art might induce female immorality if it were still untutored in self-
discipline. Thus, instinctive virtue for men translates as Christian behavior:
the love of others, preservation of the laws of God, and adherence to the
golden rule of doing unto others as you would have them do to you--whereas
for women, it translates bluntly as chastity. Women can represent the ideal
of sentimentalism, but they must not practice it.[41]

Parallel to this paradox is the confusion for the sentimentalists about the
audience. A philosophy advocating the merit of uneducated and instinctive
responses and criticizing the old writers, narrated plainly without classical
references or convoluted syntax, and sold in cheap editions or periodicals will
clearly appeal to an uneducated audience, especially an audience sensitive to
current fads in literary taste. This audience comprises women of all classes
who could read, since their "instinctive" nature seems specifically lauded; the
socially ambitious middle classes, to whom literature represents culture; and
the poor, literate classes who could afford for entertainment only these slim
miscellanies, with their anecdotes, engravings, and exotic travel tales. Yet
the high-born sentimentalists of the Scottish Enlightenment conceived of art
as the touchstone of class; they wrote for their own class, not for an
indiscriminate and undiscriminating audience. Their contempt, or hostility,

to their own public thus conflicts with their advocacy of universal good nature. Publishers had no such qualms. In their cheaper literary miscellanies, they combine "high" and popular art by using a plenitude of visual signals, mediating prefatory discourses, and a myriad of contents. Moreover, by reproducing sentimental vignettes in volumes prefaced by moral dicta, publishers provided a social context for the sentimental tale. Through miscellanies, literary sentimentalism finds a new form that bridges high and popular literary culture.

CHAPTER 7

Fighting Feeling in Gothic Sentimentalism:
The Romance of the Forest and *The Mysteries of Udolpho*

> The character of Phillipe has already been delin-
> eated in his actions; its nicer shades were blended
> with some shining tints; but these served only to
> render more striking by contrast the general
> darkness of the portrait.
>
> *The Romance of the Forest*

After the French Revolution at the end of the eighteenth century, literary sentimentalism appeared in another form that encased the post-revolutionary conservatism seen in sentimental miscellanies within sentimental stylistics: the Gothic novel. Like the sentimental fictions written before the French Revolution, these tales emphasize feeling over plot, but the feelings represented by Gothic novels include something different from sympathy and benevolence. Violence, remorse, and madness, drawn as social dangers, rather than as futile responses to oppression, counterpoint the soft feelings of melancholy borrowed from sentimental novels. While such stories as *The Man of Feeling* sacrifice causal plot to the portrait of fine, if unreal, feeling in an implied argument, novels such as Horace Walpole's early *Castle of Otranto* (1764) or Ann Radcliffe's works contextualize the immediate scenes of sensation within the causal framework of a tortuous, labyrinthine plot. Ann Radcliffe, indeed, resurrects the formula Henry Fielding followed almost half a century earlier by making her plots, obscure as they are, the vehicles of an intellectual and moral logic that pulls against the "quick fix" offered by emotive scenes. Sentimental, or sensational, stylistics thus once again work against the ideological structure of the story.[1]

Until recently, Ann Radcliffe's novels have been considered not only formally, but also aesthetically "horrid." In her Gothic parody *Northanger Abbey* (1796), Jane Austen mocks the improbable plot and simplistic characters of Radcliffe's *Mysteries of Udolpho*, particularly indicting readers like Catherine Morland who signally fail to learn the lessons of clear-sighted self-control proposed by the plot. Later readers from Coleridge to Elizabeth Napier, whose *Failure of Gothic* appeared in 1987, have winced at Radcliffe's device of the "explained supernatural," in Sir Walter Scott's words.[2] What puzzles these critics is the contradiction between Radcliffe's ostensible neoclassical ideology lauding reason, caution, and control, and her practice of describing the vacillations of doubt, fancy, and fear.[3] This contradiction, however, does not reveal a weakness in Radcliffe's technique; rather, it is itself Radcliffe's technique for managing what Daniel Cottom calls "an aesthetics in transition" bridging opposing ideologies.[4] Radcliffe exploits this contradiction with a narrative style reveling in a medley of modes, from poetry to exegesis, and shifting between logical and pictorial language. In this, she creates a form of Gothic fiction informed by sentimental stylistics: a fiction that pictures feeling as spectacle. The disjunctive styles and structures of *The Romance of the Forest* (1791) and *The Mysteries of Udolpho* (1794), the two of Radcliffe's most popular novels that include poetry extensively, aestheticize emotional reactions with the discourse of spectatorship while they also exhibit control of sentimental excess.

Radcliffe's characters themselves express the dialectic of literary sentimentalism, which indulges and criticizes feeling. While they embody sentimental clichés, they can also mock these clichés. Her loyal but weak-minded servants--the well-meaning but stupid Peter in *Romance of the Forest*, Annette, Margaret, Dorothée, and Theresa in *Udolpho*--find meaning and fulfill their natures in serving their aristocratic masters and mistresses. Still, Theresa satirizes the "fine feeling" and scruples of the heroine, her erstwhile mistress Emily, by noting "how gentlefolks can afford to throw away their happiness!"[5] By countering the patronizing view of the servant classes' indelicate pragmatism, uttered by both the heroine and the narrative voice, this comment criticizes the pretensions of sentimentalism, which ignores the business of survival to luxuriate in feeling. Peter more subtly scoffs at Adeline's idealism when he retorts in face of her exotic fears of being pursued, "Lord bless you, that is all a fudge, to frighten you; your father, *nor nobody* else has ever sent after you; I dare say, he knows no more of you than the Pope does--not he."[6] Using the homely colloquialism "fudge," Peter brushes away the fantasies of protection and power shared by Adeline and the narrative, fantasies that make the heroine important: Father, Pope, nobody--they are all the same because they are all absent. Adeline, consequently, is alone and unimportant. Throughout the novel, her feelings enforce her isolation. While these feelings mark her as a sentimental heroine, the novel conjures only an absent society to recognize this heroism.

Radcliffe also criticizes fine feeling through her Shakespearean character types, exemplified by Vivaldi's devoted servant Paulo in *The Italian* (1797). His complacent, long-winded stories, like Peter's, Dorothée's, and Margaret's, parody particularizing discourse, like that of novels, which sets the self at the center of meaning and laboriously traces every feeling and thought. By comically exhibiting bad--or absent--social training and sentimental self-importance, these servants' conversations ironically reproach both the heroes and reader for a preoccupation with plot; they remind us of the importance of good manners and self-restraint.

Characters from the other side of the class barrier also exhibit the failures of sentimental idealism. Despite his stance of impartial distance, which should ensure his power and compassion, the enlightened Count de Villefort in *Udolpho* fails to persuade his servants through reason and resorts instead to violent compulsion to combat their superstition and to retain control of his chateau. Radcliffe's attractive villains also portray the hazards of extraordinary talents and passions unrestrained by social values. Both Montoni and Montalt, whose names, alluding to "Mont," connote elevated status and leaping ambition, flush and storm without self-control, driven by mysteriously individual feelings.[7] Indeed, in *Udolpho*, the fevered Montoni mirrors the undisciplined hero Valancourt; both men's very talents threaten them when undisciplined by social duty, and both, being men, lack this discipline. Radcliffe thus modifies the proto-Romantic implications of sentimental ideology. Nature alone does not guarantee virtue. As the sentimental man is vulnerable to the perversions of society despite his goodness, so the remarkable hero requires self-restraint since, even within the self, power entails perversion. The social hierarchy should provide a structure that enforces this restraint, as the mental hierarchy of reason over feeling similarly should structure the personality. Radcliffe suggests, however, that power actually corrupts the personality, and that men, aristocrats of either sex, and rulers all abuse those beneath them.

Radcliffe's novels nevertheless veil these criticisms of the marriage of sentimental values with the social hierarchy. Her stereotyping of characters overlays her radical implications to emphasize unquestioned, familiar traits; similarities between hero and villain fade as the narrative discourse and the heroine's reactions underscore their dissimilarity. The plot argues that as the head should rule the heart, so the aristocracy must rule the servants who, as lower parts of the social body, correspondingly lack "heads." Similarly, Radcliffe's heroines voice radical notions yet return to a paternalistic order that preserves inheritance. Feminist critics have argued that Radcliffe values the emotion and imagination associated with femininity, while protesting the constraints of women, symbolized by her heroines' physical confinements and social submission to tyrannical parental figures.[8] Such protests, however, are countered by Radcliffe's reiteration of the discourse of female submission. In *Udolpho*, Montoni's blanket categorization of the virtues of a woman as "sincerity, uniformity of conduct and obedience" signals his tyrannical evil, his abuse of natural authority, and his upbringing in a superstitious, savage, and unenlightened tradition. Nevertheless, Emily agrees with this evaluation of "whatever is beautiful in the female character" (270). Moreover, she deliberately eschews what Montoni considers "contemptible foibles" in femininity: "avarice and the love of power, which latter makes women delight to contradict and to tease, when they cannot conquer" (380). These qualities indeed mark Madame Montoni (erstwhile Cheron), Emily's aunt and the prototype of Pope's maxim that "most Women have no Characters at all" (*Epistle to a Lady* [1735]). The narrative discusses her in the very language of neoclassical, antifeminist satire, excoriating her "vanity" and lust for power, considered an unnatural appetite fed by her possession of her own estates. These estates, it is important to note, fall into Emily's hands, and thence directly to Valancourt; Emily, indeed, expressly desires them only in order to return them to male hands. Montoni's speech, moreover, reinforces the overt moral lesson of *Udolpho*: the exercise of reason over passion, of intellect and self-control over force.

Radcliffe's plots also play with the subversive possibilities of incest, female dominance, and social disruption within a plot that finally reasserts the continuity of a stable social order. The problems in *The Romance of the Forest* arise from lack of self-control and of aristocratic distance: La Motte's weakness, the Marquis de Montalt's jealousy. This lack of suitable fathers to direct Adeline frees her to model correct self-restraint and reasoned behavior. Radcliffe here challenges the very notion of paternalism since, having internalized the rules of correct behavior, Adeline clearly needs no guidance. Nevertheless, the representation of self-contained virtue through the heroine appears within a plot that formally supports paternalistic and traditional authority. Adeline, apparently abandoned by her real father, betrayed by her father-substitute La Motte, and nearly raped and murdered by her false father the Marquis, resumes the position of privileged subordinate by pleading with the political father, the King, to pardon La Motte. Rather than crediting women with the power to challenge paternal authority, the weight of this discourse criticizes the abuse of the rightful authority of the father. On the one hand, Adeline regains her inheritance through her business acuity and through her public testimony; on the other hand, the fact that she is forced to appear in public is shown to be symptomatic of the corruption of society. While the plot demonstrates the objectivity of the law over corruptible society, Adeline still depends on the King's personal power to pardon her virtuous lover Theodore. Her new father thus controls her marriage.

In *Udolpho*, Emily's substitute father, the Count de Villefort, attempts to abuse his power by persuading Emily to marry Du Pont, an unimpeachable but unfavored suitor. He oversteps his authority by denying Emily her traditional right to refuse a suitor, yet Emily accords him his traditional right to prevent her marrying her own choice, Valancourt. Whereas Radcliffe's passionate heroes and heroines (even the villain Schedoni in *The Italian*, who wins our sympathy) foreshadow a proto-Romantic fascination with individual passion and an apparently revolutionary association of the order of society with violence and with sexual and social injustice, her formal character contrasts, narrative values, and plot resolutions argue her conservative dedication to the Enlightenment ideals of rationality and balance, self-control and order.

Radcliffe's plotted resolutions, like her explained supernatural effects, are almost irrelevant, however, to the real structure of the novels, even though these resolutions and explanations do indeed reflect the ideology of fiction at the end of the eighteenth century. It is not in the eventual triumph of good over evil after persistent struggle that the moral force of Radcliffe's novels lies. Rather, it is in the repeated vignettes, the mirrored scenes, the replicated postures. As sentimental miscellanies show, readers of sentimental literature "dip and skip" through long works for emotional "effects." By fragmenting the story with numberless stilled views, interchangeable characters, and elaborate narrative descriptions, Radcliffe's novels replace causality with effect. It is not the reward of virtue but the management of impressions of the moment that Radcliffe explores.

Her treatment of the theme of observation expresses Radcliffe's conservative values by conjuring a social context by which to judge all feeling and action. Throughout her work, Radcliffe contrasts ways of seeing the world and the self to recommend the disciplined observation of nature as art. One of the consequences of disobeying society's dictates in Radcliffe's work is madness, personal and social dislocation. As Michel Foucault has explored in *Madness and Civilization*, madness in the late eighteenth century is often signified by alienation from the immediate, idleness, and self-absorption.[9] Radcliffe's heroines' preoccupation with the unseen and therefore the socially irrelevant verges on madness, and it is countered, like criminalized madness, by surveillance. This surveillance is enacted both by the narrative language of spectatorship, which identifies the reader as a social guardian, and by the religious concept of divine, or paternal, supervision. These forms of surveillance reinterpret individual "visions" according to conventional categories of spiritual or social experience. After Emily's father St. Aubert dies in *Udolpho*, Emily comforts herself with the conviction that, although she cannot see him, he can still see her. Her father becomes *the* Father.[10] As a heroine, moreover, Emily models for the reader an ideal internalization of the all-seeing authority. God also watches the heroine, but he does not watch over her so she must guard herself. She watches herself. The disorderly and abandoned scenes in the castle at Udolpho--dark, confused, bloody, irrational--testify that God's surveillance does not redeem her from hell or protect her from injustice. Indeed, it is precisely her own behavior monitored by her father's principles that will help her to avoid or to endure the pains of existence.

Emily, moreover, is at risk of madness when she sees in nature only her own emotions and preoccupations. Seeing nature as a mirror, she loses sight of the difference between herself and other. It is the ability to distinguish--in scenery, in morality, in taste--that ensures both sanity, the control of nature, and power, the control of art. Surveillance throughout Radcliffe's work--the hidden Du Pont warning Montoni from the walls and watching Emily in the fishinghouse, the bands of soldiers spying on travellers and castle inmates--underscores the function of looking as a form of control. When Valancourt slips through the surveillance of his family and Emily, the same surveillance that marked his exemplary behavior at the formal dinner when Emily gets jealous, he falls into bad company and bad habits; he is unable to preserve social decorum alone. Indeed, the mad nun Agnes, who wanders mentally and physically, reinforces the necessity for social control implied throughout the novel and models the confusion that solipsism entails. Her divinely foolish song spins out social meanings into nonsense as she transforms from an angel of warning whose example Emily should avoid to a mere mad woman whose sordid death reveals the ugliness of both her social rebellion and her uncontrolled sensibility. Speaking no intelligible language except her mad melancholy music, she lives in an asylum--the convent--and torments herself with conviction of sin and exaggerated remorse. She exemplifies the insanity, which Foucault defines, that identifies itself as aberrant: "the madman, as a human being originally endowed with reason, is no longer guilty of being mad; but the madman, as a madman, and in the interior of that disease of which he is no longer guilty, must feel morally responsible for everything within him that may disturb morality and society, and must hold no one but himself responsible for the punishment he receives."[11] Agnes, as a version of what Emily might become, models the madness of unsupervised feeling. Emily, indeed, touches the edges of Agnes's madness. She herself undergoes a version of Agnes's guilt, when through absence of mind, she catches sight of some words of her father's papers, which she swore to burn without reading. Her loss of self-control when out of the sight of her father torments her throughout the novel with pain about her own identity: she creates her own doubt. Even while applauding female self-determination, Radcliffe warns readers against pursuing forbidden knowledge; even while linking sensibility and madness, she praises her heroines' fine feeling.

While theme, character, and plot in Radcliffe's novels both challenge and endorse conservative social ideas, Radcliffe's style powerfully voices, yet simultaneously muffles, contrary ideologies. This style shifts among several different modes: verse, homily, quotation, description, analysis, narrative. With pictorial language, Radcliffe figures nature as art and provides a structure for feeling. Her descriptions of tumultuous rivers, lofty peaks, and craggy depths are blueprints of Burke's theory of the sublime, and her plots similarly abruptly contrast happiness and disaster, heights and depths, light and dark, good and evil.[12] Her quoted and original poetry recounts solitary adventures or uncertain impressions. At the same time, however, her narrative contrasts the implications of these languages of aesthetic impression with the language of neoclassical rationalism, emphasizing progression, causality, logic, and restraint. In place of the individual experience celebrated in verse, the narrative voice invokes universal categories and standards. This medley of modes allows Radcliffe to hedge her praise of feeling within a frame of traditional social values.

Radcliffe's narrative voice refers constantly to an implied, absolute reality that observers can only approximate. She interlaces her descriptions with "perhaps," "probably," and "possibly," terms that discriminate levels of certainty in rational language. Radcliffe's narrative also provides multiple causes and analyses for behavior. In *Udolpho*, for example, the narrative records that St. Aubert married a woman who "perceived, or thought she perceived, that happiness and splendour were not the same, and ... did not hesitate to forego the last for the attainment of the former" (11). The narrative qualification of "or thought she perceived" emphasizes the uncertainty of self-knowledge, countering the apparent praise of disinterest with a chary note of warning against high flights of romantic prejudice. It also echoes the ironic detachment of a narrator like Fielding's who implies that he or she could say more were the reader to ask. Again, the phrase describing Madame Quesnel's actions as arising from "a wish, probably, of exciting envy" (12), explains behavior by deducing "probable" motive, according to universal patterns of human nature. Both this procedure and the kind of motive exposed--envy--identify the narrator as a satirical realist, not a sentimental reporter.[13]

The narrative also deduces plot in logical terms that emphasize the limitations of human perspective: for example, "It appeared, from these circumstances, more than probable ..." (387). Similarly, the term "perhaps" underscores the heroine's empirical uncertainty to stress the dispassionate reliability of the narrative. For example, when Verezzi, one of Montoni's boon companions, talks aloud while searching for Emily in the depths of the castle, the narrative records: "Perhaps, he was one of those heroes, whose courage can defy an enemy better than darkness, and he tried to rally his spirits with the sound of his own voice" (432). This language demonstrates the evaluative function of the authoritative narrative. While evoking probability and literary precedent to shape Emily's reasoning, the passage implies that traditional satiric judgments are the right ones: this is one of "those heroes" of whom we have read in satirical fiction. Radcliffe's narrative structure thus reasserts the reliability of comparative judgment, authorial distance, spectatorial control, and objective narration. The vacillations of experiential uncertainty are undermined by narrative fiats that emphasize motives the narrator deems common and natural, but that reflect satirical judgments of man. It is the narrator's judgment that frames and interprets the heroine's feelings.

Radcliffe also controls the reception of her meanings with the device of the epigraph. She prefaces her chapters with quotations, usually from her favorites, James Thomson or Shakespeare. Her use of these poets reflects her own stylistic method. While both poets were particularly renowned in the eighteenth century for mixing modes, Thomson especially represents the new "long poem," which includes diverse discourses and ideological contradictions yoked by skillful transitions.[14] Radcliffe uses her poetic epigraphs to introduce diverse treatments of a theme. Although these excerpts usually constitute descriptions--of a character's particular psychological state, of a scene, even of a poem within the chapter--sometimes they provide a clue to the plot or moral. In this way, these prefatory fragments control the meanings of the chapter and frame it as a fictional explication of an artistic trope. By subduing the unique aspects of the story, this technique invites familiar and stylized responses. For example, in *The Romance of the Forest*, the epigraph for Chapter 6 is, "Hence, horrible shadow! / Unreal mockery, hence!" attributed to "MACBETH" (85). The chapter chronicles the abrupt arrival at the ruined abbey of a troop of horsemen led by the Marquis of Montalt. As La Motte approaches to greet him, "the words of welcome faltered on his lips, his limbs trembled, and a ghastly paleness overspread his countenance. The Marquis was little less agitated, and, in the first moment of surprise [sic], put his hand upon his sword, but, recollecting himself, he withdrew it" (88). The epigraph evokes Macbeth's vision of Banquo in Shakespeare's play, and thus explicates a scene otherwise as incomprehensible to the reader as it is to Madame La Motte and Adeline: the attempted murder of the Marquis, the robbery, La Motte's guilt and remorse that have cast him into the mysterious gloom described in the previous pages. Significantly enough, the Marquis, unlike Banquo, is no ghost. Not only has Radcliffe revised the supernatural as the psychological, as is her wont, but she has also rewritten the story as empirical fact. The alert reader will note the difference, and, unlike Adeline (or Austen's Catherine Morland), will seek rational explanations for the phenomena in the novel. At the same time, even a knowledge of *Macbeth* cannot help the reader to unravel the details of La Motte's crime; only the narrative will tell us that. Thus, within the apparent liberty Radcliffe accords the reader to understand the plot through his or her own deductive reasoning lies another reinforcement of the authority of the narrative. Radcliffe invites a balance of active interpretation and a submissive acceptance of the control of the narrator.

Quotations provide further buried clues for the reader. These quotations underline the literary precedents of the scenes and characters, thereby evoking familiar interpretative codes by which the discriminating reader can understand the meaning of the vignette. Radcliffe, however, refines this code to emphasize Enlightenment values. In *The Romance of the Forest*, for example, the narrator concludes her description of Madame La Motte's suspicions that her husband loves Adeline, that they had met secretly, and that Adeline's innocent self-defense constitutes "a refined piece of art" by moralizing with the help of Shakespeare:

> So true is it that
>
> > ---'Trifles, light as air
> > Are, to the jealous, confirmations strong
> > As proof of Holy Writ.'
>
> And so ingenious was [Madame La Motte] 'to twist
> the true cause the wrong way.' (79)

Such self-conscious literariness proves the "realism" of her characters by generalizing them, by universalizing her particulars. The context of *Othello* and *Henry IV*, Part Two, unlocks Madame La Motte's character as a type: she is good, but weak in her inability to control her passions. These passions, as sentimental feelings often do, overwhelm even "her usual attention to good manners," and make Madame La Motte sneer at what she thinks is hypocrisy in "the artless *innocent*," Adeline. According to her perspective, social arts signal duplicity, a familiar sentimental credo. But Radcliffe certainly does not endorse this view. She emphasizes that Madame La Motte judges what she sees by her own feelings and fears, rather than by the procedure of rating empirical and objective evidence, which comprises the Enlightenment value of rational judgment. She suffers like the lonely Othello, but she has no Iago to blame beyond her own fevered passions. She is her own enemy. Like her husband and Adeline, alone in the wild forests and severed from the emotional and mental protection of society, she becomes superstitious, confusing "trifles, light as air" with "Holy Writ," and reasoning aberrantly by twisting "the true case the wrong way." The frame of the narrator's context thus controls any ambiguity of characterization or evaluation. Nevertheless, this is a detail, leading to nothing essential to the development of the story. Rather, it serves as an example of the method of reading Radcliffe advocates: interpretation directed by informed comparison.

Epigraphic poetry also allows Radcliffe safely to articulate some of the rebelliously individualistic values of sentimentalism, particularly through the theme and language of art. *The Romance of the Forest* establishes clearly the importance of the right "taste" in art, but at the same time it wavers about the powers of poetry. Throughout the book, the heroine Adeline retrieves her reason and deference from the temptations of power offered by her liberation from society and from a powerful father figure. Indeed, the novel might serve as a variation on the theme of Christ's temptation. Since Adeline is far more exemplary than Emily in her rational behavior and emotional self-control, the narrative criticizes her in language more subtle than that of *Udolpho*. Nevertheless, the same themes appear: the narrative controls Adeline's potential threat to the sexual hierarchy by framing her riotous imagination within language that condemns fancy and reasserts the supremacy of reason. Vol. 1, Chapter 11, for example, begins with an epigraph from Collins' "Ode to Fear," which associates "Fear" and fancy:[15]

> Thou! to whom the world unknown
> With all its shadowy shapes is shown;
> Who seest appall'd th'unreal scene,
> While fancy lifts the veil between;
> Ah, Fear! ah, frantic Fear!
> I see, I see thee near!
> I know thy hurry'd step, thy haggard eye!
> Like thee I start, like thee disordered fly! (152)

As is characteristic of Collins's odes, the abstract emotion Fear is personified, in this case as a figure disordered by fancy's eye, haggard with the loss of the "veil" between reality and imagination. In parallel fashion, the "seeing I/eye" of the poet perceives the "shadowy shape" of Fear itself and falls into the same disorder. The poem articulates the conventional doctrine that fear results from the attempt to overstep man's boundaries, to perceive the "unknown" world, to taste forbidden knowledge ("is shown"), and thus to lose the division, the veil or screen, between the mind and nature, between the inside and the outside. The dangers of this solipsism, this eternity of self, are, however, countered by the traditional, pictorial imagery, the frames of art that distance and order the fears of fancy. The "shadowy shapes," "hurry'd step," and "haggard eye" embody the picturesque theories of the sublime that arouses fear and awe of God's immensity, and thus tames the fancy and limits the self through judicious contemplation of Other; the pictorial scene of the fleeing, haunted figure surrounded by "bushes," which appear as "bears," also evokes a familiar iconographic or emblematic tradition. By casting the abstract as art, Collins re-establishes the distinctions his fancied Fear blurs.

These themes of the division between inside and outside, the "veil" between nature and superstition, and the dangers of fancy appear throughout the ensuing chapter. As in Collins's ode, various techniques of formal art enforce the definitions and screens between man and nature, curtailing and ordering the indulgence of disordered fancy. The chapter begins with a landscape description of the sinking sun gleaming on the ruins "which [Adeline] could not gaze upon with indifference". (152). The negative formulation emphasizes the quality Adeline lacks, indifference, so that within the ostensible praise of the heroine's sensitivity to God's nature lies a warning note that she has lost the controlled detachment that permits indifferent spectatorship. Indeed, immediately following this sentence, Adeline muses to herself:

> "Never, probably, again shall I see the sun sink below those hills ... or illumine this scene! Where shall I be when next it sets--where this time to-morrow? sunk, perhaps, in misery!" She wept at the thought. "A few hours," resumed Adeline, "and the Marquis will arrive--a few hours, and this abbey will be a scene of confusion and tumult: every eye will be in search of me, every recess will be explored." These reflections inspired her with new terror, and increased her impatience to be gone.
> (152-53)

She begins her reverie by recognizing the pictorial nature of the sight, and thus retaining some of her detachment: she calls it a "scene" that the sun "illumes" like a theatrical background of a stage, and she qualifies the melodramatic "never" with the cautious "probably." The awkwardness of this qualification, which interrupts the stylized monologue, indicates the strain between the language of rational, prosaic sense and the language of romantic, poetic sensation. In this passage, Adeline rapidly loses her detachment, as she has her indifference, and identifies herself with the dying sun, "sunk". She even weeps "at the thought," but this thought arises purely from her imagination, set loose with the sinking of the sun of reason and the coming on of twilight when the distinctions between sky and earth fade. In place of the calm scene she imagines a riotous history painting, a "scene of confusion and tumult," in which "every eye" will search her "every recess." Abandoning her detached position as the seeing eye, she becomes vulnerable to the ravishes of fancy, personified and pictorialized here as disorderly violence probing toward an absent center, herself.

This laden language implies several, related ideas. Adeline, by indulging her fancy, has annihilated the division between herself and external nature, hence relinquishing her power to control it and thus to control her own nature. The result is "confusion and tumult," loss of morality and of identity implied in the innuendo that she is open to every "I"--Pope's quintessential woman without a character at all. She indulges fears and they rule her; she is temporarily mad in having no internal self, no identity to prevent invasion.[16]

The ensuing paragraph temporarily restores Adeline to reason, and also to the control of a benevolent "eye," that of Heaven.

> Twilight gradually came on, and she now thought it sufficient-
> ly dark to venture forth; but, before she went, she kneeled
> down and addressed herself to Heaven. She implored support
> and protection, and committed herself to the care of the God
> of mercies. Having done this, she quitted her chamber, and
> passed with cautious steps down the winding staircase. No
> person appeared, and she proceeded through the door of the
> tower into the forest. She looked around; the gloom of the
> evening obscured every object. (153)

This submission to the legitimate authority of reason and God frames the ensuing portrait of Collins's "Fear" enacted by Adeline. Here, nature opposes her insubstantial, imaginary terrors. It is Adeline, not nature, who creates fear: "With a trembling heart she sought the path pointed out by Peter, which led to the tomb; having found it, she passed along forlorn and terrified. Often did she start as the breeze shook the light leaves of the trees, or as the bat flitted by, gamboling in the twilight; and often, as she looked back towards the abbey, thought she distinguished, amid the deepening gloom, the figures of men" (153). The summery breeze, the "light" leaves, the "gamboling" bat contrast with Adeline's lonely figure, looking backward toward the darkness in which she "thinks" she can "distinguish" figures. The epigraph to the chapter stresses that Adeline has, in some measure, created her own terrors. She becomes an emblem of Fear, with the emblems of death, madness, and superstition surrounding her--the tomb, bat, and abbey. The narrative further criticizes Adeline in the phrase "thought she distinguished," emphasizing her uncertain judgment and so implying that she imagines an "unreal scene," like Collins's Fear.

It is, however, characteristic of Radcliffe's style that Adeline is not, in fact, mistaken. She appears mistaken in order to underscore the emblematic meaning of the scene, to lift it, as it were, from the plot and reproduce it as a universal image of the sensation of lonely uncertainty. Almost immediately following the description above, the narrator records unambiguously that Adeline "distinguishes" correctly: "she suddenly heard ... a sound of voices, among which she distinguished that of the Marquis: they seemed to come from the quarter she was approaching, and evidently advanced. Terror for some minutes arrested her steps; she stood in a state of dreadful hesitation: to proceed was to run into the hands of the Marquis; to return was to fall into the power of La Motte" (153). Here, Adeline has "heard" and "distinguished" without narrative qualification; even the uncertainty of "seemed" is countered by "evidently." Through neat parallel phrases, the narrative underscores her rationale: "to proceed" is "to run" into danger, whereas "to return" is "to fall" into danger. As is typical of the structure of sentimental novels, this entire pattern of hesitation and action is then repeated in the chapter. Escaping from the Marquis, she leans against "a fragment of the tomb," falls into reverie, perceives and hears vague noises, and "again address[es] herself to Heaven" (154). Her spirits sink again with fear, she vacillates between refuge in a "cell" and freedom near the tomb, and fails to distinguish in the darkness the voice of her companion. The narrative convention of logical sequence battles the allusions and static postures of pictorialism.

Art as a theme and language thus provides a means in Radcliffe's works to articulate the conflict between submersion in or indulgence of nature and control over it. As Foucault notes, the observation of nature in the eighteenth century was seen as restoring or protecting sanity: "all exercises of the imagination must be excluded as being in complicity with the passions, the desires, or all delirious illusions. On the contrary, the study of what is eternal in nature and most in accord with the wisdom and goodness of Providence has the greatest efficacy in reducing the madman's immoderate liberties and bringing him to discover the forms of his responsibility."[17] Radcliffe's style reproduces the observation of nature through art. The language of art, pictorialism, also serves both to facilitate and to limit the expression of imaginary fears.

Radcliffe repeats the structure of stylistic disjunctions through her own poetry, voiced by her characters. Typically, these poems celebrate individual perception rather than neoclassical types. In *Udolpho* Emily composes her own fanciful poem "The Sea-Nymph" upon "picturing" ideas stimulated by a fresco in Montoni's "magnificent saloon." (179). Again later, as she sails from Venice, Emily recalls Greece, and "a thousand classical remembrances" that induce

> that pensive luxury which is felt on viewing the scenes of ancient story, and on comparing their present state of silence and solitude with that of their former grandeur and animation. The scenes of the Illiad illapsed [sic] in glowing colors to her fancy--scenes, once the haunt of heroes--now lonely, and in ruins; but which still shone, in the poet's strain, in all their youthful splendour.
>   As her imagination painted with melancholy touches, the deserted plains of Troy, such as they appeared in this after-day, she reanimated the landscape with the following little story. (206)

In the narrative poem that follows, Emily describes the odyssey of "a weary driver" across the plains of "Illion," his rescue by a good Samaritan shepherd, and his longing for the domestic hearth. Albeit in a nostalgic not satirical mood, Emily contrasts present decay with classical grandeur in the mock-heroic tradition. Her ability to compare marks her discipline over her imagination. Her classical education structures her imaginative activity so that she can "imitate" not *The Iliad*, but Homer, to use Young's formulation. The language of painting, however, transforms an epic action into a static picture, a still life to be contemplated by the independent mind as an emblem of time and decay. Her poem, moreover, replaces the high heroism of the ancients with Christian and domestic virtues; solitary merchants in an oriental fable supplant Homer's socially representative figures. Immediately following the poem, Emily begins "to discriminate the rich features and varied coloring of the landscape" (206) and cites a litany of fashionable trees and plants. This passage lauds the individual power to "see" art and to create emblems from nature.

Radcliffe, however, frames Emily's monologic poetry and imaginative exclamations of personal feeling and fantasy within the stylistic controls of dialogue and narrative poetry. Emily's poem "The Glow-Worm," for example, appears within a passage that urges rationality and social duty through both style and motif. Although the poem describes the Caliban-like

plaints of a lone, oppressed native, its political innuendo is countered by a
context stressing the rightness of hierarchy. The narrative introduces the
scene by a conventional description of St. Aubert as the Good Man:

> After distributing to his pensioners their weekly stipends,
> listening patiently to the complaints of some, redressing the
> grievances of others, and softening the discontents of all, by
> the look of sympathy, and the smile of benevolence, St. Aubert
> returned home through the woods,
>
> where
>
> At fall of eve the fairy-people throng,
> In various games and revelry to pass
> The summer night, as village stories tell.*
>
> *Thomson. (15)

The parallel triple phrases of "listening to the complaints of some,"
"redressing the grievances of others," and "softening the discontents of all,"
and the balanced, abstract terminology of "the look of sympathy and the
smile of benevolence" stylistically establish the public and typical nature of
this act of duty. The narrative then shifts into Thomson's poetic evocation of
folktale sociability, demonstrating St. Aubert's train of ideas as he leaves his
pensioners' simple home. The narrative next explains St. Aubert's progress
of ideas almost scientifically, with a language quite different from the
tumbling phrases of impressionistic imagery with which Emily rhapsodizes.
Isolating St. Aubert's "mind" as the "experiencing" faculty, the narrative
traces the cause of its present sensation in the specific and moral "consciousness" of "beneficent action" (15). This accounts for St. Aubert's ensuing
display of sensibility:

> "The evening gloom of woods was always delightful to me,"
> said St. Aubert, whose mind now experienced the sweet calm
> which results from the consciousness of having done a
> beneficent action, and which disposes it to receive pleasure
> from every surrounding object. "I remember that in my youth
> this gloom used to call forth to my fancy a thousand fairy
> visions, and romantic images; and, I own, I am not yet wholly
> insensible of that high enthusiasm, which wakes the poet's
> dream: I can linger, with solemn steps, under the deep shades,
> send forward a transforming eye into the distant obscurity, and
> listen with thrilling delight to the mystic murmuring of the
> woods." (15)

Through dialogue--social exchange--rather than in the single voice of a poetic persona such as Emily uses in "The Glow-Worm," this passage positions the sentimental eulogy of nature, feeling, and imagination within the language of social duty and rationalism. St. Aubert reiterates this preference for the clear, visible, or material over the mystic or mysterious. He recalls the sweets of fanciful superstition but assigns them to his youth; he trivializes his own sensibility by the negatives of "not insensible"; he revives the poetic fantasy of creation by "a transforming eye" but names this a "dream"; and he echoes the alliterative hiss and murmur of poetry, but rhymes "I," "eye," and "delight" to underscore the limitations of this private pleasure and his own stance as spectator.

In contrast to this cautious, balanced understanding of nature, which stresses the power to control it, Emily submits her reason to the impressions of nature.

> "O my dear father," said Emily, while a sudden tear started to her eye, "how exactly you describe what I have felt so often, and which I thought nobody had ever felt but myself! But hark! here comes the sweeping sound over the wood-tops; -- now it dies away;-- how solemn the stillness that succeeds! Now the breeze swells again. It is like the voice of some supernatural being--the voice of the spirit of the woods, that watches over them by night. Ah! what light is yonder? But it is gone. And now it gleams again, near the root of that large chestnut: look, sir!"

St. Aubert's "transforming eye" makes the obscure landscape clear; Emily's tearful eye blurs it. In her surprise at finding that her father shares her feelings, Emily misconceives emotion as private. She follows the sounds of the woods as they dip and swell and the light as it winks and vanishes. She is entranced by the ignis fatuus of false feeling that follows natural changes rather than locating the stable and universal truth in nature. St. Aubert reproves her by identifying the source of the light, which he names with precision.

> "Are you such an admirer of nature," said St. Aubert, "and so little acquainted with her appearances as not to know that for the glow-worm? But come," added he gaily, "step a little further, and we shall see fairies, perhaps; they are often companions. The glow-worm lends his light, and they in return charm him with music and the dance. Do you see nothing tripping yonder?" (15-16)

He represents the knowledge of nature, which controls it, rather than an "admiration of nature," which wonders at and wanders in it. Stable, universal, empirical truth, identified with Enlightenment reason and masculine control, mocks the impressionable, changeable female deluded by a conventional literary trope. Emily, however, quickly returns to her role as rational heroine, albeit she still expresses the subversively sentimental values of individual perception. Laughing with her father at her fancy a minute later, Emily switches from a model of fancy to a mistress of it, confessing that she has "anticipated" his joke by composing a poem in which a glowworm cheers fairies with his light. Emily declares that she "almost dare[s] venture to repeat" her verses, whereupon her father replies: "Nay...dismiss the *almost*, and venture quite; let us hear what vagaries fancy has been playing in your mind. If she has given you one of her spells, you need not envy those of the fairies" (16). In tones like Henry Tilney's from Austen's *Northanger Abbey*, St. Aubert corrects Emily's conventionally modest language as she prepares to exhibit her poetic language. At the same time, he denies her authorship through a cliché, albeit a playful one: it is not Emily but "fancy" who holds the pen.

Emily herself reiterates the charge of "irregularity," as her verse is "tripping" like the fairies; this is the discourse of female ignorance: "If it is strong enough to enchant your judgment, sir," said Emily, "while I disclose her images, I need *not* envy them. The lines go in a sort of tripping measure, which I thought might suit the subject well enough, but I fear they are too irregular" (16). The equation of poetry with a "spell," moreover, echoes Locke's disapproval of metaphor and imagistic language as deceptive.[18] The criticism of Emily's ambition, significantly, occurs in dialogue, the language of social exchange, a dialogue that endorses conformity and deference to authority. Emily, furthermore, answers St. Aubert's reproof with a witty compliment on his poetic judgment, acknowledging his cultural as well as personal authority.

The narrative continues, however, by collapsing the distinctions between father and daughter:

> Whatever St. Aubert might think of the stanzas, he would not deny his daughter the pleasure of believing that he approved them; and, having given his commendation, he sunk into a reverie, and they walked on in silence.

> A faint erroneous ray
> Glanc'd from th'imperfect surfaces of things,
> Flung half an image on the straining eye;

> While waving woods, and villages, and streams,
> And rocks, and mountain-tops, that long retain
> The ascending gleam, are all one swimming scene,
> Uncertain if beheld.*
>
> > > > > > > > > *Thomson.

> St. Aubert continued silent till he reached the chateau, where
> his wife had retired to her chamber. (17-18)

The narrator suspends her omniscient authority and does not reveal St. Aubert's "real" judgment of his daughter's stanzas for several reasons. Since Radcliffe herself wrote them, she refuses to praise herself by means of the ideal judge St. Aubert. His judgment, albeit a fictional creation of her own, represents male, authoritative judgment beyond her sphere.[19] Also, this retreat marks the shift in narrative from an explicatory and evaluative to a descriptive mode.[20] Like "the straining eye" in Thomson's verse, the audience's eye must picture the scene. Poetry here also represents or produces immersion in the self, the silence of St. Aubert: he cannot, therefore, rationally applaud the cause of such an effect, although as a sensitive man, he experiences "reverie." Throughout this passage, masculine, conventionally hierarchical, social values clip the ostensibly indulged feminine, sentimental, and imaginative values. Art represents a form of moral authority that alerts the discriminating reader to the fallacies of sentimental indulgence; art also serves as a vehicle for both expressing and restraining that same sentimentalism.[21]

Radcliffe's pictorial language positions the reader as artistic spectator. In *Udolpho*, Emily often appears as an icon, an idealized portrait of piety. Whereas Radcliffe's spectacles of sublime nature replace history paintings illustrating the spectacle of civilization, her prose portraits and genre scenes offer the reader the privilege of artistic patronage and aristocratic distance over more familiar scenes. By recognizing the artistic and symbolic conventions of the narrative images of Emily, Radcliffe's audience plays connoisseur and moralist.[22] When Emily is riding on Montoni's gondola, for example, the narrative alludes directly to religious painting:

> the dark blue of the upper aether began to twinkle with stars....
> The rays of the moon, strengthening as the shadows deepened,
> soon after threw a silvery gleam upon her countenance, which
> was partly shaded by a thin black veil, and touched it with
> inimitable softness. Hers was the *contour* of a Madona [sic],
> with the sensibility of a Magdalen; and the pensive uplifted

> eye, with the tear that glittered on her cheek, confirmed the
> expression of the character. (184)

The attention to background and light, which casts the single figure against
a dark "shadow," illuminated by heavenly rays, and the focus on facial and
bodily posture reinforce the allusions to the Madonna and Magdalen. In
addition, "confirmed the expression of *the* character" enforces the typicality
of the portrait; it depicts "the character" of religious devotion.[23] The portrait
conjoins reason and devotion to portray an image of rational piety.

Gestures themselves become emblematic in Radcliffe's prose. The idea
of "looking up" toward the heavens reappears: both Blanche and Emily,
gazing up from their casements, depict pure devotion, as does Adeline
praying.[24] The narrative neutrality of these descriptions hints that they need
no authorial interpretation because they are typical.[25] When, for example,
Emily, from her casement "looked, *as if for intelligence*, to the planet, which
was now risen high above the towers," both reader and narrator are
interpolating the meaning of the scene from the image (304; my italics).

Genre scenes also suggest moral meanings, although these meanings
remain implied in *Udolpho*, whereas they would be more fully explained in
Radcliffe's earlier novels. When Emily visits the peasant La Voisin who
housed her father while he was dying, we see a typical picture of rustic
domesticity:

> The old man she found sitting on a bench at his door, between
> his daughter, and his son-in-law, who was just returned from
> his daily labour, and who was playing upon a pipe, that, in
> tone, resembled an oboe. A flask of wine stood beside the old
> man, and before him, a small table with fruit and bread, round
> which stood several of his grandsons, fine rosy children, who
> were taking their supper as their mother distributed it. On the
> edge of the little green, that spread before the cottage, were
> cattle and a few sheep reposing under the trees. The landscape
> was touched with the mellow light of the evening sun, whose
> long slanting beams played through a vista of the woods, and
> lighted up the distant turrets of the chateau. [Emily] paused a
> moment, before she emerged from the shade, to gaze upon the
> happy group before her--on the complacency and ease of
> healthy age, depictured on the countnance [sic] of La Voisin;
> the maternal tenderness of Agnes, as she looked upon her
> children, and the innocency [sic] of infantine pleasures,
> reflected in their smiles. (89-90)

The static language--"stood," "spread," "reposing"--and the term "depictured" signal pictorial description, as does the careful composition of repeated triads that become stylistic groupings: La Voisin between his daughter and son-in-law, the table surrounded by the grandsons, the triplet of "healthy age," "maternal tenderness," and "infantine pleasures." While the vagueness of "daily labour" marks La Voisin's son-in-law as a generic peasant, details suggest symbolic or iconographical meanings: the pipe, peasant harmony and ancient liberty; the flask, moderation and conviviality; fruit and bread, natural nourishment from the land and Lenten purity. These details combine classical with Christian innuendo to merge associations of Horatian ease with Edenic simplicity. The dying lighting illuminates the contrast between the modest foreground scene and the majestic, protective turret in the background, implying both the loss of paternalistic control typified by St. Aubert's death and the lofty concerns of patronage. The spectating audience stands with Emily to view and to moralize the scene.

In *The Romance of the Forest*, the narrative describes the contrast between the happy scene of the refugee family and the heroine's prescient fears by shifting from a descriptive to an analytic style.

> A fire was kindled on a hearth, which it is probable had not for many years before afforded the warmth of hospitality; and Peter having spread the provision he had brought from the coach, La Motte and his family, encircled round the fire, partook of a repast, which hunger and fatigue made delicious. Apprehension gradually gave way to confidence, for they now found themselves in something like a human habitation, and they had leisure to laugh at their late terrors; but as the blast shook the doors, Adeline often started, and threw a fearful glance around. They continued to laugh and talk cheerfully for a time; yet their merriment was transient, if not affected; for a sense of their peculiar and distressed circumstances pressed upon their recollection, and sank each individual into langour and pensive silence. Adeline felt the forlornness of her condition with energy; she reflected upon the past with astonishment, and anticipated the future with fear. She found herself wholly dependent upon strangers, with no other claim than what distress demands from the common sympathy of kindred beings; sighs swelled her heart, and the frequent tear started to her eye; but she checked it, ere it betrayed on her cheek the story, which she thought it would be ungrateful to reveal. (21)

This scene moves in a series of static tableaux, characteristic of pictorial narration. The initial scene depicts the typical painterly vignette of hospitality: the family, isolated from society but mutually dependent, gathered around the emblems of fire and feast, a spot of lightness against the surrounding gloom. This scene gives way to a further tableau in which Adeline, spotlighted and separated from the other laughing characters, stares fearfully at the opening door--a picture that invites the spectator to construct a probable narrative to explain and evaluate her feelings. Finally, the joviality of feast gives way entirely to the isolation of each figure; a last tableau sees them separate and contemplative. This series of scenes, like a history progress, relies upon the reader's pictorial literacy. Only by interpreting through conventional pictorial typology the meaning of the emblems and the groupings can the audience read this scene as symbolically foreshadowing the separation of La Motte's family from Adeline and from each other. To interpret the scene, the reader must stand back and thus judge Adeline's withdrawal.

Radcliffe's narrative employs abstract terms to infuse moral meaning into her scenes and to underscore the conservative message of her fiction. Here, "the warmth of hospitality" refers both to physical and to social warmth and introduces the moral context of the ensuing tableaux. The generalized feelings of "hunger and fatigue" spice La Motte's "repast" both physically and morally to become "delicious." This phrase refers to the typos of the healthy hunger of the blameless poor, whose appetites, sharpened by toil, are finer than the rich man's and thus salt their meager fare. At the same time, La Motte's isolation from society and loss of inherited estate mark him as culpable; his poverty, his faults, and his fears divide him from his family, and them from one another.

Despite the rigorous use of visual details throughout the prose, and despite novelistic attention to details of action--Peter "spreads" the food "he had brought from the coach"--Radcliffe describes social gatherings by means of generalized emotions. "Apprehension" here bows to "confidence". From these generalized feelings of hunger and fatigue, apprehension and confidence, the narrative moves to specify the more idiosyncratic or unusual behavior of the group. They "laugh and talk cheerfully" until "a sense of their *peculiar* and distressed circumstances" sinks "*each individual* into languor and pensive silence" (my italics). Their misfortunes, sorrows, and guilt fracture their gay unity, separate and silence them: both language and universal feelings are lost. The philosophical implications of this idea--that language reflects communal conditions and describes the usual, not the unusual--appears manifest in the ensuing description of one of these isolated wanderers: Adeline. As she becomes more apprehensive, Adeline feels forlorn, remembers her private past, and begins to separate herself even further from society by imagining her future. Adeline mourns her emotional destitution, her lack of any "other claim than what distress demands from the common sympathy of kindred beings," dissatisfied with the bond of hospitality that the narrator has applauded earlier in the passage. She weeps private tears albeit stifling them for the sake of her friends. These descriptions enforce a pictorial view of her. Narrative alliteration reinforces the conventionality of her figure. "Feel," "forlorn," "reflect," "future," "fear," "found" breathe the shudders of fear; "dependent," "distress," "demands" contrast with "claim," "common," "kindred," while "sighs," "swell," and tears "start" in "sorrow." Syntactically, Radcliffe repeats aphoristic formulae: "she reflected upon the past with astonishment, and anticipated the future with fear" matches "reflection" with "anticipation"--both imaginative states--while coupling "past" with "future," and "astonishment" with "fear." By the crisp formulation, these terms that designate insubstantial feelings attain a kind of philosophical substantiation within the narrative frame. We as readers understand them as the litany of imaginative fear, as "sighs" and "tears" are those of sentimental sorrow. The aesthetic density of this language is reinforced by Radcliffe's liberal use of punctuation, which emphasizes the sonorous quality of her prose.

These portraits and genre scenes interrupt the narrative to focus on loosely emblematic representations of conventional ideas. Narrative progress thus gives way to a discourse emphasizing static, universal, typical figures in representative poses. Indeed, the ability to perceive the representative in the particular distinguishes the literate audience and the model characters. St. Aubert, for example, models enlightened sensibility and aristocratic distance. Admiring "The wonderful sublimity and variety of prospects ... and the enthusiasm with which they were viewed" by Emily and her future lover Valancourt, St. Aubert finds that "the fire and simplicity of [Valancourt's] manners seemed to render him a *characteristic* figure in the scenes around them" (49; my italics). While St. Aubert views Valancourt as part of the scenery, however, Valancourt sees the scenery as part of himself: "Of the world he seemed to know nothing; for he believed well of all mankind, and this opinion gave him the reflected image of his own heart" (49). St. Aubert's internal narrative melts into the narrative of the novel to reiterate the satiric cliché that he who believes well of mankind can know nothing of "the world." As the plot shows, moreover, Valancourt is doubly wrong, about the world and about himself, for the corrupt world corrupts him, albeit temporarily. St. Aubert, however, reconciles knowledge of the evil world with sensibility through the right use of art to order perception: the "sensible" ability to make "an art of life," as Fielding advises in the preface of *Amelia.*

St. Aubert's rational evaluation of Valancourt's character and weakness
frames the following picture of simplicity:

> St. Aubert, as he sometimes lingered to *examine* the wild
> plants in his path, often *looked* forward with pleasure to Emily
> and Valancourt, as they strolled on together; he, with a
> *countenance* of animated delight, pointing to her attention
> some grand *feature* of the *scene*; and she, listening and
> *observing* with a *look* of tender seriousness, that spoke the
> elevation of her mind. They *appeared* like two lovers who had
> never strayed beyond these their native mountains; whose
> situation had excluded them from the frivolities of common
> life whose ideas were simple and grand, like the *landscapes*
> among which they moved, and who knew no other happiness,
> than in the union of pure and affectionate hearts. St. Aubert
> smiled, and sighed at the romantic *picture* of felicity his fancy
> *drew*; and sighed again to think, that nature and simplicity
> were so little known to the world, as that their pleasures were
> thought romantic. (49; my italics)

Through the language of depiction and observation, this passage models the
way to perceive life, and St. Aubert models the way to moralize the picture.
The static gestures of the simple figures emphasize their representative
quality; St. Aubert links the "wild plants" with the scene of unspoiled human
nature before him and moralizes on "the world" in an ensuing homily
(*Udolpho* 49-50). This homily uses abstract terminology, parallel phrasing,
contrast, and questions, the rhetoric of neoclassical philosophy, to reiterate the
corruption of the modern world, and Shaftesbury's formula that virtue is
taste. This moralizing discourse surrounds and interprets the prose picture
of idyllic innocence. Watching the spectator St. Aubert, the reader is taught
to value distance and perspective.

By shifting between stylistic modes, Radcliffe's novels contextualize
sentiment in a language that enforces public reason, authority, and social
conformity and exchange. Pictorial language, poetry, homiletic dialogue, and
narrative evaluation all urge the distanced and informed observation of life
as art. Radcliffe imitates her predecessors in valuing detachment, self-
discipline, and aestheticization over emotional engagement. She permits full
expression of the charms of feeling, but also she condemns its dangers
through her weak or mad villains and ignorant heroes. In *The Mysteries of
Udolpho*, Radcliffe centers her plot and her style on the importance of
fighting fear and of knowing how to see truth. *The Romance of the Forest*

dramatizes the hazards of unobserved behavior. In both novels, Radcliffe pictorializes sentiment to control feeling by means of artistic convention. Her Gothic fictions portray the hazards of the indulgence of private feeling.

CONCLUSION

Watching Feeling in *Sense and Sensibility*

In the early years of the nineteenth century, Jane Austen reproduces the stylistic dialectic of literary sentimentalism in a novel whose title encapsulates two of its key concepts: *Sense and Sensibility* (1811).[1] This novel explores the conflicts between the heroism of feeling and that of restraining feeling. In her neat opposition, Austen effectively collapses most of the values suspended in the dialectic of literary sentimentalism while acknowledging the multivalence of these terms themselves. She also mimics the way in which sentimental fictions modify the values they borrow from earlier texts. In her novel, as in other sentimental fictions, self-restraint is valuable only when the self that needs restraining is itself valuable and exhibits virtuous feelings; at the same time, she shows that even the traditional ideal of contemplation, one of the central values of sentimental texts, comprises as much feeling as reflection. It is Austen's triumph to clarify in her novel the complexity of the choice represented by her title even while the novel itself reproduces the strains of sentimental stylistics.

Throughout her work, Austen parodies the excesses of the selfish heroes of stiffly written sentimental fictions, but she also structures her novels to dramatize the conflict between individual desire and social duty in ways designed to elicit the reader's sympathy for rebellious passion.[2] Her heroines tend to suppress their own desires for the good of their immediate society, or, like Emma Woodhouse, learn to do so, while misguided or vicious characters use others for selfish gain. In *Sense and Sensibility*, the self-disciplined Elinor Dashwood models the control of emotion, while her ebullient sister Marianne demonstrates the hazards of uncontrolled feeling. Elinor, usually representing the "sense" of the novel, resembles the mediating narrator in style and function. Silent observer or attendant of others' stories, she negotiates between her sister and the repentant Willoughby, between her mother and the rude Fanny Dashwood, between Colonel Brandon and the grateful Edward. Moderating her mother's ambition for a large house by her "prudence" (24) and "steadier judgment" (14), she hides her own wounded feelings in order to save her family pain, she sacrifices personal relief for the general good of her society. Although she indeed acts on her convictions, she apparently judges with detachment, supplying "inside views," as John Odmark observes, but from a distant perspective.[3]

Elinor's detached stance is apparent by her language. In dialogue, she uses balanced, periodical phrases that resemble those of the essayists Austen admired: Addison and Steele and Samuel Johnson.[4] By weighing one clause against another, and by impersonal predications, this rhetorical style contrasts with Marianne's unconsidered expressions to suggest a disinterested view of characters and opinions. At the same time, Elinor's deliberate phrasing cumulatively results in a tautological solemnity that echoes the parodies of Austen's juvenilia. When, for example, she describes the man she loves to her sister in an early passage that must be quoted at length, she pronounces;

> "Of [Edward's] sense and his goodness ... no one can, I think,
> be in doubt, who has seen him often enough to engage him in
> unreserved conversation. The excellence of his understanding
> and his principles can be concealed only by that shyness which
> too often keeps him silent. You know enough of him to do
> justice to his solid worth. But of his minuter propensities as
> you call them you have from peculiar circumstances been kept
> more ignorant than myself. He and I have been at times
> thrown a good deal together, while you have been wholly
> engrossed on the most affectionate principle by my mother. I
> have seen a great deal of him, have studied his sentiments, and
> heard his opinion on subjects of literature and taste; and, upon
> the whole, I venture to pronounce that his mind is well-inform-
> ed, his enjoyment of books exceedingly great, his imagination
> lively, his observation just and correct, and his taste delicate
> and pure." (20)

Elinor's assumption of the role of objective description highlights the function and style of the narrative, which is authorized to judge disinterested-ly where a heroine is not. Her mannered parallelisms, abstracts, and passive phrasing suggest an impartiality at comic variance with her motive in this speech: she is defending her love to her sister. With a self-consciousness reminiscent of the bookish Mary Bennet, Elinor reiterates clichés to validate her own judgment; she adopts the language of authoritative detachment.

Elinor's phrasing thus pulls in two directions. While it identifies her with the narrative and thus with the authority of detachment, it also serves to characterize her, since her functional ignorance as a heroine is part of what drives the plot. Parted from narrative authority, this phrasing bespeaks exces-sive caution. Elinor's interjection of irrelevant modifiers and clauses--"I think," "concealed only by that shyness which keeps him silent," "At present"--separate her agency from its object, cloaking her motive in the linguistic veil of objectivity. She confesses that she has seen "a great deal of him" from "peculiar circumstances," which she then proceeds to explain as her mother's intention; she "ventures to pronounce" on his character and belies this pomposity by what amounts to a panegyric on "minutely" dissected qualities. The objectivity of her stance thus underscores the subjectivity of her reactions, reactions so favorable to Edward that she even finds him physically handsome: "His abilities in every respect improve as much upon acquaintance as his manners and person. At first sight his address is certainly not striking; and his person can hardly be called handsome, till the expression of his eyes, which are uncommonly good, and the general sweetness of his countenance, is perceived. At present, I know him so well, that I think him really handsome; or, at least, almost so. What say you, Marianne?" (20). Elinor is attracted to Edward, yet even this most personal of responses she first expresses through passives as an objective judgment. The "expression" of his "uncommonly good" eyes and his "general sweetness," she claims, "is perceived." This aesthetic language applauds the expressive, the rare, and the good-natured concealed from the public eye. Ironically, it is this same aesthetic that characterizes the heroine opposed to "sensible" Elinor, Marianne. Whereas Marianne, however, both sees and is seen as a sentimental heroine, Elinor projects her aesthetic onto the object of her desire.[5]

By comic reversal and dramatic dialogue, this passage exposes the gender of impartiality. Just as in the sentimental vignettes of *The Spectator*, the male speaker judges women in abstractly pictorial terms, so an infatuated Darcy admires Elizabeth's eyes in *Pride and Prejudice* and Captain Wentworth mourns Anne's lost bloom in *Persuasion*.[6] Here, however, it is a woman who describes her lover through the sentimental aesthetic. Marianne, nonetheless, ignoring Elinor's assumption of an impartial authority, reads Elinor's description aright as a declaration of desire. When Elinor's confidence in her own impartiality breaks down and she asks her sister's opinion, Marianne unblushingly admits that her view of Edward will follow her desires rather than a disinterested aesthetic. "'I shall very soon think him handsome, Elinor, if I do not now. When you tell me to love him as a brother, I shall no more see imperfection in his face, than I now do in his heart'" (20-21). This rhetorical shift--from Elinor to Marianne, from description to declaration, from impartial evaluation to open partiality--dramatizes the rift between the "masculine" authority of distance and the "feminine" authority of feeling. Elinor speaks now in the "female" language of hesitation and emotion, translated from an epistolary exchange into conversation itself.

To determine how the reader should "see" and so judge Elinor, the narrative supplies a context, or a set of terms with which to construct a contrast between Elinor's view and an objective view. This is done through describing Elinor's internal thoughts. By echoing Elinor's impersonal style, this language paradoxically reveals the self-interest in Elinor's analyses, for the narrative language is ideally disinterested, whereas Elinor cannot be. After Elinor reproves Marianne's hope that Elinor will marry Edward, the narrative continues:

> Elinor had given her real opinion to her sister. She could not consider her partiality for Edward in so prosperous a state as Marianne had believed it. There was, at times, a want of spirits about him which, if it did not denote indifference, spoke a something almost as unpromising. A doubt of her regard, supposing him to feel it, need not give him more than inquietude. It would not be likely to produce that dejection of mind which frequently attended him. A more reasonable cause might be found in the dependent situation which forbad [sic] the indulgence of his affection. She knew that his mother neither behaved to him so as to make his home comfortable at present, nor to give him any assurance that he might form a home for himself, without strictly attending to her views for his aggrandizement. With such a knowledge as this, it was impossible for Elinor to feel easy on the subject. She was far from depending on that result of his preference of her, which her mother and sister still considered as certain. Nay, the longer they were together the more doubtful seemed the nature of his regard; and sometimes, for a few painful minutes, she believed it to be no more than friendship. (22)

This passage imitates Elinor's speech to Marianne in moving from observations impersonally reported, through a weighing of possibilities, to a final tumbling confession of doubt, but this passage appears not in Elinor's but in the narrative voice. The contrast between impersonal narrative and emotional language centers on the ambiguous term "real." Although Elinor's internal conflict arises from the contradiction between what she sees and what she wants, the entire passage is predicated on the difference between what Elinor has said and what she "considers," "knows," and "believes." The "real opinion" appears in the style and voice of the narrative. It is not Elinor's sincerity, nor her feelings, that are judged as "real"; it is her detached observation.

This definition of "real" underscores the difference between conversation and narration, between the languages of exchange and of information. Interpreting Edward's behavior by means of comparisons--no "more than inquietude," "A more reasonable cause," "no more than friendship"--the narrative evokes an absent context, "a something" which "speaks" to the observer. When Elinor sees Edward, rather than contemplating this absent standard, she experiences "painful" doubt. The narrative thus polarizes the function of contrast--prerogative of a disinterested perspective--and the experience of emotion.

The diction of the passage underscores the polarization of point of view. The mercantile language in which "prosperity" translates as "gain" rather than as "growth" illustrates the narrative predication on static contrast. This predication creates a strain between the narrative evaluation of present conditions and Elinor's anxiety about what will happen. The impersonal "there was" and the syntactical delay of the interjected phrase "at times" mimics Elinor's careful restraint. Her authority derives from the narrative language of impersonal description, yet this conflicts with the "female" language of emotion.

The narrative reveals the limitations of Elinor's point of view through her considered opinions of other characters. Although more suspicious of Willoughby than either Mrs. Dashwood or Marianne, Elinor nevertheless does not recognize the main danger he poses.

> Elinor saw nothing to censure in him but a propensity, in which he strongly resembled and peculiarly delighted her sister, of saying too much what he thought on every occasion, without attention to persons or circumstances. In hastily forming and giving his opinion of other people, in sacrificing general politeness to the enjoyment of undivided attention where his heart was engaged, and in slighting too easily the forms of worldly propriety, he displayed a want of caution which Elinor could not approve, in spite of all that he and Marianne could say in support (48-49).

Although she condemns Willoughby here for his "want of caution," Elinor forgives him because of it when he tells her the tale of his love of Marianne and his marriage. While Elinor rightly perceives the danger of his disregard of "persons and circumstances," his main flaw is certainly not "want of caution," but, on the contrary, a rigid adherence to a purpose his feelings oppose: marrying for money. Because of her position as a woman and a character implicated in the action, she is unable to see enough to judge with ultimate authority.

The narrative juxtaposes Elinor's evaluation of Willoughby with her
similarly cautious analysis of Colonel Brandon:

> Colonel Brandon's partiality for Marianne, which had so early
> been discovered by her friends, now first became perceptible
> to Elinor, when it had ceased to be noticed by them.... Elinor
> was obliged, though unwillingly, to believe that the sentiments
> which Mrs. Jennings had assigned him for her own satisfac-
> tion, were now actually excited by her sister.... She liked
> him--in spite of his gravity and reserve, she beheld in him an
> object of interest. His manners, though serious, were mild; and
> his reserve appeared rather the result of some oppression of
> spirits than of any natural gloominess of temper. Sir John had
> dropt hints of past injuries and disappointments, which justified
> her belief of his being an unfortunate man, and she regarded
> him with respect and compassion (49-50).

The careful opposition of Elinor's perception, derived from quiet distance, to
those of the other characters underscores the opposition between a long and
fine sight, and selfish vision. In contrast to the vulgar crowd--Mrs. Jenn-
ings--Elinor perceives "unwillingly," and with detachment, for the Colonel to
her is "an object of interest," not a subject of gossip. Elinor, moreover, likes
Colonel Brandon for many of the same reasons she appears to like Edward,
who strikes neither Marianne nor the reader as particularly charming, unless
in contrast to Willoughby. The Colonel is reserved and silent, mild-mannered
and grave, like Edward; like Edward, as we learn, he conceals a past
emotional attachment. Elinor perceives here from a position of disinterest,
and perceives accurately, but, by virtue of her gender and her place, she can
only exercise this authoritative perspective in telling the tales of others, not
in judging her own story.

As a heroine like Marianne, Elinor does not possess the ultimate
privilege of detachment; it is the narrative that will make this unique tale a
moral example to the reader by tracing the general in the particular. When
Elinor does so, or applies conventional motives to unconventional behavior,
she is almost always wrong. In her attempt to explain why Marianne and
Willoughby have not announced their engagement, she ignores her knowledge
of her sister's character for a reasonable explanation that echoes her own
beliefs and views of the general motivations of society. She attributes their
silence to Willoughby's relative poverty. Since Elinor's "fortune" resembles
Marianne's "competence," what she estimates as Willoughby's "independence" would appear to Marianne as poverty, as it does to Willoughby
himself. Yet nothing in Marianne's character suggests that she would permit

this to prevent her marriage, and indeed we learn that she never thinks of it. Elinor applies her own values to her sister's different character and deduces the same argument to explain Marianne's situation as her own with Edward. Similarly, Elinor "sees" Edward's hair ring as her own hair, her own wedding band, although in fact it is his engagement ring from Lucy Steele. Ironically, both men have other entanglements, other emotional claims, just as their actions would suggest. As elsewhere in the novel, here Elinor applies pragmatic categories to sentimental tropes. The confusion between money and feeling derives from the sentimental equation of benevolence and charity, pity and alms. Like Marianne, Elinor assumes that it is the means, not the will, that is wanting. The heart is in the right place, if the purse is not. This assumption essentially qualifies her perspective and outlines the distinction between narrative authority and the point of view of a character.

Marianne sees consistently with the spontaneity of an epistolary heroine. Her judgment of people and circumstances rests on her own emotional reactions to them. The narrative demonstrates the contrast between perception quickened by emotion in Marianne, and perception retarded by detachment in Elinor in the description of their encounter with Edward. Margaret, the youngest Dashwood sister, Marianne, and Elinor are walking in the country around their cottage and see a man in the distance riding toward their home. It is a familiar landscape scene in which distance opens possibility. Marianne, perceiving as her desires dictate, believes the man to be Willoughby, while Elinor, skeptical of desire and imagination, knows only that it is not.

> [Marianne] walked eagerly on ... and Elinor, to screen Mari-
> anne from particularity, as she felt almost certain of its not
> being Willoughby, quickened her pace and kept up with her.
> They were soon within thirty yards of the gentleman. Marianne
> looked again; her heart sunk within her; and abruptly turning
> around, she was hurrying back, when the voices of both her
> sisters were raised to detain her, a third, almost as well known
> as Willoughby's, joined them in begging her to stop, and she
> turned round with surprise to see and welcome Edward Ferrars.
>
> (86)

The narrative begins by distinguishing Marianne's motives for her hasty action from Elinor's motives for what looks like exactly the same action and underscores the difference by drawing a parallel literally, but not metaphorically, true. Whereas Elinor "keeps up with her sister" in pace, her desires lag behind her sister's. The narrative continues from Marianne's perspective. As soon as she sees that the man is not the one she desires, she sees nothing, even though to her, Edward's voice is "almost as well known as Willoughby's," for she perceives the two men in parallel ways, as suitors for her sister and herself. This connection points up the difference between her point of view and Elinor's. Had Elinor indeed "kept pace with her sister," she would have anticipated seeing Edward; that she only suspects the man is not Willoughby underscores the limitations of her perceptions. Although Marianne errs in permitting sensation to blind and deafen her, to govern her sight, Elinor errs in forbidding it to color her view at all. Most importantly, however, both sisters misperceive. The initial narrative distinction between them collapses. While the sisters strive to identify the particular figure on horseback, the narrative presents a conventional picture of figures meeting in a landscape, a picture accessible only to the structurally detached narrator and reader.

As the plot progresses, Elinor's role grows more active, and her observational distance gives way to an experiential perspective. After Marianne has fallen ill, and all of Elinor's fears have burst forth, Elinor rushes forward pursuing her hopes at the expense of reasoned "caution" in precisely the way she refuses to do in the above passage.

> The clock struck eight. Had it been ten, Elinor would have been convinced that at that moment she heard a carriage driving up to the house; and so strong was the persuasion that she *did*, in spite of the *almost* impossibility of [Colonel Brandon's and her mother's] being already come, that she moved into the adjoining dressing-closet and opened a window-shutter, to be satisfied of the truth. She instantly saw that her ears had not deceived her. The flaring lamps of a carriage were immediately in view. By their uncertain light, she thought she could discern it to be drawn by four horses; and this, while it told the excess of her poor mother's alarm, gave some explanation to such unexpected rapidity. Never in her life had Elinor found it so difficult to be calm, as at that moment. The knowledge of what her mother must be feeling as the carriage stopt at the door,--of her doubt--her dread--perhaps her despair!-- and of what *she* had to tell!--with such knowledge it was impossible to be calm. All that remained to be done was to be speedy; and therefore staying only till she could leave Mrs. Jennings's maid with her sister, she hurried down stairs.
>
> The bustle in the vestibule, as she passed along an inner lobby, assured her that they were already in the house. She

rushed forward towards the drawing-room,--she entered it,--
and saw only Willoughby. (316)

Using the same techniques of violated expectation, delay, and suspense as in
the passage describing the sister's encounter with Edward, the narrative here
also employs the punctuation and syntax of sentimental impressionism:
exclamation points, fragmented sentences, italicized words. The description
also pursues sensual impressions of sight, hearing, and feeling to recount
Elinor's actions. Elinor doubts time but trusts her confused senses, the
prerequisite to moving from a world of externals to a sphere governed by
internal feeling. She becomes a sentimental heroine.

In the following paragraph, moreover, the narrative moves from
describing Elinor's internal, sensual responses to depicting her actions in the
visually vivid detail of eighteenth-century literary sentimentalism. After
Elinor has started back, a theatrical movement, and "obeyed the first impulse
of her heart," we watch the movement of her hand, its symbolic power
accentuated by the carefully designed contrast between Elinor's heightened
expectations of emotional release with her mother, and her instant "horror"
at beholding her sister's betrayer: "Elinor, starting back with a look of horror
at the sight of him, obeyed the first impulse of her heart in turning instantly
to quit the room, and her hand was already on the lock, when its action was
suspended by his hastily advancing, and saying, in a voice rather of command
than supplication, 'Miss Dashwood, for half an hour--for ten minutes--I
entreat you to stay'" (317). Elinor enacts her feelings as she "looks" at the
dramatic "sight" of Marianne's betrayer. As her "passion" turns to action,
Elinor has changed from witness to participant, from a disinterested judge to
a sentimental heroine.

The values of detached observation, moderation, and self-control that
characterize Elinor derive from the literary tradition of the moral essay. These
values, however, appear fully realized not in the characters, but in the
narrative. By the end of the novel, the sisters speak only through tears. When
Elinor learns of her mistake in thinking Edward married to Lucy, she "burst
into tears of joy, which at first she thought would never cease" (360). When
Marianne learns of it, she reacts in almost exactly the same way: "Marianne
could speak *her* happiness only by tears" (363). The narrative now adopts the
language of epistolary spontaneity to describe Elinor's feelings:

But Elinor--How are *her* feelings to be described?--From the
moment of learning that Lucy was married to another, that
Edward was free, to the moment of his justifying the hopes
which had so instantly followed, she was everything by turns

but tranquil. But when the second moment had passed, when she found every doubt, every solicitude removed, compared her situation with what so lately it had been,--saw him honorably released from his former engagement, saw him instantly profiting by the release, to address herself and declare an affection as tender, as constant as she had ever supposed it to be,--she was oppressed, she was overcome by her own felicity;--and happily disposed as is the human mind to be easily familiarized with any change for the better, it required several hours to give sedateness to her spirits, or any degree of tranquillity to her heart. (363)

After the opening rhetorical question on method, which announces the distinction between feeling and describing, the narrative through a series of anaphoric and hasty clauses expresses Elinor's confused considerations and emotions as she witnesses and compares her situation with her fears. The narrative orders and explains this confusion by an aesthetic principle: the effect of violent contrast, which portrays the effects of the sublime on the human heart. The narrative thus frames the particular emotions Elinor experiences within a broader context that presents universal tendencies, not individuals, and so controls the sentimental particularity of the tale.

In *Sense and Sensibility*, Austen employs the stylistic patterns of literary sentimentalism within an authoritative narrative structure. Sentimental scenes appear within a discourse criticizing sentimental excess; a detached observation distinguishes a right view, yet sensation also allows a kind of truth. In *Sense and Sensibility*, Austen turns emotion into spectacle. The tensions of *Sense and Sensibility* thus do not lie between the heroines; they lie between both heroines, muffled voices of experience, and the narrative, authorized to speak by virtue of detachment. By a structure that recapitulates the literary division between "female" epistolary works narrating "authentic," internal experience and essayistic accounts of the general truth, Austen's novel exposes the political implications of narrative authority. A language endorsing contrast, impersonality, and abstract ideals opposes the language of sensation, impression, experience; consensus expressed through detachment thus rules individual experience.

Authority in Austen's world derives from detachment, the capacity (or privilege) to perceive without partiality, with what Matthew Arnold just over fifty years later would call "disinterestedness."[7] Such a source of authority denies heroines, defined by their capacity to feel, all but the power of their feelings. This creates a paradox: How can a heroine be valued for her detachment yet also for her "feeling"? In her later novels, Austen experiments with two solutions to this paradox, both of which challenge the conventions of fiction. Her "sentimental" novels use a structure that at least partially reverses the conventional sources of narrative authority. The heroines of both *Mansfield Park* and *Persuasion*, still more marginalized than Elinor by social neglect, judge society more accurately, at least until they attempt to judge their own place in it. In these novels, furthermore, the narrative voice defends the heroine's qualifications for heroism, so that often it is the narrator who speaks with feeling and the heroines with detachment. Austen thus reveals that the creation of a heroine is itself a political act, an act in which self-interest appears dressed as ideal disinterest.

In her "satirical" novels, however, Austen creates plots dramatizing the consequences of this dilemma whereby the heroine's authority is undermined by the abstract standards of the narrative voice as it articulates social authority. Elizabeth Bennet is taught that when she judges Darcy against her ideal of a gentleman, she misjudges him: her ideals are faulty, her powers of detached observation limited, and her exercise of them an exercise of vanity. Emma learns that she sees rightly only when she sees with her heart. Indeed, these heroines go astray when they usurp the disinterested viewpoint of narrative authority and attempt comparison in place of complacency. At the same time, by mimicking the objective perspective of narrative, these heroines undermine the authority of the very structure that indicts them. Again, if they dress their self-interest as disinterest, does the narrator not do the same?

Austen's attack on the politics of literary convention reflects the conflicts, structural and political, in the works of the very authors she admired. Both Samuel Richardson and Henry Fielding attempt in their final novels to blend "female" and "male" forms of narrative authority, but both encounter difficulties similar to those that Austen explores. In his epistolary novels, Richardson presents the vacillations of female sentiment as the very process of morality, but Richardson's heroines lack social power, just as the letter conventionally conjures a private audience. Austen's favorite novel, *Sir Charles Grandison*, comes closest to according a woman the power of objective judgment, for Harriet acts both as objective narrator, describing Sir Charles, and as epistolary heroine, describing her love for him. The very detachment that defines her as a heroine and qualifies her for Sir Charles, however, suggests narrative omniscience and drives the dynamic of female vacillation out of her character to leave only structured sentiment, stagnant feelings, and static letters.

Although Henry Fielding includes in his fiction inset tales as letters or stories, he subordinates these in his earlier novels entirely to an authoritative narration that presents morality as consistent feeling. *Joseph Andrews* parodies Richardson's account of moral experience in *Pamela* by dividing Pamela's virtue from her vacillations and by according the former to a man and the latter to a caricatured woman. Related by an objective narrator, Lady B's hesitations--indeed female confusions--seem merely hypocrisy, as they are in *Shamela*. Moreover, although Fielding advocates "mixed" characters, Tom Jones, a sentimental hero, experiences virtually only those feelings that consistently reflect his good nature. When in his final novel Fielding attempts to combine the authority of narrative detachment with an endorsement of female interior experience, the result, *Amelia*, suffers from a structural and tonal instability similar to that of *Sense and Sensibility*. In protesting injustice through a narrative voice that is detached but not impartial, Fielding compromises his authority and control over *Amelia*; lengthy, defensive confessions by women characters further undermine the possibility of narrative objectivity by revealing that characters see their own stories in their own way. Thus, Fielding devalues "female" literary forms, the culture vaunting female perspectives, and multiple reactions.

By the end of the century, the discourse on sentimental and aesthetic taste that Austen reflects in *Sense and Sensibility* includes discussions not only of nature and art, but also of epistemology or optics. Such discussions reveal the anxieties sentimental texts share about how to see correctly, and about threats to the hierarchies of gender and class and to the social order.[8] This can be seen in a text which, albeit not a fiction, nonetheless employs sentimental categories and language. Although it postdates the height of literary sentimentalism, Richard Payne Knight's *An Analytical Inquiry into the Principles of Taste* (1805) exemplifies this mingled discourse. An aesthetic theorist who attempted a scientific analysis of taste, Knight borrows definitions from Edmund Burke's *An Enquiry into the Origins of Our Ideas of the Sublime and the Beautiful* (1757), terms from Uvedale Price's treatises on landscape gardening, and ideas from Newtonian theories of optics, and from painterly theory to promote the appreciation of the picturesque beauties of the small Dutch masters and of genre painting. His equation of taste and sensibility segregates social from sentimental categories by dividing true feeling from violent feeling. For Knight, excess of feeling perverts feeling itself and true sensibility is detached perception, for sentiment rightly conceived is judgment itself.

Knight desires to standardize taste and feeling. Deploring in his introduction the lack of a universal standard of beauty, Knight disparages the tyranny of fashion by mocking the "revolutions" of taste in the last two centuries, especially those of women,"the most violent, sudden, and extravagant."[9] As in Frances Brooke's *Old Maid*, where, however, this equation is mocked, women, unnatural artifice, and violent revolution oppose "taste," an opposition that rephrases in sentimental language the neoclassical distinction between arrogant individuality and rational conformity in dress and in politics. Defining "taste" as a general discriminative faculty arising from "just feeling and correct judgment implanted in the mind of man by his Creator, and improved by exercise, study, and meditation," Knight underscores both the moral qualities associated with aesthetic judgment and its social dimension (18). "Just" feeling and "correct" judgment are natural, but they require experience and education for the perfection of the "discriminative" ability, taste. Only those with a choice can "discriminate"; "taste," therefore, becomes the faculty of the privileged.

Knight's optical theory illustrates the role of education in establishing universal values. Echoing Newton's theory of colors, Knight argues that "the pictures upon [the retina of the eye], by some impressions or irritations upon the optic nerves ... are conveyed to the mind, and produce the sense of vision, the most valuable of all our senses" (51). However,

> It is, therefore, only by habit and experience that we form analogies between the perceptions of vision and those of touch, and thus learn to discover projection by the eye: for, naturally, the eye sees only superficial dimension; as clearly appears in painting and all other optical deceptions, which produce the appearance of projection or thickness upon a flat surface. The faculty, however, when acquired, as it is in all adult persons who have seen from birth, is exercised as readily and instantaneously as any natural faculty whatsoever. (58)

Deducing from the example of a blind boy restored to sight, as earlier he had deduced the self-interest in aesthetic ideas from examples of primitive peoples, Knight separates "natural" or "native" from learned experience. He declares that humans literally learn to see through experience, and thus learn a new nature that can discriminate particularly perspective or distance, which "is only projection extended" (58). Nature is reformed through experience and education.

In his discussion on taste, Knight also explains the peculiar notion of the "truth" of painting that recurs throughout sentimental rhetoric. While conceding that painting "softens" real light, and thus dims the sharp contrasts of nature, Knight claims that "as the imitations of painting extend only to the visible qualities of bodies, they show those visible qualities *fairly* and *impartially--distinct from all others*, which the habitual concurrence of other senses has joined with them in the mind, in our perceptions of them in nature" (65, my italics). Knight thus accords painting the ability to represent physical nature to us distinct from prejudice: painting can show us the true appearance of things. This notion appears in sentimental literature where the moral capacity of art to show the spectator himself and thus undermine its own illusions appears through pictorialism and the self-conscious discussions of taste and of art.

Knight emphasizes that it is the "picturesque"--the aesthetic intimately associated with sentimentalism in literature--that demonstrates the "natural" pleasure of viewing. As its name indicates, however, only one who knows pictures can recognize "picturesque" beauty in nature; therefore, this natural pleasure depends on an education in art (146). Knight remarks, "persons being in the habit of viewing, and receiving pleasure from fine pictures, will naturally feel pleasure in viewing these objects in nature, which have called for those powers of imitation and embellishment "(152). Nature, as Oscar Wilde remarked, imitates art. It is a knowledge of art that facilitates the spectator's pleasure in nature. Knight further argues that "the spectator" whose mind is "enriched" with art perceives nature as art, and so enjoys "beauties which are not felt by the organic sense of vision; but by the intellect and imagination through that sense" (154). Sight itself becomes an intellectual exercise of judgment.

Spectatorship, however, has dangers:

> Good-nature is that benevolent sensibility of mind, which disposes us to feel both the happiness and misery of others; and to endeavour to promote the one, and prevent or mitigate the other: but, as this is often quite impossible; and as specta-cles of misery are more frequent and obtrusive than those of bliss; the good-natured man often finds his imagination so haunted by unpleasant images;and his memory so loaded with dismal recollections;that his whole mind becomes tinged with melancholy.... (421)

Since, according to Knight's optical theory, sight results from "irritation," spectacles can cause physical pain; the good-natured man therefore feels what he sees, be this art or nature, fact or fiction. Yet another reason appears for preserving your distance. Like Mackenzie's Harley, the sentimental man should supervise his own observations, turn spectator, and watch what he sees.

As we have seen, the methodological conflict between presenting a story from the perspective of a detached spectator and presenting it as experienced by the character carries implications for the form of later eighteenth-century fiction. By portraying experience from the inside, these novels present models of how to feel instead of proclaiming standards of how to act, a shift in emphasis with a corresponding shift in form. This shift in narrative viewpoint may contribute to what Nancy Armstrong has identified as the "feminization" of fiction: the rise of feminine authority in the novel.[10] Sentimental "autobiographies," like Laurence Sterne's *Tristram Shandy* or Henry Mackenzie's *Man of Feeling*, partly represent an attempt to accord male spectators internal, quasi-epistolary expression without compromising the ideal of authoritative detachment. These fictions deliberately fragment their narratives in order to concentrate on interpreting sensation rather than on defining moral action; however, they also mock the sentimentalism of their own heroes who lose track of their purposes in the wash of emotion. These fictions thus parody female literary conventions even while incorporating them, and hence preserve the possibility of telling the tale from an objective perspective. The supposed deletions, in fact, testify to the existence of a "whole" story, which a detached narrator could tell.

Thus, the point of view from which judgment is delivered testifies to the authority, indeed to the author, of that judgment. Eighteenth-century fiction accords detachment moral power, the right to decide who and what is valuable. This detachment, however, is conventionally prohibited to women because it is structured by a narrative point of view founded on models of writing that are informed by a neoclassical preference for generality. This viewpoint, moreover, is opposed in contemporary satire to the claims of individual feeling, portrayed in the later eighteenth century through fictions of women's experience. Austen's early challenge to this division of perspective, *Sense and Sensibility*, demonstrates that the language of judgment in eighteenth-century literature is the language of comparison, and that comparisons empower the judge to construct an ideal moral standard that muffles the expression and the authority of female experience.

In the fictions of the late eighteenth century, the stylistics of literary sentimentalism produce a dialectic between new and traditional fictional and moral values. While sentimental novels depict their characters' passionate feelings as their heroic trait, they enclose these portraits within a narrative endorsing restraint, contemplation, and self-control. While they praise individuality or uniqueness, they also attempt to socialize it through a language that evokes common values and general standards. Through strongly particularized autobiographical narrators, these novels vaunt idiosyncratic perspectives, yet the causal and moral structures of the novels in which these narrators appear document the triumph of social values. Even as these narratives invite the reader to empathize with men of feeling, they invoke conventional tropes that distance the sentimental figures and replace empathy with a sympathy structured by detachment. The techniques by which sentimental novels achieve this include pictorialism, narrative fragmentation, authoritative yet partial narrators, and multiple narrative voices and modes. These represent, by fracturing the cohesion of the novel's moral structure, the dynamics of a literary culture in flux. They license yet confine the expression of unsocial or antisocial feelings. The structure of sentimental fiction thus frames feeling to criticize the very excesses of feeling sentimental texts record and to replace sympathy with judgment.

Sentimental fictions reiterate the structures and values of the novels and periodicals of the previous fifty years. The fictions of Defoe, Richardson, and Fielding, for example, generally define characters by their behavior within a chronological plot in which initial events precipitate other events in causal sequence. While illustrating the moral maxim that people reap what they sow, such a structure also relies on an Aristotelian correspondence between the emotional and the social condition of a character, between what he feels and what he experiences. Even in the sketches of *The Spectator*, characters are understood to have come by their feelings as a consequence of personal suffering, and the importance of these feelings is their effect on Mr. Spectator himself, the surrogate of society. By their topical references and realistic detail, these novels locate meaning within the contemporary social context: their characters and their feelings are important because they illustrate the values held by society in general, even if characters endure these feelings alone. Periodicals similarly present their characters within the context of the periodical itself, as illustrations of a rhetoric of social values. Both forms underscore the connection, albeit a problematic one, between character and society.

Sentimental texts complicate this connection even as they replicate it. Whereas earlier fictions reconcile the character's feelings and the plot, the individual and society, sentimental texts adumbrate the fracture between the two. By heroicizing sufferers, sentimental stories seem to shift the center of value from action to passion; at the same time, this passion is shown to be expensive and futile in the social world, represented by the ironic voice of the narrator. Instead of defining heroes by their actions, sentimental fictions define them by their feelings even while they point out the weakness of heroic feeling in an action-dominated world. By structural fragmentation, exclamatory rhetoric and punctuation, and pictorial or aesthetic descriptions, moreover, sentimental stories present events as static vignettes, not as links in a causal plot. Such vignettes undermine the traditional moral claim of fiction that it traces the social consequences of individual actions. In place of this kind of morality, sentimental texts offer rich descriptions of mental and emotional sorrow to warn the reader of the internal consequence of social vices. In effect, the center of value is not passion, but observation, not feeling, but seeing.[11]

Beneath the erasures of the sentimental manuscript lies a buried chain of causality--the hidden story of people acting in society who produce the conditions that result in sentimental sorrow. This hidden chain is forged from the moral contexts established by social discussions in the texts of the previous generation, especially periodicals. To follow this chain, and thus to perceive the morality of the story, the reader is invited to stand at a distance from the scene and to contextualize it within a conversation on social values. She or he should not merely sympathize with the characters, but also recognize their place in the larger economy of society. This spectatorial perspective, invoked by allusions, puns, pictorialism, and textual tricks that adumbrate the fictionality of the "text," counters empathy with irony. Like earlier fictions, these self-conscious texts prod the reader to moralize for herself or himself what she or he reads. Indeed, the spectatorial perspective these fictions conjure is itself an ironic perspective, always revealing the dialectical pull of fiction to reflect and reject connections to social reality. In the very process of depicting the isolated sentimental hero confronting a cruel society, sentimental texts rely on the reader's knowledge of the conventions that organize hero and society to turn the story into a conversation on moral values.

The means by which sentimental texts establish this conversation are various. Early periodicals include sentimental vignettes, which are structured as episodes designed to induce emotion and formally disconnected from the text in which they appear, but nonetheless form part of a broader discussion on manners, society, and values. The audience of these periodicals, including women and the middle classes, further shapes the rhetoric of sentimentalism by inviting writers to emphasize domestic life and private sensation as the test of virtue. Not only *The Spectator* and *The Female Spectator*, but also Henry Fielding's *Amelia* rely on this audience to transfer public values into private behavior within the home by employing hortatory rhetoric while portraying domestic scenes. Other sentimentalists contextualize scenes of feeling within didactic narratives. Oliver Goldsmith, Henry Brooke, and Henry Mackenzie frame such vignettes inside confessions at once pseudo-autobiographical and dubiously objective; these narratives present scenes of feeling within a moral narrative on social duty. The irony provided by this structure organizes the novels of Sterne whose rhetoric ridicules sentimental indulgence even while celebrating it. The most popular forms of literary sentimentalism, epistolary novels and sentimental miscellanies, supply formal frames to express feeling; these frames position individual experience within the contexts of social exchange. As Frances Brooke's novels show, the individual effort to discipline desire into social form is modeled by the letter, which translates sensation into communication. Literary miscellanies, on the contrary, especially popular after the French Revolution, sell sentiment as social feeling contextualized as high culture. Radcliffe's Gothic sentimentalism demonstrates that the ultimate social frame lies within individual consciousness. Sentimental heroines must discipline themselves.

Sentimental texts position the new value for feeling within a social world rife with rogues, beggars, and fools. They portray feeling as painful and often useless in the social world except insofar as it stimulates benevolence, itself of limited effect. R. F. Brissenden and Jean Hagstrum have called this aspect of literary sentimentalism nostalgia, the evocation of a golden past of social unity that sanctions retreat from the current world; George A. Starr has glossed Brissenden's interpretation to see sentimentalism as personalized nostalgia or infantilism in which the characters retreat to childhood. Robert Markley has called it a bourgeois internalization or transposition of aristocratic conscience. These interpretations point to the tensions sentimental texts exhibit in moralizing the public role of feeling, but they largely ignore the identification of female values with interior feeling, and thus they overlook the implied critique of the feminization of values. This resistance to feminine values, albeit melancholy, is not nostalgic, for it appears partly through an irony that claims more--or different--things for feeling. The feeling these texts recommend should transcend that of the character and revise nostalgia into morality since it is structured on the distinction between the narrow views of fiction and the broad prospect of society. Particularly after the French Revolution, sentimental writers want not so much to return to a golden past as to control the feelings of the future; progress is their goal, albeit progress in a fashion that indeed partly resembles the past. Literary sentimentalism is supremely conscious of the need to reassert the stability of the status quo. Plots celebrating charity and pity simultaneously rationalize and defuse tensions between the poor and the patrons, women and men, the young and the old. Rhetorical formulae echoing Shaftesbury's axiom that virtue is taste flatter the quiescent audience, suggesting that private refinement comprises morality. Although it solicits new readers, sentimental literature sparks with exclusionary rhetoric designed to distinguish one "class" of readers from another, more by virtue of their educated perception than by virtue of their material or social positions. By flattering educated perception, moreover, sentimental texts suggest that readers exhibit a socialized perspective that makes their "private" feelings conform to public values.

Sentimental fictions portray feeling yet they use conventions that modify this portrayal by criticizing, satirizing, or moralizing this feeling within a conjured set of social values. They depict sentimental feeling as private experience, yet they present such private experience by formal and tonal techniques that invoke a social context or literary tradition of values that compromises its authority. Even while celebrating private feeling, sentimental fictions reinscribe its limits, curtailing the expression of emotion with formal marks, including didactic rhetoric, which urge of the necessity of restraint. The thematic corollary of this formal "framing" is the ubiquitous voice urging self-discipline: the control or channeling of feeling to keep the individual within the social frame. Sentimental fiction, in form and theme, thus positions sentiment within society, albeit a society that is contained or reproduced within a context evoked by the language of the fiction itself. The context of sentimental vignettes, furthermore, derives from a conversation on social values implied by the forerunners of the form, periodical sketches, that underscores the importance of correct judgment formed by correct perspective. Even while describing emotion, sentimental stylistics dilute empathy with an irony produced by implied contrasts. By forming a dialectic between established and new fictional values, the texts of literary sentimentalism frame feeling as spectacle. The true sentimental perspective resides in the view of the spectator, the reader of scenes of sensibility who also sees the whole picture.

NOTES FOR INTRODUCTION

1. For general analyses of sentimentalism, see Louis I. Bredvold, *The Natural History of Sensibility* (Detroit: Wayne State University Press, 1962); R. F. Brissenden, *Virtue in Distress: Studies in the Novel of Sentiment from Richardson to Sade* (London and Basingstoke: Macmillan, 1974); John K. Sheriff, *The Good-Natured Man: The Evolution of a Moral Ideal, 1660-1800* (University, Alabama: University of Alabama Press, 1982); Janet Todd, *Sensibility: An Introduction* (London and New York: Methuen, 1986).

2. J. G. A. Pocock, *Virtue, Commerce, and History: Essays on Political Thought and History, Chiefly in the Eighteenth Century* (Cambridge: Cambridge University Press, 1985) 229-30. For further accounts of the philosophical heritage of literary sentimentalism, see John Mullan, *Sentiment and Sociability: The Language of Feeling in the Eighteenth Century* (Oxford: Clarendon Press, 1988).

3. Several critics have observed that sentimental writers wrestle with contradictory ideas about human sociability, particularly Mullan, *Sentiment and Sociability*, and John Dwyer, *Virtuous Discourse: Sensibility and Community in Late Eighteenth-Century Scotland* (Edinburgh: J. Donald, 1987). Mullan uses Hume's philosophy to explain the tendency in the novels of Richardson, Sterne, and Mackenzie to counter the "desired generalization of social instincts" by turning to private and inward feeling, made public through the constructed body (15). In her Introduction to *Sensibility in Transformation: Creative Resistance to Sentiment from the Augustans to the Romantics*, Syndy McMillen Conger briefly summarizes the critical history of the origin of sentimentalism and notes the conflicts between eighteenth-century sentimental and social ideals (London and Toronto: Associated University Presses, 1990) 13-19.

4. Ian Watt, *The Rise of the Novel: Studies in Defoe, Richardson, and Fielding* (Berkeley and Los Angeles: University of California Press, 1957) 18-21, passim. See also Michael McKeon, *The Origins of the English Novel, 1600-1740* (Baltimore and London: Johns Hopkins University Press, 1987).

5. Mullan distinguishes between the religious thread in Hutcheson's theory of sentimentalism and David Hume's secularism in *Sentiment and Sociability* 31-32.

6. David Hume, *Four Dissertations* (London: A. Millar, 1757) 184-200.

7. Ann Van Sant analyzes the philosophical and psychological uses of observing sensibility in *Eighteenth-Century Sensibility and the Novel: The Senses in a Social Context* (Cambridge: Cambridge University Press, 1993) 45-59. For another treatment of sympathy as an aesthetic phenomenon or as spectacle, see David Marshall's *The Surprising Effects of Sympathy: Marivaux, Diderot, Rousseau, and Mary Shelley* (Chicago and London: University of Chicago Press, 1988) 5-13, passim. For a variety of useful discussions on the relationship between aesthetic theory and sentimentalism,

see *Studies in Criticism and Aesthetics, 1660-1800: Essays in Honor of Samuel Holt Monk*, ed. Howard Anderson and John S. Shea (Minneapolis: University of Minnesota Press, 1967). See also Walter John Hipple, Jr., *The Beautiful, the Sublime, and the Picturesque In Eighteenth-Century British Aesthetic Theory* (Carbondale: Southern Illinois University Press, 1957), and James S. Malek, *The Arts Compared: An Aspect of Eighteenth-Century British Aesthetics* (Detroit: Wayne State University Press, 1974).

8. For a key text in the development of this argument, see Lawrence Stone's *The Family, Sex, and Marriage, 1500-1800*, which traces new social attitudes to the eighteenth-century shift toward "affective individualism" (New York: Harper and Rowe, 1977). For readings of sentimentalism as promoting "female" values, including social toleration, see Jean H. Hagstrum, *Sex and Sensibility: Ideal and Erotic Love from Milton to Mozart* (Chicago and London: University of Chicago Press, 1980) 7-9, 160-218, 247-59; also Hagstrum, "'Such, Such Were the Joys': The Boyhood of the Man of Feeling," in Robert E. Moore and Jean H. Hagstrum, *Changing Taste in Eighteenth-Century Art and Literature* (William Andrews Clark Memorial Library; 17 Apr. 1971; Los Angeles: University of California Press, 1972) 47-60; Patricia Meyer Spacks, *Imagining a Self: Autobiography and the Novel in Eighteenth-Century England* (Cambridge, Mass: Harvard University Press, 1976) 1-27; Dale Spender, *Mothers of the Novel: 100 Good Women Writers Before Jane Austen* (London and New York: Pandora, 1986); Terry Lovell, *Consuming Fiction* (London: Verso, 1987) 47-73; Nancy Armstrong, *Desire and Domestic Fiction: A Political History of the Novel* (New York and Oxford: Oxford University Press, 1987); Clive T. Probyn, *English Fiction of the Eighteenth Century, 1700-1789* (London and New York: Longman, 1987) 2.

9. See, for example, John J. Richetti, "The Portrayal of Women in Restoration and Eighteenth-Century English Literature," in *What Manner of Woman: Essays on English and American Life and Literature*, ed. Marlene Springer (Oxford: Basil Blackwell, 1977) 65-97. Rita Goldberg exemplifies this view when she writes in *Sex and Enlightenment: Women in Richardson and Diderot*, "The exaltation of women in fiction really began with *Clarissa*; and the cult of tears reached its height in the decades after the novel's publication in 1748. But women were not the only clientele for the new form.... As male readers came under the sway of the new heroines, they in a sense *became* the women under attack in literature" (Cambridge: Cambridge University Press, 1984) 205. Rather than simply promoting identification with women, however, sentimental texts incorporate rhetorical signals specifically designed to distinguish between "male" and "female" readers or readerly functions. By concentrating on Richardson's sentimentalism, critics have slighted the influence of Fielding's techniques and of traditional modes of thought on sentimental texts. For a more nuanced discussion of the relationship between women's social liberation and sentimental fictions, see Katherine Sobba Green, *The Courtship Novel, 1740-1820: A Feminized Genre* (Lexington: University of Kentucky Press, 1991).

10. Robert Markley, "Sentimentality as Performance: Shaftesbury, Sterne, and the Theatrics of Virtue" in *The New Eighteenth Century: Theory, Politics, English Literature*, ed. Felicity Nussbaum and Laura Brown (London and New York: Methuen, 1987) 210-30. Markley has perceptively interpreted benevolence in

sentimental fiction as a transposition of aristocratic social roles in which middle-class "benevolists" become "naturalized" aristocrats by possessing the internal quality of sympathy. While this paradigm elucidates the sentimental identification of benevolence as a sign of instinctive "class," it does not account for the irony which runs through sentimental rhetoric.

11. Brissenden 22. Brissenden notes the tensions between the sentimental ideal of social unity and the facts of unrest, and remarks on the sentimental recognition that benevolence does not remedy social ills (82). The interpretation of sentimentalism as levelling and feminist derives largely from its association with Richardson's "female" and middle-class narratives. As this study shows, however, Richardson's form of sentimentalism, itself more   ambivalently "feminist" than generally recognized, constitutes only one version of a wider literary conception. Another argument for the "feminization" of literature through sentimentalism rests on the changing reading and literacy patterns of the century in which more women bought, read, and wrote novels. This new audience does not, however, immediately induce a literature which advocates new values; on the contrary, it stimulates a reaction to preserve the ideas of traditional literary culture within new forms.

12. Ruth Bernard Yeazell, *Fictions of Modesty: Women and Courtship in the English Novel* (Chicago and London: University of Chicago Press, 1991). See also Jonathan Rose, "Rereading the English Common Reader: A Preface to a History of Audiences," *Journal of the History of Ideas* 23 (1992): 47-70.

13. J. Paul Hunter, *Before Novels: The Cultural Contexts of Eighteenth-Century English Fiction* (New York and London: W. W. Norton, 1990) 33-34.

14. Hunter, *Before Novels* 37. For a theoretical sketch of this process, see also Wolfgang Iser's *The Implied Reader: Patterns of Communication in Prose Fiction from Bunyan to Beckett* (Baltimore and London: Johns Hopkins University Press, 1974).

15. In *The Culture of Sensibility: Sex and Society in Eighteenth-Century Britain*, G. J. Barker-Benfield examines the cultural fear of sentiment (Chicago and London: University of Chicago Press, 1992). Michael McKeon notes that "the fear that women's morals will be corrupted by reading romances" starts in the Renaissance (52; also qtd. in Patricia Meyer Spacks, *Desire and Truth: Functions of Plot in Eighteenth-Century English Novels* [Chicago and London: University of Chicago Press, 1990] 241n.).

16. J. Paul Hunter notes that the novel inherits from periodicals a polemic designating allegiance to rival traditions and tendencies in regard to perspective and politics in "'News and new Things': Contemporaneity and the Early English Novel," *Critical Inquiry* 14 (1988): 493-515.

17. See Eric Erämetsä, *A Study of the Word 'Sentimental' and of Other Linguistic Characteristics of Eighteenth-Century Sentimentalism in England* (Ser. B. Tom. 74.1. Helsinki: Annales Academiae Scientiarum Fennicae, 1951).

18. Claudia L. Johnson, "A 'Sweet Face as White as Death': Jane Austen and the Politics of Female Sensibility," *Novel: A Forum on Fiction* 22 (1989): 159-174. See also *Jane Austen: Women, Politics, and the Novel* (Chicago and London: University of Chicago Press, 1988). Whereas Mullan concentrates in *Sentiment and Sociability* on ideas of sociability expressed through the physical "language" of the body, the

present study is concerned with the cultural, social, and sexual implications of sentimental stylistics.

19. Todd, *Sensibility* 6. Noting the shift in emphasis from plot to description, Todd remarks that "The result of these various devices--asterisks, dashes, meandering narratives and fragmentation--is that readers are to some extent prevented from indulging in an identifying fantasy with a character or an author, and are forced to respond to the emotion conveyed. At the same time these devices force the literary nature of the work on to the reader by indicating the inadequacy of the medium---language--in which, despite their intrusive presence, most of the business of the work is still transacted." In contrast to this, Leo Braudy argues that fragmentation in sentimental fiction continues the tradition of "authenticity" begun by Defoe. See "The Form of the Sentimental Novel," *Novel: A Forum on Fiction* 7 (1973): 5-13.

20. See Armstrong, *Desire and Domestic Fiction*; Stone, *The Family, Sex, and Marriage*; Felicity Nussbaum, "The Politics of Difference" and Harriet Guest, "A Double Lustre: Femininity and Sociable Commerce," both in *Eighteenth-Century Studies* 23 (1990): 375-86, 479-501; Cheryl Turner, *Living by the Pen: Women Writers in the Eighteenth Century* (London and New York: Routledge, 1992).

21. Eric Rothstein remarks on structural conflicts in Fielding's narrative method, epitomized by the narrative retreat, in *Systems of Order and Inquiry in Later Eighteenth-Century Fiction* (Berkeley and Los Angeles: University of California Press, 1975).

22. Brissenden; George A. Starr, "'Only a Boy': Notes on Sentimental Novels," *Genre* 10 (1977): 501-27; Hagstrum, *Sex and Sensibility*; Robert Markley; Donna Landry, "The Resignation of Mary Collier: Some Problems in Feminist Literary History," in *The New Eighteenth Century*, ed. Nussbaum and Brown (London and New York: Methuen, 1987) 99-120.

23. Sheriff, *The Good-Natured Man* 5-6, 17.

24. Pierre Bourdieu, *Distinction: A Social Critique of the Judgement of Taste*, trans. Richard Nice (Cambridge, Mass.: Harvard University Press, 1984) 7. Identifying sentimentalism as a pre-Romantic, ambiguous portrait of the self, Stephen D. Cox blames a "curious simplicity or transparency of aesthetic motive" for the so-called poor quality of sentimental texts; see *"The Stranger Within Thee": Concepts of the Self in Late-Eighteenth-Century Literature* (Pittsburgh: University of Pittsburgh Press, 1980) 42. Homai J. Shroff illuminates associations between gentlemanly taste and current fashion, also noting a "confusion of values" in the sentimental idealization that tends "to identify intelligence with cunning, and politeness with falsehood, while naiveté and impudence tend to be associated with generosity and a good heart." See *The Eighteenth Century Novel: The Idea of the Gentleman* (Atlantic Highlands, N.J.: Humanities Press, 1978) 193.

25. John Barrell, *The Dark Side of the Landscape: The Rural Poor in English Painting, 1730-1840* (Cambridge: Cambridge University Press, 1980) 19-21, 8; Barrell, *The Idea of Landscape and the Sense of Place, 1730-1840: An Approach to the Poetry of John Clare* (Cambridge: Cambridge University Press, 1972) 4-7. See also Richard D. Altick, *The English Common Reader: A Social History of the Mass Reading Public, 1800-1900* (Chicago and London, 1957) 30-66; also Altick, *Paintings*

from Books: Art and Literature in Britain, 1760-1900 (Columbus: Ohio State University Press, 1985).

26. In *Ways of Seeing*, John Berger examines the political implications of the subjects and poses of painting, noting particularly the ways in which seventeenth-century genre paintings cast the surveyor in the role of possessor (Middlesex: Penguin, 1972) 83. The present study is indebted to Berger's work. See also Jean Starobinski, *L'Invention de la Liberté, 1700-1789* (Geneva: Skira, 1987). Roland Barthes points out in *S/Z* that all narrative "views," even "realistic" ones, are presented within limiting conditions, i.e. frames, that serve to control their depiction (qtd. in George P. Landow, *Images of Crisis: Literary Iconology, 1750 to the Present* [Boston, London and Henley: Routledge, 1982] 183).

27. Felicity A. Nussbaum, *The Brink of All We Hate: English Satires on Women, 1660-1750* (Lexington: University of Kentucky Press, 1984) 159, passim; Michel Foucault, *The Uses of Pleasure*, trans. Robert Hurley (New York: Vintage, 1985) 84.

28. For a good discussion of the ways in which reading creates "classes" in the audience, see Jon P. Klancher, *The Making of English Reading Audiences, 1790-1832* (Wisconsin: University of Wisconsin Press, 1987) 1-13. In *Society and Literature in England, 1700-1760*, W. A. Speck chronicles the increasingly rigid division between the classes throughout the century and isolates social "types" that embody political abuses (New York: Gill and Macmillan, 1983). For an excellent discussion of the social ramifications of the increasing prestige of "refinement," see also Homai J. Shroff, *The Eighteenth Century Novel.*

29. *Sensibility, Provoked by the Rival Pretensions of Pity. A Poem* (Cambridge: Cambridge University Press, 1819).

30. These titles can be found in Andrew Block's *The English Novel, 1740-1850: A Catalogue Including Prose Romances, Short Stories, and Translations of Foreign Fiction* (London: Dawsons of Pall Mall, 1961).

31. This method follows that of Walter Francis Wright in *Sensibility in English Prose Fiction, 1760-1814* (Urbana: University of Illinois Press, 1937).

32. For a definition of "style" as an ideological construct, see Mary Poovey, "Ideology and 'The Mysteries of Udolpho'," *Criticism* 21 (1979): 307-30. For an analysis of the ways in which "style" can bridge ideological contradictions, see Antonio Gramsci, *Prison Notebooks*, ed. Hoare, 404-407, qtd. in John Barrell and Harriet Guest, "On the Use of Contradiction: Economics and Morality in the Eighteenth-Century Long Poem," in *The New Eighteenth Century*, ed. Felicity Nussbaum and Laura Brown (New York and London: Methuen, 1987): 121-43.

33. Critics who have observed the Augustan elements in literary sentimentalism, especially through the influence of Shaftesbury, include Ernest Tuveson, "Shaftesbury and the Age of Sensibility," in *Studies in Criticism and Aesthetics, 1660-1800: Essays in Honor of Samuel Holt Monk*, ed. Howard Anderson and John S. Shea (Minneapolis: University of Minnesota Press, 1967) 73-93; and Leon Guilhamet, *The Sincere Ideal: Studies on Sincerity in Eighteenth-Century English Literature* (Montreal and London: McGill-Queen's University Press, 1974) 76, 284.

NOTES FOR CHAPTER 1

1. Angus Ross, "Introduction," *Selections From "The Tatler" and "The Spectator"
of Steele and Addison* (Middlesex: Penguin, 1982) 21-55, esp. 22-27.

2. Kathryn Shevelow, *Women and Print Culture: The Construction of Femininity
in the Early Periodical* (London and New York: Routledge, 1989).

3. Ruth Bernard Yeazell anatomizes a parallel conflict in contemporary attitudes
toward women's modesty in *Fictions of Modesty: Women and Courtship in the
English Novel* (Chicago and London: University of Chicago Press, 1991) 5-11.

4. Robert D. Mayo, *The English Novel in the Magazines, 1740-1815* (Evanston:
Northwestern University Press, 1962). I am indebted to this comprehensive study.

5. *The British Apollo*, Friday, Mar. 23 to Monday, Mar. 26, 1711.

6. Joseph Addison, No. 1 (1 Mar. 1711), *The Spectator*, ed. Donald F. Bond
(Oxford: Clarendon Press, 1963) 1:2. All citations from *The Spectator* refer to this
edition.

7. Ross notes that while Addison and Steele's *Tatler* was flourishing, Thomas
Baker printed *The Female Tatler* from 1709 to 1711, "helping himself to a successful
title" but using the form of one essay per number (25). While Frances Brooke also
uses this form, Eliza Haywood, writing during a different period, reverses the
direction that the periodical was taking by borrowing a periodical title for lengthy
fables. In *Women and Print Culture*, Shevelow quotes the identification of Haywood's
periodical as "'the first periodical for women written by a woman'" and notes that she
uses the form of an "essay-periodical" as a construction of difference based on gender
(London and New York: Routledge, 1989) 167-68. Shevelow notes the Female
Spectator's "culpability" as the source of her authority, her appeal to a limited,
"feminine" audience, and use of illustrative "anecdote" (168-71).

8. *The Female Spectator*. By A Lady. 5th ed. 4 vols. (London: T. Gardner, 1755)
1:12.

9. Katherine Sobba Green observes that "Haywood's constant concern is to
disabuse her readers, particularly her female ones, of their romantic notions about
marriage" (Lexington: University of Kentucky Press, 1991) 31.

10. Ian Watt, *The Rise of the Novel* (Berkeley and Los Angeles: University of
California Press, 1957); John J. Richetti, *Popular Fiction Before Richardson:
Narrative Patterns, 1700-1739* (Oxford: Clarendon Press, 1969); Margaret A. Doody,
A Natural Passion: A Study of the Novels of Samuel Richardson (Oxford: Clarendon
Press, 1974).

11. For a summary of critical views on *Amelia*, see Roger D. Sell, *The Reluctant
Naturalism of "Amelia": An Essay on the Modern Reading of Fielding* (Ser. A, vol.
62, no. 3; Abo: Akademi Aboensis, 1983). Sell notes that "in *Amelia*, society is a
whirlpool of vice and interest" drawing everyone into its evil (71).

12. Michael McKeon, *The Origins of the English Novel, 1600-1740* (Baltimore
and London: Johns Hopkins University Press, 1987) 418. In *The Impossible Observer*

(Lexington: University of Kentucky Press, 1979), Robert W. Uphaus remarks that "*Clarissa* unflinchingly represents secular life as a condition of indeterminacy, whereas *Amelia*, even in the light of such indeterminacy, yearns for a solution to this condition" (71).

13. The sentimental elements in the novel generally have disappointed critics. Frederick G. Ribble explains the confusion between portraying sensibility as a sensation and as an emotion in *Amelia* by analyzing the rhetoric of Shaftesbury and Locke in "The Constitution of the Mind and the Concept of Emotion in Fielding's *Amelia*," *Philological Quarterly* 56 (1977): 104-22.

14. John Bender traces the mixed messages in *Amelia* to Fielding's compromise of his transparent, reformist narrative by "historical realism" in *Imagining the Penitentiary: Fiction and the Architecture of Mind in Eighteenth-Century England* (Chicago and London: University of Chicago Press, 1987) 180-96, a point made earlier by Mona Scheuermann in *Social Protest in the Eighteenth-Century English Novel* (Columbus: Ohio State University Press, 1985) 13-40. Ernest Tuveson, however, traces reformism to Shaftesbury and identifies it as an aspect of sentimental rhetoric in "Shaftesbury and the Age of Sensibility" in *Studies in Criticism and Aesthetics, 1660-1800* (Minneapolis: University of Minnesota Press, 1967) 73-93.

15. J. Paul Hunter summarizes the critical objections to the novel: the plot lacks probability, the characters lack depth and subtlety, the tone lacks consistency, and the narrator seems unclear of his enemies, his attitude toward them, or his irony. See "The Lesson of Amelia" in *Quick Springs of Sense: Studies in the Eighteenth Century*, ed. Larry S. Champion (Athens: University of Georgia Press, 1974) 166-70; see also J. Paul Hunter, *Occasional Form: Henry Fielding and the Chains of Circumstance* (Baltimore and London: Johns Hopkins University Press, 1974). See also T. C. Duncan Eaves, "Amelia and Clarissa" in *A Provision of Human Nature: Essays on Fielding and Others in Honor of Miriam Austin Locke*, ed. Donald Kay (University: University of Alabama Press, 1977) 95-110.

16. See Bertrand H. Bronson, "When Was Neoclassicism?" in *Studies in Criticism and Aesthetics, 1660-1800: Essays in Honor of Samuel Holt Monk*, ed. Howard Anderson and John S. Shea (Minneapolis: University of Minnesota Press, 1967) 35.

17. See Felicity Nussbaum, *The Brink of All We Hate: English Satires on Women, 1660-1750* (Lexington: University of Kentucky Press, 1984); Paul Fussell, *The Rhetorical World of Augustan Humanism* (London: Oxford University Press, 1965); Vincent Caretta, *The Snarling Muse: Verbal and Visual Political Satire from Pope to Churchill* (Philadelphia: University of Pennsylvania Press, 1983) 250.

18. Critics who interpret the novel as a testimony to Charlotte Craddock include Wilbur Cross, Pat Rogers, and David Blewett. In contrast, Patricia Meyer Spacks explores the depictions of female evil and passivity in a plot of male power in *Desire and Truth: Functions of Plot in Eighteenth-Century Novels* (Chicago and London: University of Chicago Press, 1990) 85-113.

19. Aurélien Digeon, *The Novels of Fielding* (London: Routledge, 1925).

20. "The Portrayal of Women in Restoration and Eighteenth-Century English Literature," in *What Manner of Woman: Essays on English and American Life and Literature*, ed. Marlene Springer (Oxford: Basil Blackwell, 1977) 92.

222   Framing Feeling

21. See Max Byrd, *London Transformed: Images of the City in the Eighteenth Century* (New Haven and London: Yale University Press, 1978); Bender 63-84; Tony Tanner, *Adultery in the Novel: Contract and Transgression* (Baltimore and London: John Hopkins University Press, 1979) 24; Michel Foucault, *The History of Sexuality: Volume One, An Introduction*, trans. Robert Hurley (London: Penguin, 1976) 24-25; Sell 71; Varey 133.

22. W. A. Speck notes Fielding's use of types, particularly lawyers and professional men, in *Society and Literature in England, 1700-1760* (New York: Gill and Macmillan, 1983). Robert E. Moore examines the difference between "character" and "characters" in aesthetic and literary theory in "Reynolds and the Art of Characterization" in *Studies in Criticism and Aesthetics, 1660-1800: Essays in Honor of Samuel Holt Monk* (Minneapolis: University of Minnesota Press, 1967) 332-57.

23. Henry Fielding, *Amelia*, ed. Martin C. Battestin (Middletown: Wesleyan University Press, 1983). All citations to this text refer to this edition.

24. Ronald Paulson finds in *Amelia* a structure that expresses both resentment of oppressive guardians and criticism of the city as evil in "The Pilgrimage and the Family: Structures in the Novels of Fielding and Smollett" in *Tobias Smollett: Bicentennial Essays Presented to Lewis M. Knapp*, ed. G. S. Rousseau and P.-G. Boucé (New York: Oxford University Press, 1971) 67-69. The class signature of this analogy would strike readers: Homai J. Shroff and W. A. Speck point out that Cambridge, Oxford and Dublin maintained humiliating class distinctions in the eighteenth century; see Shroff, *The Eighteenth Century Novel: The Idea of the Gentleman* (Atlantic Highlands, N.J.: Humanities Press, 1978).

25. Jill Campbell notes Fielding's "apocalyptic vision of women's appropriation of... masculine power" in "'When Men Women Turn': Gender Reversals in Fielding's Plays," in *The New Eighteenth Century*, ed. Felicity Nussbaum and Laura Brown (New York and London: Methuen, 1987) 62-83. Terry Castle also discusses Fielding's depiction of women assuming power in *Masquerade and Civilization: The Carnivalesque in Eighteenth-Century English Culture and Fiction* (Stanford: Stanford University Press, 1986). In *Fielding and the Woman Question: The Novels of Henry Fielding and Feminist Debate, 1700-1750*, Angela J. Smallwood defends Fielding's sexual attitudes even while admitting that Fielding preserves a strong (and sentimental) sense of sexual role differentiation (New York: St. Martin's Press, 1989) esp. 152-175. Alice Browne cautions against assuming that more positive attitudes toward women were translated into social freedom in *The Eighteenth-Century Feminist Mind* (Sussex: Harvester Press, 1987) 49. In "The Changing Face of Change: Fe/Male In/Constancy," Carolyn Williams remarks on the instability of the charge of infidelity during the century (*Journal of the British Society of Eighteenth-Century Studies* 12 [1989]: 13-28). Felicity Nussbaum notes the long rhetorical heritage of the identification of women with doubleness in *The Brink of All We Hate*.

26. Varey dwells on the tension between satire and sentiment, identifying Atkinson as the "man of feeling" in *Amelia* whose individual acts of generosity are noted as exceptional in *Henry Fielding* (Cambridge: Cambridge University Press, 1986) 130-31.

27. For a discussion of the imagery of enclosure in *Amelia*, see Peter V. LePage "The Prison and the Dark Beauty of *Amelia*," *Criticism* 9 (1967): 337-54. In his

Introduction to *Amelia*, David Blewitt praises the new "realism" Fielding exhibits in the novel that allows moral development and "greater psychological accuracy" than his previous work (Middlesex: Penguin, 1987) xv. Blewitt associates this accuracy with the novel's implied connection between the "public and the private" spheres, a connection that begins with the loss of paradise and entrance into a "dark," "uncertain" world that, he claims, is Richardson's world of "sexual and psychological depths" (xi, xviii). It is also, however, the world of imprisonment, of prisons, the underside of the bright open fields of benevolent patriarchy, the metaphorical equivalent of what happened to spontaneous, generous Tom Jones when he got married.

28. Terry Belanger in *Books and Their Readers*, ed. Isobel Rivers (New York: St. Martin's Press, 1982) 9.

29. Nussbaum, *Brink* 159.

30. This argument appears differently developed in Barbara M. Benedict, "The Tensions of Realism: Oppositions of Perception in Some Novels of Fielding and Austen," diss., University of California, Berkeley, 1985.

31. Armstrong, *Desire and Domestic Fiction: A Political History of the Novel* (New York and Oxford: Oxford University Press, 1987) 51.

32. See Eric Rothstein, *Systems of Order and Inquiry in Late Eighteenth-Century Fiction* (Berkeley and Los Angeles: University of California Press, 1975) 160-62, 183-84.

NOTES FOR CHAPTER 2

1. John Bender traces the "ruptures in fictional continuity" and ideological contradictions in *The Vicar of Wakefield* to its reformist rhetoric in "Prison Reform and the Sentence of Narration in *The Vicar of Wakefield*," in *The New Eighteenth Century*, ed. Felicity Nussbaum and Laura Brown (New York and London: Methuen, 1987) 168-88.

2. For a lucid discussion of the development of aesthetic theory, see Walter John Hipple, Jr., *The Beautiful, the Sublime, and the Picturesque in Eighteenth-Century British Aesthetic Theory* (Carbondale: Southern Illinois University Press, 1957).

3. This idea of the world as a coded moral fable shows the influence of Puritan and Dissenting literature on sentimental practice. Defoe's episodic novels, while widely different in tone from sentimental fiction, portray a similar double-message by, on the one hand, emphasizing the minutiae of realistically conveyed experience, and, on the other, insisting on a concealed religious narrative. See George A. Starr, *Defoe and Spiritual Autobiography* (Princeton, N.J.: Princeton University Press, 1965).

4. As John Mullan argues in "The Language of Sentiment: Hume, Smith, and Henry Mackenzie," the sentimentalists of the eighteenth century used the notion of sympathy to counteract the increasing competition in society, which set men's interests at odds with each other (*The History of Scottish Literature, 1660-1800*, vol.

2, ed. Andrew Hook [Aberdeen: Aberdeen University Press, 1987] 273-88). In a similar way, the aesthetic of distance valorizes a noncompetitive social relationship.

5. Although the first edition of two volumes was published in 1766 (London: Printed for W. Johnston in Ludgate-Street), the traditionally authoritative edition is the five volume one, published serially from 1766 to 1770. Henry Brooke has very recently found his way into eighteenth-century literary surveys, as demonstrated by Clive T. Probyn's *English Fiction of the Eighteenth Century, 1700-1789* (London and New York: Longman, 1987).

6. Oliver Goldsmith, *The Vicar of Wakefield*, ed. Arthur Friedman (Oxford and New York: Oxford University Press, 1974) 83. All citations from this text refer to this edition.

7. In his Introduction to the novel, Arthur Friedman explains the book as a comic novel with a sentimental plot and argues that Goldsmith's hero is modelled on Fielding's Abraham Adams and equally free from authorial satire (*The Vicar of Wakefield*, ed. Arthur Friedman [Oxford and New York: Oxford University Press, 1974] ix-xvii). Parson Adams, however, is not free from satire; rather, he is forgiven for the weaknesses that the narrator mocks. As Friedman admits, moreover, Goldsmith's narrative method, which entrusts the story to the hero, introduces ambiguity where Fielding's omniscient narrator prohibits it; this difference reflects a difference in method rather than ideology.

8. Robert H. Hopkins, *The True Genius of Oliver Goldsmith* (Baltimore: Johns Hopkins University Press, 1969).

9. G. S. Rousseau claims that contemporary readers detected no satire in *The Vicar of Wakefield*, but in his attack on the Hopkins reading he glosses over the criticisms even in the selective contemporary reviews he reprints. Fanny Burney, for example, objects to the disparity between Primrose's tone and his subjects, especially regarding his wife and his reformist views. Since Rousseau contends that discovering irony or satire in Goldsmith's novel results from historical misreading, it should be noted that he admits that Goethe observed its "'high, *benevolent irony'*" and other critics took exception to aspects of its form; see *Goldsmith: The Critical Heritage*, ed. G. S. Rousseau (London: Routledge, 1974) 12-13, 25 n.35, 51-53. See also Sven Backman, *This Singular Tale: A Study of "The Vicar of Wakefield" and Its Literary Background* (Lund Studies in English, 40, Lund: C. W. K. Gleerup, 1971). John K. Sheriff in *The Good-Natured Man: The Evolution of a Moral Ideal, 1660-1800* (University, Alabama: University of Alabama Press, 1982) argues that Goldsmith treats Primrose ironically but that Primrose exposes the villainy of society (30- 34). Sheriff also summarizes the critical debate on whether *The Vicar of Wakefield* supports or attacks sentiment (30-32). See D. W. Jefferson's "*The Vicar of Wakefield* and Other Prose Writings: A Reconsideration" for a rebuttal of Hopkins' argument that *Vicar* is ironic and an assertion of its fundamentally Christian structure (in *The Art of Oliver Goldsmith*, ed. Andrew Swarbrick [London: Vision, 1984] 17-32).

10. John Bender has accounted for the contradictions in the book by identifying a conflict in the text between an idea of a modern, state ideology and the rhetoric of paternalism. Brissenden finds in Goldsmith conflicts between sentimental theory and the increasing awareness of its faulty practice, as well as conflicts in cultural and political ideas. For an argument suggesting that Goldsmith is antagonistic to Rousseau

and politically conservative, see W. F. Gallaway, Jr., "The Sentimentalism of Goldsmith," *PMLA* 48 (1933) 1167-81. In *Sensibility: An Introduction* (London and New York: Methuen, 1986), Janet Todd notes that "authorial irony diffuses the female plot of seduction" and that the sentimental heroes of both Goldsmith and Sterne invite ironic readings from contemporary as well as modern audiences (106, 109). See Bender, "Prison Reform," and R. F. Brissenden, in *Virtue in Distress: Studies in the Novel of Sentiment from Richardson to Sade* (London and Basingstoke: Macmillan, 1974), esp. 249 where Brissenden locates a conflict between the plot, which produces suffering, and Primrose, who models virtuous sentiment (249).

11. Bender compares Goldsmith and Fielding as novelists whose reformist rhetoric violates their novelistic structures, "splitting off into a separate discourse lodged within but not integral to the structure of the novel itself" in *Imagining the Penitentiary: Fiction and the Architecture of Mind in Eighteenth-Century England* (Chicago and London: University of Chicago Press, 1987) 207.

12. As Backman observes, Goldsmith's chapters run the same length as the average *Spectator* essay and echo the narrative economy and social commentary of the periodical (143-57).

13. Robert H. Hopkins discusses Goldsmith's political conservatism and traditionalism in "Matrimony in *The Vicar of Wakefield* and the Marriage Act of 1753," *Studies in Philology* 74 (1977) 322-39. See also Seamus Deane, "Goldsmith's *The Citizen of the World*" for an analysis of Goldsmith's "Enlightenment" satire and ironic criticism of travel literature; Deane also observes Goldsmith's criticism of the sentimentality of Altangi himself, which impairs his objectivity (*The Art of Oliver Goldsmith*, ed. Swarbrick [London: Vision, 1984] 33-50, esp. 46-47).

14. Richard Sennett, *The Fall of Public Man* (New York: Knopf, 1977).

15. Backman 25.

16. In *The Discourse of the Mind in Eighteenth-Century Fiction* (The Hague: Mouton, 1974), John A. Dussinger sees Goldsmith's novel as a fusion of contrary values that reasserts patriarchal, economic class relations (162-63).

17. Swarbrick draws attention to Goldsmith's use of "the conventions of civilized *conversation*...[in] style, subject, form, manner of address" (*Art of Oliver Goldsmith* 14).

18. *Vicar of Wakefield* 46. Friedman compares this to a similar passage in *The Spectator* no. 211 for 8 Nov. 1711 (*The Vicar of Wakefield* 194, n.1).

19. Friedman 195. Janet Todd notes that Goldsmith "claimed that he could tell the gender of a writer by the style and 'a nameless somewhat in the manner'" (*The Sign of Angelica: Women, Writing and Fiction, 1660-1800* [New York: Columbia University Press, 1989] 126).

20. Stephen Coote, noting the "trivialization" of aesthetic standards, identifies this as Goldsmith's only literary use of the ballad *per se* (*The Vicar of Wakefield*, ed. Stephen Coote [Midddlesex: Penguin, 1982] 204, n. 204).

21. Coote claims the painting is merely "absurd" and "confused" (*The Vicar of Wakefield* 207-208) but Terry Castle remarks that it comprises a sort of masquerade (*Masquerade and Civilization: The Carnivalesque in Eighteenth-Century English Culture and Fiction* [Stanford: Stanford University Press, 1987] 69).

22. This type appears in *The Spectator*, no. 328; in Johnson's *Rambler*, no. 138, and *Idler*, no. 13, as well as in Colman and Thornton's *Connoisseur*, no. 91 (23 Oct. 1755). See Backman 204-206.

23. It is not insignificant that this type is female, for it is the female--and what Terry Lovell terms the "feminization of culture"--at this period in history that embodies physicality--desire, appetite, materialism; see *Consuming Fiction* (London: Verso, 1987). Sentimental fiction translates this association; it does not revise it.

24. For a discussion of Primrose's dual function, see G. A. Starr, "'Only a Boy': Notes on Sentimental Novels," *Genre* 10 (1977) 501-27; and Dussinger 149.

25. *The True Genius of Oliver Goldsmith* 27.

26. Eighteenth-century aesthetic theory, at least in the first half of the century, maintained the neoclassical view that fundamental forms expressed beauty, while color was merely decorative, and occasionally delusive, a theory reflected even in Locke's notions of the "coloring" of metaphorical language to basic ideas. Although Backman denies that Goldsmith draws attention to the material fact of his text, other critics including John Bender note Goldsmith's linguistic games.

27. J. M. S. Tompkins, Brissenden, and Probyn express this view. Probyn observes that "Essentially, *The Fool of Quality*, as all the novels in this sub-genre, exhibits an argument for mutual sympathy and tolerance, for charity and an emotional expansion of the individual universe in which the boundaries and possibilities have nothing to do with gender, birth-right, social place, or culture" (*English Fiction of the Eighteenth Century* 156). Brooke's tragedy *Gustavus Vasa* was renowned in its time, while *Universal Beauty* was reprinted in miscellanies until the end of the century. See *The Poetical Works of Henry Brooke, Esq.. In Four Volumes; with a Portrait of this Author and his Life*. By Miss [Charlotte] Brooke. Dublin: Printed for the Editor, 1792.

28. Henry Brooke, *The Fool of Quality; or, the History of Henry Earl of Moreland*. 2nd ed. 5 vols. London: Johnston,. 1767-70. All citations refer to this edition. Mona Scheuermann, *Social Protest in the Eighteenth-Century English Novel* (Columbus: Ohio State University Press, 1985) 42.

29. Patricia Meyer Spacks points to this episode to illustrate the radical implications of Brooke's novel, which maintains that the characters' "situation alone defines their right to sympathy, and thus to benevolence"; see *Desire and Truth: Functions of Plot in Eighteenth-Century English Novels* (Chicago and London: Chicago University Press, 1990) 120-21. She also notes the paradoxical enforcement of the separation between benefactor and the spectacular object of sympathy that undermines the radical implications of sentimental ideology.

30. The success of the first two volumes of *The Fool of Quality* in 1766 prompted the new, five volume edition. The frames, as Mackenzie observes, of dialogue between author and reader diminish as the novel proceeds and finally vanish; it is perhaps this that prompts Isaac D'Olier, the biographer of Brooke's nephew Henry Brooke, to remark of the uncle that "His novels were the last of his writings; and it should not be concealed that the fifth volume of *The Fool of Quality*, and his subsequent novel of *Juliet Grenville* were written after the wheels of his mental chariot began to drive slow. In these we trace...the magnificent ruins of genius" (*Memoirs of the Life of the late Excellent and Pious Mr. Henry Brooke* [Dublin: R. Napper, 1816] 89-90).

31. Henry Brooke. *Juliet Grenville; or, the History of the Human Heart.* 3 vols. London: G. Robinson, 1774. All citations refer to this edition.

32. Brooke also sounds this theme in his poetic fables. James Raven argues that *The Fool of Quality* defensively justifies the merchant classes in response to contemporary attacks on luxury and a readership hostile to trade; see *Judging New Wealth: Popular Publishing and Responses to Commerce in England, 1750-1800* (Oxford: Clarendon Press, 1992) 87. Goldsmith shares this contemporary concern with luxury and overspending, and both authors shunt the blame for this cultural degeneration particularly onto women.

33. While it is certainly possible that Brooke may be punning on "the pit" and "Mr. Pitt," I think it more likely that this is a misspelling since the text is full of errors.

NOTES FOR CHAPTER 3

1. Ian Ross Campbell, ed. and intro., *The Life and Opinions of Tristram Shandy, Gentleman*, by Laurence Sterne, World Classics Ed. (Oxford and New York: Oxford University Press, 1983) 8. Laurence Sterne, *A Sentimental Journey through France and Italy*, ed. Graham Petrie, intro. A. Alvarez (Baltimore: Penguin, 1967). All citations will refer to these editions.

2. See also Tristram's query, 4: x, 225: "is a man to follow rules--or rules to follow him?"

3. In "Clocks, Calendars, and Names: The Troubles of Tristram and the Aesthetics of Uncertainty," J. Paul Hunter argues that *Tristram Shandy* reflects eighteenth-century anxieties about inheritance and identity; see *Rhetorics of Order/Ordering Rhetorics in English Neoclassical Literature*, ed. J. Douglas Canfield and J. Paul Hunter (Newark: University of Delaware Press, 1989) 173-98, esp. 193.

4. John Traugott, *Tristram Shandy's World: Sterne's Philosophical Rhetoric* (Berkeley and Los Angeles: University of California Press, 1954) 74.

5. Janet Todd, *Sensibility: An Introduction* (London and New York: Methuen, 1986) xvi. See also Robert Markley, "Sentimentality as Performance: Shaftesbury, Sterne, and the Theatrics of Virtue," in *The New Eighteenth Century*, ed. Felicity Nussbaum and Laura Brown (London and New York: Methuen, 1987) 210-30.

6. Richard A. Lanham, *"Tristram Shandy": The Game of Pleasure* (Berkeley and Los Angeles: University of California Press, 1973); John M. Stedmond, *The Comic Art of Laurence Sterne: Convention and Innovation in "Tristram Shandy" and "A Sentimental Journey"* (Toronto: University of Toronto Press, 1967) 53-63. See also Pat Rogers, "Sterne and Journalism," in *The Winged Skull: Papers from the Laurence Sterne Bicentenary Conference*, ed. Arthur H. Cash and John M. Stedmond (London and New York: Methuen, 1971) 132-43.

7. John Mullan, *Sentiment and Sociability: The Language of Feeling in the Eighteenth Century* (Oxford: Clarendon Press, 1988) 147-200.

8. In a version of this argument, J. Paul Hunter sees Tristram's hostility to his mother as a symptom of his failure to embrace "subversive creative Imagination" as he clings to the febrile male line; see "Clocks, Calendars, and Names" 198.

9. Critics who have noted Sterne's tonal ambiguity in sexual matters include Max Byrd, *Tristram Shandy* (Unwin Critical Library. London: G. Allen & Unwin, 1985) 51, 103-20; Mark Loveridge, *Laurence Sterne and the Argument About Design* (London and Basingstoke: Macmillan Press, 1982) 151-66; Joseph Chadwick, "Infinite Jest: Interpretation in Sterne's *A Sentimental Journey*," *Eighteenth-Century Studies* 12 (1978-79): 190-205; Frank Brady, "*Tristram Shandy*: Sexuality, Morality, and Sensibility," *Eighteenth-Century Studies* 4 (1970): 41-56. See also Mullan 182 and 199; and Stedmond, *Comic Art* 49-53.

10. "The Portrayal of Women in Restoration and Eighteenth-Century English Literature," in *What Manner of Woman: Essays on English and American Life and Literature*. ed. Marlene Springer (Oxford: Basil Blackwell, 1977) 67.

11. *Sentiment and Sociability* 154. John Mullan interprets this as a device to counter the intensity of feeling evoked by the story; it also, however, links this frame with others in the novel.

12. Richetti 84.

13. See Fritz Gysin, *Model as Motif in Tristram Shandy*. The Cooper Monographs, No. 31 (Basel, Switzerland: Francke Verlag Bern, 1983); also Lanham; and Stedmond, *Comic Art*.

14. Mullan discusses the contemporary idea of the dangers of reading, as does Richard D. Altick in *The English Common Reader: A Social History of the Mass Reading Public, 1800-1900* (Chicago and London: University of Chicago Press, 1957). See also Loveridge, who quotes Edmund Burke to conclude, "To read is to lay oneself open...to 'Contagion'. The sympathy of reading is like the sympathy of sentiment..." (208). In *Textual Exile: The Reader in Sterne and Foscolo* (American University Studies, Ser, 3, vol. 15 [New York, Berne, Frankfurt am Main: Peter Lang, 1985]), Sante Matteo argues that reading is central to *A Sentimental Journey* since Yorick "invites" the reader into the text to read the bodies of women like texts (187).

15. Nancy Armstrong, *Desire and Domestic Fiction* (New York: Oxford University Press, 1987) 8. In a contrasting view in "Clocks, Calendars, and Names," J. Paul Hunter points to Tristram's dubious paternity as an example of Sterne's allegiance to the creative female line over the degenerating male line.

16. See Patricia Meyer Spacks, *Imagining a Self: Autobiography and Novel in Eighteenth-Century England* (Cambridge: Harvard University Press, 1976) for a discussion of the relations between women and the novel; see also Robert Alter: *Partial Magic: The Novel as a Self-Parodying Genre* (Berkeley and Los Angeles: University of California Press, 1975) 30-56.

17. See Bruce Stovel, "*Tristram Shandy* and the Art of Gossip," in *Laurence Sterne: Riddles and Mysteries*, ed. Valerie Grosvenor Myer (London: Vision, 1984) 115-25. Also Eugene Hnatko's "Sterne's Conversational Style," in *The Winged Skull: Papers from the Laurence Sterne Bicentenary Conference*, ed. Arthur Hill Cash and John M. Stedmond (London and New York: Methuen, 1971) 229-36. Martin C. Battestin notes Sterne's formal conversational rhetoric in "*A Sentimental Journey* and

the Syntax of Things," in *Augustan Worlds*, ed. J. C. Hilson, M. M. B. Jones and J. R. Watson (Leicester: Leicester University Press, 1978) 223-39.

18. "Response as Reformation: *Tristram Shandy* and the Art of Interruption" *Novel: A Forum on Fiction* 4 (1971): 132-46.

19. R. F. Brissenden notes the uncertainty in sentimentalism in *Virtue in Distress* (London: Macmillan, 1974); C. J. Rawson also notes the tensions in late eighteenth-century notions of ideal control in *Henry Fielding and the Augustan Ideal Under Stress* (London and Boston: Routledge, 1972).

20. Traugott notes that the reader is intended to sympathize with but not to emulate the "group of humor characters" in the novel (74-75).

21. Among the most recent is Janet Todd, *Sensibility* 5-6.

22. "Some Sexual Beliefs and Myths in Eighteenth-Century Britain," in *Sexuality in Eighteenth-Century Britain*, ed. Paul-Gabriel Boucé (Manchester: Manchester University Press, 1982) 32.

23. For discussions of Sterne's use of the eye, see Gysin; W. B. Carnochan, *Confinement and Flight: An Essay on English Literature of the Eighteenth Century* (Berkeley and Los Angeles: University of California Press, 1977) 54-59; Jean-Jacques Mayoux, "Laurence Sterne" in *Laurence Sterne: A Collection of Critical Essays*, ed. John Traugott (Englewood Cliffs, N.J.: Prentice-Hall, 1968) 66-89. In *The Curious Perspective: Literary and Pictorial Wit in the Seventeenth Century*, Ernest B. Gilman notes Sterne's use of the hurdy-gurdy image (New Haven and London: Yale University Press, 1978).

24. Gysin 8.

25. Arther Hill Cash, *Sterne's Comedy of Moral Sentiments: The Ethical Dimension of the "Journey"* (Duquesne Studies, Ser. 6 (Pittsburgh: Duquesne University Press, 1966) 36; also 105, 108.

26. The ambiguous attitude of literary sentimentalism toward this desire grows into disapproval in the fiction written after the French Revolution. For example, Maria Bertram quotes these words as she yearns to break her engagement with Rushworth, elope with Henry Crawford, and thus escape social and sexual bonds in Jane Austen's *Mansfield Park* (1814).

NOTES FOR CHAPTER 4

1. See R. F. Brissenden, *Virtue in Distress: Studies in the Novel of Sentiment from Richardson to Sade* (London: Macmillan, 1974); and John K. Sheriff, *The Good-Natured Man: The Evolution of a Moral Ideal, 1660-1800* (University, Alabama: University of Alabama Press, 1982). Both these works emphasize the expressive and individualistic element of sentimentalism at the expense of recognizing the pleas for social responsibility and restraint in sentimental fiction. John Dwyer notes the minatory strand in Scottish sentimentalism in several places; see especially "Clio and Ethics: Practical Morality in Enlightened Scotland," *Eighteenth Century* 30 (1989):

45-72, and *Virtuous Discourse: Sensibility and Community in Late Eighteenth-Century Scotland* (Edinburgh: J. Donald, 1987).

2. In *The Popular Novel in England, 1700-1800*, J. M. S. Tompkins distinguishes Fanny Burney's and Brooke's "reasonable" plots from the mass of unreasonable novels (Lincoln: University of Nebraska Press, 1961) 60.

3. For an examination of Brooke's theatrical career, see K. J. H. Berland, "Frances Brooke and David Garrick," *Studies in Eighteenth-Century Culture* 20 (1990): 217-30.

4. For a thorough account of Frances Brooke and her works, see   Lorraine McMullen's *An Odd Attempt in a Woman: The Literary Life of Frances Brooke* (Vancouver: University of British Columbia Press, 1983). Pointing to the reviews of her novels in the contemporary *Monthly Review* and *Critical Review*, as well as to the acid exchange between Bonnell Thornton and George Colman's *The Connoisseur* and *The Old Maid*, McMullen demonstrates the popularity of Frances Brooke, and her experience in the literary world of the mid-century. McMullen argues that Brooke probably wrote *All's Right at Last; or, The History of Miss West*, published in 1774 and set in Canada (141).

5. *The Old Maid*. London: Printed for A. Millar, in the *Strand*, and sold by S. Bladon, in *Pater-noster-Row*. McMullen argues that Frances Brooke's periodical, lighter than both Eliza Haywood's *Female Spectator* and Samuel Johnson's *Rambler*, imitated the "wit, irony, and didacticism" of *The Spectator* (15, 16).

6. James Clifford notes a similar frontispiece to Father Lafitau's *Moeurs de sauvages ameriquains* showing "a young woman sitting at her writing table amid artifacts from the New World," Greece, and Egypt, with her pen identified as the source of truth, and Time flying above religious allegorical vistas behind her in *The Predicament of Culture: Twentieth-Century Ethnography, Literature and Art* (Cambridge, Mass.: Harvard University Press, 1988) 21. Such illustrations represent the control of foreign culture by the writer's translation; see Barbara M. Benedict, "The 'Curious Attitude' in Eighteenth-Century Britain: Observing and Owning," *Eighteenth-Century Life* n.s. 14 (1990): 59-98.

7. For a discussion of gender in the periodical, see Kathryn Shevelow, *Women and Print Culture* (London and New York: Routledge, 1989). Shevelow explains that Brooke imitated Haywood's *Female Spectator* but departed from "the centrality of the essay-periodical" by its diverse contents (151, 175).

8. In "A Tax on Old Maids and Bachelors: Frances Brooke's *Old Maid*," K. J. H. Berland argues that the periodical centers on "the way marriage meets (or fails to meet) the needs and expectations of women," and thus anatomizes the corruptions of the marriage marketplace that compel spinsterhood (*Eighteenth-Century Women and the Arts*, ed. Frederick M. Keener and Susan E. Lorsch [New York: Greenwood, 1988]) 29-30, passim.

9. Marie-Jeanne Riccoboni, *The Letters of Juliet Catesby, To her Friend Lady Henrietta Campley*, trans. Frances Brooke, 4th ed. (London: R. and J. Dodsley, 1764).

10. In 1770, Brooke translated *Memoirs of the Marquis de St. Forlaix* by Nicholas Etienne Framery (1745-1810); in 1771, she translated the Abbé C. F. X. Millot's *Elements of the History of England, from the invasion of the Romans to the reign of George the Second*. Undoubtedly most famous for her translations of Marie-Jeanne

Riccoboni's *Letters of Juliet Catesby*, Brooke clearly borrowed aesthetic descriptions of organized nature from the French source.

11. Frances Brooke, *The History of Lady Julia Mandeville*. 2 vols. (Dublin: J. Potts, 1763) 1:4. All citations refer to this edition. In the absence of any authoritative edition of these texts, I have preserved the original errors of punctuation and spelling as also reproduced in the 1764 edition (London: Dodsley).

12. This combination of sentimental and aristocratic virtues comprises the sentimental social ideal: see Robert Markley, "Sentimentality as Performance: Shaftesbury, Sterne and the Theatrics of Virtue," in *The New Eighteenth Century: Theory, Politics, English Literature*, ed. Felicity Nussbaum and Laura Brown (New York and London: Methuen, 1987) 210-30.

13. Robert Rosenblum, *Transformations in Late Eighteenth Century Art* (Princeton, N.J.: Princeton University Press, 1967) 7, 40.

14. John Mullan interprets the physical "language" of sentimental emotion as a transparent display of instinctive virtue, but such a view ignores the conventionally painterly language of such descriptions; see *Sentiment and Sociability: The Language of Feeling in the Eighteenth Century* (Oxford: Clarendon Press, 1988). See also Janet Todd, *Sensibility: An Introduction* (London and New York: Methuen, 1986).

15. See Barbara M. Benedict, "Pictures of Conformity: Sentiment and Structure in Ann Radcliffe's Style," *Philological Quarterly* 68 (1989): 363-77.

16. In *The Later Women Novelists, 1744-1818*, B. G. MacCarthy notes the "Gothic terrors" in this passage (Oxford: Basil Blackwell, 1946) 71. Michel Foucault discusses the eighteenth-century association of forgetfulness and madness in *Madness and Civilization: A History of Insanity in the Age of Reason*, trans. Richard Howard (New York: Vintage, 1965).

17. Frances Brooke, *The History of Emily Montague*, ed. Mary Jane Edwards (Ottawa: Carleton University Press, 1985). All citations refer to this edition.

18. Katherine Sobba Green, while noting that the novel begins from the man's point of view and recommends friendship in marriage, interprets *Emily Montague* as endorsing women's use of sensibility as a justification for opposing their guardians in *The Courtship Novel, 1740-1820* (Lexington: University of Kentucky Press, 1991) 62-66.

19. Carl F. Klinck avers that Brooke approves imperialism and entertains "conventional intolerance," but in fact her careful structure of parallels and contrasts between different cultures suggest that she is using the conventions of imperialism and cultural intolerance to argue for women's freedom and protection, not for imperialism per se. See Klinck, Introduction, *The History of Emily Montague*, by Frances Brooke (Toronto: McClelland and Stewart, 1961) v-xiv.

20. Carol Barash explores the overlaps between sexual and colonial exploitation in slave narratives that use the device of dreaming and the language of possessive dominance; see "The Character of Difference: The Creole Narrator as Cultural Mediator in Narratives about Jamaica," *Eighteenth-Century Studies* 23 (1990): 406-24.

21. Clifford observes that dominant cultures view colonized or "primitive" people as without history (32); Frye, on the contrary, identifies *The History of Emily Montague* as a chronicle of the "primitivism" of the New World that is almost

historical in its empirical detail; see "Eighteenth-Century Sensibility," *Varieties of Eighteenth-Century Studies* 24. Spec. issue 2 (1990-91): 157-72.

22. Ann Messenger notes the play with names, and the similarity between Pope's style and Brooke's character's style in *His and Hers: Essays in Restoration and Eighteenth-Century Literature* (Lexington: University of Kentucky Press, 1986) 148-71.

23. K. J. H. Berland traces the philosophical sentimentalism behind Brooke's transformation of philanthropy into "the gratification of the natural affections" in "The True Pleasurable Philosopher: Some Influences on Frances Brooke's *History of Emily Montague*," *Dalhousie Review* 66 (1986): 286-300, 287. While stressing Brooke's sentimental orthodoxy and use of natural scenery to evoke ideal nature, Berland does not discuss Brooke's self-conscious use of art.

24. Frances Brooke, *The Excursion*. 2 vols. (London: T. Cadell, in the Strand, 1777).

NOTES FOR CHAPTER 5

1. John Dwyer has identified Mackenzie's role in the "Mirror" club and in the Edinburgh elite in *Virtuous Discourse: Sensibility and Community in Late Eighteenth-Century Scotland* (Edinburgh: J. Donald, 1987); here and elsewhere he argues for Mackenzie's fear of social disruption, although he underrates Mackenzie's irony and literary sophistication. See also Dwyer and Alexander Murdoch, "Paradigms and Politics: Manners, Morals and the Rise of Henry Dundas, 1770-1784," in *New Perspectives on the Politics and Culture of Early Modern Scotland*, ed. John Dwyer, Roger A. Mason, and Alexander Murdoch (Edinburgh: J. Donald, 1982) 220-37, esp. 222-24.

2. Henry Mackenzie, "Account of the German Theater," *The Transactions of the Royal Society of Edinburgh* (London: T. Cadell, 1790) 2:2, 192. This speech was given in 1788.

3. Critics who interpret *The Man of Feeling* as uncritically advocating sentiment include J. M. S. Tompkins, *The Popular Novel in England, 1770-1800* (Lincoln: University of Nebraska Press, 1961) 53-55; Robert D. Mayo, *The English Novel in the Magazines, 1740-1815* (Evanston: Northwestern University Press, 1962) 125; R. F. Brissenden in *Virtue in Distress: Studies in the Novel of Sentiment from Richardson to Sade* (London: Macmillan, 1974); Brian Vickers, Introduction, *The Man of Feeling* by Henry Mackenzie (Oxford: Oxford University Press, 1987) vii-xxiv; and Ann Van Sant, *Eighteenth-Century Sensibility and the Novel: The Senses in a Social Context* (Cambridge: Cambridge University Press, 1993). John K. Sheriff finds literary merit in Mackenzie's novel, arguing for the "complex and artistic" attack on Harley's "vanity" through the narrative frames in *The Good-Natured Man: The Evolution of a Moral Ideal, 1660-1800* (University, Alabama: University of Alabama Press, 1982) 82-91, esp. 83, 90. Even while noting the "disparity between virtue and the indulgence of benevolent feelings" in Mackenzie's work, Sheriff, however, interprets

the book according to Mackenzie's consistent "Humean ethical stance," ignoring the literary humor in the novel (85-86).

4. Vickers xxii-iii.

5. Henry Mackenzie, *The Man of Feeling*, ed. Brian Vickers (Oxford, 1987) 5. All citations to this text refer to this edition.

6. See three letters on Brooke's novel in *Henry Mackenzie: Letters to Elizabeth Rose of Kilvarock. On Literature, Events and People, 1768-1815*, ed. Horst W. Drescher (Edinburgh and London: Oliver and Boyd, 1967) 52-53, 53-54, 68.

7. For a theoretical explication of the dialogic structure of novelistic discourse, see M. M. Bakhtin, *The Dialogic Imagination*, ed. Michael Holquist, trans. Caryl Emerson and Michael Holquist (Austin: University of Texas Press, 1981).

8. Kenneth Simpson notes Mackenzie's attack on opulence in one issue of *The Mirror*; see *The Protean Scot: The Crisis of Identity in Eighteenth-Century Scottish Literature* (Aberdeen: Aberdeen University Press, 1988) 180. See also Barbara M. Benedict, "'Service to the Public': William Creech and Sentiment for Sale," *Eighteenth-Century Life* n.s. 15 (1991): 119-46. In "Women Writing/Writing Women: Pope, Dulness and 'Feminization' in the *Dunciad*," Catherine Ingrassia notes contemporary attacks on the promulgation of "female" fancy (*Eighteenth-Century Life* n.s. 14 [1990]: 40-41). See also Terry Lovell, *Consuming Fiction* (London: Verso, 1987) 36-45. James Raven quotes Mackenzie as blaming the aristocracy for infecting the middle classes with extravagance, as in *The Mirror* no. 12 (6 Mar. 1779); in *Judging New Wealth: Popular Publishing and Responses to Commerce in England, 1750-1800* (Oxford: Clarendon Press, 1992) 181-82.

9. Graeme Tytler, "Letters of Recommendation and False Vizors: Physiognomy in the Novels of Henry Fielding," *Eighteenth-Century Fiction* 2 (1990): 105. Tytler analyzes the overlap of religious and sentimental attitudes to physiognomy in *Physiognomy in the European Novel: Faces and Fortunes* (Princeton, N.J.: Princeton University Press, 1982) esp. 8-10. Addison and Steele discussed physiognomy; see, for example, *The Spectator* no. 86 (8 June 1711).

10. See Lavater's "*Essays on Physiognomy*, Designed to promote the Knowledge and Love of Mankind," trans. Henry Hunter (London: John Murray, 1789) esp. 20. In "Mackenzie's Martyr: The Man of Feeling as Saintly Fool," Robert L. Platzner observes that Mackenzie interprets benevolence as personal forgetfulness, and that Harley, in his fusion of love and pain, enacts a saintly identification with the reviled (*Novel: A Forum on Fiction* 10 [1976]: 59-64).

11. George A. Starr notes Harley's immaturity in "'Only a Boy': Notes on Sentimental Novels," *Genre* 10 (1977): 501-27.

12. Episodes from Mackenzie's work, both his periodicals and his novels, were also published separately toward the end of the eighteenth century and into the nineteenth, especially "The Story of La Roche" and "Louisa Venoni" from *The Lounger* and "The Story of Father Nicholas" from *The Mirror*. "Harley's Visit to Bedlam," "The Misanthrope," and "The Seduction of a Young Girl" all appear in collections of sentimental or moral tales. See Barbara M. Benedict, "Literary Miscellanies: The Cultural Mediation of Fragmented Feeling," *ELH* 57 (1990): 407-30. See also Chapter 6, "Canonizing and Popularizing Sentimental Literature" 137-55.

13. Henry Mackenzie, *The Works of Henry Mackenzie, Esq.* 8 vols. (Edinburgh and London: Ballantyne, 1808) 3:168-72.

14. Mackenzie, *Works* 3: 7. In "Imitation and Ideology: Henry Mackenzie's Rousseau," Kim Ian Micasiw documents Mackenzie's revision of the Rousseau's *Julie* into a more moderate, even mixed, recommendation of sentiment (*Eighteenth-Century Fiction* 5 [1993]: 153-76). Mackenzie mentions Madame Riccoboni disapprovingly several times, as in *The Lounger* no. 92, for example.

15. Reprinted in *"The Beauties of Mackenzie; selected from his various Works. To which is prefixed a Short Sketch of His Life and Writings"* (London: R. Tullis, 1813) 58. This character sketch emphasizes the domestic morality of Mackenzie. Citations from this story refer to this edition.

16. National Library of Scotland mss. 598, f.2, received by Mackenzie on 10 March 1779. I examine the full text in "'Service to the Public': William Creech and Sentiment for Sale."

17. National Library of Scotland mss. 598, f.31, signed A.Z.

18. Henry Mackenzie, *The Lounger. A Periodical Paper, published at Edinburgh in the Years 1785 and 1786* (Edinburgh: W. Creech, 1787) no. 51 (208). See also nos. 16, 20, 51, and 21, "Danger to young ladies of being introduced into and society and style of manners above their natural situation in life." Henry Mackenzie, *The Mirror: A Periodical Paper, published at Edinburgh in the Years 1779 and 1780*, 4th ed. 3 vols. (Edinburgh: W. Strahan, T. Cadell, and W. Creech, 1782). All citations to these texts refer to these editions.

NOTES FOR CHAPTER 6

1. In *The Making of English Reading Audiences, 1790-1832*, Jon Klancher analyzes the way periodical publications helped to define social groups or "classes" (Madison: University of Wisconsin Press, 1987). For examinations of the ways in which poorer urban classes imitated the tastes of the gentry, see Roy Porter, *English Society in the Eighteenth Century* (Middlesex: Penguin, 1982) 67-90; and J. H. Plumb, "Commercialization and Society" in *The Birth of a Consumer Society: The Commercialization of Eighteenth-Century England* by Neil McKendrick, John Brewer, and J. H. Plumb, (London: Hutchison, 1982) 269, 284.

2. The Eighteenth Century Short Title Catalogue and the British Museum Library suggest that the first two decades of the eighteenth century saw a proliferation of poetic and technical collections while by mid-century these had been replaced by prose or multi-genre literary miscellanies.

3. For this insight into the implications of literature by blindmen, see David Daiches, *Literature and Gentility in Scotland* (Edinburgh: University of Edinburgh Press, 1982) 90-100. For the popularity of rogues' biographies, see G. A. Starr, *Defoe and Spiritual Autobiography* (Princeton, N.J.: Princeton University Press, 1965). For the popularity of the catechism, see Donald Davie, *A Gathered Church: The Literature of the English Dissenting Interest, 1700-1930* (London: Routledge, 1978).

4. Ronald Paulson, *Popular and Polite Art in the Age of Hogarth and Fielding* (Notre Dame and London: University of Notre Dame Press, 1979) 16.

5. Such anonymity reflects the prevalence of piracy, unauthorized reprints of material by publishers and booksellers who did not hold rights to the copy; the scrambling method of production of miscellanies, however, which were sometimes compiled by booksellers from spare copy in their shops, also allowed them to neglect attributing the works to specific authors.

6. Paulson notes only early "Sentimental Beauties," and collected "beauties" of Sterne, Fielding, and Richardson from the first half of the century, but such collections continued into the 1800s (*Popular and Polite Art* 141). See also James Raven, *Judging New Wealth: Popular Publishing and Responses to Commerce in England, 1750-1800* (Oxford: Clarendon Press, 1993) 13-14, 53-55. Altick notes the 1783 collection of engravings entitled "Picturesque Beauties of Shakespeare" (*Paintings from Books* [Columbus: Ohio State University Press, 1985] 42).

7. James Sutherland, *The Restoration Newspaper and Its Development* (Cambridge: Cambridge University Press, 1986) 42. John Brewer notes the "printers' and booksellers' eagerness to seize the main chance, and to respond swiftly to changes in taste and fashion"; see "Commercialization and Politics" in *The Birth of a Consumer Society: The Commercialization of Eighteenth-Century England* by Neil McKendrick, John Brewer, and J. H. Plumb, (London: Hutchison, 1982) 258.

8. George Nicholson, ed., *The Literary Miscellany; or, Elegant Selections of The Most Admired Fugitive Pieces, and EXTRACTS from Works of the Greatest Merit: with Originals in Prose and Verse* (London, 1796) 1. In his *Lives of the English Poets*, Johnson censured the extravagance, roughness, and obscurity of Collins's verse.

9. John Dixon Hunt, *The Figure in the Landscape: Poetry, Painting and Gardening During the Eighteenth Century* (Baltimore and London: Johns Hopkins University Press, 1976) 8-12. The psychological emphasis on landscaping, which controlled nature in order to please the mind of man, is also reflected in the framing techniques of publishers in the late eighteenth century: the reader's experience takes precedence over the original "meaning" or context of the literature.

10. In *Popular and Polite Art*, Ronald Paulson cites both Addison's *Spectator* and Chesterfield's *Letters* as mediations between "the learned and the new reading public" (115). He also notes that Chesterfield's letters "perfectly reflect Locke's argument that education is not to secure the child's obedience, not to tyrannize, but to prepare him for an eventual emergence into the world--a moment of liberation" (139). In *Popular Culture in Early Modern Europe*, Peter Burke notes that dancing becomes a central touchstone of class, as treatises on the subject proliferate and the upper classes adopt a self-conscious, restrained, and courtly manner (London: Temple Smith, 1978) 271.

11. Nicholson clearly exploits the popularity of Robert Dodsley's *A collection of poems, by several hands* (1748-58), revised and extended by Pearch (1775). This collection of poems from the Graveyard School, finely illustrated, helped to establish the contemporary taste for sentimental verse.

12. Hunt remarks that, in the early half of the century, landowners hired hermits to inhabit the picturesque hermitages they had built on their estates, paying them to scuttle away from visitors, wear humble rags and sandals, and refuse to speak to

anyone (8). Victor E. Neuburg discusses chapbook depictions in *Popular Education in Eighteenth-Century England* (London: Woburn, 1971) 116-18.

13. This definition by negatives, which emphasizes that a good woman "says nothing," resembles the moral language of both Samuel Johnson and Jane Austen and characterizes moral behavior by its restraint rather than by its positive action.

14. See Katherine Tillotson, *Novels of the Eighteen-Forties* (Oxford: Clarendon Press, 1954).

15. For a discussion of the superiority of friendship to love in the early eighteenth century, see Jean Hagstrum, *Sex and Sensibility: Ideal and Erotic Love from Milton to Mozart* (Chicago and London: University of Chicago Press, 1980) esp. 104-106.

16. James Mitchell, ed. *Sentimental tales &c.* (Newcastle-upon-Tyne: J. Mitchell, 1801). All citations refer to this edition.

17. Altick, *Paintings from Books* 38.

18. This characteristic imitates that of the chapbook, the main form of printed popular literature in the seventeenth and eighteenth centuries. See the collection entitled "Entertaining and Instructive Tales," vol.2 (British Library, 1078.k.4: 1813) bound by the British Museum as *Chapbooks Printed in Scotland, 1805-21*; also see Victor E. Neuburg, *The Penny Histories: A Study of Chapbooks for Young Readers over Two Centuries* (London: Oxford University Press, 1968).

19. Pat Rogers, *Literature and Popular Culture in Eighteenth-Century England* (Sussex: Harvester Press, 1985) 163. See also Peter Burke's discussion of the two-way cultural crossover between "high" and "popular" culture in *Popular Culture in Early Modern Europe* (London: Temple Smith, 1978) 23-28.

20. R. F. Brissenden discusses the connections between revolutionary theory and sentimentalism in *Virtue in Distress: Studies in the Novel of Sentiment from Richardson to Sade* (London: Macmillan, 1974) 56-64. For a discussion of the pastoralism and nostalgia of sentimentalism, see Roger Sales, *English Literature in History, 1780-1830: Pastoral and Politics* (New York: St. Martin's Press, 1983) 15-18. On English Jacobinism, see Marilyn Butler, *Romantics, Rebels, and Reactionaries: English Literature and Its Background, 1760-1830* (Oxford: Oxford University Press, 1982). To aid pedagogy and attract children, Marmontel's tales were often enhanced with engravings in the neoclassical style.

21. See Plumb 331-32. In 1774, William Hooper published a book called *Rational Recreations*, which advertised magic lanterns. See also Michael Fried, *Absorption and Theatricality: Painting and Beholder in the Age of Diderot* (Berkeley and Los Angeles: University of California Press, 1980). In *Cultural History: Between Practices and Representations* (trans. Lydia G. Cochrane [Cambridge, Mass.: Polity, 1988]), Roger Chartier develops Pierre Bourdieu's thesis in *Distinction: A Social Critique of the Judgement of Taste* (trans. Richard Nice [Cambridge: Harvard University Press, 1984]) to argue that imagery operated both in illustrations and in texts to promote myths praising peasant harmony and reading as domestic comfort (164). See also Francis Haskell, *The Painful Birth of the Art Book* (New York: Thames and Hudson, 1987), which discusses the consumption of masterpieces as aesthetic objects accessible to a general audience after 1760 (57).

22. John Barrell, *The Dark Side of the Landscape: The Rural Poor in English Painting, 1730-1840* (Cambridge: Cambridge University Press, 1980) 8.

23. John Berger, *Ways of Seeing* (Middlesex: Penguin, 1972). See also Peter Burke, *Popular Culture in Early Modern Europe* for a theoretical analysis of the ways in which "peripheries" can inform the historian--social or literary--of cultural signals and values (9-15).

24. Altick, *Paintings from Books* 34.

25. Altick 40-41.

26. See Jeffrey R. Smitten, "Gesture and Expression in Eighteenth-Century Fiction: *A Sentimental Journey*" *Modern Language Studies* 9 (1979): 85-97. Also Robert Markley, "Sentimentality as Performance: Shaftesbury, Sterne, and the Theatrics of Virtue," in *The New Eighteenth Century: Theory, Politics, English Literature*, ed. Felicity Nussbaum and Laura Brown (London and New York: Methuen, 1987) 210-30.

27. Henry Mackenzie, *The Anecdotes and Egotisms of Henry Mackenzie, 1745-1831*, ed. with an intro. Harold William Thompson (Oxford: Oxford University Press, 1927) 245. For a perceptive analysis of the sexual and political implications of epistolarity, see Annabel Patterson, *Censorship and Interpretation: The Conditions of Writing and Reading in Early Modern England* (Madison: University of Wisconsin Press, 1984) 203, 232. It is possible that the feminine script of so many pocket series also evokes the implied "censorship" Patterson discusses, reinforcing the minatory and instructive character of these miscellanies.

28. Margaret Spufford, *Small Books and Pleasant Histories: Popular Fiction and Its Readership in Seventeenth-Century England* (Cambridge: Cambridge University Press, 1981) 72-75.

29. Plumb 292.

30. In the next thirty years, this identification between the uneducated, women, and children will stimulate the Romantic interest in medieval chivalric poetry and popular ballads; the naiveté of these literary forms will be seen as the expression of the innocence and purity of those uncorrupted by social education or the shadow of the prison house. For a discussion of sentimentalism as Oedipal and proto-Romantic, see Robert E. Moore and Jean H. Hagstrum, *Changing Taste in Eighteenth-Century Art and Literature* (William Andrews Clark Memorial Library: 17 Apr. 1971; Los Angeles: University of California Press, 1972) 60-61.

31. Spufford 72.

32. Spufford 12; R. A. Houston, *Scottish Literacy and the Scottish Identity in Scotland and Northern England, 1600-1800* (Cambridge: Cambridge University Press, 1985) 164-65. *The Lounger. A Periodical Paper, published at Edinburgh in the Years 1785 and 1786* (Edinburgh: W. Creech, 1787) 237-40. All citations to this text refer to this edition.

33. We cannot know certainly because Lord Abercromby insisted on preserving the authorial anonymity of specific contributions to *The Lounger* and hence his own reputation as the best-educated man in Scotland. Creech, however, also founded the Speculative Society in 1764, one of the series of intellectual clubs that dominated the literary character of Edinburgh during the second half of the Scottish Enlightenment.

34. For the history of the eighteenth-century debates over the influence of the past, see Joseph M. Levine, *The Battle of the Books: History and Literature in the Augustan Age* (Ithaca: Cornell University Press, 1991).

35. See Terry Lovell, *Consuming Fiction* (London: Verso, 1987) 36-45. Lovell dates the "feminization of literary culture" somewhat vaguely as beginning early in the eighteenth century but flowering at the beginning of the nineteenth, but in fact the association of corrupt culture with female values predates the novel. See Jean H. Hagstrum 37. Hagstrum observes that Milton bequests to eighteenth-century letters the recognition that sexuality levels social and sexual hierarchies and that women's will, in the Biblical tradition, effeminizes men; thus, submitting to female sexuality becomes prostitution and effeminization.

36. Alistair Duckworth, *The Improvement of the Estate: A Study of Jane Austen's Novels* (Baltimore: Johns Hopkins University Press, 1971); Plumb 332.

37. J. Paul Hunter suggests that this association between winding and sex may have predated and so informed Sterne's *Tristram Shandy*, in which the winding of the clock is associated with sexual intercourse. See "Clocks, Calendars, and Names: The Troubles of Tristram and the Aesthetics of Uncertainty," in *Rhetorics of Order/Ordering Rhetorics in English Neoclassical Literature* ed. J. Douglas Canfield and J. Paul Hunter (Newark: University of Delaware Press, 1989) 174.

38. Hagstrum isolates Sterne from other sentimental writers for his unique carnality, but the association of sentimentalism with sexual promiscuity is clear throughout the period (252).

39. Fielding makes this connection in *Amelia* (1751) by attributing the sexual infidelity of the hero Booth to his religious freethinking and by portraying the gambler, blackmailer, and thief Robinson as a freethinker. Mackenzie also associates sexual libertinism with freethinking in *The Man of Feeling*, in which Captain Atkins teaches his daughter Emily his own freethinking, which in turn leads to her prostitution. In fact, the very similarity between the names of the characters in the two novels--Emily and Amelia, Atkins and Atkinson--suggests that Mackenzie used *Amelia* as his model, deliberately preserving the thesis that freethinking leads to promiscuity.

40. Berger ch. 5.

41. Hagstrum traces this contradiction to Rousseau, for whom sexuality was represented by the maternal. See Moore and Hagstrum 51, 54-59.

NOTES FOR CHAPTER 7

1. For an account of the way in which contradictory discourses or "ideologies" such as those Radcliffe displays can be read as coherent, see Antonio Gramsci, *Selections from the Prison Notebooks*, ed. Hoare, 404-407, quoted in "On the Use of Contradiction: Economics and Morality in the Eighteenth-Century Long Poem," John Barrell and Harriet Guest, (*The New Eighteenth Century: Theory, Politics, English Literature*, ed. Felicity Nussbaum and Laura Brown (New York and London: Methuen, 1987) 123.

2. See Elizabeth R. Napier, *The Failure of Gothic: Problems of Disjunction in an Eighteenth-Century Literary Form* (Oxford: Clarendon Press, 1987) 52-53.

3. Several critics have questioned the relationship between reason and emotion in Radcliffe's works. In "A Constant   Vicissitude of Interesting Passions: Ann Radcliffe's Perplexed Narratives," Gary Kelly simplifies this relationship by arguing that "Reason schools Sensibility and then marries her" (*Ariel: A Review of International English Literature* 10 [1979]: 52). Wylie Sypher locates in *Udolpho* "an unresolved conflict between an essentially bourgeois and a radical or romantic point of view" in the opposition between the moral advocacy of caution, and aesthetic indulgence in "Social Ambiguity in a Gothic Novel" (*Partisan Review* 12 [1945]: 54).   Napier echoes Sypher's view (71-2, 100). By   underrating Radcliffe's sentimental heritage, these critics overlook the connection between "caution" and aesthetic distance.

4. Daniel Cottom, *The Civilized Imagination: A Study of Ann Radcliffe, Jane Austen, and Sir Walter Scott* (Cambridge: Cambridge University Press, 1985) 43. This excellent book identifies the aristocratic implications in the discourse on taste and on objectivity in the eighteenth century, but fails to examine Radcliffe's prose in detail.

5. Ann Radcliffe, *The Mysteries of Udolpho*, ed. Bonamy Dobrée, World's Classics Edition (New York: Oxford University Press, 1966) 626. All citations will refer to this edition. Chloe Chard, editor of Ann Radcliffe's *The Romance of the Forest*, observes in a footnote that the "comically naive" Peter, "given to prolixity, digression, and   confusion" re-enacts a Gothic convention established by Walpole (World's Classics Edition [New York: Oxford University Press, 1986] 373). The technique of interrupting the dramatic action while a servant proses on, however, belongs rather to Shakespeare; and it is to Shakespeare that Radcliffe explicitly refers even in the very epigraph of the novel. In *Gothic Strains and Bourgeois Sentiments in the Novels of Mrs. Ann Radcliffe and Her Imitators*, John Garrett notes the "choral function" of Radcliffe's peasants and her fundamental political conservatism ([New York: Arno, 1980] 269, 231-37).

6. Ann Radcliffe, *The Romance of the Forest*, ed. Chloe Chard, World's Classics Edition (New York: Oxford University Press, 1986) 145. All citations to this text refer to this edition.

7. The repetition of this allusion in sentimental nomenclature--Mackenzie's Mountford, Montford in Mitchell's *Sentimental tales, &c.*--suggests the persistence in sentimental prose fictions of the notion that heroes or antiheroes are distinguished by their moral (if not also social) height, a notion that Radcliffe complicates here.

8. See, for example, Margaret A. Doody, "Deserts, Ruins and Troubled Waters: Female Dreams in Fiction and the Development of the Gothic Novel," *Genre* 10 (1977): 529-72; Norman N. Holland and Leona F. Sherman, "Gothic Possibilities," *New Literary History* 8 (1977): 279-94; Cynthia Griffin Wolff, "The Radcliffean Gothic Model: A Form for Feminine Sexuality," *Modern Language Studies* 9 (1979): 98-113. In *Visits to Bedlam: Madness and Literature in the Eighteenth Century* (Columbia, S. C.: University of South Carolina Press, 1974), Max Byrd observes that "Both Sterne and Mackenzie also correct to some extent the Augustan misogyny by making their pathetic victims women. Far from being objects of Popean and Swiftian scorn, women now appear as creatures of extraordinary delicacy, sensitivity, genius; these mad ladies ... are first drafts of the virtuous heroines of Mrs. Radcliffe's Gothic novels" (92-93).

9. Michel Foucault, *Madness and Civilization: A History of Insanity in the Age of Reason* (trans. Richard Howard [New York: Vintage, 1973]) 220, 58, 217. All citations to this text refer to this edition.

10. In "The Spectralization of Other in *The Mysteries of Udolpho*" (*The New Eighteenth Century*, ed. Nussbaum and Brown [New York and London: Methuen, 1987])," Terry Castle discovers in this scene the obsession with death and the denial of its finality characteristic of *Udolpho*, and explicitly dismisses the religious significance of the book (248). While it is true that religion serves political and social purposes in the novel, it is a misreading to ignore the emphatic references throughout the book to the good manners of believing in God.

11. Foucault 246; see also Foucault 156, 207, 219, 262.

12. For discussions of Radcliffe's use of landscape, see Cottom 35-50; Lynne Epstein, "Mrs. Radcliffe's Landscapes: The Influence of Three Landscape Painters on her Nature Descriptions," *Hartford Studies in Literature* 12 (1969): 107-20; and Chloe Chard's "Introduction" to *The Romance of the Forest*, vii-xxiv.

13. In "A Constant Vicissitude of Interesting Passions: Ann Radcliffe's Perplexed Narratives," Gary Kelly argues that Radcliffe "stabilizes" her novels through the even-tempered objective narrative voice of "good taste," drained of expressive language or syntax (61). Kelly ignores both the characteristics of the narrative voice, and the conflicts between stylistic modes in Radcliffe's works.

14. See Barrell and Guest, "On the Use of Contradiction: Economics and Morality in the Eighteenth-Century Long Poem" (*The New Eighteenth Century: Theory, Politics, English Literature*, ed. Felicity Nussbaum and Laura Brown [(New York and London: Methuen, 1987]: 121-43). I am indebted to this essay for its discussion of mixed-genre poetry and ways of reading in the eighteenth century, esp. 132-35.

15. Radcliffe also quotes Collins's "Ode to Fear" in *The Mysteries of Udolpho* and *The Italian*, and the text was a favorite one in late century literary miscellanies.

16. Foucault 157, 247.

17. Foucault 248. In the conclusion of *Madness and Civilization*, Foucault argues that the presence of art indicates the absence of madness, and vice versa (284). However, Clementina in Richardson's *Sir Charles Grandison*, Lucy in Mackenzie's *Man of Feeling*, and Agnes in *Udolpho* all exhibit the madness of frustrated nature expressed through fine art, while earlier in the century the mad mathematicians and dreamers in Hogarth's asylums connect madness with artistic fantasy.

18. Terry Castle observes Radcliffe's attention to Locke's "Rentention" of mental images in "The Spectralization of Other" 247.

19. In *Imagining a Self: Autobiography and Novel in Eighteenth-Century England* (Cambridge, Mass.: Harvard University Press, 1976), Patricia Meyer Spacks argues that eighteenth-century women write novels "to affirm the social order that limits them," defining their heroines by their weakness but acknowledging the cost of such weakness (57-58).

20. For a discussion of classical rhetorical ornaments and the relations between description and narrative, see Gerard Genette, "Boundaries of Narrative," trans. Ann Levonas, *New Literary History* 8 (1976): 1-13.

21. See Donna Landry's "The Resignation of Mary Collier: Some Problems in Feminist Literary History" (*The New Eighteenth Century*, ed. Nussbaum and Brown

[New York and London: Methuen, 1987] 99-120). Radcliffe here not only demon-strates the knowledge of neoclassical technique and allusion requisite for a poet, but also "discloses ... the necessary 'intertextuality' of all literary enterprise," thus "demystifying" literary art (110-11). Radcliffe's reliance on contemporary aesthetic theory, however, tends to argue against the ultimate subversiveness of her literary voice.

22. For Radcliffe's audience, see Richard D. Altick, *The English Common Reader: A Social History of the Mass Reading Public, 1800-1900* (Chicago: University of Chicago Press, 1957) 63. For the visual literacy of the audience, see Ronald Paulson, *Emblem and Expression: Meaning in English Art of the Eighteenth Century* (London: Thames and Hudson, 1975) 47; J. H. Plumb, "Commercialization and Society," in *The Birth of a Consumer Society: The Commercialization of Eighteenth-Century England*, ed. Neil McKendrick, John Brewer, and J. H. Plumb (London: Hutchinson, 1982) 329; John Dixon Hunt, *The Figure in the Landscape: Poetry, Painting, and Gardening during the Eighteenth Century* (Baltimore and London: Johns Hopkins University Press, 1976) 18; Jean H. Hagstrum, *The Sister Arts: The Tradition of Literary Pictorialism and English Poetry from Dryden to Gray* (Chicago: University of Chicago Press, 1958) 130.

23. For a depiction of this posture, see Caesar Ripa, *Iconologia: Or, Moral Emblems*, trans. Isaac Fuller (London: Benjamin Motte, 1709) 5; Fig.17.

24. For other examples of heaven-gazing, see *Udolpho* 151, 184, 329, 475. Jeffrey R. Smitten discusses gesture as sentimental language in "Gesture and Expression in Eighteenth-Century Fiction: *A Sentimental Journey*," *Modern Language Studies* 9 (1979) 85-87.

25. Hagstrum xvi-xxii, 10, 33, 38.

NOTES FOR CONCLUSION

1. Jane Austen, *Sense and Sensibility*, ed. R. W. Chapman (Oxford: Oxford University Press, 1923). All citations to this text refer to this edition.

2. James Thompson remarks on the difficulty of determining Austen's attitude to romantic love or to marriage as an institution that is at once idealistic and materialis-tic in "*Sense and Sensibility*: Finance and Romance,"in *Sensibility in Transformation: Creative Resistance to Sentiment from the Augustans to the Romantics: Essays in Honor of Jean H. Hagstrum*, ed. Syndy McMillan Conger (London and Toronto: Associated University Presses, 1990) 147-71. See also James Thompson, *Between Self and World: The Novels of Jane Austen* (University Park: Pennsylvania State University Press, 1988).

3. John Odmark, *An Understanding of Jane Austen's Novels: Character, Value, and Ironic Perspective* (Oxford: Basil Blackwell, 1981) 58.

4. Frank Bradbrook examines Austen's debt to, and ambivalence towards, Addison and Steele and Samuel Johnson in *Jane Austen and Her Predecessors* (Cambridge: Cambridge University Press, 1966) 3-17. J.F. Burrows defends Austen's

careful stylistics and suggests that they recapitulate stereotypical gender distinctions in *Computation into Criticism: A Study of Jane Austen's Novels and an Experiment in Method* (Oxford: Oxford University Press, 1987). For a study of Austen's shifting viewpoint, see also Howard S. Babb, *Jane Austen's Novels: The Fabric of Dialogue* (Ohio: Ohio State University Press, 1962).

5. In examining the critique of sensibility in the novel, Kenneth L. Moler argues that Austen intends us to view Elinor's "sense" skeptically; see *Jane Austen's Art of Allusion* (Nebraska: University of Nebraska Press, 1968) 44. In *The Proper Lady and the Woman Writer: Mary Wollstonecraft, Mary Shelley, and Jane Austen*, Mary Poovey suggests that Elinor experiences a conflict between feeling and control ([Chicago and London: University of Chicago Press, 1984]: 185-87).

6. John Barrell analyzes the eighteenth-century value for a detached, disinterested, comprehensive viewpoint in *English Literature in History, 1730-80: An Equal, Wide Survey* (New York: St. Martin's Press, 1983) 33-40.

7. In "The Function of Criticism at the Present Time" (1864), Matthew Arnold traces the corruption of disinterested culture to the French Revolution, which he argues politicized culture.

8. Stephen Cox convincingly argues in "Sensibility as Argument" that sentimental writers increasingly distinguish between different kinds of sensibility to preserve the value of social decorum. See Conger, ed. *Sensibility in Transformation* 63-82.

9. Richard Payne Knight, *An Analytical Inquiry into the Principles of Taste*, 3rd. ed. (London: T. Payne, 1806) 1:2. All citations to this text refer to this edition.

10. Nancy Armstrong, "The Rise of Feminine Authority in the Novel," *Novel: A Forum on Fiction* 15 (1982): 127-45.

11. Miriam Hobson discovers that optical theory in the eighteenth century supported the notion of absolute judgments in *The Object of Art: The Theory of Illusion in Eighteenth-Century France* (Cambridge: Cambridge University Press, 1982) 30. Charles L. Batten, Jr., explains travel as the education of the eye in *Pleasurable Instruction: Form and Convention in Eighteenth-Century Travel Literature* (Berkeley and Los Angeles: University of California Press, 1978) 119, passim.

BIBLIOGRAPHY

Addison, Joseph, and Sir Richard Steele. *The Spectator.* 5 vols. Ed. Donald
F. Bond. Oxford: Clarendon Press, 1963.

Alter, Robert. *Partial Magic: The Novel as a Self-Parodying Genre.*
Berkeley, Los Angeles, and London: University of California Press, 1975.

Altick, Richard D. *The English Common Reader: A Social History of the
Mass Reading Public, 1800-1900.* Chicago and London: University of
Chicago Press, 1957.

_____. *Paintings from Books: Art and Literature in Britain, 1760-1900.*
Columbus: Ohio State University Press, 1985.

Anderson, Howard, and John S. Shea, ed. *Studies in Criticism and Aesthetics,
1660-1800: Essays in Honor of Samuel Holt Monk.* Minneapolis: University of Minnesota Press, 1967.

Armstrong, Nancy. *Desire and Domestic Fiction: A Political History of the
Novel.* New York and Oxford: Oxford University Press, 1987.

_____. "The Rise of Feminine Authority in the Novel." *Novel: A Forum
on Fiction* 15 (1982): 127-45.

Austen, Jane. *Sense and Sensibility.* Ed. R. W. Chapman. Oxford: Oxford
University Press, 1923.

Babb, Howard S. *Jane Austen's Novels: The Fabric of Dialogue.* Ohio:
Ohio State University Press, 1962.

Backman, Sven. *This Singular Tale: A Study of "The Vicar of Wakefield"
and Its Literary Background.* Lund Studies in English, 40. Lund: C. W.
K. Gleerup, 1971.

Bakhtin, Mikhail M. *The Dialogic Imagination.* Ed. Michael Holquist.
Trans. Caryl Emerson and Michael Holquist. Austin: University of Texas
Press, 1981.

_____. *Problems of Dostoevsky's Poetics.* Trans. R. W. Rostel. Ann Arbor,
Michigan: Ardis, 1973.

_____. *Rabelais and His World.* Trans. Hélène Iswolsky. Cambridge, Mass.:
MIT Press, 1968.

Barash, Carol. "The Character of Difference: The Creole Narrator as Cultural
Mediator in Narratives about Jamaica." *Eighteenth-Century Studies* 23
(1990): 406-24.

Barker-Benfield, G. J. *The Culture of Sensibility: Sex and Society in Eighteenth-Century Britain*. Chicago and London: University of Chicago Press, 1992.

Barrell, John. *The Dark Side of the Landscape: The Rural Poor in English Painting, 1730-1840*. Cambridge: Cambridge University Press, 1980.

_____. *English Literature in History, 1730-80: An Equal, Wide Survey*. New York: St. Martin's Press, 1983.

_____. *The Idea of Landscape and the Sense of Place, 1730-1840: An Approach to the Poetry of John Clare*. Cambridge: Cambridge University Press, 1972.

_____, and Harriet Guest. "On the Uses of Contradiction: Economics and Morality in the Eighteenth-Century Long Poem," in *The New Eighteenth Century*, ed. Felicity Nussbaum and Laura Brown. New York and London: Methuen, 1987: 121-43.

Barrows, J. F. *Computation into Criticism: A Study of Jane Austen's Novels and an Experiment in Method*. Oxford: Oxford University Press, 1987.

Batten, Charles L., Jr. *Pleasurable Instruction: Form and Convention in Eighteenth-Century Travel Literature*. Berkeley and Los Angeles: University of California Press, 1978.

Bender, John. *Imagining the Penitentiary: Fiction and the Architecture of Mind in Eighteenth-Century England*. Chicago and London: University of Chicago Press, 1987.

_____. "Prison Reform and the Sentence of Narration in *The Vicar of Wakefield*," in *The New Eighteenth Century: Theory, Politics, English Literature*, ed. Felicity Nussbaum and Laura Brown. London and New York: Methuen, 1987: 168-88.

Benedict, Barbara M. "The 'Curious Attitude' in Eighteenth-Century Britain: Observing and Owning." *Eighteenth-Century Life* n.s. 14 (1990): 59-98.

_____. "Literary Miscellanies: The Cultural Mediation of Fragmented Feeling." *ELH* 57 (1990): 407-30.

_____. "The Tensions of Realism: Oppositions of Perception in Some Novels of Fielding and Austen." Diss., University of California at Berkeley, 1985.

_____. "Pictures of Conformity: Sentiment and Structure in Ann Radcliffe's Style." *Philological Quarterly* 68 (1989): 363-77.

_____. "'Service to the Public': William Creech and Sentiment for Sale." *Eighteenth-Century Life* n.s. 15 (1991): 119-46.

Berger, John. *Ways of Seeing*. Middlesex: Penguin, 1972.

Berland, K. J. H. "Frances Brooke and David Garrick." *Studies in Eighteenth-Century Culture* 20 (1990): 217-30.

_____. "A Tax on Old Maids and Bachelors: Frances Brooke's *Old Maid.*" *Eighteenth-Century Women and the Arts*, ed. Frederick M. Keener and Susan E. Lorsch. New York: Greenwood, 1988: 29-35.

_____. "The True Pleasurable Philosopher: Some Influences on Frances Brooke's History of Emily Montague." *Dalhousie Review* 66 (1986): 286-300.

Black, Jeremy. *The English Press in the Eighteenth Century.* London: Croom Helm, 1978.

Blewett, David. Introduction. *Amelia.* By Henry Fielding. Middlesex: Penguin, 1987: ix-xx.

Block, Andrew. *The English Novel, 1740-1850: A Catalogue Including Prose Romances, Short Stories, and Translations of Foreign Fiction.* London: Dawsons of Pall Mall, 1961.

Boucé, Paul-Gabriel, ed. *Sexuality in Eighteenth-Century Britain.* Manchester: Manchester University Press, 1982.

Bourdieu, Pierre. *Distinction: A Social Critique of the Judgement of Taste.* Trans. Richard Nice. Cambridge, Mass.: Harvard University Press, 1984.

Bradbrook, Frank. *Jane Austen and Her Predecessors.* Cambridge: Cambridge University Press, 1966.

Brady, Frank. "*Tristram Shandy*: Sexuality, Morality, and Sensibility." *Eighteenth-Century Studies* 4 (1970): 41-56.

Braudy, Leo. "The Form of the Sentimental Novel." *Novel: A Forum on Fiction* 7 (1973): 5-13.

Bredvold, Louis I. *The Natural History of Sensibility.* Detroit: Wayne State University Press, 1962.

R. F. Brissenden. *Virtue in Distress: Studies in the Novel of Sentiment from Richardson to Sade.* London and Basingstoke: Macmillan, 1974.

Brooke, [Charlotte], ed. *The Poetical Works of Henry Brooke, Esq. In Four Volumes; with a Portrait of this Author and his Life.* Dublin: Printed for the Editor, 1792.

Brooke, Frances. *The Excursion.* 2 vols. London: T. Cadell, 1777.

_____. *The History of Emily Montague.* Ed. Mary Jane Edwards. Ottawa: Carleton University Press, 1985.

_____. *The History of Lady Julia Mandeville.* 2 vols. Dublin: J. Potts. 1763.

_____. *The Old Maid*, London: A. Millar, 1755-56.

Brooke, Henry. *The Fool of Quality; or, the History of the Henry Earl of Moreland* 2 vols. W. Johnston: London, 1766.

_____. *The Fool of Quality; or, the History of the Henry Earl of Moreland.* 2nd ed. 5 vols. W. Johnston: London, 1767-70.

_____. *Juliet Grenville; or, The History of the Human Heart.* 3 vols. London: G. Robinson, 1774.

Browne, Alice. *The Eighteenth-Century Feminist Mind*. Sussex: Harvester, 1987.

Burke, Peter. *Popular Culture in Early Modern Europe*. London: Temple Smith, 1978.

Burrows, J.F. *Computation into Criticism: A Study of Jane Austen's Novels and an Experiment in Method*. Oxford: Oxford University Press, 1987.

Butler, Marilyn. *Romantics, Rebels and Reactionaries: English Literature and Its Background, 1760-1830*. Oxford: Oxford University Press, 1981.

Butt, John, ed. *Of Books and Humankind: Essays and Poem Presented to Bonamy Dobrée*. London: Routledge, 1964.

Byrd, Max. *London Transformed: Images of the City in the Eighteenth Century*. New Haven and London: Yale University Press, 1978.

_____. *Tristram Shandy*. London: G. Allen & Unwin, 1985.

_____. *Visits to Bedlam: Madness and Literature in the Eighteenth Century*. Columbia, S.C.: University of South Carolina Press, 1974.

Campbell, Jill. "'When Men Women Turn': Gender Reversals in Fielding's Plays," in *The New Eighteenth Century: Theory, Politics, English Literature*, ed. Felicity Nussbaum and Laura Brown. New York and London: Methuen, 1987: 62-83.

Caretta, Vincent. *The Snarling Muse: Verbal and Visual Political Satire from Pope to Churchill*. Philadelphia: University of Pennsylvania Press, 1983.

Carnochan, W.B. *Confinement and Flight: An Essay on English Literature of the Eighteenth Century*. Berkeley and Los Angeles: University of California Press, 1977.

Cash, Arthur Hill. *Sterne's Comedy of Moral Sentiments: The Ethical Dimension of the "Journey"*. Duquesne Studies, Ser.6. Pittsburgh: Duquesne University Press, 1966.

_____, and John Stedmond. *The Winged Skull: Papers from the Laurence Sterne Bicentenary Conference*. London: Methuen, 1971.

Castle, Terry. *Masquerade and Civilization: The Carnivalesque in Eighteenth-Century English Culture and Fiction*. Stanford: Stanford University Press, 1986.

Chadwick, Joseph. "Infinite Jest: Interpretation in Sterne's *A Sentimental Journey*." *Eighteenth-Century Studies* 12 (1978-79): 190-205.

Champion, Larry S., ed. *Quick Springs of Sense: Studies in the Eighteenth Century*. Athens: University of Georgia Press, 1974.

Chapbooks Printed in Scotland, 1805-21. Vol. 2, 1813. London: British Museum f.1078.k.4.

Chartier, Roger. *Cultural History: Between Practices and Representations*. Trans. Lydia G. Cochrane. Cambridge: Polity, 1988.

Conger, Syndy McMillen, ed. *Sensibility in Transformation: Creative*

Resistance to Sentiment from the Augustans to the Romantics: Essays in Honor of Jean H. Hagstrum. London and Toronto: Associated University Presses, 1990.

Coote, Stephen. Introduction and Notes. *The Vicar of Wakefield*. By Oliver Goldsmith. Harmondsworth, Middlesex: Penguin, 1982: 7-24; 200-213.

Cottom, Daniel. *The Civilized Imagination: A Study of Ann Radcliffe, Jane Austen, and Sir Walter Scott*. Cambridge: Cambridge University Press, 1985.

Cox, Stephen D. *"The Stranger Within Thee": Concepts of the Self in Late-Eighteenth-Century Literature*. Pittsburgh: University of Pittsburgh Press, 1980.

Clifford, James. *The Predicament of Culture: Twentieth-Century Ethnography, Literature and Art*. Cambridge, Mass.: Harvard University Press, 1988.

Daiches, David. *Literature and Gentility in Scotland*. Edinburgh: University of Edinburgh Press, 1982.

Davie, Donald. *A Gathered Church: The Literature of the English Dissenting Interest, 1700-1930*. London: Routledge, 1978.

Digeon, Aurélien. *The Novels of Fielding*. London: Routledge, 1925.

D'Olier, Issac. *Memoirs of the Life of the late excellent and pious Mr. Henry Brooke*. Dublin: printed by R. Napper, 1816.

Doody, Margaret A. "Deserts, Ruins and Troubled Waters: Female Dreams in Fiction and the Development of the Gothic Novel." *Genre* 10 (1977): 529-72.

_____. *A Natural Passion: A Study of the Novels of Samuel Richardson*. Oxford: Clarendon Press, 1974.

Duckworth, Alistair. *The Improvement of the Estate: A Study of Jane Austen's Novels*. Baltimore: Johns Hopkins University Press, 1971.

Dussinger, John A. *The Discourse of the Mind in Eighteenth-Century Fiction*. The Hague: Mouton, 1974.

Dwyer, John. "Clio and Ethics: Practical Morality in Enlightened Scotland." *Eighteenth Century* 30 (1989): 45-72.

_____, Roger A. Mason, and Alexander Murdoch, eds. *New Perspectives on the Politics and Culture of Early Modern Scotland*. Edinburgh: J. Donald, 1982.

_____. *Virtuous Discourse: Sensibility and Community in Late Eighteenth-Century Scotland*. Edinburgh: J. Donald, 1987.

Edwards, Mary Jane, ed. *The History of Emily Montague*. Ottawa, Canada: Carleton University Press, 1985.

Erämetsä, Eric. *A Study of the Word 'Sentimental' and of Other Linguistic Characteristics of Eighteenth-Century Sentimentalism in England*. Ser. B., Tom. 74.1. Helsinki: Annales Academiae Scientiarum Fennicae, 1951.

Epstein, Lynne. "Mrs. Radcliffe's Landscapes: The Influence of Three Landscape Painters on her Nature Descriptions." *Hartford Studies in Literature* 12 (1969): 107-20.

Fielding, Henry. *Amelia*. Ed. Martin C. Battestin. Middletown: Wesleyan University Press, 1983.

_____. *Joseph Andrews*. Ed. Martin C. Battestin. Middletown: Wesleyan University Press, 1967.

Foucault, Michel. *The History of Sexuality: Volume One. An Introduction.* Trans. Robert Hurley. London: Penguin, 1976.

_____. *Madness and Civilization: A History of Insanity in the Age of Reason.* Trans. Richard Howard. New York: Vintage, 1973.

_____. *The Uses of Pleasure: History of Sexuality, Volume Two.* Trans. Robert Hurley. New York: Vintage, 1985.

Fried, Michael. *Absorption and Theatricality: Painting and Beholder in the Age of Diderot.* Berkeley and Los Angeles: University of California Press, 1980.

Frye, Northrop. "Eighteenth-Century Sensibility." *Varieties of Eighteenth-Century Studies* 24.2, special issue (1990-91): 157-72.

Fussell, Paul. *The Rhetorical World of Augustan Humanism.* London: Oxford University Press, 1965.

Gallaway, W. F., Jr. "The Sentimentalism of Goldsmith." *PMLA* 48 (1933): 1167-81.

Garrett, John. *Gothic Strains and Bourgeois Sentiments in the Novels of Mrs. Ann Radcliffe and Her Imitators.* New York: Arno, 1980.

Genette, Gerard. "Boundaries of Narrative." Trans. Ann Levonas. *New Literary History* 8 (1976): 1-13.

Gilman, Ernest B. *The Curious Perspective: Literary and Pictorial Wit in the Seventeenth Century.* New Haven and London: Yale University Press, 1978.

Goldberg, Rita. *Sex and Enlightenment: Women in Richardson and Diderot.* Cambridge: Cambridge University Press, 1984.

Goldsmith, Oliver. *The Vicar of Wakefield.* Ed. Arthur Friedman. Oxford and New York: Oxford University Press, 1974.

Gramsci, Antonio. *Selections from the Prison Notebooks.* Eds. Quintin Hoare and Geoffrey Nowell Smith. New York: International, 1972.

Green, Katherine Sobba. *The Courtship Novel, 1740-1820: A Feminized Genre.* Lexington: University of Kentucky Press, 1991.

Guest, Harriet. "A Double Lustre: Femininity and Sociable Commerce." *Eighteenth-Century Studies* 23 (1990): 479-501.

Guilhamet, Leon. *The Sincere Ideal: Studies on Sincerity in Eighteenth-Century English Literature.* Montreal and London: McGill-Queen's University Press, 1974.

Gysin, Fritz. *Model as Motif in Tristram Shandy*. The Cooper Mongraphs, no. 31. Basel, Switzerland: Francke Verlag Bern, 1983.

Hagstrum, Jean H. *Sex and Sensibility: Ideal and Erotic Love from Milton to Mozart*. Chicago and London: University of Chicago Press, 1980.

____. *The Sister Arts: The Tradition of Literary Pictorialism and English Poetry from Dryden to Gray*. Chicago and London: University of Chicago Press, 1958.

Hart, Francis Russell. *The Scottish Novel: A Critical Survey*. London: John Murray, 1978.

Haskell, Francis. *The Painful Birth of the Art Book*. New York: Thames and Hudson, 1987.

Haywood, Elizabeth. *The Female Spectator*. 5th ed. 4 vols. London: T. Gardner, 1755.

Hilson, J. C., M. M. B. Jones and J. R. Watson. *Augustan Worlds*. Leicester: Leicester University Press, 1978.

Hipple, Walter John, Jr. *The Beautiful, the Sublime, and the Picturesque in Eighteenth-Century British Aesthetic Theory*. Carbondale: Southern Illinois University Press, 1957.

Hobson, Miriam. *The Object of Art: The Theory of Illusion in Eighteenth-Century France*. Cambridge: Cambridge University Press, 1982.

Holland, Norman N., and Leona F. Sherman. "Gothic Possibilities." *New Literary History* 8 (1977): 279-94.

Hook, Andrew, ed. *The History of Scottish Literature*. Vol. 2, 1660-1800. Aberdeen: Aberdeen University Press, 1987.

Hooper, William. *Rational Recreations*. London, 1774.

Hopkins, Robert H. "Matrimony in *The Vicar of Wakefield* and the Marriage Act of 1753." *Studies in Philology* 74 (1977): 322-39.

____. *The True Genius of Oliver Goldsmith*. Baltimore: Johns Hopkins University Press, 1969.

Houston, R. A. *Scottish Literacy and the Scottish Identity: Illiteracy and Society in Scotland and Northern England*, 1600-1800. Cambridge: Cambridge University Press, 1985.

Hume, David. *Four Dissertations*. London: A. Millar, 1757.

Hunt, John Dixon. *The Figure in the Landscape: Poetry, Painting and Gardening During the Eighteenth Century*. Baltimore and London: Johns Hopkins, 1976.

Hunter, J. Paul. *Before Novels: The Cultural Contexts of Eighteenth-Century Fiction*. New York and London: W. W. Norton, 1990.

____. "Clocks, Calendars, and Names: The Troubles of Tristram and the Aesthetics of Uncertainty," in *Rhetorics of Order/Ordering Rhetorics in English Neoclassical Literature*, ed. J. Douglas Canfield and J. Paul Hunter. Newark, N.J.: University of Delaware Press, 1989: 173-98.

____. "News and new Things: Contemporaneity and the Early English Novel." *Critical Inquiry* 14 (1988): 493-515.

____. *Occasional Form: Henry Fielding and the Chains of Circumstance.* Baltimore and London: Johns Hopkins University Press, 1974.

____. "Response as Reformation: *Tristram Shandy* and the Art of Interruption." *Novel: A Forum on Fiction* 4 (1971): 132-46.

Ingrassia, Catherine. "Women Writing/Writing Women: Pope, Dulness and "Feminization" in the *Dunciad.*" *Eighteenth-Century Life* n.s. 14 (1990): 40-58.

Iser, Wolfgang. *The Implied Reader: Patterns of Communication in Prose Fiction from Bunyan to Beckett.* Baltimore and London: Johns Hopkins University Press, 1974.

Johnson, Claudia. *Jane Austen: Women, Politics, and the Novel.* Chicago and London: University of Chicago Press, 1988.

____. "A 'Sweet Face as White as Death': Jane Austen and the Politics of Female Sensibility." *Novel: A Forum on Fiction* 22 (1989): 159-74.

Kay, Donald, ed. *A Provision of Human Nature: Essays on Fielding and Others in Honor of Miriam Austin Locke.* University: University of Alabama Press, 1977.

Kelly, Gary. "A Constant Vicissitude of Interesting Passions: Ann Radcliffe's Perplexed Narratives." *Ariel: A Review of International English Literature* 10 (1979): 45-64.

Klancher, Jon P. *The Making of English Reading Audiences, 1790-1832.* Madison: University of Wisconsin Press, 1987.

Knight, Richard Payne. *An Analytical Inquiry into the Principles of Taste.* 3rd ed. London: T. Payne, 1806.

Klinck, Carl F. Introduction. *The History of Emily Montague.* By Frances Brooke. Toronto: McClelland and Stewart, 1961: v-xiv.

Landow, George P. *Images of Crisis: Literary Iconology, 1750 to the Present.* Boston, London and Henley: Routledge, 1982.

Landry, Donna. "The Resignation of Mary Collier: Some Problems in Feminist Literary History," in *The New Eighteenth Century: Theory, Politics, English Literature*, ed. Felicity Nussbaum and Laura Brown. New York and London: Methuen, 1987: 99-120.

Lanham, Richard A. *"Tristram Shandy": The Game of Pleasure.* Berkeley and Los Angeles: University of California Press, 1973.

Lavater, Johann Casper. *"Essays on Physiognomy*, Designed to promote the Knowledge and Love of Mankind." Trans. Henry Hunter. London: John Murray, 1789.

Lea, Sydney L. W., Jr. *Gothic to Fantastic: Readings in Supernatural Fiction.* New York: Arno, 1980.

LePage, Peter V. "The Prison and the Dark Beauty of *Amelia.*" *Criticism* 9 (1967): 337-54.

Levine, Joseph M. *The Battle of the Books: History and Literature in the Augustan Age.* Ithaca: Cornell University Press, 1991.

Lovell, Terry. *Consuming Fiction.* London: Verso, 1987.

Loveridge, Mark. *Laurence Sterne and The Argument About Design.* London and Basingstoke: Macmillan Press, 1982.

MacCarthy, B. G. *The Later Women Novelists, 1744-1818.* Oxford: Basil Blackwell, 1946.

Mackenzie, Henry. "Account of the German Theatre." *The Transactions of the Royal Society of Edinburgh.* London: T. Cadell, 1790.

_____. *The Anecdotes and Egotisms of Henry Mackenzie, 1745-1831.* Ed. Harold William Thompson. Oxford: Oxford University Press, 1927.

_____. *The Beauties of Mackenzie.* London: R. Tullis, 1813.

_____. *Henry Mackenzie: Letters to Elizabeth Rose of Kilvarock. On Literature, Events, and People, 1768-1815.* Ed. Horst W. Drescher. Edinburgh and London: Oliver and Boyd, 1967.

_____. *The Lounger. A Periodical Paper, published at Edinburgh in the Years 1785 and 1786.* Edinburgh: W. Creech, 1787.

_____. *The Man of Feeling.* Ed. Brian Vickers. Oxford: Oxford University Press, 1987.

_____. *The Mirror. A Periodical paper, published at Edinburgh in the Years 1779 and 1780.* 4th ed. 3 vols. London: W. Strahan, T. Cadell, and W. Creech, 1782.

_____. *The Works of Henry Mackenzie, Esq. In Eight Volumes.* Edinburgh and London: Ballantyne, 1808.

Malek, James S. *The Arts Compared: An Aspect of Eighteenth-Century British Aesthetics.* Detroit: Wayne State University Press, 1974.

The Man of Benevolence. London: 1789.

Markley, Robert. "Sentimentality as Performance: Shaftesbury, Sterne, and the Theatrics of Virtue," in *The New Eighteenth Century: Theory, Politics, English Literature*, ed. Felicity Nussbaum and Laura Brown. New York and London: Methuen, 1987: 210-30.

Marshall, David. *The Surprising Effects of Sympathy: Marivaux, Diderot, Rousseau, and Mary Shelley.* Chicago and London: University of Chicago Press, 1988.

Matteo, Sante. *Textual Exile: The Reader in Sterne and Foscolo.* American University Studies, Ser. 3, vol. 15. New York: Peter Lang, 1985.

Mayo, Robert D. *The English Novel in the Magazines, 1740-1815.* Evanston: Northwestern University Press, 1962.

McKendrick, Neil, John Brewer, and J. H. Plumb. *The Birth of a Consumer Society: The Commercialization of Eighteenth-Century England.* London: Hutchison, 1982.

McKeon, Michael. *The Origins of the English Novel, 1600-1740.* Baltimore and London: Johns Hopkins University Press, 1987.

McMullen, Lorraine. *An Odd Attempt in a Woman: The Literary Life of Frances Brooke.* Vancouver: University of British Columbia Press, 1983.

Messenger, Ann. *His and Hers: Essays in Restoration and Eighteenth-Century Literature.* Lexington: University of Kentucky Press, 1986.

Micasiw, Kim Ian. "Imitation and Ideology: Henry Mackenzie's Rousseau." *Eighteenth-Century Fiction* 5 (1993): 153-76.

Mitchell, James, ed. *Sentimental Tales, &c.* Newcastle-upon-Tyne: J. Mitchell, 1801.

Moler, Kenneth L. *Jane Austen's Art of Allusion.* Nebraska: University of Nebraska Press, 1968.

Moore, Robert E. and Jean H. Hagstrum. *Changing Taste in Eighteenth-Century and Literature.* William Andrews Clark Memorial Library: 17 Apr. 1971; Los Angeles: University of California Press, 1972.

Mullan, John. *Sentiment and Sociability: The Language of Feeling in the Eighteenth Century.* Oxford: Clarendon Press, 1988.

Myer, Valerie Grosvenor, ed. *Laurence Sterne: Riddles and Mysteries.* London: Vision, 1984.

Napier, Elizabeth R. *The Failure of Gothic: Problems of Disjunction in an Eighteenth-Century Literary Form.* Oxford: Clarendon Press, 1987.

Neuburg, Victor E. *The Penny Histories: A Study of Chapbooks for Young Readers over Two Centuries.* London: Oxford University Press, 1968.

_____. *Popular Education in Eighteenth-Century England.* London: Woburn, 1971.

Nicholson, George, ed. *The Literary Miscellany; or, Elegant Selections of The Most Admired Fugitive Pieces, and EXTRACTS from Works of the Greatest Merit: With Originals in Prose and Verse.* London, 1793-1802.

Nussbaum, Felicity. *The Autobiographical Subject: Gender and Ideology in Eighteenth-Century England.* Baltimore and London: Johns Hopkins University Press, 1989.

_____. *The Brink of All We Hate: English Satires on Women, 1660-1750.* Lexington: University of Kentucky Press, 1984.

_____. "The Politics of Difference." *Eighteenth-Century Studies* 23 (1990): 375-86.

_____, and Laura Brown, ed. *The New Eighteenth Century: Theory, Politics, English Literature.* New York and London: Methuen, 1987.

Odmark, John. *An Understanding of Jane Austen's Novels: Character, Value, and Ironic Perspective.* Oxford: Basil Blackwell, 1981.

Patterson, Annabel. *Censorship and Interpretation: The Conditions of Writing and Reading in Early Modern England.* Madison: University of Wisconsin Press, 1984.

Paulson, Ronald. *Emblem and Expression: Meaning in English Art of the Eighteenth Century.* London: Thames and Hudson, 1975.

_____. "Life as Journey and as Theater: Two Eighteenth-Century Narrative Structures." *New Literary History* 8 (1976): 43-58.

_____. *Popular and Polite Art in the Age of Hogarth and Fielding.* Notre Dame: University of Notre Dame Press, 1979.

Platzner, Robert L. "Mackenzie's Martyr: The Man of Feeling as Saintly Fool." *Novel: A Forum on Fiction* 10 (1976): 59-64.

Pocock, J. G. A., *Virtue, Commerce, and History: Essays on Political Thought and History, Chiefly in the Eighteenth Century.* Cambridge: Cambridge University Press, 1985.

Poovey, Mary. "Ideology and 'The Mysteries of Udolpho'." *Criticism* 21 (1979): 307-30.

_____. *The Proper Lady and The Woman Writer: Mary Wollstonecraft, Mary Shelley, and Jane Austen.* Chicago and London: University of Chicago Press, 1984.

Porter, Roy. *English Society in the Eighteenth Century.* Harmondsworth, Middlesex: Penguin, 1982.

Probyn, Clive T. *English Fiction of the Eighteenth Century, 1700-1789.* London and New York: Longman, 1987.

Radcliffe, Ann. *The Mysteries of Udolpho.* Ed. Bonamy Dobrée. World's Classics Edition. New York: Oxford University Press, 1966.

_____. *The Romance of the Forest.* Ed. Chloe Chard. World's Classics Edition. New York: Oxford University Press, 1986.

Raven, James. *Judging New Wealth: Popular Publishing and Responses to Commerce in England, 1750-1800.* Oxford: Clarendon Press, 1992.

Rawson, C. J. *Henry Fielding and the Augustan Ideal Under Stress.* London: Routledge, 1972.

Ribble, Frederick G. "The Constitution of the Mind and the Concept of Emotion in Fielding's *Amelia.*" *Philological Quarterly* 56 (1977): 104-22.

Riccoboni, Marie-Jeanne. *The Letters of Juliet Catesby, To her Friend Lady Henrietta Campley.* Trans. Frances Brooke. 4th ed. London: R. and J. Dodsley, 1764.

Richetti, John J. *Popular Fiction Before Richardson: Narrative Patterns, 1700-1739.* Oxford: Clarendon Press, 1969.

_____. "The Portrayal of Women in Restoration and Eighteenth-Century English Literature," in *What Manner of Woman: Essays on English and American Life and Literature,* ed. Marlene Springer. Oxford: Basil Blackwell, 1977: 65-97.

Ripa, Caesar. *Iconologia; Or, Moral Emblems*. Trans. Isaac Fuller. London: Benjamin Motte, 1709.

Rivers, Isobel, ed. *Books and Their Readers in Eighteenth-Century England*. New York: St. Martin's Press, 1982.

Rogers, Pat. *Literature and Popular Culture in Eighteenth-Century England*. Sussex: Harvester Press, 1985.

Rose, Jonathan. "Rereading the English Common Reader: A Preface to a History of Audiences." *Journal of the History of Ideas* 23 (1992): 47-70.

Rosenblum, Robert. *Transformations in Late Eighteenth Century Art*. Princeton, N.J.: Princeton University Press, 1967.

Ross, Angus, ed. *Selections from "The Tatler" and "The Spectator" of Steele and Addison*. Middlesex: Penguin, 1982.

Rousseau, G.S., ed. *Oliver Goldsmith: The Critical Heritage*. London: Routledge, 1974.

_____, and P.-G. Boucé, eds. *Tobias Smollett: Bicentennial Essays Presented to Lewis M. Knapp*. New York: Oxford University Press, 1971.

Rothstein, Eric. *Systems of Order and Inquiry in Later Eighteenth-Century Fiction*. Berkeley and Los Angeles: University of California Press, 1975.

Sales, Roger. *English Literature in History, 1780-1830: Pastoral and Politics*. New York: St. Martin's Press, 1983.

Scott, Walter, Sir. *Lives of Eminent Novelists and Dramatists*. London: Frederick Warne, 1887.

Sedgwick, Eve Kosofsky. "The Character in the Veil: Imagery of the Surface in the Gothic Novel." *PMLA* 96 (1981): 255-70.

Sell, Roger D. *The Reluctant Naturalism of "Amelia": An Essay on the Modern Reading of Fielding*. Ser. A., vol.62, no.3. Abo: Akademi Aboensis, 1983.

Sennett, Richard. *The Fall of Public Man*. New York: Alfred A. Knopf, 1977.

"Sensibility, Provoked by the Rival Pretensions of Pity. A Poem." Cambridge: Cambridge University Press, 1819.

Scheuermann, Mona. *Social Protest in the Eighteenth-Century English Novel*. Columbus: Ohio State University Press, 1985.

Sheriff, John K. *The Good-Natured Man: The Evolution of a Moral Ideal, 1660-1800*. University, Alabama: University of Alabama Press, 1982.

Shevelow, Kathryn. *Women and Print Culture: The Construction of Femininity in the Early Periodical*. London and New York: Routledge, 1989.

Shroff, Homai J. *The Eighteenth Century Novel: The Idea of the Gentleman*. Atlantic Highlands, N.J.: Humanities, 1978.

Simpson, Kenneth. *The Protean Scot: The Crisis of Identity in Eighteenth Century Scottish Literature*. Aberdeen: Aberdeen University Press, 1988.

Smallwood, Angela J. *Fielding and the Woman Question: The Novels of Henry Fielding and Feminist Debate, 1700-1750.* New York: St. Martin's, 1989.

Smitten, Jeffrey R. "Gesture and Expression in Eighteenth-Century Fiction: A Sentimental Journey." *Modern Language Studies* 9 (1979): 85-97.

Spacks, Patricia Meyer. *Desire and Truth: Functions of Plot in Eighteenth-Century English Novels.* Chicago and London: University of Chicago Press, 1990.

_____. *Imagining a Self: Autobiography and the Novel in Eighteenth-Century England.* Cambridge, Mass.: Harvard University Press, 1976.

Speck, W. A. *Society and Literature in England, 1700-1760.* New York: Gill and Macmillan, 1973.

Spender, Dale. *Mothers of the Novel: 100 Good Women Writers Before Jane Austen.* London and New York: Pandora, 1986.

Springer, Marlene, ed. *What Manner of Woman: Essays on English and American Life and Literature.* Oxford: Basil Blackwell, 1977.

Spufford, Margaret. *Small Books and Pleasant Histories: Popular Fiction and Its Readership in Seventeenth-Century England.* Cambridge: Cambridge University Press, 1981.

Starobinski, Jean. *L'Invention de la Liberté, 1700-1789.* Geneva: Skira, 1987.

Starr, George A. *Defoe and Spiritual Autobiography.* Princeton, N.J.: Princeton University Press, 1965.

_____. "'Only a Boy': Notes on Sentimental Novels." *Genre* 10 (1977): 501-27.

_____. "Sentimental De-education," in *Augustan Studies: Essays in Honor of Irvin Ehrenpreis*, ed. Douglas Lane Patey and Timothy Keegan. Newark: University of Delaware Press, 1985: 253-62.

Stedmond, John M. *The Comic Art of Laurence Sterne: Convention and Innovation in "Tristram Shandy" and "A Sentimental Journey".* Toronto: University of Toronto Press, 1967.

Sterne, Laurence. *The Life and Opinions of Tristram Shandy, Gentleman.* Ed. Ian Campbell Ross. World Classics Edition. Oxford: Oxford University Press, 1983.

_____. *A Sentimental Journey through France and Italy.* Ed. Graham Petrie. Harmondsworth, Middlesex: Penguin, 1967.

Stone, Laurence. *The Family, Sex, and Marriage in England, 1500-1800.* Abridged edition. New York: Harper and Rowe, 1977.

Sutherland, James. *The Restoration Newspaper and Its Development.* Cambridge: Cambridge University Press, 1986.

Swarbrick, Andrew, ed. *The Art of Oliver Goldsmith.* London: Vision, 1984.

Sypher, Wylie. "Social Ambiguity in a Gothic Novel." *Partisan Review* 12

(1945): 50-60.

Tanner, Tony. *Adultery in the Novel: Contract and Transgression*. Baltimore and London: Johns Hopkins University Press, 1979.

____. *Jane Austen*. Cambridge, Mass.: Harvard University Press. 1986.

Thompson, Harold William. *A Scottish Man of Feeling: Some Account of Henry Mackenzie, Esq. of Edinburgh and of the Golden Age of Burns and Scott*. London: Oxford University Press, 1931.

Thompson, James. *Between Self and World: The Novels of Jane Austen*. University Park: Pennsylvania State University Press, 1988.

Tillotson, Kathleen. *The Novels of the Eighteenth Forties*. Oxford: Clarendon Press, 1954.

Todd, Janet. *Sensibility: An Introduction*. London and New York: Methuen, 1986.

____. *The Sign of Angelica: Women, Writing and Fiction, 1660-1800*. New York: Columbia University Press, 1989.

Tompkins, J. M. S. *The Popular Novel in England, 1770-1800*. Lincoln: University of Nebraska Press, 1961.

Traugott, John, ed. *Laurence Sterne: A Collection of Critical Essays*. Englewood Cliffs, N.J.: Prentice-Hall, 1968.

____. *Tristram Shandy's World: Sterne's Philosophical Rhetoric*. Berkeley and Los Angeles: University of California Press, 1954.

Turner, Cheryl. *Living by the Pen: Women Writers in the Eighteenth Century*. London and New York: Routledge, 1992.

Tuveson, Ernest. "Shaftesbury and the Age of Sensibility." *Studies in Criticism and Aesthetics, 1660-1800: Essays in Honor of Samuel Holt Monk*, ed. Howard Anderson and John S. Shea. Minneapolis: University of Minnesota Press, 1967: 73-93.

Tytler, Graeme. "Letters of Recommendation and False Visors: Physiognomy in the Novels of Henry Fielding." *Eighteenth-Century Fiction* 2 (1990): 93-111.

____. *Physiognomy in the European Novel: Faces and Fortunes*. Princeton, N.J.: Princeton University Press, 1982.

Uphaus, Robert W. *The Impossible Observer*. Lexington: University of Kentucky Press, 1979.

Van Sant, Ann. *Eighteenth-Century Sensibility and the Novel: The Senses in a Social Context*. Cambridge: Cambridge University Press, 1993.

Varey, Simon. *Henry Fielding*. Cambridge: Cambridge University Press, 1986.

Watt, Ian. *The Rise of the Novel: Studies in Defoe, Richardson, and Fielding*. Berkeley and Los Angeles: University of California Press, 1957.

Williams, Carolyn. "The Changing Face of Change: Fe/Male In/Constancy."

Journal of the British Society for Eighteenth-Century Studies 12 (1989): 13-28.

Wolff, Cynthia Griffin. "The Radcliffean Gothic Model: A Form for Feminine Sexuality." *Modern Language Studies* 9 (1979): 98-113.

Wright, Walter Francis. *Sensibility in English Prose Fiction, 1760-1814.* Urbana: University of Illinois Press, 1937.

Yeazell, Ruth Bernard. *Fictions of Modesty: Women and Courtship in the English Novel.* Chicago and London: University of Chicago Press, 1991.

Zimmerman, Everett. "Fragments of History and *The Man of Feeling*: From Richard Bentley to Walter Scott." *Eighteenth-Century Studies* 23 (1990): 283-300.

INDEX

AMS Studies in the Eighteenth Century, No. 26
ISSN: 0196-6561

Other titles in this series:

1. Modern Language Association of America. *Proceedings of the 1967-68 Neoclassicism Conferences.* Edited and with a Selected Bibliography, 1920-68, by Paul J. Korshin. 1970.
2. Francesco Cordasco. *Tobias George Smollett: A Bibliographical Guide.* 1978.
3. Paula R. Backscheider, ed. *Probability, Time, and Space in Eighteenth-Century Literature.* 1979.
4. Ruth Perry. *Women, Letters, and the Novel.* 1980.
5. Paul J. Korshin, ed. *The American Revolution and Eighteenth-Century Culture.* 1986.
6. G. S. Rousseau, ed. *The Letters and Papers of Sir John Hill (1714-1775).* 1982.
7. Paula R. Backscheider. *A Being More Intense: A Study of the Prose Works of Bunyan, Swift, and Defoe.* 1984.
8. Christopher Fox, ed. *Psychology and Literature in the Eighteenth Century.* 1987.
9. John F. Sena. *The Best-Natured Man: Sir Samuel Garth, Physician and Poet.* 1986.
10. Robert A. Erickson. *Mother Midnight: Birth, Sex, and Fate in Eighteenth-Century Fiction (Defoe, Richardson, and Sterne).* 1986.
11. Malcolm Jack. *Corruption and Progress: The Eighteenth-Century Debate.* 1989.
12. Christopher Fox, ed. *Teaching Eighteenth-Century Poetry.* 1990.
13. Richard Dircks, ed. *The Letters of Richard Cumberland.* 1988.
14. John Irwin Fischer, Hermann J. Real, and James Woolley, eds. *Swift and His Contexts.* 1989.
15. Kenneth W. Graham, ed. *Vathek and the Escape from Time: Bicentenary Revaluations.* 1990.
16. Kenneth W. Graham. *The Politics of Narrative: Ideology and Social Change in William Godwin's Caleb Williams.* 1990.
17. Richard J. Dircks. *The Unpublished Plays of Richard Cumberland.* 1990.
18. Kevin L. Cope, ed. *Enlightening Allegory: Theory, Practice and Contexts of Allegory in the Late Seventeenth and Eighteenth Centuries.* 1992.
19. O M Brack, Jr., ed. *Writers, Books, and Trade: An Eighteenth-Century English Miscellany for William B. Todd.* 1992.
20. Malcolm, Jack. *William Beckford: An English Fidalgo.* 1992.
21. Peter J. Schakel, ed. *Critical Approaches to Teaching Swift.* 1992.
22. James Walton, ed. *"The King's Business": Letters on the Administration of Ireland, 1742-1762.* 1994.
23. Ruth P. Weinreb. *Eagle in a Gauze Cage: Louise d'Epinay, femme de lettres.* 1993.
24. O M Brack, Jr., ed. *Shorter Prose Writings of Samuel Johnson.* 1994.
25. Ann Messenger. *Pastoral Tradition and the Female Talent: Studies in Augustan Poetry.* 1994.
26. Barbara M. Benedict, *Framing Feeling: Sentiment and Style in English Prose Fiction, 1745-1800.* 1994.
27. Ann Messenger, *Woman and Poet in the Eighteenth Century: The Life of Mary Whateley Darwall (1738-1825).* 1994.
28. Carla H. Hay, ed.*The Past As Prologue: Essays to Celebrate the Twenty-Fifth Anniversary of ASECS.* 1994.

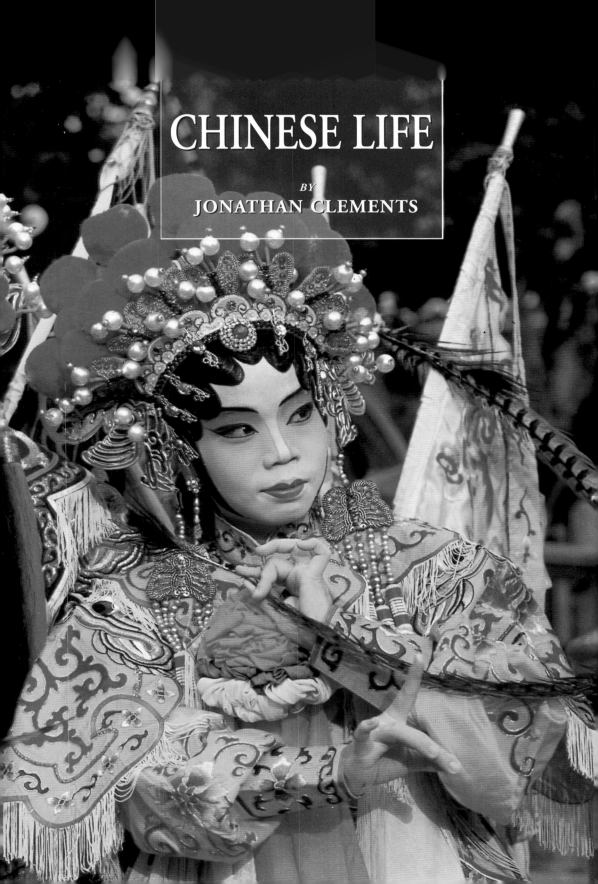

CHINESE LIFE

BY
JONATHAN CLEMENTS

Who were the Ancient Chinese?

YANGSHAO CULTURE

The Yangshao people were one of the earliest recorded civilizations in China, thriving in around 4500 BC. They lived in pyramid-shaped thatched huts, reared dogs and pigs and made pottery. The tribes were ruled by women, property passed in the female line from daughter to daughter and women had richer, better-furnished graves than their male counterparts.

China is big. It stretches from the frozen wastes of Siberia to the tropical islands of the Equator. Life was so precarious on the banks of its giant Yangzi and Yellow rivers, and the people so numerous, that whoever has wanted to rule part of China has been forced to seize, or try to seize, the whole. China's borders have changed constantly throughout the thousands of years of its civilization, which is one of the world's oldest and most advanced cultures. Originally made up of several squabbling states, the country was united in 221 BC when King Chen of Qin conquered his enemies and proclaimed himself the First Emperor. His family, or dynasty, ruled for only a few years until it was overthrown. Since then, each period of Chinese history has been named after the family that ruled it.

IMPERIAL RICHES

Since the Qin, there have been many different dynasties (ruling families), each claiming to rule the world on behalf of Heaven. The Chinese emperors' power was far reaching and brought them tribute taxes from all over Asia. Through the ages, their wealth attracted brilliant craftsmen, such as the creators of this Ming Dynasty vase.

THE LAST EMPEROR

Not all emperors were Chinese. The Yuan Dynasty were Mongol invaders descended from Genghis Khan. The Manchurian Qing Dynasty ruled for more than 200 years. Their rule ended in 1912 when their Emperor Xuan Tong (personal name: Pu Yi) was ousted. Born in 1906 and made emperor at the age of 3, Pu Yi was to be the Last Emperor.

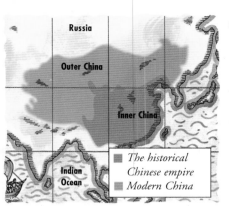

INNER & OUTER CHINA

China is commonly divided into two areas. Inner China, the area around the basins of the Yellow and the Yangzi rivers, is the core of the historical Chinese empire, and has sustained a continuous civilization since the Stone Age. Modern or Outer China includes Manchuria, Inner Mongolia, Xinjiang and Tibet – vast areas of land that were considered by the Chinese to be foreign countries until relatively recently.

The historical Chinese empire
Modern China

THE MIDDLE KINGDOM

The Chinese name for their country is Zhong Guo (The Middle Kingdom), supposedly the centre of the world. The symbol for middle consists of a line going straight through the centre of a hole. The symbol for kingdom shows a king with a jewel, surrounded by a square to signify the borders of his kingdom.

EARLY MONEY

The bronze coin above (*c.* 220 BC) is circular to represent the Earth, with a square hole to represent Heaven. The symbol to the right of the hole means 'shell', since earlier in the Shang Dynasty, cowrie shells were used as money. Early Chinese states soon developed their own currencies, including bricks of tea and metal chits. During the reign of the First Emperor, coins were standardized throughout the empire.

CHINESE DYNASTIES

2100–1600 BC
Xia Dynasty (Legendary)
1600–1100 BC
Shang Dynasty (North China only)
1100–221 BC
Zhou Dynasty (North China only)

IMPERIAL CHINA

221–207 BC
Qin Dynasty
206 BC – AD 220
Han Dynasty
220–280
Three Kingdoms Period
265–420
Jin Dynasty
420–589
Southern and Northern Dynasties (including Song, Qi, Liang, Chen, North, East & West Wei, North Qi and Northern Zhou)
581–618
Sui Dynasty
618–907
Tang Dynasty
907–979
Five Dynasties and Ten Kingdoms
960–1279
Song Dynasty (North and South)
916–1125
Liao Dynasty
1115–1234
Kin Dynasty
1260–1368
Yuan Dynasty (Mongols take over)
1368–1644
Ming Dynasty
1644–1912
Qing Dynasty (Manchus take over)
1912
Last Emperor deposed

POST-IMPERIAL CHINA

1912–1949
Republic
1949–present day
People's Republic (Communist rule)

THE EXAM SYSTEM

In times of war, prowess on the battlefield could help someone rise through the ranks in society. In times of peace, the only way to advance was by becoming a civil servant. To do so, Chinese scholars had to sit gruelling exams consisting of memorized passages from poems and histories. But a pass-mark only lasted for a limited period. They had to resit their exams regularly or they lost their qualifications.

Life for the Rich

Chinese society had a rigid hierarchy, with the emperor at the top and the common peasants at the bottom. Much of what remains of ancient China concerns the life of the rich and powerful, as only their artefacts have stood the test of time. Since the ancient Chinese invented paper, many of their documents have disintegrated faster than those of less advanced cultures, whose documents were carved in stone or written on parchment. Few buildings remain standing but artefacts found in graves have provided us with evidence of how people lived in ancient China.

CONSULTING THE ORACLE

Since the earliest days of the Shang Dynasty (1600–1100 BC), those who could afford divine guidance sought it from a soothsayer. A hot pointer was pressed against the underpart of a tortoise shell while questions were asked. The cracks that formed were interpreted and the answers etched into the shell as a permanent record.

DECLINING NOBILITY

There were five ranks in ancient Chinese nobility, the Gong, Hou, Bo, Zi and Nan, roughly equivalent to duke, marquis, earl, viscount, and baron. Chinese peerages were hereditary but declined over time. If a family did nothing to justify their honour, each successive generation would fall one rank, until the great-great-great grandson of the original nobleman became a humble commoner. However, the heir of Confucius (see page 28) always kept the highest rank.

A RICH MAN'S HOUSE

The layout of a person's house was said to directly affect the occupant's fortune. Those who could afford it would ensure that their house was positioned to avoid evil spirits and ill winds. The presence of other people's bad fortune could bring disaster, and the perfect gentleman's house was said to be in the quiet countryside; city-dwelling was an evil to be avoided.

TOO RICH TO WORK

Long fingernails were a sign of a person who was wealthy enough not to have to do manual work. Many Chinese let at least one fingernail grow long but the very rich would grow all ten. Nail protectors were worn by the Qing Empress Dowager Zi Xi (1835–1908) to protect her long, carefully manicured nails.

THE SEAL OF AUTHORITY

Letters, documents, orders and even paintings were marked with the owner's seal: a stylized representation of their name. Documents were not accepted as authentic without such a mark. Commoners and low-ranking officials would stamp in red, while high-ranking officials used mauve. During times of national mourning, all seals would use blue ink. Modern seals are roughly a centimetre square, but the emperor's official signature was so large it had to be lifted by two people.

MAGIC STONE

Jade was a prized commodity among the rich. Like all stone, it could be broken but never twisted, making it a symbol of honour and constancy. Jade was also rumoured to have magical powers. An extremely difficult stone to shape, it had to be worn into the required form by laborious sanding.

Life for the Poor

Physical labour was a job for the poor and they were forced to become labourers, builders and farmers to support the rich. Taxation was introduced in about 600 BC, and peasants had to support wars by serving in the army or providing materials, food and money. Peasant families relied heavily on those members who could work while dependents, such as old people and children, were a constant burden. But the old were looked after out of respect, and children were reared to share the work. Respect for elders lasted even after death when, in their afterlife, ancestors were believed to offer prayers to help and protect the family. Many peasants did not own their land. They were tenant-serfs of landlords who could punish them for not working hard enough, which meant they had little opportunity to earn extra money to buy land.

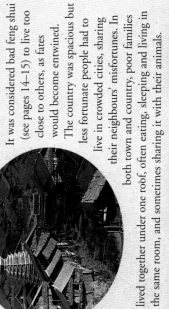

OX POWER

Ideally, an ox was used to pull a plough in the rice paddies. Oxen were not always easy to come by, as most animal herds were on the steppes of Outer China, whereas the farms were in Inner China. Some areas had 'ox-lords' who rented out animals, but many peasants were too poor even to rent one, so had to prepare their fields by hand.

LIFE IN THE CITY

It was considered bad feng shui (see pages 14–15) to live too close to others, as fates would become entwined. The country was spacious but less fortunate people had to live in crowded cities, sharing their neighbours' misfortunes. In both town and country, poor families lived together under one roof, often eating, sleeping and living in the same room, and sometimes sharing it with their animals.

HARD LABOUR

Chinese farm life was hard. In May and June each year there was a whirl of activity: planting, harvesting, moving young rice plants into the fields and harvesting silk worms. Between November and February, with little to do, the large summer workforce became hungry mouths to feed. Working barefoot in rice paddies strewn with manure left the coolies (hired workers) prone to diseases. Such hardships led the Chinese to replace 'coolie' with the word for bitterness and strength: kuli.

LAND LUBBERS

Those who were poor and who lived near the sea often became fishermen, a harsh job, with constant risk from pirate attack. Chinese fishermen rarely strayed far from the coast, and usually sailed in pairs for safety. A small Chinese boat is called a sampan, although today big and small boats both tend to be known as junks (from the Malay word, jong: large boat).

Food & Drink

CORMORANT FISHING

Rods and lines were not the only way to catch fish. Lamps on fishing boats lured fish to the surface where trained cormorants scooped them from the water. Each bird had a collar around its neck to prevent it from swallowing its catch. The fisherman forced the bird to spit the fish out, then sent it back into the water for more. Cormorant fishing is still practised today.

China's vast size meant that its different regions were almost like foreign countries. Each had its own very different crops and dishes, and the distinctive styles of cooking still exist today. In south China, Cantonese food was cooked swiftly in hot oil, while farther north in the Yangzi Valley, more time was taken to prepare sweet-and-sour sauces. Unlike other regional cooking, Tibetan, Mongolian and Manchurian cuisines used a lot of dairy products, whereas the coastal province of Fujian specialized in delicate seafood dishes. The distinctive spicy flavours of Sichuan cooking were only possible after the introduction of the Central American chilli in the 16th century AD.

RICE & RICE CULTURE

During the Tang Dynasty (AD 618–907), quick-ripening varieties of rice were introduced from Vietnam. Canals built to aid transport and famine relief around China also brought water to outlying areas. It was lifted into the fields by a chain-and-paddle system operated by a turning crank. These changes, plus the development of new tools, such as the harrow, made rice-growing essential to feeding China's expanding population. But reliance on one food could cause trouble. If the rice crop failed, the famine affected the entire population.

WHEAT & MILLET

The staple food in ancient China was millet, which was ground into a kind of rough flour. Around AD 500 improvements in milling techniques made wheat more popular, and this formed the major ingredient in most noodle dishes.

ALL THE TEA IN CHINA

Tea, or *cha*, was a popular drink among both rich and poor, and was available in many different varieties to suit every taste and pocket. For the familiar red tea, the leaves were roasted. Other kinds, which used different flavourings and processes, could be sampled in a tea-house – a popular meeting place in ancient China. In the local dialect of south China, cha was pronounced *tay*, from which came the English word. All varieties of modern tea are descended from the Chinese original.

CHOPSTICKS

Metal was often in short supply, and so cooks in ancient China would cut up the food before it was brought to the table. The tiny bite-sized morsels were easy to pick up with wooden sticks, or chopsticks. The Chinese word for chopsticks is *kuaizi* (hasteners), because they hasten the food into the mouth. Chopsticks were used with a hand-held bowl so that the user could manipulate the food more easily.

A TASTE OF THE EXOTIC

Many exotic fruits and vegetables were grown in ancient China. They included lychee fruits (see left), longans (dragon's eyes), water-chestnuts, snow-peas, bitter melons and Chinese cabbage (*bak choi*: 'white vegetable'). All of which helped to give Chinese food its distinctive flavour and texture.

Pastimes

BOOK OF CHANGES

The I Ching is an ancient system of fortune-telling. Advice and answers to important personal questions were, and still are, sought by referring to a text, in which a chapter between 1 and 64 is consulted at random by throwing sticks or coins. The picture shows the eight three-line trigrams that are combined with one another to create the 64 numbers.

There were good and bad pastimes according to the Imperial government. Singing the praises of the emperor, watching approved dramas and martial training were all thought to be good ways of strengthening the nation. Excessive drinking, gambling and lewd behaviour were all frowned upon. Plays that ridiculed the ruling dynasty were outlawed.

CHINESE CHESS

Chess was invented in India, but the Chinese had already adopted it by AD 570. Chinese chess is very different to the common version. It is played on a board of 64 squares but the pieces move along the lines between them, and the kings cannot leave their four-square palaces. The 32 pieces are all the same size and shape, each one inscribed with its functions. As well as horses, chariots, ministers and soldiers, the Chinese chessboard has elephants, guardsmen and cannons.

CHINESE OPERA

Performances of music and song, popular since the 7th century AD, eventually developed into Chinese opera. All the actors had to be male. They were divided into four classes of character, known as Sheng (emperors, generals, gentlemen), Qing (villains, rebels, outlaws), Dan (female roles) and Chou (comic relief).

READING THE FUTURE

Ancient China had its own unique systems for telling fortunes, including face reading, which looked at marks and lines on the face, and the I Ching. Other systems developed over time and palm readers and astrologers could often be found telling fortunes on the streets.

BOOK OF SONGS

In order to report the mood of the people to the emperor, a government agency called the *Yue-fu* was established in 120 BC. Its officials regularly travelled through the countryside writing down the songs they heard. These reports survive as the Book of Songs – perhaps the oldest pop charts in the world. Some of the earliest Chinese instruments included stone chimes, bamboo flutes, the *pipa* (lute), *huiqin* (fiddle) and *qin* (zither), all of which are illustrated here.

HIGH-FLYING

As early as the 2nd century BC, kites were used for military signalling in China. Physicians recommended kite-flying as an activity for young boys to make them throw back their heads and open their mouths, thereby cooling the body's energy levels. Early kites were shaped like a kite, the bird from which they were named, but later developments included dragon-shapes (that fought to cut each other's tails), kites that could carry a human scout, and exploding kites that carried firecrackers on their strings. This modern kite looks like a space-age version of a coiled dragon.

PUPPET MASTERS

Puppetry originated in China and is still a common form of entertainment throughout Asia. But not just an entertainment, puppetry once saved an emperor's life. In 206 BC, giant puppets were moved around on the walls of a city in order to convince the besieging rebels that Emperor Gao Zi was still within. By the time the ruse was discovered, he had already made his getaway.

Fashion

Common people in ancient China mainly wore clothes made of hemp or ramie-grass. In the 14th century AD, they began growing cotton brought in from South Asia, which was found to be warmer and more profitable to grow. Clothes were not just items to keep the body warm. They were important indicators of status, and high-ranking officials had to take great care with their appearance. Chinese clothes were often decorated with mythical animals to protect the wearer from harm and bring them good fortune.

KEEPING COOL

Early fans were flat, rigid panels used by both men and women to keep cool. The folding variety was invented in Japan in the 4th century AD, and eagerly adopted by the Chinese before the 11th century. It was important among the rich to have the right fan for the right season, and writing or painting on someone's fan was a sign of friendship. A deserted wife was called an 'autumn fan'.

Most dragons were drawn with three or four claws on each limb. Five-clawed dragons were reserved for the Imperial family.

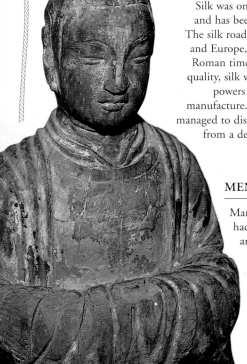

THE SILK MYSTERY

Silk was one of China's most important commodities, and has been manufactured for well over 2,000 years. The silk road was the lengthy trade route between Asia and Europe, where Chinese silk was prized as early as Roman times. A light, soft fabric with a shimmering quality, silk was in great demand abroad, and foreign powers were desperate to know the secret of its manufacture. In the 6th century AD, European spies managed to discover the incredible truth: it was made from a delicate gossamer thread unwound from the cocoons of silkworm moths.

MEN OF THE CLOTH

Mandarins and other officials had to wear elaborate clothing and jewels to show their rank. But monks and priests took a vow of poverty and wore very simple, humble robes.

MANDARIN STYLE

From the 12th century onwards, the Manchu people of northern China began to create fashions to honour their most faithful servant, the horse. These styles eventually caught on in other parts of China. Sleeves were worn wide and placed over the hands to resemble the horse's hoof, and servants were made to wear their hair shaven at the front and plaited at the back, to resemble a horse's tail.

HIGH & MIGHTY

A mandarin was a member of any of the senior grades of bureaucracy. His footwear kept him high above lesser mortals, and away from troublesome dirt. Such shoes could be difficult to walk in, but only a peasant or common labourer would need to get himself about. The richer the mandarin, the more likely he was to be carried everywhere!

FOOT-BINDING

Small feet were considered a sign of beauty – the smaller the better. From around AD 1000 girls had their feet tightly bound to help increase their chances of getting a good husband. Eventually the instep broke, creating a kind of gnarled hoof. Walking was agony, yet poets praised the deformed results of foot-binding as 'golden lilies'. This tradition continued in China until the early 20th century.

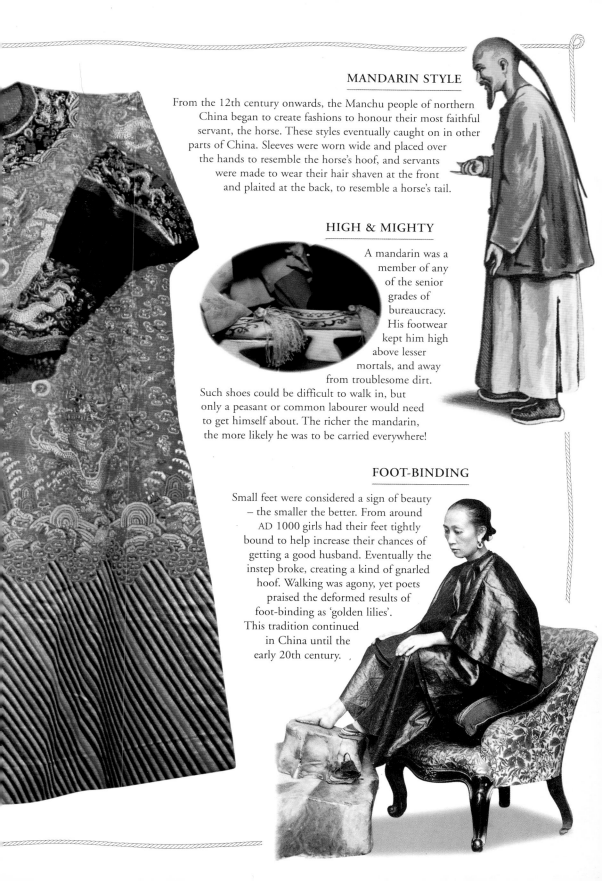

Art & Architecture

FINE FIGURES

Sculpture was highly-regarded from early times. This white earthenware horse was found in the grave of Zhang Shigui, a nobleman from the Tang Dynasty (AD 618–907).

The wealth and sophistication of ancient China created some of the most valuable treasures in the world. In times when the empire was strong and stable, such as at the height of the Song and Tang Dynasties, Chinese arts flourished in every conceivable medium, including bronze statuary, silken textiles, lacquer work, ink paintings and decorated porcelain. Chinese architecture avoided hard edges and corners in favour of soft curves as seen in the wing-like shape of Chinese roofs. It was believed that this softer style created good *qi* (energy). A similar emphasis on flowing shapes and natural harmony is found in the other arts. Chinese painters often concentrated on landscape scenes of *shan shui* (mountains and water), with swirling mists and tiny human figures dwarfed by the beauty of nature.

FENG SHUI

Feng shui (wind and water) is that which can be felt but not seen, grasped but not held. Originally used to find auspicious sites for graves in the 3rd century AD, this set of beliefs and superstitions was adapted to help the living counter unlucky influences in their homes. Even today, feng shui masters use a complex compass, such as this one, to determine the lucky and unlucky influences caused by the position of a house.

BRONZE-AGE ART

The Shang people flourished in north China around 1000 BC, and were incredibly advanced forgers of bronze ware, which they decorated with images of mythical-monster masks and animal figures. Some pictures were broken up into square thunder-pattern spirals, or leiwen, with just an eye remaining to indicate it symbolized a living creature.

THE FORBIDDEN CITY

The capital city of China, Beijing, was designed along regular, square, grid patterns, which were good for transport. The north–south and east–west alignment of the square deliberately evoked the feng shui of ancient times. In 1420 a walled citadel was built in the middle as a home for the emperor and his family. Closed to outsiders, it was known as the Forbidden City.

Health & Medicine

Chinese medicine is based on herbal cures and the theory of qi – an energy believed to be in all living things. A person's qi had to be kept healthy and balanced, otherwise they would fall ill. Qi was maintained through eating a healthy diet and getting sufficient exercise. However, while the ancient Chinese had medical beliefs, they lacked medical science. Some cures worked by accident, while others did more harm than good. No system was in place to prove those cures that worked and those that didn't. Matters were not helped by shyness; doctors could not touch female patients, and instead had to use a doll to indicate where the pain was.

MOXIBUSTION

Some aches and pains were treated with moxibustion, which involved making pastilles from the dried leaves of the moxa plant, applying them to the skin and setting them on fire (normally under a glass to contain the heat). This practice is still in use today.

MAN ROOT

Ginseng, which became widespread after the 12th century AD, is an aromatic root, often shaped like a man and highly prized for its medicinal properties. All ginseng in China was considered the property of the emperor, though he would often bestow quantities of it upon his loyal subjects. It was believed that the ginseng plant would turn into a white-blooded man if left undisturbed for 300 years and that the blood of such a man could raise the dead.

ACUPUNCTURE

The Chinese believed that energy circulates throughout the body but could be unbalanced if the channels became blocked. In the 1st century AD, the science of acupuncture was devised to treat this problem. It involved sticking needles into the body at special points as shown on this statue. Still in use today, it is thought to stimulate the body's own defence mechanisms, and is also used as an anaesthetic.

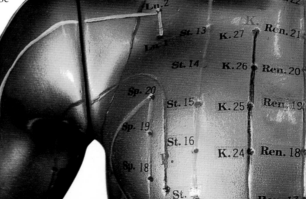

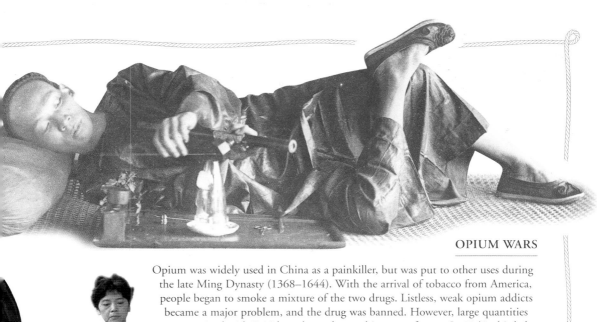

OPIUM WARS

Opium was widely used in China as a painkiller, but was put to other uses during the late Ming Dynasty (1368–1644). With the arrival of tobacco from America, people began to smoke a mixture of the two drugs. Listless, weak opium addicts became a major problem, and the drug was banned. However, large quantities arrived with British traders, who used it to pay for tea. In 1840, this led to the Opium War which ended with China defeated and Britain occupying Hong Kong as part of the settlement.

MORNING EXERCISE

The Chinese have always believed that exercise and clean living strengthens the body's energy and extends the natural lifespan. One such exercise was *tai qi,* a combined regime of callisthenics that could also be used as a martial art. Strengthening the body, it was said, would also strengthen the mind. Other physical exercises included gong fu boxing, which we know today as kung fu.

MYSTERY CURES

The lack of scientific method in Chinese medicine has meant that some cures work well, whereas others are merely based on superstition. Deer horns were imported in vast quantities for use in medicines, most probably because the word in Chinese for deer sounds a little like 'ease' in some dialects.

Love & Marriage

LOVE BIRDS

Because mandarin ducks mate for life they have become the Chinese symbol of a loving and faithful marriage. Wild geese in flight were the symbols of communication from afar. They crop up in many poems about lovers forced to live apart, waiting for news of each other.

In ancient China people were expected to put their family duty ahead of their personal feelings. Marriages were arranged by professional matchmakers, sometimes before the bride and groom were even born. Such alliances turned enemies into in-laws who were then obliged to respect and help each other. A bride had to leave her family behind and become a member of her husband's family. In her new home, she would have to worship his ancestors and obey his parents.

SECOND-CLASS WIVES

A man could have only one wife who would share any title or honours he gained during his life. However, he was free to take concubines to increase his chances of having more children. As a second-rank 'wife', a concubine was liable to be badly treated by both her 'husband's' mother and his first wife.

DIVORCE

A man could divorce his wife if she was barren, lascivious or jealous, or if she had a disease, stole anything or neglected to honour her in-laws. She could even be divorced if she talked too much. However, he could not divorce her during a period of mourning, if he had come into money or if she had no home to return to.

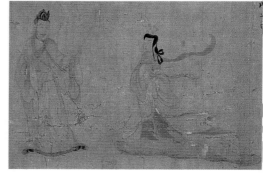

FATAL ATTRACTION

The most beautiful woman in Chinese history was said to be Yang Guifei, an 8th century companion of Emperor Xuanzong. He was so infatuated with her that he neglected his kingdom and appointed members of her family to high offices. The last straw came when he made her cousin prime minister. There was a rebellion and she was killed.

MARRIAGE RITUALS

Before a marriage took place, the year, month, day and hour of the bride and groom's birth were checked to ensure that the union would bring good fortune. On the chosen (lucky) day, the bride wore red and was taken to the groom's home in a sedan chair. The pair worshipped the groom's ancestors together, leaving the shrine as man and wife. Until the beginning of the Sui Dynasty (AD 581), Chinese women had to wear veils when they went outside the house. This custom is still practised at many Chinese weddings today.

LU'S LOVE LOST

The Zhinan temple complex in Taiwan is sacred to Lu Dongbin, one of the eight Immortals of Chinese legend, who was thwarted in love. It is unlucky for lovers to visit the temple together, lest they be parted by the Immortal's jealous anger.

Women & Children

POMEGRANATE

A pomegranate is a fruit bursting with seeds, and so became a Chinese symbol of fertility. Pomegranates were placed in the homes of couples who hoped to have more children. However, couples who already had too many mouths to feed tried to avoid them at all costs.

According to ancient Chinese philosophy the universe was a place in constant search of harmony and balance. As applied to men and women it was considered the man's duty to command and the woman's duty to obey. Real life, however, wasn't so simple. Women could exert great authority over their children, and several emperors were puppets of their powerful mothers. Though sworn to obey her husband, a wife was the boss at home. Even the philosopher Confucius once complained: *'When she's close, she's insolent. When she's far away, she nags.'*

THE EMPRESS DOWAGER

The Empress Dowager Zi Xi (1835–1908) was the last of many female rulers, stretching back to the 1st century AD, who put a weakling on the throne so she could rule from behind the scenes. The weakling in question was her own son, the Tongzhi Emperor. Although an emperor was all-powerful, he was still obliged to obey his surviving parents, and sometimes a mother could use her power over her son to rule the whole nation.

UNICORN FATE

The Chinese unicorn, or *jilin*, was said to have appeared shortly before the death of Confucius, and to herald a time of great peace and prosperity. A unicorn is thought to bring luck to parents in the form of a genius child, and images of them were often kept near cradles. Such legends of fantastical creatures were reinforced when Admiral Zheng-He brought back a giraffe from his sea journey to Africa, and astounded the Chinese court.

CELESTIAL BIRDS

As the dragon was the symbol of the male, the phoenix was the symbol of the female. Phoenix designs can be found on many articles of female clothing and jewellery throughout Chinese history.

CHILDREN

Children were expected to work from a very young age. Peasant sons worked in the fields with their parents. As young as seven, children were given adult tasks and responsibilities. Chinese ages were counted from one, not zero, so children were one year old the moment they were born. Instead of having birthdays, everyone would add a year to their age at each Chinese New Year, so it was technically possible for a child born on New Year's Eve to be two years old the following morning.

SILK SPINNING

While their brothers were in the fields, girls had to spin and weave. A poor family dreaded the birth of a girl. She would be one more mouth to feed until they could marry her off, at which point they would have to pay a dowry to her prospective husband's family. Whatever happened, the bride rarely had much say in her fate. According to Confucian tradition, a girl was supposed to obey her parents until she married, her husband until his death and her eldest son until her own death.

ALIEN INVADERS

The Great Wall didn't always work. In the 4th century AD, it was crossed by the Tabgatch people of Inner Mongolia, who founded the Wei Dynasty. In the 12th century, the people of the steppes were united under their strongest ruler ever, Genghis Khan. His grandson Kublai conquered China and founded the Yuan Dynasty in 1271. It was breached for the last time in the 17th century, when the Manchus invaded and stayed to rule China right up until the early 20th century.

ARMOUR

Robes restricted movement, so Chinese soldiers wore trousers to make horse-riding easier. Tough leather protected most parts of the body, with extra quilting to reduce the impact of blows. Cavalrymen wore extra leg protection. Metal plates were uncommon, except on the chest in later years. Most soldiers had small metal studs to deflect enemy blades. Chinese soldiers often painted a tiger's head on their shields, or even wore imitation tiger-skins, complete with a fake tail. As 'King of Beasts', an image of the tiger was meant to strike fear into the hearts of China's enemies.

CLAY SOLDIERS

We know a great deal about Chinese warfare from the evidence found at archaeological sites, especially the Qin Emperor's famous Terracotta Army. It consisted of over 6,000 lifelike statues guarding his tomb. Most of the soldiers, however, are empty-handed. The real weapons they had carried were looted during a rebellion in 206 BC.

War & Weaponry

In some parts of China the climate will support only farming; in others, only herding. The northern border zone supports both, and so throughout history, it has been fought over constantly. The greatest threats to China came from the plains of Asia, from horse-riding tribes such as the Mongols and the Xiong-nu (Huns). China's soldiers had advanced weaponry to fight off the barbarian (foreign) invaders. Iron weapons replaced inferior bronze during the 7th century BC, around the time that the Chinese invented the crossbow. From 500 BC, horses were ridden instead of simply being used to pull chariots. Triple ranks of archers and crossbowmen kept up a continuous rain of arrows, charioteers and horsemen charged through enemy ranks, and humble footsoldiers attacked with swords and spears.

FIRE POWDER

Gunpowder was first used in fireworks during the 7th century AD. Today, firecrackers are still used to scare off evil spirits at important occasions. Some were also used for military purposes, fired into enemy ranks to cause chaos. Actual guns of Western origin were first used in China by Mongol invaders under Genghis and Kublai Khan.

GREAT WALL

The First Emperor ordered the Great Wall of China to be built as a defence against invasion by the nomadic tribes of the plains beyond China. Overall, it was about 6,000 km (4,000 miles) long and had a series of watchtowers along its length. Although parts of it date from the 3rd century BC, the most famous views we see are those restored in the Ming Dynasty during the 15th and 16th centuries. At its western end, it is little more than a bank of mud.

POMP & CEREMONY

Not all weapons were for warfare. This Shang Dynasty axe has a bronze handle and a blade of jade which would not have been much use in battle. More likely, it was used for ceremonial purposes. A jade blade was believed to have magical properties.

Crime & Punishment

Several types of punishment were used against wrong-doers in ancient China. The mildest were flogging or being locked into wooden stocks. The next level involved banishment, either for a limited period or permanently. A death sentence also varied with the severity of the crime. The simplest method was a straightforward beheading, but truly evil criminals (such as those who had murdered their parents) were treated to the terrible 'lingering death', by which they were slowly cut to pieces whilst still alive.

HEAVEN'S JUDGE

Chinese judges would have had images of cranes in their courtrooms, and the bird eventually became a symbol of justice itself.

STREET WISE

Strict rules governed the right-of-way on Chinese streets. Pedestrians had to make way for coolies carrying heavy loads. Coolies had to make way for empty sedan chairs. Empty sedan chairs had to make way for occupied sedans. Chairs had to make way for horses, and *everyone* had to make way for a wedding procession or an important official. Because it was polite to dismount to greet friends, pedestrians often used a fan to hide their face from acquaintances who were on horseback or in a sedan chair. Otherwise, the friend would be obliged to get down to say hello.

THE CRIMINAL'S YOKE

Petty thieves and other minor criminals were forced to wear a heavy wooden collar called a *cangue*. It was generally taken off at night but during the day they would have to rely on their friends for help, as they couldn't feed themselves.

OFF WITH HIS HEAD

Executions were performed with a sword that was heavily weighted to deliver the cleanest and swiftest downward stroke possible. An executioner's sword was too unwieldy for use in combat; it was only good for chopping off heads.

CANING

Some criminals were flogged with a lash made from a strip of bamboo that had been planed smooth. There were two kinds of instrument, the heavy and the light, and the criminal would be struck across the back. However, Emperor Kang Xi of the Qing Dynasty decreed that beating the buttocks was preferable, as there was less risk of damaging internal organs.

METHODS OF TORTURE

Magistrates were allowed to use torture to extract confessions. Men were flogged, and women could be slapped on the cheeks with a piece of leather. Chinese water torture involved the slow dripping of water onto the victim, who was usually wrapped in a cloth. As it slowly became soaked it made it almost impossible for the person to breathe. There was also a device for squeezing the fingers or the ankles until the bones rubbed together painfully.

WHEELBARROWS

The earliest plans for the Chinese wheelbarrow date back to the 1st century AD. With the wheel under the main part, it could easily lift 135 kg (300 lb) of weight, and was used extensively to replace a cart on narrow tracks.

WATER CLOCKS

Time was kept with a clepsydra or water clock, which originally consisted of several jars. They each emptied after a set time, and more exact measurements could be made with a bamboo dipstick to see how much water (and time) was remaining. Water clocks are a very old invention in China, but were not mentioned in literature earlier than the 1st century BC.

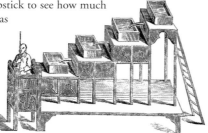

PAPER, PULP & PARCHMENT

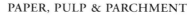

Though a form of parchment was in use in China during the Han Dynasty, the legendary inventor of paper was Cai Lun, who died in AD 114. He is said to have made his first sheets from old linen, tow, and pieces of fishnet. Paper made from rice straw or bamboo pulp was used in the normal way. Stronger papyrus sheets were used in windows as a cheap alternative to glass. It was considered extremely bad luck to step on paper inscribed with words, or even to throw it away. It had to be carefully burned to avoid ill fortune. This picture shows the fresh wet paper being laid out on racks to dry in the sun.

THE BURNING OF THE BOOKS

In 213 BC, the Qin Emperor, on advice from his prime minister, decided to burn all records of previous dynasties and all books that were not for soothsaying or of medical or agricultural use. The Qin Dynasty was believed to be so great that no previous literature could be of interest. Important and irreplaceable documents and records of discoveries were burnt. This also helped the Qin Emperor control what the population read. Hundreds of people were burned alive when they were found to be hiding books. Books from before this period have only survived by accident. Several hundred years later, in the Liang Dynasty, Emperor Yuan burned another 140,000 books for similar reasons.

Transport & Science

Despite occasional disasters, such as the Burning of the Books, the Chinese were an advanced civilization. In warfare they had crossbows and fireworks, and in industry they were using water wheels to power bellows in forges as early as the 1st century AD. But 'science', as a method of improving earlier ideas, was almost unknown. In later centuries, China was limited by its own education system. Even in the 19th century, the only way to get ahead was by studying the classics, and officials frowned upon people with knowledge of new-fangled arts like engineering, steam trains or medicine.

COUNTING BOARDS

Mathematics in China was done with an abacus, or counting board, often said to be a primitive form of computer. Each row represents units, tens, hundreds, thousands and so on, and calculation can be as fast as with a pen and paper. But, with pen and paper it's possible to check back for mistakes. Our word abacus comes from the Hebrew for dust on a tabletop (abak), in which people wrote their sums.

CATCHING QUAKES

The scientist Zhang Heng invented this earthquake detector in AD 132. An internal pendulum would knock against the sides if there was a tremor, causing a ball to fall from a dragon's mouth into a frog's mouth. Exactly which frog caught which ball would show the direction of the quake. A year before his death in AD 1   ng used the device to detect an earthquake 373 miles away.

SEDAN CHAIRS

Important officials would be carried by a team of men in a sedan chair. The emperor was allowed sixteen bearers, princes and governors had eight and other officials had four. Others who could afford it were only permitted two.

Religion

DAOISM

Daoism was founded in the 6th century BC by Lao Zi. It was a philosophy that preached harmony in all things, represented by the uniting of chaos and law, negative and positive and earth and sky in the yin-yang symbol.

*I*n ancient China, it was considered rude to impose upon those who were too high above or far below oneself in rank, and this even applied in the afterlife. Worshippers could only pray to their ancestors and family, or spirits of a similar class. The Chinese believed that the next world was very like our own, and that they could send aid to their ancestors by burning paper effigies in the real world. The emperor prayed to the most powerful gods, to keep the land free of flood and famine. Natural disasters were sometimes used as excuses for revolts, blamed on an emperor who was failing in his divine duties. As in China today, there was no single religion, but several belief systems which existed side-by-side.

CONFUCIANISM

Confucius sought to make the world a better place with precise rules on a small scale. He thought that if each person knew their place in the family, then each village, city and province would be strengthened, and ultimately the entire state would become perfect. Confucianism preached loyalty and respect to the ancestors.

BUDDHISM

Buddhism first arrived in China from India in the 1st century AD, though there are earlier stories about Buddhist missionaries imprisoned by the Qin Emperor and rescued by an angel. Initially an urban religion, it slowly spread into the countryside as believers mixed it with elements of Daoism. Buddhists believe that you can only be truly happy when you stop wanting things and work to remove all desire from your life. Their ultimate aim is to achieve enlightenment through reincarnation.

BURNING INCENSE

Incense is made from the dust of certain sweet-smelling woods, mixed with clay. The sticks then burn slowly to fill the air with their perfume; some were even marked to show the passing of time. In ancient China, incense was burned as a way of honouring the gods.

HOROSCOPES

Chinese horoscopes were an important part of everyday life. Fortune-tellers would ascertain which of twelve different animals ruled the year of someone's birth. The animals were the Rat, Ox, Tiger, Rabbit, Dragon, Snake, Horse, Sheep, Monkey, Rooster, Dog and Pig, at which time the cycle would return to the Rat. The year 2000 was ruled by the Dragon, so you can count forward or backward to work out which animal rules you.

FOREIGN FAITHS

Buddhism is not the only foreign import. Many of China's ethnic groups have their own beliefs, including thousand-year-old communities of Christians and Muslims. This is the Potala palace, the former home of the religious leader of Tibet, the Dalai Lama.

EVIL SPIRITS

The magical art of feng shui sought to protect the living from predatory ghosts and evil spirits. It was believed that symbolic guardians could keep supernatural threats at bay, hence statues like this fearsome stone lion, found outside a Chinese tomb.

Legacy of the Past

The greatest legacy of ancient China is modern China. Unlike many other past civilizations, it is still with us today, bigger and more powerful than before. But there are many different Chinas. There is the ancient historical civilization, the vast Communist state, the 'little dragon' Chinese nations like Singapore and Taiwan and the millions of people all around the world who are ethnic Chinese. There are no emperors any more, but China is still a great superpower and central in world politics and trade. The people still call their nation Zhong Guo, 'the Middle Kingdom'.

HONG KONG

Taken by the British after the Opium War, Hong Kong was returned to China in 1997. In the interim, it had grown into a centre of commerce, the tiny area of land turning into a forest of skyscrapers. This giant building is owned by the Bank of China, and was designed in accordance with the rules of feng shui. Some locals disagreed, suggesting that it looked like a giant dagger: very bad luck.

THE BALLAD OF MULAN

In the 6th century AD, songs were sung about Hua Mulan ('Magnolia Flower'), a girl who joined the army in her father's place. She fought for 12 years disguised as a man, but when she was offered a place in the Khan's court (China at the time was ruled by foreign Tabgatch nomads), she begged instead to be given a camel on which she could ride home to her family. The story is still famous today.

FISTS OF FURY

Bruce Lee (1940-1973) is still one of the most well-known Chinese faces around the world. Born in the United States, Lee became a martial arts teacher on the west coast of America. He is best remembered for his kung fu films such as *Enter the Dragon*. Lee and his successors popularized Chinese martial arts as a sport abroad.

THE EAST IS RED

The Last Emperor was overthrown in 1912, but the Republic of China soon had difficulties. After Japanese invasion and a civil war, the Republicans were forced to retreat to the island of Taiwan and Chairman Mao, a former librarian, proclaimed the People's Republic in 1949. Though the Communists were unquestionably the masters of China, the Republicans in Taiwan still claimed to be the true rulers. The United States did not recognize the Communists until 1973, when President Nixon went on a goodwill visit.

DID YOU KNOW?

There are thousands of Chinese characters?
The total number of Chinese characters
and variants is estimated at 40,000,
though nobody could possibly list or
learn them all. The majority are ancient,
extinct words or extremely complex ideas
in specialist fields. To reach a reasonable
level of Chinese reading ability, you
would need to memorize a much
smaller number: maybe just 5,000.

**That martial artists once fought a war
against Christians?** Christianity took
root in parts of China from AD 631.
When organized bands of missionaries
arrived many centuries later, the locals
were heard to complain that the sharp
church spires erected by the 'Jesus devils'
upset the area's feng shui. Towards the
close of the Qing dynasty in 1899, poor
areas saw the Boxer Uprising against
Christianity and all other foreign
influences. The Boxers were martial
artists who claimed to have a magic
invulnerability to foreign blades and
bullets. Some would enter trances to
be possessed by the God of War.

That goldfish are baby dragons? According
to some Chinese tales, a goldfish turns into a
dragon when it dies and passes through the
Gates of Heaven. It will return to wreak
vengeance if owners have mistreated
it, or grant them great fortune if they
were kind to it.

Gold and silk can kill? In ancient
Chinese records, if someone was said
to have 'swallowed gold' it meant they
drank poison and killed themselves.
If an official was 'presented with silk',
it was a command from the emperor
that they should be strangled.

**Midnight guessing games were
banned?** Chai Mui is a game played
by two people holding up a hand
each, with some, all or none of the
fingers displayed, and simultaneously
shouting out a guess at the sum of
the two hands. The closest guess was
the winner. During the Qing dynasty,
games of Chai Mui became so loud that
the Governor of Hong Kong banned
them between 11pm and 6am.

PRONUNCIATION

**Most of the Chinese words in this book sound as they look to you.
The following letters are pronounced differently:**

c = ts, I = ee after all consonants except c, ch, s, z, and zh, when it sounds like yrrh.
q = ch, x = hs (pronounced fast) z = dz, zh = j

ACKNOWLEDGEMENTS

For Ellis Tinios

We would like to thank: Helen Wire, David Hobbs and Elizabeth Wiggans

Copyright © 2000 ticktock Publishing Ltd.

First published in Great Britain by ticktock Publishing Ltd., The Offices in the Square, Hadlow, Tonbridge, Kent, TN11 0DD. All rights reserved.
No part of this publication may be reproduced, stored in a retrieval system, or transmitted in any form or by any means electronic, mechanical,
photocopying, recording or otherwise, without prior written permission of the copyright owner.
A CIP catalogue record for this book is available from the British Library. ISBN 1 86007 159 7 (paperback). ISBN 1 86007 226 7 (hardback).

Picture research by Image Select. Printed in Spain.

Picture Credits:
t=top, b=bottom, c=centre, l=left, r=right, OFC=outside front cover, IFC=inside front cover, IBC=inside back cover, OBC=outside back cover

AKG Photos; 4bl, 4tl, 5tl, 9t,9br, 11tr, 11cl, 13br, 16bl, 17t, 24cr, 25tr, 26tr & OBC bc, 26/27c, 27bl, 28/29c, OFC (main pic) & OFCcr. Ancient Art &
Architecture Collection; 2tl, 2bl, 3br, 4cb, 12bl, 21tr, 21bl, 25tl, 27tr, 29cl, 29tr. The British Museum; 18br. Ann Ronan @ Image Select; 2/3c, 6tr, 6/7, 13tr
& OBC cr, 14/15, 20cr, 20/21cr, 28bl, 32c. Corbis; 4c, 10cl, 12tl, 13cl, 17br, 20tl, 25br, e.t. archive; 8cr, 19tr, 22tl, OFCtr, OFCtc & OFCbr. Heather
Angel; 16tl. Holt Studios International; 8bl, 9bl. The Hutchinson Library; 18/19c. Images Colour Library; 10tl, 14/15tr, 16/17c. Image Select; 6bl, 6br,
22bl, 23bl, 26bl, 29tl, 30br, 31bl. Jean Loup Charmet; 26c. Oxford Scientific Films; 18tl, 24tl. Ronald Grant Archive; 30bl, 31. Science & Society; 27br.
Spectrum; 10/11c & IFC, 11cr, 17cl, 19br, 23tr. Still Pictures; 30tr. Tony Stone Images; 8tl & OBCtr, 22cr. Werner Foreman Archive; 5tr, 11br, 12/13c,
20bl, 23b, 29br. 24/25c *Everyday Life through the Ages* by Reader's Digest.

Every effort has been made to trace the copyright holders and we apologize in advance for any unintentional omissions.
We would be pleased to insert the appropriate acknowledgement in any subsequent edition of this publication.

snapping-turtle
guide

INDEX